AMERICAN EDUCATION:
Its Origins and Issues

AMERICAN EDUCATION:

Its Origins and Issues

Adrian M. Dupuis, Ph.D.

and

Robert C. Craig, Ph.D.

THE BRUCE PUBLISHING COMPANY • MILWAUKEE

Library of Congress Catalog Card Number: 63–17495

© 1963 The Bruce Publishing Company
Made in the United States of America

To our parents
    Ed and Emilie Dupuis
    Frank and Sylva Craig

INTRODUCTION

Many faculty members in teacher education institutions, as well as administrators and teachers in the field, are convinced that the future teacher needs a broad understanding of the psychological, historical, philosophical, and administrative aspects of the field of education before he begins a study of each specific area.

Generally speaking, each of the special areas is treated quite independently of the others. Thus, the educational psychologist devotes his class time almost exclusively to the study of the basic growth patterns of the child, the laws and theories of learning, psychological and physiological differences in pupils, and so on. The course (or units) in tests and measurements delves deeply into the techniques of testing intelligence, achievement, personality and interests, grading and reporting, with little or no time spent on the historical or philosophical foundations of education in general or of testing itself for that matter. Similarly, the other specialized courses in education are not concerned with the general foundations of professional education. Perhaps this approach to the special areas is as it should be — there is only so much time available in a "three-credit" course. But the authors of this book feel that an overview of the entire field of professional education will assist the student to see the relationships among the specialized fields, thereby enabling him to integrate the knowledge acquired piecemeal in each area.

Another advantage of an overview of the field of education arises from the stimulus the student should receive to relate his studies in the general area of the sciences, the social sciences, and the humanities to his professional studies. Practically every course in history contains a wealth of knowledge and insights having a direct bearing on education. Parallels can be drawn between literary periods and educational epochs. The scientific movement in the academic world gives rise to the application of scientific method to the solution of educational problems. Courses in philosophy and theology are replete with ideas which have affected educational theory and practice. To cite one such instance, Platonic or Aristotelian theory of knowledge (epistemology) dominated learning theory for centuries. Seemingly, then, a student should be able to derive much from his liberal arts or general education courses which can serve his professional goals. Nor should such use of academic courses detract from their liberalizing aspects. On the contrary, the content of these courses can lend greater depth to the future teacher's grasp of the fields in a liberal education, which he in turn might incorporate into his own teaching. Thus, a knowledge of the foundations of education can further the liberal arts education of the student and also assist him in gleaning professional knowledge from liberal arts courses.

Yet another function this book will serve lies in the effort to show the continuity of educational theory and practice. Wherever possible, similarities between the traditional and the modern are pointed up. Whenever an ancient view or practice appears in modern dress, the student's attention is called to this phenomenon. The specific purpose for reminding the twentieth-century student of this fact is that he often believes that no worthwhile educational theories or practices existed prior to the twentieth century. Since this "superiority complex" is so prevalent among American college students, a little reminder of the educational achievements of the past might generate the needed modicum of intellectual humility.

The responsibility for the content of this book is assumed by each author for his own area. R. C. Craig has done the chapters on the structure of American public and private school systems, and on the psychological foundations of education (Chapters II–V; XII–XVI). The responsibility for the remaining areas covering the historical and philosophical foundations of education and issues in education rests with A. M. Dupuis.

Both authors sincerely hope that this foundations text will prepare the student to enter the study of the specialized areas in the professional education sequence with a broader perspective of education as a field of study.

CONTENTS

Part I

THE AMERICAN SCHOOL SYSTEM

Chapter I

THE STUDY OF EDUCATION—

ITS SCOPE AND CHALLENGE

Although there are some who might question the claim that education is a legitimate field of study, the authors of this text are of the opinion that there is now a sufficiently large enough body of knowledge to warrant attention to education as a separate area of study for the future teacher. This chapter presents to the student a glimpse of the scope of education, the two generally conflicting viewpoints in education (the traditional and the new), and the challenge that the study of education places before the student.

Teaching, like any other profession, requires a certain amount of post-high school education. But the education of a teacher is a many-faceted enterprise. Collegiate institutions preparing teachers usually divide the student's program into (1) general (or liberal) education (courses all college students take), (2) professional education (courses specifically designed to prepare the student for teaching), and (3) specialized education (courses leading to a "major" in some academic or professional subject). The study of professional education generally is divided into the areas of educational psychology (human growth and development), methods, history and philosophy of education, educational measurement, and student teaching. Many institutions preface the professional program with an introduction to the field of professional education. Such is the purpose of this book, to introduce the student to professional education as a field of study or inquiry.

Before the student embarks upon his study of education he is usually very much interested in knowing something about the teaching profession. He has heard much about "blackboard jungles," low

3

pay, discipline problems, long hours spent on correcting papers, and evenings spent supervising dances or athletic events. But since this is not the complete picture, one part of this book is devoted to presenting the student with an overview of the teaching profession.

Teachers and administrators in the field and their colleagues in teacher education institutions are convinced that the future teacher should have a knowledge and understanding of the school systems where he will teach. One part of the book will present the history, structure, and organization of both public and private school systems, and the role of other educational agencies cooperating with the schools in the all-important task of educating youth. With this background the future teacher should be able to discern his professional relationship as a teacher to the school administration, the parents, the community, and all the agencies which assist him in achieving his professional goals.

Another foundational area often neglected in the training of future teachers is the historical development of education, especially in the Western world. The authors' experience with teachers and administrators in the field suggests that many of them know very little about the historical background of modern education. Many of them labor under the illusion that nothing particularly significant took place in education prior to the nineteenth and twentieth centuries. Perhaps there are some grounds for this general innocence of history of education. Formerly, a course in the history of education was taken by all prospective teachers. Often the course consisted in a listing of names and dates of important personages and events in education, but with no effort to relate them to the modern educational scene, or even to the educational beliefs of the times in which the events took place. It is no wonder that in a survey made in the 1920's teachers rated history of education the least helpful course in their professional preparation. Cramming the mind of the student with the mass of names, dates, and events of twenty-five centuries certainly does not have a very "liberalizing" effect. To offset this very real difficulty and yet to give the student some historical perspective of the development of education in the Western world, key persons and ideas have been selected who have contributed in a significant manner to modern educational thought.

As the student shall learn in the course of his professional studies, modern education draws heavily upon the science of psychology.

Most texts in this field concentrate on the presentation of the findings of psychology and their implications for educational practice without devoting much attention to the psychological foundations of traditional education or to the pioneering activities of the early scientific psychologists. Some knowledge and understanding of the psychological foundation of education are essential if the student is to grasp the rationale underlying the different points of view which he is sure to encounter in his study of educational psychology. Such background knowledge should dispel the naïve belief that psychologists are in agreement on the basic principles of their scientific discipline, and on the educational implications of those principles.

From what has been noted above and from the perusal of both popular and professional publications, no doubt the student already has come to the conclusion that education is one of the most controversial fields of study. Next to politics, people probably argue about education more than any other subject. One reason for this condition is that education touches very intimately upon the lives of all people. Practically every American under fifty years of age has spent from eight to sixteen years in school. Many older people are convinced that the education they received was superior to that received by their children. There is much harking back to the "good old days" when schools were *schools* rather than social centers. Such statements never go unchallenged, as many educators rise in defense of the superiority of modern education. Charges and countercharges are exchanged, often in very heated and emotive language. Name-calling is the order of the day in most of these discussions.

To acquaint the student with some of these differences of opinion, four chapters are devoted to critical issues in education. Since all issues in education cannot be treated in the limited space of a foundations text, some selection was necessary. In general, contemporaneity, frequency of appearance in print, and relevance to the part of the book they conclude are the criteria for selection of these issues. Undoubtedly, the instructor or his students using the same criteria may consider other issues just as significant as the ones selected by the authors.

The method of presenting the issues also should be noted. Usually, extreme positions on the issues are given, along with some of the main arguments in their behalf. Obviously, more moderate views on the issues are held by many educators, but usually the representatives of the diametrically opposed positions are heard from the most. Thus, a statement of the opposing views in their radical form should give some clues to the fundamental differences between the warring factions. Just as the student might prefer to be a moderate Republican or Democrat, so he might choose a "middle-of-the-road" position on many of the issues.

A word of warning is in order, however, with regard to the philosophical issues. Here there is frequently no "middle of the road" — you are either for or against one side or the other. To illustrate, one cannot consistently hold that the pupil is merely a biological organism and at the same time view him as a composition of body and soul. Such, however, is not the case for most of the issues discussed. For example, whether one prefers the teachers' union to a professional organization such as the National Education Association (N.E.A.) usually is not derived from one's theological or philosophical beliefs about the nature of man. One's preference in these "practical matters" may be based on a variety of reasons so that it is possible to have two representatives of the same school of philosophy holding opposing views on a particular issue.

TRADITIONAL VS. NEW EDUCATION

Throughout this book the authors have used the terms "traditional" and "modern" education to contrast the more conservative from the newer views in educational theory and practice. Modern education is not to be confused with progressive education, although there are many facets of modern education which have their origins in the progressive movement. Rather, modern education is to be viewed as encompassing the findings of scientific psychology and measurement, as well as the acceptable practices of both traditional and progressive education. The term "new education," on the other hand, generally is used to denote the educational theories and practices of the nineteenth- and early twentieth-century educators as described in Chapter X. In general, these innovations were considered very revolutionary at the time they were proposed. Also, at that time many theories and practices of traditional education were rejected by the advocates of the new education simply because they were traditional rather than on the basis of sound logic or experimentation.

A visit to any American school today, public or private, will reveal that both the traditional and the modern are operative in the educational process. To illustrate, the typical elementary school concerns itself with basic skills and subject-matter mastery as well as with the development of the "whole child." In most secondary schools, the objectives of subject-matter mastery and the ability to solve contemporary problems are both considered important and necessary. Many other instances of the blending of the old and the new in today's schools might be cited to show that very few are either exclusively traditional or new.

The major differences, then, between the traditional school and the new are more likely to appear at the level of philosophic belief rather than in the classroom. But one's philosophic outlook does have some effect on classroom practice, and the trained observer will be able to indicate whether any school leans more in one direction than the other. Thus, even though the "traditional" and the "new" cannot be applied as black-white classifications, these terms can be applied in the sense that a school is more or less on one side than on the other. The following summary might serve as a guide to the student in classifying educational beliefs and practices as they are described in this book and in the other texts the student will use in his professional courses.

I. OBJECTIVES OF EDUCATION

Traditional

1. The school should develop the intellectual or mental powers of the pupil.

2. The school should help the pupil rise above his material environment by emphasizing intellectual pursuits and a mastery of the "cultural heritage."

New

1. The school should develop all the growth potential of the pupil — mental, physical, emotional, etc.

2. The school should assist the student to adjust to and within his environment by emphasizing the problems arising in that environment and by working toward their solution.

II. ROLE OF THE SCHOOL IN SOCIETY

It is not the task of the school to change the social order; nevertheless, it must equip students with the knowledge and insights needed to make necessary social changes after they leave school.

The school should be the vanguard of social change — it should direct social change. Students should begin effecting changes in the social order while they are in school through the practice of democratic methods in the solution of contemporary problems.

III. CURRICULUM

1. Academic and liberal education should be clearly separated from vocational education. Liberal education is of a "higher" order than vocational education.

1. Academic and liberal education should be fused according to the needs of the students. Vocational education is not considered inferior to academic or liberal education.

2. The curriculum should contain those subjects representing the basic fields of human achievement, past and present. Such knowledge will provide the student with the means for solving contemporary problems.

2. The curriculum should consist of the real-life experiences and problems of the students. Knowledge of the past is of value only insofar as it contributes to the solution of a contemporary problem.

3. The curriculum should be largely prescribed to insure mastery of the basic areas of human knowledge by all students.

3. Prescription should be kept to a minimum. Individual (or group) needs and interests should determine the choice of problems and vocational subjects to be studied.

4. The subject matter should be organized in logical or chronological fashion with a definite sequence of content.

4. Subject matter should be psychologically organized, i.e., the needs, interests, and problems of the students should determine the sequence.

IV. TEACHING-LEARNING PROCESS

1. The teaching-learning process is teacher-centered.

1. The teaching-learning process is pupil- (or group-) centered.

2. The teacher stresses general principles to be learned; specific applications to individual and social situations are to be applied in out-of-school situations.

2. Direct student experience with concrete situations is stressed; general principles are to be derived from these direct experiences.

3. The teaching-learning process stresses common abilities. Thus all students are taught all subjects at the same level common to a certain age group.

3. Individual aptitudes, interests, and needs determine the teaching-learning process.

4. The teacher emphasizes higher motives for learning. The student should rise above his basic needs and interests. Spiritual or cultural motivation (extrinsic motivation) is employed.

4. The learner is motivated to study by his own need for or interest in a certain problem, subject, or vocational field.

5. The teacher uses drill not only to establish correct responses but frequently to develop and discipline the mental habits of students.

5. Drill is seldom used, and then only when it develops insight or achieves some goal related to the activity at hand.

6. The teacher approaches subject matter from the logical or chronological (historical) point of view. Each subject is "covered" systematically.

6. The teacher starts with the students' problems or interests in a subject rather than with a specific period in history or the first chapter of a textbook.

7. Transfer of training is achieved by emphasizing those subjects which best develop the mental powers of students. When these mental powers have been developed the student can solve specific problems as they arise.

7. Transfer is achieved by helping the student to generalize from his own experiences in solving problems so that new problems might be solved as they arise.

V. EVALUATION

Mastery of facts, concepts, and principles will determine the student's "grade" in a subject.

Evaluation of each pupil is given in terms of total growth, not only in subject matter but also in attitudes, ideals, and deepened interest in solving problems.

These differences between the two views of education will be developed throughout the book, but especially in the chapters on issues in education. After a study of the issues the student should be able to determine what are the essential differences between the traditional and new views and which aspects are accidentals that might be acceptable to both parties. The student will also discover that many of the innovations of the new education are based upon the findings of the recently developed behavioral sciences rather than upon the philosophical views of many protagonists of the new education. It is for this reason, perhaps, that many traditionalists have adapted the methodology and scientific findings of the new education to their own philosophic creed.

EDUCATION AS A FIELD OF STUDY

There are various ways of approaching education as a field of study. As mentioned above, many teacher education institutions approach the study of professional education from the avenues of the specialized areas such as educational psychology, philosophy, methods, and measurement. This division of the subject matter of professional education lends itself well to scheduling and other administrative functions, but it does not distinguish the nature or source of statements made within these various areas. Thus, a methods class might involve statements of quite different nature, although they might be treated by the instructor or text as though they were the same. Perhaps a more accurate approach to education as a field of study might be derived from a classification of the statements made about and in education according to the area of application, their origin, etc.

Thus one can make statements which apply to different areas such as: (1) the learner and the learning process, (2) the teacher and the teaching process, (3) the educational environment (school, community, classroom), or (4) curriculum (subject matter to be learned).

Specific statements about these four different areas may be derived from such sources as the sciences (chiefly psychology and sociology), history, philosophy, or theology. For example, the assertion that "the learner is a rational being destined for life in the hereafter" is derived from one's philosophical and/or theological beliefs, and of course applies to the nature of the learner. The statement that "pupils are more alert and learn more subject matter per period at a room temperature of 72 degrees than at a temperature of 80 degrees" is based on the findings of psychology, and also applies to the learner and the learning process. That "Plato and Aristotle believed that only the gifted should receive higher education" is a fact noted for us from the history of education. "Every American classroom should be a miniature democracy" is a statement based on one's philosophy of education and applies to the third area, the educational environment.

Thus it is evident that educational statements have different origins, with the result that much discussion about the truth of such statements is futile unless one sees very clearly their origin and nature. In most instances, one will find almost universal agreement on statements derived from scientific observation. For example, no one who has any knowledge of elementary and secondary education would doubt the truth of the statement that there is a wide range of mental ability in any one age group. Some ten-year-old pupils are very bright, others mentally retarded, and the largest percentage between these two extremes. However, one will not find such universal acceptance of the statement, "Every American classroom should be a miniature democracy." The reason is quite simple for, as mentioned above, this statement is based upon a philosophy of education which some educators accept and others reject.

But a school cannot be operated on simple statements derived from science, history, philosophy, or theology. To meet this practical demand, *policies* are formulated which outline in a very general way how the basic statements from science, history, philosophy, and theology will be utilized in running a school system. In turn, educational *practices* will be devised which are in harmony with the policy. To illustrate with the example used above: the science of psychology shows that there is a wide range of individual differences in mental ability for each age group of school children. One's philosophy of education might demand that schools meet the needs of all ability levels. Then the following *educational policy* might be derived from the statements of science and philosophy: "All schools in Glen Echo will make adjustments to the individual differences of the learners."

To implement this general policy, School "X" in the Glen Echo system might employ the educational *practice* of "sectioning" the students into separate classes according to their ability level. Thus, in School "X" one might find three separate classes of sixth graders — the bright, the average, and the retarded. School "Y" might implement the same general policy in another manner, such as using small classes of 20 to 30 unselected pupils with a great deal of individualized instruction to develop the talents of the different levels of ability. Then, both School "X" and School "Y" are carrying out the general policy of the Glen Echo school system even though they are employing different educational *practices*.

Perhaps another example will serve to illustrate these important distinctions. "Education consists essentially in preparing man for what he must be and for what he must do here below, in order to attain the sublime end for which he was created. . . ." This statement, taken from Pope Pius XI's encyclical on Christian Education, finds its origin in Christian philosophy and theology since it refers to man's nature and final destiny. A general *policy* derived from this statement might be: "Any sound program of Christian education will meet the spiritual, mental, and physical needs of the pupil." A specific diocese in the United States might restate this policy in such a manner that *all* schools in the diocese will have well-rounded programs of physical and health education, academic and vocational education, and religious instruction. The actual implementation of this policy in terms of specific *practices* might differ from school to school and teacher to teacher. School "X" in the diocese might have no separate courses in religion but integrate religion in academic courses, especially the social sciences and humanities. School "Y" might implement the policy by having separate courses in religion. Similarly, one school might have a separate health course whereas another might integrate health education with biology courses.

These examples indicate that an educational *practice* involves a way of handling specific situations, whereas educational *policy* usually covers a large number of cases and merely points up the broadest outlines of the desired end result. But the specific *practices* should serve as harmonious implementations of the *policy*; and the policies should be in harmony with the findings of science and one's philosophy and theology.

From the foregoing pages it is evident that education, unlike most other subjects the student studies in college, is very broad in scope. College algebra, chemistry, American history, and other subjects have a very definite content. But the courses in professional education involve the natural sciences, mathematics (statistics), history, psychology, politics, sociology, philosophy, and theology.

That the content of professional education is derived from so many areas of knowledge is both an advantage and a disadvantage. On the negative side of the ledger one might mention the difficulty involved in "pinning" the content down to the nice neat packages found in academic areas such as mathematics or science. As a result the student is often at a loss to decide exactly what should be known by the future teacher. Second, he never is quite certain whether the instructor (or the text) is speaking of educational principles, policies, or practices, as all three levels might appear in the same paragraph or even the same sentence. Third, the statements made may sound somewhat familiar to the student as he may know some of the concepts and generalization from his basic courses in psychology, sociology, philosophy, or theology. Consequently, he feels that this is "old stuff" and does not demand any further study. Because of this superficial knowledge, he does not probe more deeply into the course content and fails to realize the educational implications of the knowledge and insights derived from other branches of knowledge.

On the positive side of the ledger, and herein lies the challenge of education, many advantages might be derived from the study of education. First, this study constitutes one of the greatest opportunities for the student to integrate the knowledge he has acquired from other academic fields and put it to work to achieve his professional goals. What other professional training program requires so much knowledge from outside sources? Even the age-old professions of medicine, law, and theology do not demand as much background in the liberal arts as does the teaching profession.

Second, the challenge of professional education is as vital and important as the clientele which the teacher serves, the youth of the nation. If the educational system of a country fails, it is due in large part to the failure of its teachers and administrators. After the home, the school is the most influential agency in the modern world for molding the mind and character of youth. If the school fails in this task, there will be inadequate personnel for staffing the other professions. The role of the teacher is particularly crucial in this latter half of the twentieth century because the home often has neglected its primary function of character education. Thus in our times one may say that a nation is as strong as its schools.

Third, a much broader education is required to be a good teacher than is demanded by other jobs calling for a college education. For example, a mathematician, scientist, or engineer who will spend the rest of his days in a research laboratory does not need the array of personal qualities, skills in dealing with children and youth, and the knowledge of several academic fields required of the teacher. The research expert need not possess the qualities of a first-aid expert, counselor, guide, substitute parent, or what have you, to be a success in his job. But the teacher needs most (or all) of these qualities to be successful. Undoubtedly, many of you possessed these traits to some degree before you entered college. But you can be assisted in developing those qualities to their highest potential by proper guidance and supervision. Those of you who, through lack of experience or maturity, do not recognize or understand the need for such qualifications can be helped in the task of recognizing your own deficiencies and in attempting to remove them before launching on a career of teaching. Thus both education as a field of study and teaching as a career present one of the greatest challenges to the youth of today.

SELECTED READINGS

Adler, M., "In Defense of the Philosophy of Education," *Philosophies of Education*, Forty-First Yearbook of the National Society for the Study of Education, Part I (Chicago: University of Chicago Press, 1942), Chap. V.
    Deals with the relationship between theory, principles, and practices in education based upon Aristotelian philosophy.
Harris, Chester (ed.), *Encyclopedia of Educational Research* (New York: Macmillan Co., 1960), "Teacher Education," pp. 1452–1473.
    A good summary of the professional training for teachers viewed as a separate field of study.
Haskew, Laurence D., *This is Teaching* (Chicago: Scott, Foresman, and Co., 1956), pp. 147–150.
    Shows how science, philosophy, religion, the social order, and educational theory are used in education as a field of study.
Mayer, Martin, *The Schools* (New York: Harper & Row, 1961), Chap. 19.
    A layman looks at the "Tools and Technology" of modern American education and gives a nontechnical evaluation of educational theory. (This book is now available in a paperback edition published by Doubleday Anchor Books.)
Power, Edward J., *Education for American Democracy* (New York: McGraw-Hill Book Co., 1958), Chap. 10.
    Shows the evolution of the status of the teacher and of his professional training in America.
Reeder, W. G., *A First Course in Education* (New York: Macmillan Co., 1958), Chaps. II, XXIII, and XIV.
    Discusses the contributions of philosophy, the science of education, and observation of school and class procedures to education as a separate field of study.

Chapter II

ORIGIN AND DEVELOPMENT OF THE AMERICAN PUBLIC SCHOOL SYSTEM

American educational developments are best viewed as part of the vast social and political movement which began with colonization and continues as an experiment in democracy. American traditions were first built on Old World patterns and then adapted, adopted, or abandoned to meet the needs of American life. The colonial education of New England met religious needs through colleges for the ministry and "reading" schools for congregations expected to study the Bible. Then emphasis on education declined for a time as industrialization, Western expansion, and the Revolution took priority over all other interests. After the Revolution, the states assumed the responsibility of developing able leaders, and informed and productive citizens. Free public schools were their tools, and these schools began to assume some of their present characteristics. Curricular changes, new types of institutions, and innovations of all kinds have been tried as Americans have embraced an experimental philosophy which consciously seeks to modify existing ways and means to meet more modern conditions. All levels of education from the kindergarten to graduate and professional schools have been affected.

This chapter provides an overview of some of the elements and events of American education in order that the student may better understand the present and prepare for the future. The more general aspects of the following are considered: origins of the public schools, types of institutions, curricular developments, and enrollment trends. Patterns of organization and support for public schools of the past and present are reviewed in greater detail in Chapter III, and a thorough treatment of the effects of philosophical and psychological developments on school goals and practices will be found in the chapters of Parts II and III.

ELEMENTARY EDUCATION

The search for religious and political freedom, the chance to own land, to find gold, and to seek adventure were the chief motives for settling in the New World. In spite of the fact that these early immigrants came to this country to get away from what they disliked in their mother countries, and tended to establish institutions different from those they had known in Europe, most early American schools were patterned after European models (cf. Chapter IV).

The main educational agencies in colonial America, as in Europe of the time, were the churches, for they wanted their members to be able to read enough to follow the Bible and learn the catechism. Many elementary schools were "dames' schools," that is, schools operated by housewives for their own and a few of the neighbors' children. Of course, the wealthy were able to provide tutors for their children or even send them abroad for schooling. But there was no public education, even though communities often bore part of the cost of schools. In fact, the first systematic attempts at organizing a system of free elementary schools, open to all, should probably be dated in the first half of the nineteenth century. Hence, there were some 200 years of American education before effective moves were made toward establishing public elementary schools as we know them today.

The colonists supported education in principle, however, as is shown by some notable early steps. Colleges were founded, including Harvard (1636), Yale (1661), and Princeton (1746). A law requiring the establishment and maintenance of lower schools was passed in Massachusetts in 1647, the "Old Deluder Satan Act." The preamble of this act stated that reading the Bible was a protection against Satan, and communities with fifty or more families were directed to establish "reading and writing" schools. But this act did not compel children to attend a school even though some provision was made for one. Many parents were presumed to be able to teach their children at home. An earlier ordinance of 1642 obligated them to do so or be fined. This 1642 act was partly a labor law, and the children of parents who did not comply could be apprenticed to more responsible adults. Despite these early efforts, elementary education continued to be somewhat haphazard. Many colonists not only failed to insist upon systematic schooling for their children, they were unable or loath to have their children take the time for it. The demands of colonial life were often heavy but seldom of a nature which seemed to require more than a token education.

As immigration continued and colonization spread, new concerns slowed the development of education still further. The colonists and new immigrants who were caught up in the Westward movement usually left opportunity for formal schooling behind. Newly opened territories were sparsely settled, and the number of children in any one place was seldom enough to warrant a school or support a teacher. All too frequently, moreover, just the business of staying alive demanded the full attention of children as well as parents.

In Eastern communities, as in Europe, the Industrial Revolution began to lure children into the factories. Immigrant children, in particular, were exploited so completely that their education was impossible.

At about the same time when Westward expansion and industrialization turned many Americans from education, relations with England began to deteriorate. The Revolution which followed and its aftermath absorbed the interests and the energy of the American people and their leaders for the last quarter of the eighteenth century.

Thus organized public education, the concern of this chapter, developed slowly in America. Public schools first began to assume their present characteristics in the nineteenth century, when the people of the new United States were able to turn from war and devote their energies to educational progress in harmony with the national ideal of equality of opportunity for all (cf. Chap. III). As late as 1825 public schools of any standing existed only in a few communities. The dominant view in many parts of the country was still that the support of schools was an individual, philanthropic, or religious responsibility, not a public one. There was widespread opposition to using tax money to support schools; and, strangely enough, the demand for free schools was not even made by those who needed them most, the poor. Actually the leadership for the movement to establish free public education arose in the ranks of the privileged classes or within organizations such as the Pennsylvania Society for the Promotion of Public Schools, the New York

Public School Society, the American Institute of Instruction, the Western Academic Institute, and a few local or regional labor organizations. Chapter IV includes a discussion of the part played by the New York Public School Society.

In the second quarter of the nineteenth century the first effective measures were taken toward establishing public elementary education. James Carter (1795–1840) and Horace Mann (1796–1859) succeeded in getting the state of Massachusetts to pass a law setting up a state board of education with definite powers in the field of education (1837). Carter also succeeded in getting the legislature to appropriate funds for education in the local districts and to establish a normal school to train teachers. Mann was the first secretary of the state board of education in Massachusetts. In this position he succeeded in convincing people of the value of public education. His lectures and his publication, *The Common School Journal*, were avenues for educating professional educators and the people to the necessity of public education in a democracy.[1]

Henry Barnard (1811–1900) became the first executive officer of the state board which Connecticut established in 1839, just two years later than Massachusetts. Barnard's role in Connecticut was similar to Mann's in Massachusetts. In Pennsylvania and New York there were others who began to work zealously for a state-wide system of tax-supported schools and for teacher standards. A few decades later, the principle of free public schools had been generally accepted.

The school population and the importance of schools grew rapidly as the population expanded (see Fig. 1). In 1900 approximately fifteen million children were in the public elementary schools and another million were in independent schools. By 1961–1962 the enrollment in public elementary schools reached twenty-nine million, nearly double that of 1900, and there were five million in independent elementary schools. Less than 50 percent of the children of elementary school age attended schools of any kind in 1850, but 86 percent of children between seven and thirteen years of age and 35 percent of the five- and six-year-olds were in schools by 1910. By 1930 these same figures were 95 percent and 43 percent. In 1960 virtually all children between seven and thirteen years of

---

[1] See M. T. Mann, *Life of Horace Mann* (New York: Lee & Shepard Co., 1865), for a very moving description of this great educator.

Fig. 1. Enrollment in Grades K–8 of Public and Independent Schools
of the United States, 1900–1970

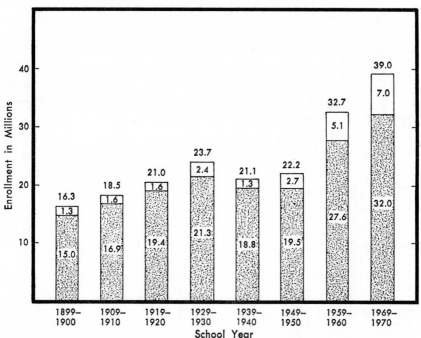

NOTES:

1. Shaded portion of bar indicates public school enrollment. White portion indicates independent school enrollment.
2. Figures through 1960 are actual enrollments based upon U. S. Office of Education data. Principal source: *Statistical Summary of Education: 1957–58,* Biennial Survey of Education in the United States, 1956–58, Chapter 1 (OE–10003–58) (Washington, D. C.: United States Government Printing Office, 1962), p. 5, Table 4.
3. Figures for 1970 are projections assuming 1950 to 1960 trends.

age, and about 64 percent of those five and six, were in regular attendance, 85 percent of them in the public schools.[2]

Changes in the content of the elementary school curriculum through the years are shown in Figure 2. At about the beginning of the twentieth century, the curriculum included reading, writing, arithmetic, spelling, geography, history, some music and drawing, hygiene and physical education, elementary science and business subjects. This was a far cry from the "reading, writing, and religion"

---

[2] U. S. Bureau of the Census, *U. S. Census of Population: 1960, General Social and Economic Characteristics, United States Summary.* Final Report PC (1)–1C (Washington, D. C.: U. S. Government Printing Office, 1962), pp. 1–206, Table 74.

Fig. 2. Additions to the Content of the Elementary School Curriculum

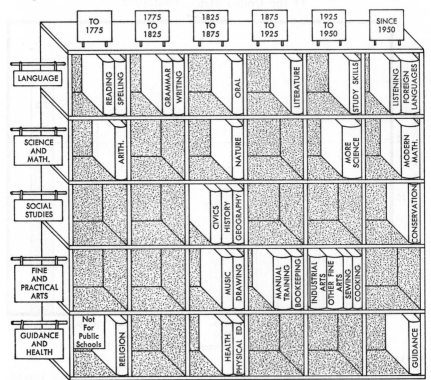

program of the colonial elementary school. In 1900 it was assumed that many graduates of the elementary schools would go on to high schools where they would continue the study of many elementary school subjects at a more advanced level. Now, cooking, sewing, manual training, literature, and even foreign language have been added. Some content has been drastically revised, as in mathematics and art, or regrouped, as when history, government, and other older subjects are combined in social studies.

With the increased enrollment and expanded curriculum came the broadening of the purposes of elementary education. The curriculum which was predominant in the elementary school in the early decades of the twentieth century was designed primarily to teach basic skills and give essential knowledge. This pattern was in harmony with the goals of traditional education, but with the advent of the new education (cf. Chapter X) new aims were developed for the elementary school. The belief that the "whole child" is the concern of the educational process was felt first in the elementary school. Emphasis was soon placed also on the following themes: (1) the elementary school should foster the physical, emotional, mental, and social development of the child; (2) the elementary school should not be merely preparation for high school or future life but an actual experience in living, through working on current problems and satisfying the individual and social needs of the students; (3) the school should be an integral part of the community, participating in its life and activities, with its members, especially the parents, active in the affairs of the school.

The 1960's have brought determined efforts on the part of the public and the profession to insure that the intellectual aims of the school are not neglected. Specifically, there is greater insistence on achieving more learning in less time, finding better ways to adjust instruction to individual differences, and turning to specialists for help with content in the sciences, humanities, and other fields. It is wise to reaffirm our concern for intellectual goals at this point in our national history. At the same time, we should avoid losing sight of other worthy goals in the areas of health, human relations, vocational skills, and attitudes and values.

In spite of the many changes in elementary education since the turn of the twentieth century, some schools adhere to the basic eight-grade organization which was traditional then. Some designate Grades 1 to 3 as primary, 4 to 6 as intermediate, and 7 and 8 as upper elementary. Others put Grades 7 and 8 in a new institution, the junior high school. The remaining six grades may be organized in a continuous six-grade elementary school, or the equivalent of the first three grades may be designated as lower elementary and the next three as upper elementary.

The ungraded or nongraded elementary school has been developed in a few places to encourage and enable each child to advance at his own rate of development, rather than at a grade rate set by the calendar. A five- to nine-year block of uninterrupted time is provided during which children are grouped to learn as rapidly as possible or as slowly as necessary. In schools of this kind the usual child completes the elementary program in seven years, but some take as little as five, whereas others may take nine without being labeled failures or pressured to move faster.

KINDERGARTEN EDUCATION

Today the kindergarten, rather than the first grade, is usually the first step on the public school educational ladder. There are nursery schools for three- and four-year-olds, but these are generally not a part of public school systems. In the kindergarten five-year-olds are given experiences which will prepare them for the life and work of succeeding grades.

The kindergarten is a latecomer, relatively speaking, in American education. The first true kindergarten in the United States seems to have been founded in 1855 at Watertown, Wisconsin, by Mrs. Carl Schurz. A German immigrant, Mrs. Schurz was a disciple of Froebel, the "Father of the Kindergarten,"[3] who had died in 1852. Another American kindergarten was begun in Boston in 1859 by Horace Mann's wife. Both the Watertown and the Boston schools, however, were private, not public. The first public school kindergarten in the United States was founded by Susan Blow in 1873 in St. Louis, while W. T. A. Harris was superintendent.

The kindergarten movement spread so rapidly that shortly after the turn of the century most school systems in the larger cities had added it. Today, kindergarten is considered an essential part of elementary education. Statistical reports often include kindergarten enrollments in the elementary figures, although only about two thirds of the five-year-olds are in kindergarten.

There are at least two reasons why the percentage in kindergarten is not larger. First, not all school systems have kindergartens. A number have been dropped in recent years because of rising educational costs and a shortage of classrooms. Another reason is that attendance at school is usually not compulsory before the age of seven.

The purposes of Froebel's kindergarten and that of the 1960's in the United States have something in common. Froebel placed the major emphasis of kindergarten on the interests and free activities of the child. He saw this period as one in which the child could discover himself and learn to adjust to the environment. This process is not furthered by teacher domination but by "pupil unfolding." The principle of self-realization through self-activity is almost synonymous with the name of Froebel, and probably accounts for the great emphasis in most kindergartens on play activities, creative work projects, and cooperative activities among the children.

---

[3] See Chapter X, pp. 245–246, for Froebel's theory of education.

One secret of the success of Froebel's kindergarten and its modern American counterpart, as well as the Montessori preschool classes which are currently winning support in the United States, can undoubtedly be found in the materials which make up a "controlled environment." Perceptual materials of all kinds are used to develop reading and number readiness, spatial relations, and "social readiness." Singing, dancing, and arts and crafts are used extensively. In general, there are not subject matter requirements as found in most elementary schools.

A perusal of the literature on kindergartens reveals that most modern ones have one or more of the following goals:

1. To develop readiness for the reading, writing, and arithmetic which will be started in the first grade.

2. To offer opportunities for children and teachers to discover special aptitudes and interests which can be developed in the years of formal schooling.

3. To promote habits of health and safety in the children.

4. To give opportunities for children to learn how to get along and work with other children and adults (chiefly teachers).

5. To give opportunities for children to develop the ability to work alone (self-reliance).

6. To develop within the individual child the ability to concentrate on a task when other activities are going on around him.

The emphasis given each of the foregoing goals may vary from school to school and teacher to teacher. Some concentrate on activities which are basically social in nature, such as developing respect for one's own property and that of others, sharing of materials, learning to plan in groups, developing habits of listening and skills of speaking in groups, and evaluating group experiences. Others place the major emphasis in kindergarten activities on developing readiness for the subject matter and skills of the first grade. Some kindergartens actually encourage the pupils to begin the process of mastering the basic skills of reading, writing, and computation.

SECONDARY EDUCATION

The history of public secondary education in America is less devious than that of elementary. The Latin grammar school and the academy are recognized as the forerunners of the American public high school. The first Latin grammar school was founded in Boston about 1635, to prepare students for college, particularly Harvard, which was founded about a year later. Since the Latin grammar schools were not completely supported by taxes they cannot be classified as public schools in the modern sense of the term. As might be expected, the curricular patterns in these schools were very similar to those of the humanistic period in Europe, which are described in Chapter IX. As the name indicates, the study of Latin grammar and classical literature constituted the core of the curriculum. These subjects were considered the best means for developing the intellectual powers of the student.

Obviously, such schools did not cater to students of low ability or those interested in practical pursuits. They were designed instead to lay the foundations of intellectual life needed for the ministry and the honored professions of medicine and law. That this type of school served at least one of the important purposes of post-elementary education is evident. Within six decades after the first Latin grammar school was founded in Boston, there were nearly fifty such institutions in the Colonies.

But it does not demand the vision of an astute student of society to see that the Latin grammar school did not meet the needs of a pioneering people. The colonists and their immediate descendants didn't need training in Latin as much as in agriculture; they demanded leadership in the practical fields rather than in the cultural. Whereas European society could afford cultural education, American society had jobs to be done, frontiers to be opened, forests to be conquered, and waterways to be developed. Certainly the knowledge of Latin grammar and the classics was of little value in solving problems of this type.

The man who took up the battle for the practical curriculum was Benjamin Franklin. About the middle of the eighteenth century Franklin and his friends opened the first academy.[4] The curriculum of the school was broader than that of the Latin grammar schools; and, what is perhaps more significant, it admitted students who were not going to American and European colleges or universities. This represents the first break in the traditions of secondary education; that is, it no longer was viewed primarily as a college-preparatory phase. Secondary education was soon to become a terminal rather

---

[4] Thomas Woody, *Educational Views of Benjamin Franklin* (New York: McGraw-Hill Co., 1931).

than a preparatory period, replacing elementary schooling as the essential foundation for an enlightened electorate.

The academy rapidly replaced the Latin grammar school as the typical secondary school. Girls academies (seminaries) began providing both cultural and practical training for the daughters of middle- and lower-class families, although young women were permitted to enroll in some of the regular academies. This was the start of the coeducational high school in America.

The academy movement reached its peak about 100 years after the founding of its prototype, going from approximately 100 schools in 1800 to nearly 500 in 1850 in the States on the Atlantic seaboard alone. In the entire United States of 1850 there were over 6000 academies with over 250,000 pupils enrolled and taught by over 12,000 teachers. A few academies are still in operation today. The more recent history of the academies is reviewed in Chapter IV.

As mentioned above, the curriculum of the academies was much broader than that of the Latin grammar school, including both classical and practical subjects. For example, when the Philadelphia Academy (Franklin's school) opened in 1751 its curricular offerings were Latin, Greek, English, French, German, history, geography, chronology, logic, rhetoric, writing, arithmetic, merchants accounts, geometry, surveying, gauging, navigation, astronomy, drawing in perspective, and other mathematical sciences, etc.[5] With such broad offerings it is no wonder that the popularity of this institution grew so rapidly. By the middle of the nineteenth century the offerings of some of the academies included as many as seventy-three subjects.[6] For example, the Wesleyan Seminary (Academy) offered all subjects of the Philadelphia Academy (though under different titles), plus such courses as chemistry, anatomy, physiology, mineralogy, geology, animal chemistry, agricultural chemistry, evidences of Christianity, natural theology, elements of criticism, governmental instruction (civics or political science), bookkeeping, botany, elocution, and others.[7]

But the academy still was not a secondary school for all the children of all the people. True, some academies received public support, but basically they were tuition schools, and many students

---

[5] From an announcement in the *Pennsylvania Gazette*, January 1, 1750.

[6] See I. L. Kandel, *History of Secondary Education* (New York: Houghton Mifflin Co., 1930), p. 455.

[7] *Ibid.*, p. 415.

could not afford to attend them. Such schools were looked upon by many as undemocratic institutions because of their exclusiveness and the difficulty of even the "practical" subjects. Furthermore, the academies never came completely under public control, even when some public funds were used. Little or no regulation led to many weak schools. These taught almost everything and all of it poorly.

The first truly *public* secondary schools were founded in Boston in 1821 and 1826 — the first for boys, the second for girls. This type of school came to be known as the English high school, shortly after its founding, since the classical and foreign languages were not in the curriculum. The founding of the first two English high schools was followed in 1827 by the High School Act of the Massachusetts legislature, which required towns with 500 or more families to maintain a school to teach the high school subjects — United States history, algebra, geometry, surveying, and bookkeeping. In 1859 another law, enacted by the legislature of the same state, enlarged upon the subjects to be offered, and also permitted neighboring towns to cooperate in forming high schools.

Other Northern states soon followed Massachusetts' lead, and by the Civil War had accepted the principle of free secondary school education and provided for the establishment of high schools in their towns and cities. Few rural high schools were established before 1900, however. In the South, public high schools also developed very slowly. The upper social classes of Southern states attended private schools; the lower classes did not expect more than an elementary education. As a result, public high schools were not established in any numbers until Georgia led the way in 1906 with a law which provided for agricultural schools.

A number of citizens in all parts of the country opposed tax-supported high schools, for they felt that public support for elementary education fulfilled their obligation to the youth of the country. Any educational expense beyond the elementary level, they argued, should be borne by those wishing such education. The first legal test of taxation for the support of public high schools came in Michigan in 1874 in the well-known Kalamazoo Case. The Supreme Court of Michigan decided that it was legal for school districts to levy taxes for the support of secondary schools. Other states followed Michigan's example, thereby giving legal approval to a practice that started with the first free public high school over 50 years earlier.

The curriculum of the first public high school in Boston was basically the same as that of the academies, except for the dropping of the classical languages. But the Boston pattern was not to be followed in all future high schools. Latin was returned to the high school curriculum and remains to this day as an elective. The primary reason for reinstating "traditional" subjects was the simple fact that admission to college still demanded a certain pattern of high school courses.

The offerings of public high schools varied also from community to community, in response to the needs and demands of the residents. Thus, by the beginning of the twentieth century one could point to no single dominant pattern of courses in American secondary schools except the college-preparatory "track." But just at the turn of the century voluntary accrediting agencies sprang up. The Middle States and the North Central Associations of Secondary Schools and Colleges were organized, and certain requirements for membership were established. One of their first tasks consisted in formulating more specific college-entrance requirements. For example, the North Central Association recommended (in 1900) that its member colleges admit only those students who had graduated from a four-year high school (or its equivalent) with two years of English, two of mathematics, one of science, and one of history, for a total of six units. Ten other elective units were to be added to these six. Today the regional accrediting agencies set standards for buildings and equipment, curriculum, teacher preparation and salaries, length of class periods and school year, pupil-teacher ratios, libraries, and a few other school characteristics.

At about the same time, 1892, the National Education Association, the professional organization of teachers, appointed a committee of ten experts to attempt to put some order in secondary education. After a year of conferences the committees listed the following subjects for secondary schools: Greek, Latin, English, German, French, Spanish, algebra, geometry and trigonometry, general history (United States, European, ancient, etc.), astronomy, meteorology, botany, zoology, physiology, geology, ethnology, physical geography, physics, and chemistry. Obviously, these courses were offered primarily for the college-bound student, and in general it was believed that each of them developed the students' mental powers. These were the "prestige subjects"; but the vocational subjects were not removed from the curriculum and were still taken by many students who were intellectually unable to handle the academic curriculum or uninterested in it.

Some influential progressive educators objected to the exclusively academic nature of the committee's proposed curriculum and argued for one clearly designed to fit the needs of all students.[8]

In many respects the curriculum of contemporary high schools is similar to that of early twentieth-century schools. Opportunities are offered for the college-bound student to get the academic requirements necessary for college entrance; and a variety of vocational, cultural, and recreational offerings are available to those with other pursuits in mind. The number and variety of courses offered depends, however, upon the size of the school and the socioeconomic level of the high school clientele. For example, a large comprehensive high school in an area with middle-class and some lower-class families will offer college-preparatory work in mathematics, the sciences, Latin and modern foreign languages, social studies (including history, geography, and civics), and English. Several of these subjects may be combined in a "core" program. A full complement of home economics courses (as many as a dozen) and industrial arts and business education courses are offered for the terminal student. In addition, physical education, driver training, music (band, chorus, etc.), art, dramatics, speech are available.

A high school serving rural areas usually will have at least one full-time agriculture teacher to provide training in "scientific farming." Some high schools offer a variety of courses in arts and crafts and other subjects designed to help students use their leisure time well, e.g., fly casting and social dancing. Thus the high school curriculum of today may range all the way from an "educational cafeteria" with hundreds of units in some large schools, to only the basic subjects of the traditional high school. Many activities which were formerly considered extracurriculur now are an integral part of the high school program, thus expanding it further without adding new courses.

The Smith-Hughes Act of 1917 greatly stimulated vocational education by subsidizing high school offerings in agriculture, home economics, and industrial education, and by providing for the preparation of teachers in these areas. This act is a notable instance

---

[8] See Charles De Garma, "Critique of the Report," *Educational Review*, March, 1894.

of federal action to correct neglect of an important phase of education by the local communities (cf. Chap. III). Funds appropriated by Congress under the Smith-Hughes Act are made available to states on the basis of student population; but, to receive this federal money, a state and its communities must spend an equal amount of their own money for programs of the same type.

Whatever the curriculum of the modern high school happens to be, most educators at that level feel it should, as nearly as possible, achieve the objectives which have been proposed by the National Association of Secondary School Principals of the N.E.A.[9] These objectives are aimed at producing: the vocationally prepared youth; the healthy, cooperative, and democratic citizen; the wise consumer; the good father or mother of a family; a person who appreciates beauty in art, music, and literature; one who uses his leisure time well; and, finally, the person who can think rationally, express his thoughts clearly, read and listen intelligently, and understand the role of science in modern life.

The several organizational patterns of secondary education in the United States are clarified by Figure 3 (see p. 30). When the elementary school includes the first eight grades, the high school usually embraces Grades 9 through 12. When the elementary school reaches only through Grade 6, the junior high school generally encompasses Grades 7 through 9, and the senior high school, 10 through 12. These two are the most common organizational patterns, although some states include Grades 13 and 14 in secondary education. However, since these grades are usually designated as junior college, they shall be discussed separately.

The junior high school, a relative newcomer in secondary education (1910), is difficult to describe. It is more advanced than elementary school, yet not quite so sophisticated as senior high school. Perhaps one of the most significant purposes of the junior high school is to move the pupil gradually from the single curriculum and self-contained classroom of the elementary school to the subject-matter specialization of the senior high school. For the first time the student can select an elective in the areas of science, mathematics, foreign languages, shopwork, arts and crafts, or elsewhere. In

---

[9] National Association of Secondary School Principals, "Planning for all American Youth" (Washington, D. C., 1951), p. 9. See Chapter X, below, for analysis of these objectives.

Fig. 3. The Structure of Elementary and Secondary Education
in the United States

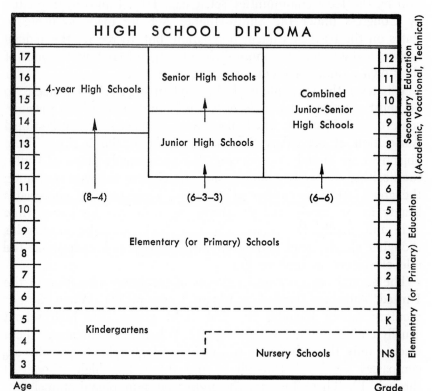

Source: U. S. Office of Education, *Progress of Public Education in the United States of America, 1961–62* (OE–10005–62–B) (Washington, D. C.: U. S. Government Printing Office, 1962).

general, the work of a junior high school student is more exploratory and less penetrating and thorough than that of a senior high school student. Through "homerooms" and double periods he still has some of the advantages of the elementary school, along with his initiation into the specialization of senior high school. Not all school districts maintain junior high schools. Further, not all junior high schools are basically transitional schools of the type described above. Some are as clearly departmentalized as are senior high schools.

The preceding paragraphs portray the expansion of the curriculum and purposes of the public secondary schools. Certainly, in these matters, the high school of today is a far cry from its forebears, the Latin grammar school and the academy. But these changes are far less startling than the enrollment changes which are shown in Figure 4. As mentioned previously, the peak enrollment in the tuition academies was a little over 250,000 in 1850. By 1900 there were only about five hundred thousand students in the free public secondary schools. In 1920 there were over two million; in 1940, over six million; in 1962 the unofficial count was approximately 12½ mil-

Fig. 4. Enrollment in Grades 9–12 in Public and Independent Schools of the United States, 1900–1970

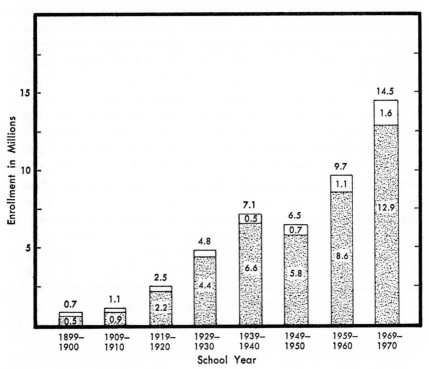

NOTES:

1. Shaded portion of bar indicates public school enrollment. White portion indicates independent school enrollment.

2. Figures through 1960 are actual enrollments based upon U. S. Office of Education data. Source: *Progress of Public Education in the United States of America, 1961–62* (OE–10005–62–B) (Washington, D. C.: U. S. Government Printing Office, 1962), p. 48, Table 2.

3. Figures for 1970 are projections assuming current trends.

lion. The estimated enrollment for 1970 is around the 15 million mark.[10]

What is more significant than numbers, perhaps, is the percentage of youth of high school age enrolled in school. In 1960, nearly 90 percent were in school — nine of ten in public schools. (In European countries today only about 15 percent of the youth of secondary school age are enrolled.) In 1889–1900 only 6.7 percent of the youth of high school age were enrolled in high schools, both public and private. It was not until 1930 that 50 percent of American youth of high school age were enrolled in public or private high schools.[11] Of course the number of teachers rose correspondingly from 12,000 in 1850 to 578,400 in the public secondary school system in 1962.

As has been stated in the preceding paragraphs, most modern high schools offer some form of more practical education such as industrial arts, agriculture, business and secretarial training, and homemaking arts. However, there are some schools within the public educational system that are designed primarily for preparing youth for immediate placement in business and industry upon graduation. Such schools are often called "technical" or "trade" high schools; usually they are located in the larger cities, where there is great demand for trained personnel in the skilled trades. In most of these schools the student will take a majority of his courses in his special area of training and enroll only in a few of the general education courses of the high school, such as English and history. Most often the courses in the mathematics and science areas are designed to develop the student's competence in his specialty, e.g., industrial chemistry, business mathematics, and the like. Many of the schools of this type are not coeducational, with a larger number enrolling only boys. The opinion seems to be that most of the coeducational high schools offer enough vocational courses for girls as part of the regular high school program, thus reducing the demand for separate vocational schools for girls.

Some of these vocational schools are under the administrative control of the same organizational unit as the regular public high school.

---

[10] "School Statistics: 1961–62," *N.E.A. Research Bulletin*, Vol. 40, No. 1, February, 1962, p. 4.

[11] U. S. Office of Education, *Progress of Public Education in the United States of America, 1961–62* (OE–10005–62–B) (Washington, D. C.: U. S. Government Printing Office, 1962), p. 48, Table 2.

Others have an independent administrative structure, even though they receive public tax money for their support.

PUBLIC HIGHER EDUCATION

The history of higher education prior to 1850 is in the main a history of independent or church-related education. Some state colleges and universities were founded before 1850, but the real expansion of public higher education did not take place until the last few decades of the nineteenth century and the first half of the twentieth century. Georgia can claim credit for establishing the first state college or university (1785). North Carolina, Vermont, Tennessee, Ohio, Maryland, Virginia, Alabama, Indiana, Delaware, Kentucky, Michigan, Mississippi, Iowa, and Wisconsin followed Georgia's lead in the order listed. All were founded before 1850. But many of today's "Ivy League" schools had been founded even earlier, and they were the influential institutions. Harvard, William and Mary, Yale, Princeton, Pennsylvania, Columbia, Brown, Rutgers, and Dartmouth were all in operation prior to 1770.

Early American institutions of higher learning had the education of the ministry as their chief goal. This was true of all colleges established before the Revolution except the University of Pennsylvania, which had its start as an academy.[12] But it was evident that the public institutions had to select nonsectarian purposes in order to remain public institutions, although sectarian interests often made the distinction a dubious one. Practical, secular goals were dominant, however, in the new state institutions of higher education.

Thomas Jefferson was among the first of those who emphasized the secular goals of higher education. In his plans for the public university of his own state, Virginia, he wished that all the subjects considered "useful" for "modern times" be taught. Moreover, he argued that the natural sciences, political science, history, and modern languages be considered as worthwhile as the classical curriculum. Another point he made was that the goals of public institutions should embrace leadership training for the country's statesmen, training for the professions, and pure research in all academic fields. Since he considered these broad goals so essential to the welfare of

---

[12] Stewart G. Cole, *Liberal Education in a Democracy* (New York: Harper & Brothers, 1940), p. 4.

the nation, Jefferson believed that the universities should be supported by the state and made free from sectarian bias and control.

The Morrill Act of 1862 represents another milestone in the development of the ideal of the American university as a service institution in the practical or useful areas. This act appropriated lands in every state to be used to promote education in agriculture, mechanical arts, and the natural sciences (cf. Chap. III). Some appropriations under the Morrill Act went to independent schools which negotiated contracts with their respective states. Cornell University in New York, a privately controlled university, is still affiliated with the program.

Research, another important goal of the public universities, was brought to this country from Germany before the public institutions were even founded. American students attending German universities had returned with a "research mind" and began pushing this ideal in opposition to the prevalent one of a liberal, religious education based on the "disciplinary value" of a prescribed course in the classics. Experimentalism and specialization became the accepted pattern in many American universities even at the undergraduate level.

Charles W. Eliot, president of Harvard, for the last three decades of the nineteenth century and the first decade of the twentieth, also worked for removal of the prescribed curriculum and advocated that students be given the freedom to select the course of studies most suited to their needs, interests, and abilities. His view was that a person could be "liberally educated" by modern studies such as the physical sciences, social sciences, and modern languages, just as well as by the classical curriculum of the humanistic schools.

Another very significant event in American higher education was the admission of women to the ranks of college and university students. Oberlin College became the first coeducational institution in the country when it opened its doors to women in 1837, and gave them the opportunity to work for the same A.B. degree as men. One year later the first college for women was opened in the U. S., Mount Holyoke in Massachusetts. Most of the women's colleges are still under independent control. Public educational opportunities for women are found almost exclusively in the coeducational state colleges and universities.

As one might anticipate, increased enrollments in secondary

schools, coupled with the enlarged demands of a technological society, were followed by increased enrollments in institutions of higher learning. This is evident from the statistics presented in Figure 5. In 1900 there were 90,684 students in public universities and colleges and 146,903 in independent institutions of the same type. The ratio of the total college and university enrollment to the college-age population (18 to 21) was only 4 per cent; and less than four of every ten of these students were in public schools. In the fall of 1961 there were about 2,400,000 degree-seeking students in publicly con-

Fig. 5. Enrollment in Public and Independent Institutions of Higher Education in the United States, 1900–1970

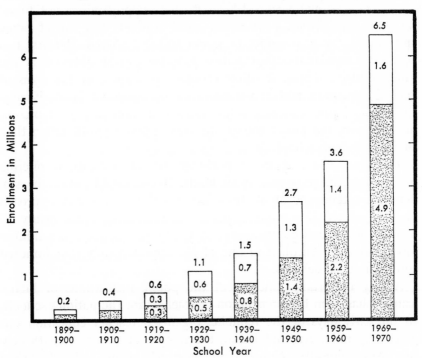

NOTES:

1. Shaded portion of bar indicates enrollment in public institutions. White portion indicates independent school enrollment.
2. Figures through 1960 are based on U. S. Office of Education figures. Principal source: *Statistical Summary of Education, 1957–58*, Chap. I, "Biennial Survey of Education in the United States, 1956–58" (OE–10003–58) (Washington, D. C.: U. S. Government Printing Office, 1962), p. 5, Table 4.
3. Figures for 1970 are projections assuming current rate of change of ratio of college population to high school population and a continued decline in the proportion of students attending independent colleges and universities.

trolled colleges and universities, and about two thirds of that number or 1,500,000 in independent institutions of the same level. Now six of every ten are in public institutions. The total for both public and independent schools is nearly 4 million and the ratio of students to the total college-age population has risen to 38 percent. These latest figures include about half a million junior college students in courses designed to prepare students for further study leading to a bachelor's level degree, but omit those preparing for immediate employment in a number of occupations. Sixty-two percent of today's college students are men.[13]

The junior college may well be the institution that will experience the most growth in the next decade. Even though it is a latecomer on the educational scene (1902), it offers opportunities not found in other institutions. First of all, most students can live at home and attend the community or junior college. Second, the first two years of a regular four-year college program can be obtained at the junior college. Third, it offers terminal education in the areas of general education and in vocational or occupational fields. Finally, the public junior college has low tuition or none at all. At present nine of every ten junior college students attend a public rather than an independent school.

There are other types of post-high school institutions offering one-to-four-year programs of all kinds. If one could count the students in attendance at all these schools the sum would approach or even exceed five million; and to that amazing total, nearly 50 percent of the college-age group, we might add as many as a million more who have enrolled in one of the approximately four hundred correspondence schools.

A very important function of the public institutions of higher learning has been the preparation of teachers for the nation's schools. In the early days of the republic, organized teacher education was practically unknown; but before the middle of the nineteenth century Massachusetts, Connecticut, and Michigan had established state schools for elementary teachers (normal schools). Even before this time some of the tuition academies had been given tax funds to offer training in pedagogy for elementary teachers.

As normal schools were established, they were often attached to

---

[13] Edith M. Huddleston, "Opening College Enrollment, Fall 1961," *Higher Education*, Vol. XVIII, No. 4, January-February, 1962, pp. 12–16.

local high schools, and high school teachers might act as instructors. The high school teachers of the time were usually trained in colleges, where the aim was mastery of the content of the teaching fields plus, of course, disciplining the mind. A rather large number of high school teachers began as elementary teachers and were "promoted" as they took additional college work. The usual normal school gave a one-year course in which the prospective teacher was drilled in the fundamentals of the elementary school subjects and the constitution of the United States, and was given some training in teaching methods. Often there was a model or practice school connected with the normal school in which the prospective teacher might "observe and imitate" the master teacher.

The school that set the pattern for the later normal schools was founded in Oswego, New York, in 1866. Oswego's distinction was the incorporation of Pestallozi's theories of education into its teacher-training methods (cf. Chap. X). Two-year normal schools are still in existence in a few states of the union (e.g., Wisconsin).

As the professional level of the elementary schools rose, the normal school began raising requirements until, around the end of the nineteenth century, applicants were expected to have completed high school before being admitted to the normal school. Illinois State Normal University, founded in 1857, was one of the first to make high school graduation a requirement.

In 1879 the University of Michigan registered another "first" in the history of teacher education by establishing a full-time professorship in education. Then, around 1890, New York University and Columbia began graduate work in teacher education.[14]

By 1920 the normal schools began to wane and were replaced by the state teachers' colleges. At mid-twentieth century many state teachers' colleges were in turn being transformed into state colleges with schools or departments of education. In addition, practically every state university had a school or department of education by the end of World War I. Thus the typical teacher of today is prepared in an institution which has the same common stock of college courses found in all institutions of higher learning, as well as those "education courses" needed for state certification. Certainly

---

[14] For dates on founding of normal schools and education departments see E. W. Knight, *Fifty Years of American Education* (New York, Ronald Press Co., 1952), Chap. 6.

the education of today's teacher is a far cry from the first normal school training in the fundamentals of reading, 'riting and 'rithmetic, plus a course or two in pedagogy.

In one recent year (1957) for which data are available, about 15 percent of qualified teacher graduates had studied in schools designed especially for teacher training. About 40 percent were graduated from universities, and another 40 percent came from multipurpose colleges.[15] It seems safe to predict that within the new few decades most teachers will receive their education in a four- or five-year program in an institution with comprehensive offerings, where future teachers will not be isolated or separated from college students preparing for other careers.

Although the trend is away from separate teachers' colleges, the student population of these institutions will not decline in an era of teacher shortages. On the contrary we may expect their enrollments to grow so rapidly that they will be transformed into multipurpose institutions. This is what has happened in the past. As a matter of fact, the schools presently classified as teachers' colleges enjoyed an 11.8 percent increase in enrollment from 1960–1961 to 1961–1962, greater than that experienced by any other major type of college except the junior colleges, which were up 14.9 percent.

In 1961–1962 the teachers' colleges enrolled 402,000 students, of whom approximately 20,000 were graduated in June of 1962.[16] From all institutions an estimated 106,000 new teachers were available in September, 1962. Five or six thousand more were trained for teaching at less than the baccalaureate level. But this is far from enough! In fact, 240,000 new teachers were needed in 1962.[17] In Figure 13 in Chapter XVII the 1962 shortage of qualified teachers is estimated at substantially more than 130,000.

GRADUATE AND PROFESSIONAL EDUCATION

The granting of degrees beyond the bachelor's degree, viz., master's and doctor's degrees, was very haphazard prior to the beginning of the twentieth century. In the first part of the nineteenth century most were "unearned" or honorary degrees which were not recog-

---

[15] Lindley J. Stiles, A. S. Barr, Carl R. Douglass, and Hubert H. Mills, *Teacher Education in the United States* (New York: The Ronald Press Co., 1960), p. 104.

[16] Huddleston, *op. cit.*

[17] National Education Association, *Teacher Supply and Demand in Public Schools, 1962*, Research Report, 1962–R8 (Washington, D. C.: The Association, 1962), p. 21.

nized by any respectable European university. As the end of the nineteenth century approached, American educational leaders offered scathing criticism of the practice of granting supposedly advanced degrees with no systematic instruction in the related subject fields.

The United States commissioners of education, and influential publications like *Educational Review*, were especially vigorous in their attacks on the "diploma mills." Of course not all schools of the late decades of the nineteenth century gave advanced degrees without requiring certain evidences of scholarship beyond the A.B. level. Respectable schools like Johns Hopkins University, which had opened in 1876 for the sole purpose of providing graduate work, were naturally outraged by such fraudulent practices. But it is not within the scope of this chapter to do a qualitative analysis of the whole problem of advanced degree granting.[18] Suffice it to say that a long-overdue academic "housecleaning" was under way by the turn of the century.

One of the "new brooms" used effectively about this time was the Association of American Universities, which was founded in 1900. This organization worked tirelessly on the standards for advanced degrees. Other professional organizations contributing to the upgrading of standards were the American Philological Association, American Association for the Advancement of Science, National Association of State Universities, the American Association of University Professors, Association of Land-Grant Colleges and Universities, and the National Catholic Education Association (College and University Department). As a result, by the outbreak of World War II anyone connected with graduate work was able to learn whether the holder of an advanced degree possessed a recognized degree or merely a worthless piece of sheepskin. The U. S. Office of Education compiled a list of recognized graduate schools, and similar information can be found elsewhere. Although an advanced degree from one school may be considered "better" than that of another, the line between recognized and unrecognized advanced degrees is now very clear.

Graduate enrollments in true degree programs (not honorary)

---

[18] See: National Society for the Study of Education (Chicago: University of Chicago Press, 1951): *Fiftieth Yearbook*, "History of Graduate Instruction in the United States."

have grown, as have the enrollments in undergraduate programs. This is clearly indicated in the number of earned degrees conferred. In 1870 only one was reported; by 1900 there were 1583 master's and 382 doctor's. Thirty years later, in 1930, nearly 15,000 master's and over 2000 doctor's were recorded. The pace has not slackened since. An estimated 76,000 master's and 10,000 doctor's degrees were awarded in 1959–1960.[19]

The field of professional education is a relative latecomer in the business of granting advanced degrees. As noted earlier in this chapter, New York University and Teachers College, Columbia University, were the first universities to offer graduate work in education. But the state universities soon followed suit, and only a few decades later many teachers were getting advanced degrees in professional education. In recent years more than a third of all master's degrees and a seventh of all doctorates awarded were in education. This increase in advanced degrees in education (especially master's) is probably due to: (1) advantages gained on salary schedules of the public schools by the holders of advance degrees and (2) increased requirements in professional education study by certification agencies.

A word about the professional schools might be in order in this short survey of higher education. The professional education of teachers was discussed above in sufficient detail for the purposes of this chapter.

The first professional schools in this country were designed to train the ministry. In fact the first purpose of all higher education was preparation for the ministry. Education for other professions, such as medicine, dentistry, and law, was not specifically provided for in the early days of our country. Most of our outstanding physicians, for example, were trained in European schools. Lawyers were usually trained through an apprenticeship program.

Dentistry might be used as an example of the development of programs of education for a number of professions in this country. About the middle of the nineteenth century the dental curriculum consisted of two lecture courses of four months' duration coupled with some preceptorial training. At that time there were no ad-

---

    [19] U. S. Office of Education, *Progress of Public Education in the United States of America: 1961–62* (OE–10005–62–B) (Washington, D. C.: Government Printing Office, 1962), p. 54, Table 8.

mission requirements. By 1910 the program had grown to three years in length and required at least two years of high school for admission. By 1930, dental schools required at least two years of college for admission to a full four-year program. The modern dental curriculum combines clinical practice with highly technical training in microbiology, pathology, biochemistry, pharmacology, physiology, and other basic sciences. With all of this content the dental program of studies will probably soon be extended to five years.

A similar metamorphosis in professional training has been experienced by other professions. Like dentistry, they have gone from practically no admission requirements and short programs of preparation to relatively selective admission requirements and a long program of preparation. Actually, many who oppose further extension of professional programs believe that too much time is spent on schooling. A medical doctor, for example, has difficulty getting through school and an internship before he is thirty years old.

Much of the improvement in professional training has been brought about through the efforts of the professional organizations for dentists, doctors, and lawyers. Another significant factor is the educational studies which the Carnegie Foundation has sponsored for these professions. These activities and problems are discussed in Chapter XVII.

As is the case in teacher education, education for other professions is not carried on exclusively in public institutions of higher learning. In some professions, such as the ministry, training is given only in private schools. For medicine, dentistry, engineering, and law, the burden today is shared by public and independent schools.

Enrollments have increased in the professional schools as in other higher educational institutions. For example in the first decade of the twentieth century medical schools enrolled about 12½ thousand students. By mid-century the enrollments had just about doubled. Relatively this increase is small, however. During the same period enrollments in higher education in general increased eightfold. In 1905 there was one medical student to every six students in college; at mid-century the ratio was one to a hundred. By the 1960's the shortage of medical doctors was becoming critical. What has been happening in medicine has occurred in greater or less degree in other professions. As the general population becomes more highly educated, the demand for highly trained people in all the professions will continue to increase and pose ever greater problems for our educational system.

ADULT EDUCATION

Since most adult-education activities are carried on in the post-high school years, adult education is sometimes classified as higher education. However, it must be clearly differentiated from college and university adult education, which are forms of higher education leading to recognized college degrees. The purposes are vocational, avocational, or simply self-improvement. To keep the discussion within manageable limits the immense amount of informal education carried on for similar purposes by libraries, theaters, radio, TV, clubs, and other agencies will not be included. Rather, we shall limit the topic to organized formal classes for the post-high school age group not seeking degree credit.

Prior to the Civil War several attempts were made to organize adult education classes. About the middle of the seventeenth century a few evening schools were organized in New York State. In 1808 Yale University offered what we now call extension courses. The state of Ohio can be given credit for sponsoring the first public institutions for adult education, when it passed a law in 1839 making it possible for communities to offer evening classes.

The post-Civil War period saw the first great expansion of public adult education. Some of the first public school evening courses for adults were designed to prepare the host of immigrants for American citizenship. Greater proficiency in the English language was a related goal. This type of adult education is still common in urban areas, where most immigrants settle.

Many new courses were added to adult programs in the first decades of the twentieth century. Some examples are typing, shorthand, general business, music appreciation, arts and crafts, folk and ballroom dancing, and gardening or agricultural methods. In large urban areas today adult-education programs offer just as many (and sometimes more) courses as are found in the high school curriculum. During World War I the federal government lent support to adult education via the Smith-Lever Act which provided funds specifically for adult education in the field of agriculture.

The enrollments of early adult-education programs are not available and even those of today are somewhat unreliable. In 1955 it was estimated that there were approximately 50 million students enrolled in all forms of public and private adult-education courses. This figure represents a 20 million increase in the five-year period from 1950 to 1955, a 28 million increase in 20 years, and a 35 million increase since World War I.[20]

The recent rapid growth of adult-education activities in the United States has its reasons. First, psychologists have been relatively successful in convincing the public that learning is not limited to the time of youth, but rather that one can learn as long as one lives. Second, the great demand for the specialized skills of business and industry have put pressure on adults to get more formal education if they are going to "get ahead on the job." Third, the increasing amount of leisure time brought about by technological advances has provided the worker and housewife with time for further study.

In 1926 the first coordinating organization for adult education was founded, the American Association for Adult Education. The National Education Association had a Department of Adult Education within its organization which later joined forces (1951) with the American Association for Adult Education to form the Adult Education Association. This latter organization is the largest centralizing force in the many-faceted activities of adult education in the United States. The 624-page 1960 *Handbook* of this organization is perhaps the best single source of information on adult education in this country. According to this source certain generalizations about adult education may be made.

1. Adult education has risen in response to the needs and interests of people rather than as a result of a planned program of post-high school education;

2. Adult-education programs, even though they enroll extremely large numbers of students, still occupy a status in the American educational scene which is subsidiary or inferior to the regular programs of elementary, secondary, and higher education;

3. In spite of the great advances made in centralizing the activities of adult education each institution tends to formulate and keep its own program without tying it to any general "adult-education movement";

---

[20] See M. Knowles, "Adult Education in the U. S.," *Adult Education*, Vol. 5, 1955, p. 75 ff.

4. Agencies designed for other purposes (e.g., church work, civic service) tend to sponsor the institutional forms of adult education;

5. The development of adult education has not followed the same pattern as that of public education in general and appears to have been somewhat unrelated to other education developments.[21]

Summary

The antecedents of American education, as we know it today, are to be found in history. The first colonial schools of all levels were church projects serving church purposes by European methods. Still, a tradition of community responsibility for education arose in Puritan Massachusetts where social, political, and religious authority was one. It was there that community support for secular education in the national interest, as conceived by the leaders of the new nation, first took root, then spread rapidly to other states. The enabling legislation by all states was virtually complete before 1900.

The curriculum of the schools at all levels has evolved in response to an experimental philosophy and the needs of the nation. Reading and the basic skills were the concerns of the first American elementary schools; but by the time these became public, they added several courses as an introduction to the newer high school subjects. Vocation and avocational studies have been added to the elementary school program in this century as schools abandoned their traditional preoccupation with intellectual goals and launched a many-sided effort to improve almost every aspect of pupils' lives. New developments of the past several years suggest a renewed emphasis on intellectual goals, however.

The secondary schools were strictly college preparatory at first and offered only traditional subjects. Franklin's vocationally oriented school held the center of the stage before the public high school, offering both vocational and college-preparatory work, developed. Accrediting agencies are now active in establishing standards for the offerings of the modern high school in terms of the needs of its clientele. Such offerings are often very comprehensive, rivaling those of the colleges. Extensive offerings of vocational, avocational, or self-improvement courses for the high school graduate who is not seeking an advanced degree are sponsored by many public schools.

---

[21] M. S. Knowles (ed.), *Handbook of Adult Education* (Chicago: Adult Education Association, 1960), p. 26.

Schools on the collegiate or university level passed through a long period in which their offerings were limited largely to religion and the classics. During the nineteenth century they gradually added "modern subjects," such as physical sciences, social sciences, modern languages, and art and music. Soon students could specialize, as they may now, in an academic area or in one of the professional courses — agriculture, education, business, engineering, and others. Graduate study in academic and professional fields was pioneered by Johns Hopkins University in 1876. Most professions have a "past" of practically no standards and requirements of preparation, but today's universities have evolved selective admissions practices and programs of rigorous study and training.

Today, the curriculum at all educational levels is changing more rapidly than ever before. New factors making for change are a tremendous expansion of knowledge in all areas, new leaders, support from the federal government and philanthropic organizations, and intense international competition.

The traditional types of schools have changed also. The well-known elementary school (six or eight grades) and the high school (three or four grades) were more and more often preceded by a kindergarten year for self-discovery and social adjustment, and separated by a transitional institution, the junior high school (Grades 7 to 9). Special vocational or trade schools became common. A two-year "junior college," developed to provide the first two years of a college education or terminal training for a number of occupations in the local community, was a distinctive American institution.

Two- or three-year normal schools for training teachers were numerous during the nineteenth century. Most normal schools have now been replaced by the four-year teachers' college, and many of these have added liberal arts studies to become multipurpose institutions. Large universities are distinguished by their graduate programs for training research scholars and college teachers in academic fields, and by a variety of associated professional schools. Colleges and universities endowed by federal land grants of the nineteenth century are known for schools of agriculture and domestic and mechanical arts.

The American school population has never stopped growing. Steady increases for institutions at all levels have been noted in almost every decade since the Revolution. The rate of increase for public institutions rose steadily from 1900 to 1950 and very rapidly thereafter.

From about 15 million in 1900, public elementary and secondary school enrollment has jumped to nearly 40 million or over 80 percent of the school-age group. The main factor has been population growth, although the schools also serve a larger portion of school-age youth, particularly on the high school level.

Enrollments on the college level have grown dramatically and now include about 38 percent of the age group (18 to 21) with nearly three million in public institutions and 1½ million in independent schools. Additional thousands train for specific occupations in public nondegree programs after high school graduation, and millions enroll for some avocational, vocational or self-improvement courses. Graduate schools now award nearly 90,000 graduate degrees annually, as compared to less than 2000 in 1900. Large numbers of highly qualified professionals are trained each year at both the undergraduate and graduate levels, but not enough, since our demand for professional services has grown even faster than our population. The shortage of qualified teachers is particularly acute.

SELECTED READINGS

Conant, James B., *The American High School Today* (New York: McGraw-Hill Book Co., 1959).
    An influential book by a former president of Harvard which characterizes a select group of comprehensive high schools and gives recommendations for improving the teaching of knowledges and skills. The point of view is that of an administrator rather than of a student of human learning.

Cottrell, Donald P. (ed.), *Teacher Education for a Free People* (Oneonta, N.Y.: American Association of Colleges for Teacher Education, 1956).
    Suggests principles and policies and illustrates practices. Chapter II by Charles W. Hunt sketches the historical development of teacher-education agencies and standards.

Cubberley, Elwood P., *Public Education in the United States*, rev. ed. (New York: Houghton Mifflin Co., 1934).
    Standard factual treatment. Chapters 6 and 7 discuss the "battle for free public schools" and the "struggle to extend the system upward."

Cubberley, Elwood P. (ed.), *Readings in Public Education in the United States* (New York: Houghton Mifflin Co., 1934).
    Original sources and documents of importance in the history of education are reproduced.

DeYoung, Chris A., *American Education* (New York: McGraw-Hill Book Co., 1960), Part II.
    A concise review of pioneer efforts and the expansion of public education at each level from nursery school to higher and adult education. Useful historical charts relate national and educational developments.

Drake, William E., *The American School in Transition* (New York: Prentice-Hall, 1955), Chaps. 6, 7 and 10.

Historical background on the nineteenth-century public schools and influences which shaped them. Chapter 10 deals with curriculum changes.

Elicker, Paul E., "The Next Twenty-five Years in Secondary Education," *Education Digest*, Vol. 23 (March, 1958), pp. 9–11.

A penetrating look ahead and a prediction of new respect for teachers.

French, William M., *American Secondary Education* (New York: Odyssey Press, 1957), Chaps. 2–6.

Describes the European heritage in secondary education, the Latin grammar schools, the academies and the battle for free high schools.

Good, Harry G., *A History of American Education*, 2 ed. (New York: The Macmillan Co., 1962).

A comprehensive chronological survey of the development of public schools which relates changes to social and political events. Chapters 18 and 19 analyze changes since World War II.

Irwin, Mary (ed.), *American Universities and Colleges* (Washington, D. C.: American Council on Education, 1960).

Includes several chapters on the history and status of higher education as well as detailed information on major colleges and universities.

Knight, Edgar W., *Education in the United States* (Boston: Ginn & Co., 1951), Chap. 5.

Outstanding description of early frontier schools.

Knowles, Malvern S., "Adult Education in the United States," *Adult Education*, Vol. 5 (Winter, 1955), pp. 67–75.

A brief history of adult education at local and national levels.

Mayer, Martin, *The Schools* (New York: Harper Bros., 1961).

A reporter's first-hand account of what he finds happening in today's schools plus interesting sketches of life in yesterday's schools (Chaps. 2 and 3).

Medsker, Leland L., "The Junior College Picture," *NEA Journal*, Vol. 47 (December, 1958), pp. 628–630.

Describes the different types of junior colleges and their advantages and disadvantages.

National Education Association, *Early Education* (Washington, D. C.: the Association, 1956).

Sixteen authoritative statements on early childhood education.

Power, Edward J., *Education for American Democracy* (New York: McGraw-Hill Book Co., 1958).

First of the publisher's Catholic Series in Education. Chap. 2 describes the origins and essential features of education in the United States; Chaps. 6–8, the historical development, objectives, curriculum and methods of elementary, secondary and higher education respectively.

Stiles, Lindley J., Barr, A. S. Douglass, Harl R., and Mills, Hubert H., *Teacher Education in the United States* (New York: Ronald Press Co., 1960), Chaps. 5 and 6.

Classification and description of types of institutions and programs for teacher education.

Chapter III

THE ADMINISTRATION OF
PUBLIC EDUCATION

This chapter is about the way the free, tax-supported schools of America are administered, financed, and controlled. Traditionally, public schools have been and today are run by the local communities, although the states have the greater legal responsibility. The United States is unique among the great nations of the world in having no national educational system. Still, the federal government must discharge its responsibility to "provide for the common defense and general welfare" (Constitution, Clause 1, Section 8 of Article I) and prevent any abridgment of "the privileges or immunities of the citizens of the United States" (Constitution, Fourteenth Amendment).

This chapter provides information about the organization and activities of educational agencies at the local, state, and national levels in order to show the way in which the different governmental units have worked together in sharing responsibility for schools and in providing for their operation by administrators and teachers.

THE LOCAL COMMUNITY AND EDUCATION

Local control of the schools is one of the oldest American traditions. There were strong religious motives for Bible reading in the early New England colonies, and towns established schools with this purpose in mind. In two historic acts the Massachusetts Bay Colony empowered officials to fine parents who did not teach their children to read (1642), and required all towns of at least fifty families to provide an elementary school (1647). The responsibility was to rest with the parents and the town. Other New England colonies soon took similar action; and, as settlers spread out from the towns, school districts were established in outlying areas.

Other early American colonies had different educational needs, and did not share the New England pattern. The Middle Atlantic colonies had a number of religious sects; and each sect preferred separate, rather than community-wide, schools. The South had one dominant religion, Anglicanism, but lacked the New England fervor for extending education to all classes.

Local support and control of education appears to have been well suited to the needs of frontier communities. At least we know that this Yankee element was prominent in the schools founded by Western settlers of the eighteenth and nineteenth centuries. Indeed it is scarcely less so in modern schools. All educational powers not specifically reserved in law to the federal and state governments are considered the concern and responsibility of the local school authorities. In effect, as we shall see, this makes the *policies* of the local authorities *law* in many respects, at least in the details of carrying out federal and state requirements with respect to education.

School Boards and Districts

One New England innovation, the school district, became the most popular unit for the administration of education at the local level. Originally, the district was just a local arrangement within or outside of towns to determine which families should be served by different schools. Later, district boundaries were established by state law. Several states use towns, townships, or counties as the local school units, however, and do not establish special districts.

In colonial days the governing bodies of communities often chose a school committee to hire a teacher and arrange for a school. These school committees were the forerunners of our local boards which have the responsibility for managing schools within each school district. The members of most school boards are elected, although some are appointed by governmental officials. Members of the board should be truly dedicated persons, for their position is one of responsibility and authority, requiring a great deal of time and offering little or no pay.

The school board is responsible for the total instructional program of the schools, and for insuring that the particular needs of the community and the requirements of the state are met. First, it must employ qualified school personnel, especially a chief administrative officer or superintendent. It must also furnish the facilities and funds for education. In most states about two thirds of the money for schools derives from local taxes; the rest may come from state taxes and special funds. All funds must be budgeted and spending carefully supervised.

The sources of school funds and the types of expenditures for all the nations' elementary and secondary schools are summarized in Figures 6 and 7. Current expenditures alone average $414 a student each year, although Mississippi spends only "$220 per pupil annually while New York spends $615."[1]

Numerous other responsibilities demand the time, energy, and wisdom of the board. A few examples are: pupil transportation, cafeterias, athletic programs, community relations, research, and development.

The principle of local control, once established, has helped to insure local efforts to provide competent schools; but when one considers that the smallest school districts may have only a few families,

Fig. 6.   Estimated Receipts for Public Elementary and Secondary Schools, by Source: Continental United States, 1959–60*

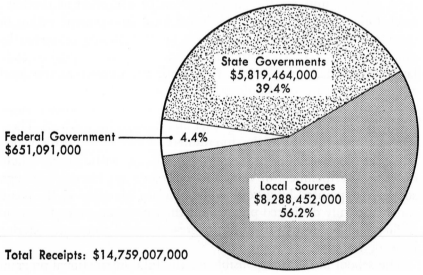

State Governments
$5,819,464,000
39.4%

Federal Government —————→ 4.4%
$651,091,000

Local Sources
$8,288,452,000
56.2%

Total Receipts: $14,759,007,000

* Reproduced from U. S. Office of Education, *Progress of Public Education in the United States of America, 1961–62* (OE–10005–62–B) (Washington, D. C.: U. S. Government Printing Office, 1962), p. 44, Figure 6.

[1] National Education Association, "Where Does Your State Stand," *Research Bulletin*, Vol. 40, No. 1, February, 1962, pp. 9–13.

Fig. 7. Summary of Expenditures for Public Elementary and Secondary
Schools: Continental United States, 1959–60*

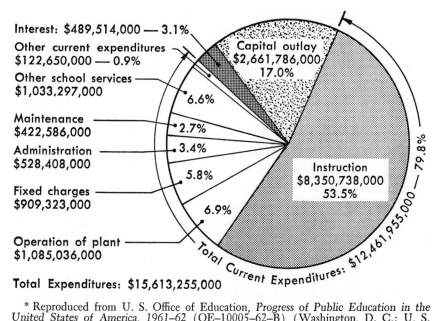

Interest: $489,514,000 — 3.1%

Other current expenditures
$122,650,000 — 0.9%

Other school services
$1,033,297,000

6.6%

Capital outlay
$2,661,786,000
17.0%

Maintenance
$422,586,000

2.7%

Administration
$528,408,000

3.4%

5.8%

Instruction
$8,350,738,000
53.5%

79.8%

Fixed charges
$909,323,000

6.9%

Operation of plant
$1,085,036,000

Total Expenditures: $15,613,255,000

Total Current Expenditures: $12,461,955,000

* Reproduced from U. S. Office of Education, *Progress of Public Education in the
United States of America, 1961–62* (OE–10005–62–B) (Washington, D. C.: U. S.
Government Printing Office, 1962), p. 45, Table 7.

and the largest, millions (New York City), it is evident that there
are vast differences in the ability of the boards to provide facilities
and programs. The original school districts, which were established
to support elementary schools, are often unable to maintain satisfactory secondary schools as well. For the past twenty years attempts
have been made to consolidate the smaller districts in order to bring
together students and teachers and pool resources. Although local
sentiment for old schools is still strong, the number of districts has
been reduced by 50 percent in the past ten years. Five states, however, still have over 2000 independent school districts.[2]

Superintendents and Principals

As school attendance increased and problems became more complex, school boards found it impossible to handle all details of

[2] In 1959–1960 over half of the school districts of the United States enrolled less
than 50 pupils. National Education Association, "What Do You Know About Today's
Schools," *Research Bulletin*, Vol. 39, No. 1, February, 1961, p. 27. Cf. also "School
Statistics, 1961–62," *ibid.*, Vol. 40, No. 1, February, 1962, p. 5.

managing the school. They reluctantly delegated some of their responsibility to a teacher or other person retained for the purpose. At first the duties of this position were largely of a clerical or accounting nature. It was inevitable, however, that with the further growth of schools such an individual would be given more and more duties such as hiring and supervising teachers, disciplining students, and planning courses. This executive officer of the board came to be called a superintendent. Several large cities, beginning with Buffalo, reported the establishment of the superintendency around 1837.[3] Finally, when business matters were in the superintendent's hands also, the role of the board became what it is today, that of policy-making. The superintendent is the board's chief administrator and the responsible head of the school system, charged with carrying out the policies of the board. His central role in the administrative organization of a large school district is shown in Figure 8 (see p. 53).

The superintendent is expected to be the community's educational leader. He must have broad professional competence and a high degree of skill in human relations and administrative processes. In systems of even moderate size he cannot master all the technical aspects of managing schools but must rely on his skill in choosing and supervising a staff. The superintendent of a large school system has deputy, associate, or assistant superintendents to help him. Sometimes each assistant assumes responsibility for a different educational level, such as elementary, junior high, or senior high school. In other places there are assistant superintendents for business, personnel, instruction, and other phases of school operations. Usually, assistant superintendents for both broad areas of administration are found. In 1961 the 23 largest cities had a total of 180 such officers intermediary between the superintendent and individual schools of the system.[4] In addition, the central office of large school systems usually has a number of specialists who act in a consulting or advisory role to the superintendents and to the principals and staff of each school.

The title of principal probably evolved from an earlier term, that of principal teacher. The principal of today may teach a full load or

---

[3] American Association of School Administrators, *The American School Superintendency*, Thirtieth Yearbook (Washington, D. C.: National Education Association, February, 1952), p. 55, Table 3.

[4] National Education Association, "Assistant Superintendents," *Research Bulletin*, Vol. 40, No. 1, February, 1962, p. 25.

Fig. 8. Possible Organization of the Administrative Staff of a Large School District*

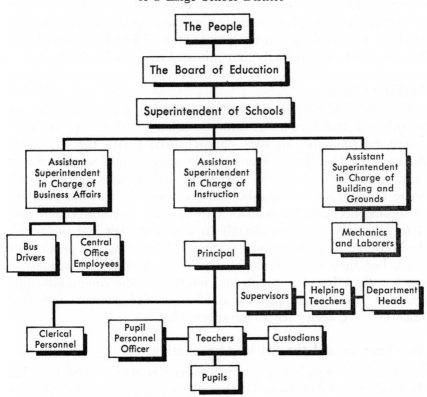

* Reproduced from Edward W. Smith, Stanley W. Krouse, Jr., and Mark M. Atkinson, *The Educator's Encyclopedia* (Englewood Cliffs, N. J.: Prentice-Hall, Inc., 1961), p. 150, Figure III-I.

not at all, but he is the responsible professional head of the school. His role in the individual school is similar to that of the superintendent in the school system. He is the chief executive of the school, the supervisor and coordinator of both instructional and noninstructional programs, and the educational appraiser. He is responsible to the superintendent or to an intermediate administrative official, such as a district superintendent. His relations with other central office personnel vary greatly from system to system.

A larger school may have assistant principals, directors of various subordinate activities, and department heads. Little or much responsibility may be delegated to these persons. Ordinarily they serve as liaison agents between individual members of the staff and the principal. They may be asked to help new teachers, lead in revisions of the curriculum, plan in-service programs, or assign and evaluate teachers. It is evident that a department head in a large school may have as much responsibility as a principal in a small school.

Advisory Groups

Citizens' advisory committees have become a popular means of providing better liaison between the schools and the community. There are thousands of such groups working with the schools of the country. Usually membership is by invitation of school officials only. Many lay groups are largely fact-finding arms of the board. Some have organized a number of subcommittees to work in behalf of specific needs of the schools. Others make specific recommendations for study or action directly to school officials and the board. The purpose of all lay groups is conceded to be in part public relations, but they are of undoubted value in keeping the schools in touch with different segments and interests of the community. Professional advisory groups of specially qualified persons, including teachers, have been used to advantage also.

The Teacher and the School Organization.

The school organization and administrative structure exist so that the teacher may do his job. Teachers do not, as a rule, feel themselves part of the administration while in the classroom. They may, of course, turn to administration at some time in their career.

Nevertheless, teachers do have some responsibilities that are quite clearly administrative. At the classroom level they take over as executors of the policies of the board and school office. They are responsible for keeping records of attendance and other reports, ordering books and materials, supervising student conduct, working with parents, and representing the school in the community.

Almost all teachers and administrators feel that teachers as professional persons should participate in policy formation which affects their own welfare or work directly.[5] Such matters include: curriculum development, pupil personnel policies, salary schedules and related matters, the philosophy and objectives of the school, evalua-

---

[5] National Education Association, "Ten Criticisms of Public Education," *Research Bulletin*, Vol. 35, No. 4, December, 1957, pp. 135–136.

tion of the program, and in-service educational activities. The extent to which such democracy exists among school faculties varies widely, of course, but the trend is definitely in this direction.

New teachers may expect to find many recommendations for changes originating in faculty committees or being acted upon in faculty meetings. The Educational Policies Commission has said:

> Educational policies should be formulated initially by the professional staff of the school system, through a "cooperative process capitalizing on the intellectual resources of the whole staff. The participation in the development of educational policies should not be thought of as a favor granted by the administration, but rather as a right and an obligation. After policies have been developed by the staff, they should be submitted to the board of education for final review and approval."[6]

The administrators see that policies so conceived and adopted are carried out, but some responsibility may be placed on individual teachers. When the teachers help make policy they are usually more willing and more able to accept such responsibility. Doing so gives them a better understanding and pride in their professional role, and tends to make them partners in the administration rather than hired hands. We will see more developments of this nature, but there are several limitations on a teacher's role in administration. The board and the superintendent are legally responsible and must work within the law. Again, many practical decisions cannot wait for the often meandering course of group deliberations. Finally, it is simply too expensive to free any significant number of teachers from instructional duties to spend large amounts of time on administrative matters.

THE STATE AND EDUCATION

Early schools were the result of local initiative, but the concept of state responsibility emerged very early. As we have seen, Massachusetts saw fit to require local communities to provide for education. Other colonies and newly formed state governments followed suit. The general practice until about 1800 was to encourage and strengthen local control of the schools, however, rather than to assume control at the state level. There was no serious attempt to

---

[6] Educational Policies Commission, *Learning the Ways of Democracy: A Case Book in Civic Education* (National Education Association, 1940), p. 331, quoting the Commission's earlier volume, *The Structure and Administration of Education in American Democracy* (National Education Association, 1938), p. 67.

make education a state rather than a local function until after the adoption of the Tenth Amendment to the Constitution in 1791. This amendment reads: "The powers not delegated to the United States by the Constitution, nor prohibited by it to the States, are reserved to the States, respectively, or to the people." The Constitution does not delegate educational powers to the Congress nor prohibit them to the states; therefore, this legislation has been interpreted as giving the states the right to organize and administer schools.

After about 1800, states began to develop educational systems for discharging their responsibilities. State constitutions were revised to give state governments explicit authority in education, and other laws were passed to establish local districts and boards, authorize taxation for school support, and regulate expenditures. An administrative structure was required, giving rise to the establishment of state boards of education and executive officers.

The state superintendency was actually the first type of superintendency to appear at any level. New York led the way by appointing a state superintendent in 1812, but later abolished the office for a time because of local resentment. Other states found it necessary to experiment also. Maryland's first superintendent lasted only two years. Michigan, on the other hand, has had a state superintendent continuously since 1829.

For a time many states used the secretary of state as the chief school officer. By 1850 nearly all states had made some official responsible for the use of school funds, and the collection of statistics on schools. Gradually, as the duties and responsibilities of the office became more than routine, all states made provisions for a department of education and for the election or the appointment of a state superintendent of public instruction. In states where this officer is appointed by a state board of education he is generally known as the commissioner of education. In 1948, only nine states appointed their chief school officer; by 1958, twenty states were doing so. Appointment by a state board has the advantage of taking the office out of the realm of politics and insuring the choice of a competent professional educator. An elected superintendent may not be fully qualified and he is not directly responsible to the state board but has independent authority. Conflicts between the state board and an independent state school officer may lead to an impasse which would affect education adversely. This cannot happen when the board appoints the chief state school officer.

The State Board of Education

In all but nine states the superintendent or commissioner is responsible to a central board of education. New York established the Board of Regents in 1784, and in 1825 North Carolina established a board to control a state educational fund. The state boards established in Massachusetts (1837) and Connecticut (1839) proved of greater historical importance because of the men chosen as executive officers — Horace Mann in Massachusetts and Henry Barnard in Connecticut. Both were among the greatest of American educators, and they campaigned tirelessly to overcome the abuses and inequities caused by strictly local control. When they assumed office they found tuition schools for those who could pay and workhouse schools for paupers, the latter staffed by anyone who would work for little or nothing. Their efforts won public support for a state-wide system of tax-supported schools and certification standards for teachers. Through their writings, both encouraged better practice everywhere and helped set the pattern for organization in other states. Barnard later became the first United States Commissioner of Education.

State boards function in much the same manner as boards at the local level. The state board is responsible for educational policies, which the state superintendent then administers. State boards vary in size from about three members to nearly twenty-five. In most states, board members are appointed by the governor and approved by the legislature. In seven states they are elected; in one or two others they have membership on the board by virtue of their governmental office.[7] Some states have additional boards responsible for vocational agricultural education, and special programs of institutions, such as those for the handicapped. State colleges and universities often have separate governing boards which may or may not be responsible to the central board of education.

The State Department and Its Work

The state superintendent and his staff constitute a state department of education, which functions at the state level much as the

---

[7] Edgar Fuller, "State School Systems," in Chester W. Harris (ed.), *Encyclopedia of Educational Research* (New York: Macmillan Co., 1960), p. 1387.

city superintendent's office does at the local level. There are sub-
ordinates responsible for such matters as teacher certification, curriculum development, school laws and legislation, and public relations. Several of the larger states have several hundred professional
persons in their education departments. New York has over 500 and
California nearly 1000.

The activities and contributions of the state department vary. In
some states the department is little more than a fact-finding and
reporting agency, compiling statistical data, issuing reports on the
schools, and computing and distributing school monies. Other state
departments serve schools in an advisory and regulatory capacity.
They interpret the statutes with respect to education, and encourage
or require the compliance of local and intermediate districts and
the colleges. The state department's chief weapon in enforcing state
requirements is the withholding of accreditation or state funds. As
a further inducement many states grant special funds for special
programs, such as those for handicapped children.

Some state departments are assigned specific operational tasks by
the legislature. They may be required to establish or supervise the
establishment of programs in conservation, citizenship, adult education, or vocational rehabilitation. In some instances the state operates individual schools — for example, the state university, teachers'
colleges, and schools for the blind, deaf, or otherwise handicapped.

As a matter of policy, most state departments try to encourage as
much local independence and responsibility as the state law allows.
The state departments seek a leadership role in their relations with
the local system. Many bulletins, guides, and other printed materials
are issued, and personnel of the department work directly with local
school officers in the improvement of their programs.

All states help in the *financing* of schools. The state's direct
dollar contribution to educational costs averages about 40 percent of
the total bill throughout the United States. But this figure varies
widely from 5 percent in Nebraska to 85 percent in Delaware. Federal funds, amounting to 3 or 4 percent of the total, also are administered by the state.[8]

Money for education at either the local or state level comes from
taxes, although small amounts may come from the interest on funds
set aside by the legislature or contributed by the wealthy. On the

[8] *Ibid.*, p. 1390.

state level, school monies are usually raised by gasoline, income, or general sales taxes, rather than by property taxes. States can raise large sums of money by taxation more easily than local communities. The chief advantage, however, of state financing of schools is that the state can plan the distribution of funds so that the very poor school districts, as well as the relatively wealthy, can pay for better facilities and programs. A common method of determining the funds each district should receive is to relate them to the number of students actually attending school in the district. Other factors, such as the local school budget and the number of classrooms or local property values, are considered in some states.

The state determines who may teach in the public schools. Each state has certification requirements which must be met by those who wish to teach. Each candidate for a teaching certificate must apply to the state department and submit evidence that he has met the requirements. In practice, state departments may rely on the teacher-training institutions to see that preparation requirements are fulfilled and issue certificates on the strength of an endorsement by the institution from which the prospective teacher was graduated.

The state department usually has authority from the state board of education to regulate what is taught in the schools. Many states publish courses of study which must be followed. In about half of the states, textbooks are chosen on a state-wide basis; others merely recommend suitable texts. Probably every state prescribes certain courses such as United States or state history, health education, or conservation.

The leadership of the state department in the area of curriculum and instruction is probably more important than its regulations. The following activities, adapted from a longer list by Beach,[9] are believed typical of state department personnel:

1. Advising on local problems of curriculum and instruction.

2. Conducting conferences, institutes, and workshops.

3. Providing demonstrations or exhibits of improved materials and methods.

4. Conducting or advising on pilot and experimental schools or classes.

5. Participating in research studies to evaluate educational programs.

---

[9] Fred F. Beach, *The Functions of State Departments of Education*, U. S. Office of Education, Federal Security Agency, Miscellaneous No. 12, 1950, p. 40.

6. Preparing and publishing resource material for instruction.

7. Developing programs of child study as a basis for curriculum revision.

8. Conducting a clearinghouse for information on new developments.

The state department may also regulate and supervise the construction of school buildings throughout the state in order to insure that minimum standards are met and that full value is received for school monies spent for this purpose. Architectural and financial advice is provided, and in some instances state funds.

Increasingly state departments are assuming the responsibility for long-range planning for education within the state. They recommend legislation and may be active in securing its passage. Ordinarily, the department provides the experts to whom the governor and the legislature turn for advice with respect to both professional and public opinion on all educational developments. To meet this responsibility the state department attempts to assess and be responsive to the opinion of the public, tries to keep the public informed, and seeks its support.

The County and Education

In a number of states where there are a number of local school districts within each county, some of the state's functions and responsibilities are delegated to an appointed or elected county board or officer. We are not speaking here of the states where the county is the local school administrative unit, but of states where the county forms an intermediate unit between the state and local units. Occasionally geographical or political units other than the county may be established as intermediate between the state and local units for educational purposes, but we will discuss the county as the most typical of such units.

The county superintendent's responsibilities vary from state to state, but "the distinguishing feature of the intermediate unit is that its officer or board exercises only supervisory or service functions in relation to the basic units."[10]

As a rule, city systems operate quite independently of the county educational organization, but rural schools often turn to the county

[10] National Commission on School District Reorganization, *Your School District* (Washington, D. C.: Department of Rural Education, National Education Association, 1948), p. 52.

or other intermediate unit for leadership and service of much the same type that the state departments provide. Any county superintendent probably has routine duties, such as assembling statistics for his area, assisting in distributing state funds, checking teachers' qualifications, and enforcing various state regulations. Some county officers have, in addition, helped the smaller schools cooperate in gaining many of the advantages of larger ones. The following are listed as typical activities and services of county superintendents by the Commission on the American School Superintendency of the American Association of School Administrators:[11]

1. Instructional supervision
2. Pupil transportation
3. Health and dental examinations and services
4. Educational and vocational guidance programs
5. Specialized services for handicapped and problem children
6. Curriculum laboratories
7. In-service education workshops
8. Fine arts and industrial arts consultants
9. County libraries
10. Audio-visual aids and services
11. Specialization in different schools
12. Centralized purchasing and maintenance
13. Cooperative study of financial problems

As local citizens who know local problems, many county superintendents have been particularly effective in securing support for the state's school district reorganization efforts, so that gradually smaller districts are being consolidated. The need for a county educational organization may soon vanish.

THE FEDERAL GOVERNMENT AND EDUCATION

While the framers of the Constitution did not mention education specifically, they did intend that the federal government would "provide for the common defense and general welfare of the United States. . . ." This thought was expressed in the Preamble to the Constitution, and again in the section that empowers Congress to levy and collect taxes. Actually, the federal government was involved

---

[11] Commission on the American School Superintendency, *The American School Superintendency*, Thirtieth Yearbook (Washington, D. C.: The American Association of School Administrators, 1952), p. 363.

in educational activities even before the adoption of the Constitution in 1789.

General Land Grants

Under the Articles of Confederation Congress passed ordinances in both 1785 and 1787 which granted land for the benefit of the public schools. The 1785 ordinance reserved the lot number 16 of every township for the maintenance of public schools; and the Ordinance of 1787 for the government of the territory northwest of the Ohio River, stated that "Religion, morality, and knowledge being necessary to good government and the happiness of mankind, schools and the means of education shall be forever encouraged."

Since 1850, when California was admitted, new states have generally received two sections of land per township for the support of education. Several states have been allowed four sections because of the low value of the lands. Each state has used its school land without federal interference. Most was sold cheaply, the money being squandered, or yielding but a small amount of interest. On the other hand some states, particularly those admitted relatively recently, have managed school lands wisely and profitably for education.

The federal government has at various times aided public education within the states by additional gifts of forest lands, swamp lands, and salt lands. Other funds have come from a percentage of the proceeds from sale of public lands, the income from national forests, and royalties for mineral rights on public lands. In 1836, $28,000,000 from a most unlikely source, a surplus in the national treasury, was returned to the states. Most used this windfall to establish or swell permanent school funds.

Legislation for Specific Purposes

The federal aid described so far was for general rather than specific educational purposes. Federal legislation has provided funds for specific purposes as well. The following is a partial list:

1. The Morrill Acts of 1862 and 1890 set aside 30,000 acres of federal land within each state for each senator and representative in Congress. The land was to be sold and the proceeds used by each state to establish colleges of agricultural and the mechanical arts. The individual states received from $50,000 to $750,000, and a total of 69 "land-grant" colleges were established, some in connection

with existing state universities (California, Illinois, Minnesota, Wisconsin) and some as separate institutions (Iowa State, Michigan State, Purdue).

2. The Hatch Act of 1887 set aside $15,000 annually to each state and territory having an agricultural college, to help establish an experimental station to promote agricultural science. Later legislation greatly increased these funds.

3. The Smith-Lever Act of 1914 provided for county agricultural agents, 4-H leaders, and other vocational specialists and for the training of teachers in these areas.

4. The Smith-Hughes Act of 1917, and other legislation from 1929 to the George-Barden Act of 1946, provided funds for vocational education in agriculture, trades, industry, the distributive occupations, and homemaking, and also for teacher training in these fields.

5. The Federal Surplus Commodities Corporation of 1935 and the National School Lunch Act of 1946 gave both funds and surplus foods to schools.

6. The Surplus Property Act of 1944 granted land, buildings, and equipment to private as well as public schools.

7. Public Law 507 of 1950 established the National Science Foundation which has furthered education in science through research grants, conferences, institutes, and in-service programs for teachers. The National Science Foundation has enlisted the aid of scientists and educators in redesigning and updating elementary and secondary school science and mathematics course material.

8. The Lanham Act of 1941 and later legislation in 1950 gave federal assistance for the construction and operation of schools in areas where federal activities have created financial hardships for local communities. Federal military installations, for example, often bring several hundred families but pay no taxes.

9. Public Law 16 and Public Law 346 of 1944 ("G.I. Bill") and Public Law 550 of 1952 (the "Korean G.I. Bill") provided financial assistance to millions of veterans who desired to continue their education in high schools, colleges, universities, specialized vocational schools, or adult-education classes. In terms of cost and influence these laws made possible more federal participation in education than any others in our history.

10. The National Defense Education Act of 1958 (Public Law

85–864) authorized a four-year program under which more than a billion dollars would be expended in support of education from kindergarten to the graduate school. The intent of this complex and far-reaching act was the expansion of educational opportunities for the individual, who is to be regarded as our first line of defense. Under this act funds have been provided for: (1) loans to college students, (2) fellowships for students preparing for college teaching; (3) facilities and state supervisory services for strengthening instruction in science, mathematics, and foreign languages; (4) guidance, counseling, and testing programs for able students and training institutes for counselors; (5) centers for the study of foreign languages and institutes for the advanced preparation of language teachers; (6) research and experimentation in the use of television, radio, motion pictures, and other media; (7) vocational education programs to supplement the provisions of earlier acts; (8) more adequate dissemination of science information; and (9) the improvement of state systems for collecting and reporting data on education. The tradition of local control of education was continued in provisions which made the states, and the communities and institutions within them, wholly responsible for all programs established under the National Defense Education Act.

Federal Schools

No listing of federal aid or activity in the field of education can be exhaustive. There are federal schools for the District of Columbia, for American Indians, for American dependents abroad, and for territories and possessions. The Departments of Justice, Interior, State, and Treasury operate training schools for their employees. There are innumerable schools associated with the military services in addition to the well-known military academies.

Our national government has campaigned actively for the improvement of education in other countries through the United States Point Four Program, the Technical Assistance Program, the Peace Corps, and especially through its leadership role in UNESCO.

Some Supreme Court Decisions

The judicial branch of the federal government has played a most important role in education. Of greatest significance are the Supreme

THE ADMINISTRATION OF PUBLIC EDUCATION

Court rulings with respect to: (1) state and federal powers in education, (2) private or religious education, and (3) segregation.

The first cases pertaining to education which were tried before the Supreme Court were related to the rights and responsibilities of the federal and state governments. We have reviewed the part the decisions played in the evolution of the state's role in education. Most recently, civil-rights questions have occupied the center of the stage. Among the most important decisions of recent years were the May 17, 1954, finding that segregation and "separate but equal" facilities for the education of white and colored have no place under our Constitution, and the February 19, 1962, ruling holding unconstitutional a 1961 Louisiana law permitting parishes (counties) of that state to close public schools rather than segregate them.

Three types of cases have affected the independence of church-related schools. In 1923 (*Meyer vs. Nebraska*) and in 1925 (*Pierce vs. the Society of Sisters*) the high court upheld the rights of the individual in his free choice of an educational institution. In other words, children cannot be required to attend public schools rather than independent ones.

The McCollum and Zorach cases, of 1948 and 1952 respectively, dealt with the constitutionality of public schools providing released time for religious instruction. The decision in the McCollum case was that such a program was unconstitutional when held on the school premises and made an integral part of the public school programs. In the Zorach case four years later, however, the court held that released time for religious instruction off the school grounds was constitutional and that religion and government may cooperate, for "We are a religious people."

Decisions in the cases of Cochran vs. Board of Education, 1930, and Emerson vs. Board of Education, 1947, held that public funds can be used to provide secular textbooks for all students, including those in church-related schools (1930) and to pay for the transportation of children for the secular benefits of education, even though they attend church-related schools (1947). Federal aid to private education will be considered as an issue in Chapter VI.

The Office of Education

There is one federal agency whose only concern is education. The federal government intends this agency, the Office of Education, to exert national leadership and to extend cooperation and assistance to other governmental agencies, the states, professional groups and institutions, citizen groups, and individuals.

The Office of Education was established in 1867 in the Department of the Interior, transferred (first) in 1939 to the Federal Security Agency and then again in 1953 to its present place in the Department of Health, Education, and Welfare. Its chief officer, the United States Commissioner of Education, is appointed by the President upon the recommendation of the Secretary of Health, Education, and Welfare. The organizational structure of the Office of Education is shown in Figure 9.

Neither the Commissioner nor the Office which he heads has any administrative authority over the schools of the country. The four major areas of activities in which the Office engages and examples of each have been listed in a summary report of the Office:[12]

1. Gathering and disseminating statistics and other information. The extensive *Biennial Survey of Education in the United States*, for example, provides a summary of educational conditions throughout the country; *School Life* is the monthly official journal of the Office.

2. Conducting educational surveys and research. Projects study-

Fig. 9.   Organization of the U. S. Office of Education

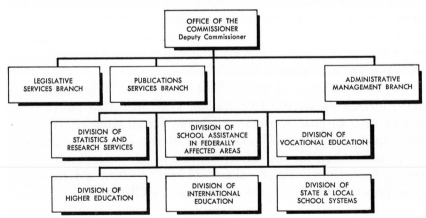

Source: U. S. Office of Education, *Handbook* (Washington, D. C.: U. S. Government Printing Office, 1959), inside back cover.

[12] Office of Education, *Progress of Education in the United States of America* (OE–10005) (Washington, D. C.: U. S. Government Printing Office, 1960), pp. 4–5.

ing almost every aspect of education are supported by the Cooperative Research Program and the Educational Media Branch of the Office. Through the Office, the educational profession is striving for more adequate funds for educational research. The budget proposed in 1962 included about five million dollars for research. This figure might be compared with the approximately 500 million dollars for health research.

3. Offering consultative services to state and local units and to both public and independent institutions. Personnel of the department are active in workshops, conferences, and other efforts of the profession to improve itself.

4. Distributing federal funds for education. The funds provided by federal legislation for the purposes and activities which have been reviewed in this chapter are administered by the Office. In 1960 such funds amounted to more than 431 million dollars.

This brief review of the federal government's role in education should leave no doubt that we have both federal aid to education and a measure of federal control. The questions of how much aid and how much control and whether one can be increased without the other are serious and controversial. Federal involvement in education will be presented as a current issue in Chapter VI.

Summary

A tradition of local control originated in the New England colonies, and spread west with the frontier. Although the state has been the legal unit for education since the formation of the Union, much responsibility continues to be delegated to local boards. Local boards make the policies, but over the years they have turned more and more of their management of the schools over to professionals — the superintendents, the principals, and their staffs. Citizens' advisory groups help the boards and administrators of larger districts to keep in touch with the people. At the classroom level the teacher has administrative responsibilities, and increasingly a democratic concept of administration has involved teachers in policy decisions as well.

The local communities are primarily responsible for providing the facilities and funds for education. Different communities differ greatly in their ability to provide these, and there has consequently been a trend toward the consolidation of smaller and poorer districts and the collection of a larger share of taxes for school support on the state level. The state then distributes these funds in a manner which will enable all districts to offer at least a minimum program.

With state participation in education came the need for an administrative organization. State boards and their executive officers, who are known as superintendents or commissioners, emerged in the first half of the nineteenth century. Horace Mann in Massachusetts and Henry Barnard in Connecticut were among the first state officers, and they influenced subsequent developments significantly. The chief state officers and their staffs form state departments of education. Although the work of these departments varies, in most states they collect and disseminate information about education, distribute and supervise the use of state funds, assist in curriculum study and revision, establish certification requirements for teachers, provide consultative services to schools, governmental agencies, and officials, and discharge the specific functions assigned them by the state board or the legislature. They may, for example, operate special schools for the handicapped or prepare courses in state history or conservation. The better departments provide leadership for educational planning and development throughout the state.

Intermediate administrative organizations, such as those on the county level, have assisted the state in its educational efforts especially in rural areas. The better county superintendents have been invaluable in encouraging the sharing of resources and other forms of cooperation among local districts and in encouraging the consolidation of smaller districts.

There is no question that the federal government has greatly aided education. The executive branch has established agencies with educational responsibilities. The legislature has made land grants to the states for general educational purposes and has provided funds for specific purposes as well. The judiciary has defined the rights and powers of the states and protected the rights of individuals. The United States government operates a variety of schools for special groups of citizens or employees. The United States Office of Education in the Department of Health, Education, and Welfare provides leadership to the profession on the national level and is active in gathering and disseminating statistics on education, offering consultative services, and in managing federal funds for education. There is also an extensive program of cooperation with other nations to improve education internationally.

The policy of the federal government has been called "leadership without domination and financial assistance without interference."[13] The traditional role of the state in its relations with local schools is similar. With federal and state participation in education increasing we are, however, faced with the question of how well this relationship can be retained. It is certain that unless the weaker or poorer communities recognize and make determined efforts to solve their own problems, it will be difficult to prevent the erosion of local controls.

SELECTED READINGS

American Association of School Administrators, *School Board-Superintendent Relations*, Thirty-Fourth Yearbook (Washington, D. C.: National Education Association, 1956), Chaps. 2–4.
    Describes the organization and the work of school boards and their relationships with the Superintendent.
Beach, Fred F. and Will, Robert F., *The State and Education* (Washington, D. C.: U. S. Office of Education, 1955).
    Comprehensive description of the organization and operation of the educational system of each state.
Bereday, George Z. F. and Volpicelli, Luigi (eds.), *Public Education in America* (New York: Harper & Bros., 1958).
    Seventeen educational leaders appraise the functioning of our school systems.
Cooper, Shirley and Fitzwater, Charles O., *County School Administration* (New York: Harper & Bros., 1954).
    History and development of county units with recommendations for the future.
Cubberley, Elwood P., *Public School Administration* (Boston: Houghton Mifflin Co., 1922), Chap. 7.
    A classical account of the evolution of school organization and administration.
DeYoung, Chris A., *American Education* (New York: McGraw-Hill Book Co., 1960).
    Chaps. 1–4 give prospective teachers a professional overview of educational organization and administration, as seen from the national, state, county and local levels. Chap. 16 shows how tax dollars are used for educational progress.
Educational Policies Commission, *Public Education and the Future of America* (Washington, D. C.: National Educational Association, 1938), Part IV.

---

[13] Office of Education, *Progress of Public Education in the United States of America, op. cit.*, p. 2.

A classic statement of the proper role and function of the federal government in education.

Edwards, Newton, *The Court and the Public Schools* (Chicago: Univ. of Chicago Press, 1955), Chap. 1.
Describes the legal role of the state in education and cites judicial decisions.

Gross, Neal, *Who Runs Our Schools?* (New York: John Wiley & Sons, 1958).
Interesting "inside stories" of the interaction of boards, superintendents and community pressure groups.

Hansen, Kenneth H., *Public Education in America* (Englewood Cliffs, N. J.: Prentice-Hall, 1956), Chap. 12.
One of the better descriptions of the teacher's role in administration.

Hughes, James M., *Education in America* (Evanston, Ill.: Row, Peterson & Co., 1960), Chaps. 11–13.
The origins, current status and probable future of powers and functions over school matters at the local, state and federal levels, including a helpful chart which clarifies the division of educational control among these levels, pp. 318–319.

Hunt, Herold C. and Perce, Paul R., *The Practice of School Administration* (Boston: Houghton Mifflin Co., 1958).
Two experienced school men review the practical aspects of administering the schools. See Chap. 8 on developing relations with the home and community.

National Education Association, "Can America Afford Better Schools?" *NEA Journal*, Vol. 48 (February 1959), special insert.
The problems of financing education are presented in simplified graphical form.

National Education Association, Research Division, *Rankings of the States*, an annual bulletin.
Compares the states with respect to wealth, school expenditures, teacher salaries etc.

Power, Edward J., *Education for American Democracy* (New York: McGraw-Hill Book Co., 1958), Part II and Appendix.
Historical development, organization and activities of educational agencies of local, state and federal governments. The Appendix contains abstracts of Supreme Court statements on educational questions.

Thomas, Lawrence G., Kinney, Lucien B., Coladarci, Arthur P. and Fielstra, Helen A., *Perspective on Teaching* (Englewood Cliffs, N. J.: Prentice-Hall, 1961), Chap. 6.
Clear presentation of the factors in increasing school costs and a discussion of new plans for school financing.

U. S. Office of Education, *Handbook* (Washington, D. C.: U. S. Government Printing Office, 1959).
Describes the organization and operation of the U. S. Office of Education.

Chapter IV

INDEPENDENT SCHOOLS

IN AMERICA

In the United States one of six elementary school children, one of ten secondary school students, and one of three college or university students attend independent schools.[1] The schools attended by these seven and one-half million students are "independent" because they are not supported by public taxation and are relatively free from political control. These schools can select their own objectives, faculties, courses, and students. The term "private," as an antonym for public, will not be used here, for these schools serve the public by educating millions of Americans. Many independent schools are neither church-related nor segregative.

As a matter of fact, these schools are notable for the differences which their independence makes possible. They may be denominational or nondenominational, and this distinction provides a convenient division in some of the discussion which follows. They may be military or civilian, boarding schools or day schools, exclusive or democratic, traditional or progressive. They may be kindergartens or universities. In other words, there are independent schools of all types and purposes. One university president has said that the term covers "everything from Harvard to an Indian Reservation School in Rosebud, Montana."[2]

The first schools in America were all independent. Such schools provided most of the educational opportunities in this country down to the middle of the nineteenth century. Today, America's educa-

---

[1] U. S. Bureau of the Census, *Statistical Abstract of the United States: 1961*, Eighty-Second Edition (Washington, D. C., 1961), p. 107, Table 136.
[2] Ernest Barrett Chamberlain, *Our Independent Schools* (New York: American Book Co., 1944), p. 9.

tional system recognizes the responsibilities and rights of the parents, church, and state in education. At the elementary and secondary level independent school enrollments are on the increase. The influence of these schools in American education seems to grow also. Although the public colleges are growing more rapidly than the independent schools, the "independents" are still the first choice of many college-bound Americans. Year after year the top independent colleges and universities attract more winners of national scholarship competitions than do any of the public institutions, large or small.

This chapter sketches the development and the characteristics of independent schools at the elementary, secondary, and higher education levels during the colonial period, in the new American nation, and in modern times.

RELIGION AND EDUCATION IN THE COLONIAL PERIOD

The early settlers in America came from European countries with a tradition of religious interest in education. Since the fall of the Roman Empire religion had been the dominant influence in European schools. At first only the Roman Catholic Church kept learning alive, but after the Reformation Protestants were required to read the Bible, and schools were established for just this reason. Even when the financial support of the schools was assumed by some European states, and when commercial interests established schools in the sixteenth and seventeenth centuries, the religious purposes and influences of the dominant faith persisted. Thus an intimate relationship between religion and education in colonial America was a carry-over from Europe.

Elementary Schools

The New England colonies were "Bible states," solidly Puritan or Calvinist, with a political authority more or less synonymous with religious authority. Almost from the beginning, schools were established under the supervision of the ministers "to make little Puritans." At first these schools were efforts of the individual communities or of private individuals, but a uniformity of beliefs and interests encouraged the compulsory establishment and maintenance of schools to teach the common doctrine. In 1642 Massachusetts ordered the selectmen of towns to see to it that all children were able "to read and understand the principles of religion, & the capitall lawes of this country." Children neglected by their parents were to be apprenticed to masters who were then responsible for their instruction. A short time later Massachusetts (1647) and Connecticut (1650) ordered every town of fifty families to employ a teacher of reading and writing.

The New England town school was in session six days a week, six hours a day, in a shanty furnished with a teacher's desk which resembled a pulpit, and rough plank benches for the students. The method here, as in other schools of the time, was that of individual recitation, usually at the teacher's desk, supplemented by copying and spelldowns. A student probably received about ten minutes of teaching for each hour or so of sitting. But the materials of instruction are of most interest here. These were the Bible and the Psalter, the hornbook and the primer. The hornbook had been in general use since the fifteenth century and was the earliest form of textbook. It was really a board shaped like a paddle which carried a single sheet of paper protected by a strip of transparent horn. The alphabet, the vowels, and a few prayers were learned from the hornbook. The *New England Primer* was in use for nearly two hundred years after its original publication about 1690. It contained rhymes and illustrations for teaching the alphabet, word lists, and moral and religious lessons, including a catechism. John Cotton's "Spiritual Milk for American Babes Drawn out of the Breasts of Both Testaments, for Their Soul's Nourishment" suggests the nature of some of the content.

Since the education offered in these schools was often of poor quality, well-to-do parents generally preferred to engage tutors. Girls were often excluded from these schools, along with any boys who had not learned the alphabet. The needs of these youngsters had to be met at home also, or in the dames' schools described in Chapter II.

The town schools of New England declined as the frontiers moved outward and the population of the colonies dispersed. The teachers began to move from community to community, dividing their time among different localities. Commercial and political activities and wars with the French and Indians began to break down the Puritan exclusiveness and unity. The legal profession began to challenge the supremacy of the ministry. The result was legislation making the establishment, support, and operation of schools more clearly a public function and the responsibility of school districts established for this purpose.

The middle colonies lacked the religious unity characteristic of New England. There were Catholics in Maryland, Quakers in Pennsylvania, and Dutch Calvinists in New York, but also Adventists, Baptists, Congregationalists, Episcopalians, Lutherans, and others. Each religious group tended to establish its own schools. Five Jesuits were with the first Maryland settlers in 1634, for example, and they devoted themselves to the development of Catholic schools. Whenever a new mission was established there was an attempt to start a new school. The Society for the Preservation of the Gospel in Foreign Parts of the Anglican Church established charity schools, partly to win back the Quakers. The Quakers were, however, most zealous in establishing their own schools to preserve their beliefs. The quality of the schools available was always variable, however, and often depended on how much the parents could contribute toward their support. The apprenticeship system was the most common form of instruction available to the laboring class. As the frontier moved west, religious differences in education often broke down, and neighborhood schools set up by the cooperation of several families became common.

The geography and economics of plantation life discouraged any general educational program by the dominant Anglican Church in the Southern colonies. Those parents who could afford private tutors for their children employed them; the children of those who could not, often remained illiterate. Here and there, it is true, a few free schools were established by private individuals; and many boys and girls were apprenticed to masters who were supposed to provide instruction, and occasionally did.

The Southern views on education were the traditional English ones — each according to his means. The children of aristocrats were educated at home and, when they were older, in English schools abroad. The children of laborers, it was believed, should labor also. To teach them to think would be a waste of time and could only make them dissatisfied with their lot.

As has been noted, Catholicism did not play a major role in educational developments within the original thirteen colonies. There is a long history of pioneering efforts by the Catholic teaching orders within the present boundaries of the United States beyond the English colonies, however. The Franciscans were teaching in Florida in the late sixteenth century, where they established a seminary at St. Augustine in 1606. The first of many elementary mission schools for Indians began in New Mexico in 1629, and somewhat later others were founded in Texas, Louisiana, California, and the Northwest Territory.

The Latin Grammar School

The Latin grammar school, which was described in Chapter II, was at first the only secondary school of the English colonies. The avowed purpose of the earliest one was to prepare boys for Harvard and, consequently, for the ministry. Only the sons of the elite, socially and professionally, were admitted to the schools. Tuition was required of all, although in New England some tax support came from the towns.

Massachusetts tried to force the establishment of grammar schools in 1647 by the same ruling which required the establishment of elementary schools. Every town of 100 families was ordered to support a grammar school as well as an elementary school. This part of the law was not widely obeyed by the towns, in spite of penalties and strong support and supervision by the Puritan ministry.

Outside of New England, the Latin Grammar schools were even more definitely independent and church-related, but similar in purpose and course of study except for the particular religious creed emphasized. The Dutch of New Amsterdam, the Quakers and other religious groups in New Jersey and Pennsylvania, and the Anglicans and Presbyterians of Maryland, Virginia, and the Carolinas established a few such schools. In Maryland special duties on imports and exports, supplemented by contributions, made possible the establishment of King William's School (which later became St. John's College) for the study of Latin and Greek. The catalog of this famous school claims as graduates "practically all the Anapolis men who held leading positions in the Colonial government from 1720 until the Revolutionary War."

Until 1850 Catholic secondary education in America was largely the work of the Jesuits. A school which lasted only a few years had been established in Newton, Maryland, in 1640. Another in New York failed also. Bohemia Manor in Maryland dates from about

1740. Here boys of all ages were accepted on a tuition basis. A non-Jesuit but Catholic contribution was an early, perhaps the earliest, secondary school for girls. This was a convent school established by the Ursuline nuns in New Orleans in 1727. The growth of this school was remarkable, with several hundred students in residence about 1800.[3]

Colonial Church Colleges

The role of the grammar school, as previously stated, was to prepare boys for college and the ministry. Beginning with Harvard, founded by the Puritans in 1636, eight denominational colleges were established before the colonies broke with England. Only one nondenominational college, the College of Philadelphia, appeared in this early period. In addition to Harvard, the denominational colleges were: William and Mary, Anglican, 1693; Yale, Congregational, 1701; Princeton, Presbyterian, 1746; King's (now Columbia), Anglican, 1754; Brown, Baptist, 1764; Rutgers, Reformed Dutch, 1766; and Dartmouth, Congregational, 1769. All began as small liberal arts colleges with the tutorial system of English schools. There was no professional training for medicine or law or other fields.

The philosophy underlying the program was not unlike that of the medieval universities for the training of Catholic priests, except that it was built around Protestant creeds. The studies included the liberal arts of the Middle Ages: the philosophy of Aristotle (as then interpreted), the classical languages, and theology. Like the European universities, the colonial church colleges believed that the highest truth would be revealed through philosophical and theological speculation. There is evidence that the colonial college student sometimes waivered in his devotion to the pursuit of a classical curriculum in the midst of a frontier world, even under strict regimentation and the threat of public whippings.[4]

From the beginning it was necessary to seek diverse means of support for the colleges. Lotteries were commonly used, and there were small endowments from a few wealthy persons. Usually some money was received from England. Tobacco taxes helped William and Mary, and Yale benefited from a tax on rum.

[3] William E. Drake, *The American School in Transition* (New York: Prentice-Hall, 1955), p. 268.

[4] Edgar W. Knight and Clifton L. Hall, *Readings in American Educational History* (New York: Appleton-Century-Crofts, Inc., 1951), p. 67.

There were twelve Catholic universities in the New World, several dating from around 1550, before there was a single institution of higher education in North America. Prior to the Revolutionary War, however, there were only a few Catholics in the English colonies, and these found acceptance and expansion difficult. Some evidence suggests that there was a college course in connection with the Jesuit school at Newton, Maryland, in 1677.[5]

Private Venture Schools of the Colonial Period

A number of schools of the colonial period were conducted by individuals for profit. These appear to have been especially numerous in the large cities of the East in the early 1700's, but were found elsewhere too.[6] They were established to meet the need, especially in commerce, for a practical education which the Latin grammar schools did not provide. The emphasis was usually upon applied mathematics, bookkeeping, penmanship, modern languages, and English grammar. There were also private teachers or tutors who offered instruction in practically anything to anybody, girls included, and at any time, in the evening to those who worked days. These private teachers prepared students for college entrance and for a variety of vocations and professions. They helped a few girls to get an education beyond that given in the dames' schools.

INDEPENDENT SCHOOLS OF THE NEW NATION, 1778–1900

An account of the nation's youthful groping for a system of schools which would best meet the needs of the republic was presented in the preceding two chapters. The nation's early leaders laid great stress on the need for informed and educated citizens. Some, such as Thomas Jefferson, saw that private efforts alone would not insure universal education of high caliber. It was not so much a matter of the lack of quality in the independent schools that existed, but in some places there just were no independent schools. Where independent schools existed they were not intended for all, and all could not afford them. Most important was the financial instability of many independent schools of the period. Tuition, gifts, and lotteries

---

[5] Edward J. Power, A History of Catholic Higher Education in the United States (Milwaukee: The Bruce Publishing Co., 1960), p. 27.

[6] Galen Saylor, "Secondary Education — Development," in Chester W. Harris (ed.), Encyclopedia of Educational Research (New York: The Macmillan Co., 1960), p. 1233.

could not be depended upon. Some of these problems were particularly evident to Jefferson. He was a Southern planter, although an unusual one. His fellow Southern aristocrats, it will be recalled, had no intention of educating the children of all men. As might be expected, Jefferson's early proposal for a system of public schools in Virginia came to naught. Perhaps he would have been more successful in securing support for his ideas in New England. There the Puritans considered some education for all a religious need. It was in New England that Horace Mann, Henry Barnard, and others finally succeeded in laying the foundations for a system of tax-supported public schools.

In the period from the Revolution to the Civil War many halfway measures were tried, for there was a reluctance on the part of many both to giving up independent control of the schools and to assuming the full financial burden for them. Some of these schemes actually encouraged the growth of independent schools. One plan paid the private schools to educate the poor. In Pennsylvania, for example, the Constitution of 1790 and laws of 1802 and 1804 required teachers of reading and writing to instruct paupers. Payment of costs was from relief funds. One of the greatest evils of this system was that it marked the poor for ridicule. Many preferred to remain uneducated. When the poor did come in large numbers, those who could sought more exclusive independent schools. Another plan was to place a local tax, called the "rate bill," on every parent who had children in school. The rate bill supplemented tax monies, but it kept away those who could not pay and many who would not pay.

Every state experimented with a state school fund to endow education, so that tax support would be easier or unnecessary. The proceeds from the sale of public lands, special taxes, and public lotteries went into these funds. Some federal money became available. Many states squandered these funds. At any rate, they did not prove sufficient for any state.

Public school societies were established in New York and Philadelphia to provide free education for the poor and at low rates for others who could not afford to go elsewhere. These societies were supported by grants from the state and private philanthropists. Although society schools were open to all, they were definitely Protestant, though nondenominational, and they taught religion. Some

Protestant denominations, for example the Bethel Baptist Church in 1822, sought and also received New York public funds for the support of schools. Catholic schools were also helped at one time. The New York Public School Society, foreseeing similar demands by a multitude of denominations, agitated for and secured legislation prohibiting the use of public funds to support religious schools. This left the Society, which claimed that its schools were not religious because they were not denominational, in a favored position. The Catholics, led by Archbishop John Hughes (1797–1864), continued to seek support periodically, without success, and bitterly protested the use of the Protestant Bible and textbooks with passages unsuitable for Roman Catholics.

There were a number of other attempts to achieve Catholic purposes within the framework of a common school system. For nearly twenty years the Poughkeepsie Board of Education leased a Catholic school building for one dollar a year, and accepted the Sisters of Charity and other Catholics as teachers. The school was open to all denominations. Religious instruction was given after regular school hours only. This plan, also in effect in other states from time to time, was declared illegal in New York in 1898 because of the denominational influence of Sisters in religious garb.[7]

The New York controversy had extremely important aftereffects. The Catholic hierarchy, feeling the struggle for equal rights and benefits hopeless, accelerated the development of an independent parochial school system. The First Plenary Council of Baltimore (1829) judged it "absolutely necessary" to establish schools "in which the young may be taught the principles of faith and morality, while being instructed in letters."[8] New York State finally amended its constitution (1894) to prohibit the use of public money to aid or maintain, directly or indirectly, "any school or institution of learning wholly or in part under the control or direction of any religious denomination, or in which any denominational tenet or doctrine is taught." Similar legislation became the national pattern and policy.

The Development of Independent Elementary Schools

Schools without religion were unacceptable to Roman Catholics and

[7] Rev. Joseph T. Tinnelly, C.M., "The Right to Education — The Role of Parents, Church, State," Proceedings and Addresses (55th Annual Meeting), National Catholic Educational Association, August, 1958, p. 42.

[8] Ibid., p. 40.

several Protestant denominations. The Third Plenary Council in Baltimore specifically directed that a school should be erected near each church within two years. Further, the Council stated that all Catholic parents were bound to send their children to these parish or parochial schools "unless at home or in other Catholic schools they may sufficiently and evidently provide for the Christian education of their children, or unless it be lawful to send them to other schools on account of sufficient cause, approved by the bishop, and with opportune cautions and remedies."[9]

Catholic parish schools multiplied very rapidly once the policies for their development were laid down. By 1900 over 5 percent of all American elementary school children were in the more than 3000 parochial schools. In the beginning these schools were staffed largely by the teaching orders, often from Europe. At first parishes made whatever arrangements they wished for supervision; but, after the Third Council of Baltimore, diocesan school boards were established for this purpose. As time went on, it became general practice to appoint a priest as superintendent of diocesan schools. This superintendent took over much of the board's responsibility. The teaching orders of Sisters, Brothers, and priests also had supervisors for their schools who worked in cooperation with the diocesan officials.

With the development of public schools the nineteenth-century Protestants very largely gave up their attempts to maintain independent schools. Only two denominations — the Lutherans and the Quakers — were actively working to expand their elementary school systems during this period.

Eighteenth-century German immigrants had established Lutheran elementary schools wherever they settled. One of the Lutheran problems was language, and they were inclined to retain German as the language of church and school. In Pennsylvania, where the Lutherans were strongest, they had established 240 schools by 1820. Then they apparently lost their drive — perhaps because they were learning English. At any rate the number of schools operated by this particular group of Lutherans dropped very rapidly and finally disappeared altogether.[10]

During the nineteenth century, a second wave of Lutheran immi-

[9] Quoted in J. A. Burns, *Growth and Development of the Catholic School System in the United States* (New York: Benziger Bros., 1912), p. 195.

[10] Walter H. Beck, *Lutheran Elementary Schools in the United States* (St. Louis: Concordia Publishing Co., 1939), p. 74.

grants moved into the Midwest, where the Lutheran Church — Missouri Synod was organizing congregations and establishing schools.[11] In 1843, Missouri Synod Lutherans made provisions for the training of Lutheran male teachers at its college in Perry County, Missouri, and later, in 1857, transferred the teacher education program to Fort Wayne, Indiana. In 1864, the Synod centralized teacher education in a special Lutheran teachers' seminary at Addison, Illinois, which was later relocated at River Forest, Illinois. By 1900 this Lutheran group was operating about 1700 schools, mostly of the rural one-teacher kind. The six- to seven-hour day was devoted to catechism, Bible reading, mental arithmetic, alphabet study, penmanship, history, English, and German. There was much hymn singing and regular prayers. Discipline was reported as particularly strict.

No tuition was charged in the first elementary schools of the Missouri Synod. The schools were integrated into the entire church program and budget. The pastor even taught in the school. The practice of requiring each member of the congregation to set aside part of his property for the church swelled the funds available. Somewhat later students were sometimes charged a small monthly tuition.

The Society of Friends or Quakers was among the last of the other Protestant groups to allow their schools to be absorbed into the public school system during the nineteenth century. The Quakers sought the "guarded religious education" of their children, and by 1800 there were sixty or seventy Quaker elementary schools in Pennsylvania and a number in other states as well.[12] The Quakers fought against surrendering to the movement for universal elementary education under public auspices but were handicapped by their scattered numbers and few teachers. Still, they maintained and expanded the number of their schools until shortly after the Civil War. The collapse of the system was rapid after 1885, however, and was very nearly complete by 1900.

While it survived, Quaker education had some notable characteristics. The Quakers' lack of adornment in dress is well known, and the same devotion to simplicity and practicality characterized their schools. The practical skills, including manual training and laboratory methods, were emphasized. Other Quaker principles were those

---

[11] At that time the name of the Lutheran Church — Missouri Synod was The Evangelical Church of Missouri, Ohio, and Other States.

[12] Elbert Russell, *History of Quakerism* (New York: The Macmillan Co., 1942), p. 207.

of pacifism and equality. In education this meant nonviolent, loving discipline and the acceptance of pupils and teachers of all races, sexes, and classes. The Quakers were among the first to promote an education for girls which would be equivalent to that provided boys, and Negroes were accepted into their schools from the beginning.

The Reformed Jews, chiefly German immigrants, did not generally favor the establishment of parochial schools. A few day and boarding schools were established by New York German congregations. In 1854 there were seven Hebrew day schools.[13] The work of these schools centered around languages, with German as the medium for instruction. Tuition was charged. By about 1870 the most popular means for Jewish religious instruction were schools which the synagogues conducted on Sunday. In addition, the Jews of New York City founded an industrial school for girls in 1879 and a technical institute for Jewish boys in 1884. A Jewish kindergarten was set up in 1882.

In the 1800's Russian Jewish immigrants established several types of schools. One type, the Talmud-Torah, started as charitable schools for poor. They were operated as communes. Although the Talmud-Torah were regarded as pauper schools at first and were plagued by low standards as well, they gradually improved and became quite numerous and popular.

There were a number of contributions of private-venture schools to the elementary education of this period. As was noted in Chapter II, independent schools led the way in establishing kindergartens along lines suggested by Frederich Froebel. The first was established in Watertown, Wisconsin, in 1855. Others followed rapidly. A kindergarten training school in Boston and a kindergarten demonstration at the Philadelphia Exposition in 1876 stimulated the spread of the movement so that there were five hundred or more by 1900.[14]

The first schools for the handicapped were independent. Dr. John Fisher started with a school for the blind in Boston in 1832, after visiting the world's first school of this kind in France. The first American school for deaf-mutes was established in 1817 at Hartford, Connecticut. Thomas Henry Gallaudet promoted this school which,

---

[13] Department of Public Relations, Torah Umesorah, National Society for Hebrew Day Schools, Facts and Figures on the Growth of the Hebrew Day School (mimeographed), November, 1960, p. 1.

[14] Drake, op. cit., p. 281.

like others that followed, used a manual sign-language method of instruction. Clarke Institute of Northampton, Massachusetts, introduced the oral or spoken language and lipreading methods in 1867.[15]

Secondary Schools

The academy, described in Chapter II, was the most popular institution for secondary education during the period being discussed. Although historically important as a transitional institution in the history of public education, the academy was an independent school.

The first academies were not operated for profit and tuition was kept as low as possible. Endowed institutions were common. They were regarded as part of the nation's scheme of education, for the people and states frequently gave them money and land. As a further evidence that they performed a valuable public function they were given exemption from taxation. Perhaps in line with their service to communities, a number became coeducational.

Another interesting feature of the early academies was the great variety of students. The first class at Andover in 1778 ranged in age from six to twenty-nine. After the Revolution many veterans enrolled. The growth of the academy movement and its lack of regulation as well as other characteristics of early academies have been described in Chapter II. At their worst the academies were very poor, indeed. Their decline was only hastened by the withdrawal of major public support after the rise of public high schools. Their own internal decay and disorder made their future uncertain.

When the Kalamazoo case of 1874 gave tax-supported high schools legal status, high schools increased and the academies decreased. A few of the better academies survived, however, and became exclusive boarding schools preparing children of the well-to-do for equally exclusive private colleges.

Some of the "new academies" acquired the traditions and prestige of the great secondary schools of England. Their advantage, compared to the high school, was their selectivity and the fact that they could offer culture and character development twenty-four hours a day. The two Phillips Academies at Andover, Massachusetts (1778), and Exeter, New Hampshire (1782), taught the classics and sciences and, in addition, "the great end and real business of living," and

---

[15] *Ibid.*

promoted "true piety and virtue."[16] Deerfield Academy (1797) used athletics, community activities, and dramatics to develop the personality of boys. Bradfield Junior College, originally a coeducational academy, became an exclusive girls' school in 1836. Miss Sarah Porter, a sister of one of Yale's presidents and founder of Miss Porter's School in Farmington, Connecticut (1843), was credited with having given "hundreds of the best-born women of the land that poise and stability of character, that combination of learning and good manners, which is a mark of the noblest American Womanhood."[17]

After the Civil War, and perhaps because of it, the independent military schools began to appear. Among the first of this type were Howe Military School (1884) and Bordentown Military Institute (1885). More than a quarter of the military schools still in existence today were founded in the period between 1869 and 1894.[18]

A rapid rise in secondary school enrollments near the end of the nineteenth century affected the exclusive independent school as well as the public high school. A number of the most famous were founded in this period, including Shady Side, 1881, Groton, 1884, and Thacher, 1889. Thacher in Ojai, California, prepared boys for Eastern universities while featuring Western outdoor life.

The typical academy emphasized Protestant religious, ethical, and moral training, but was not narrowly sectarian. A few, particularly Episcopal schools, such as St. Paul's in Concord (1856), were and have remained definitely denominational. Several Quaker academies established before 1800 later grew into colleges.

The first Catholic secondary school to be established after the Revolution was in Baltimore. St. Mary's Seminary, founded by the Sulpicians in 1791, opened an academy near the turn of the century and a college in 1805. This school trained students who moved west to establish other Catholic academies. College-preparatory work at the secondary level was offered by practically all Catholic colleges of the time. Several college-level institutions offered vocational training as well. Another development was the founding of secondary schools for girls by several French orders of nuns. Some of the

---

[16] Porter E. Sargent, A Handbook of Private Schools (Boston: Porter Edward Sargent, 1943), p. 159. Quoted by Ernest Barrett Chamberlain, Our Independent Schools (New York: American Book Co., 1944), p. 59.

[17] Sargent, op. cit., p. 231, quoted by Chamberlain, op. cit., p. 53.

[18] Chamberlain, op. cit., p. 54.

success of these schools probably was due to the popularity of French manners and customs about this time. One example was the school of the Brown County Ursulines at St. Martin, Ohio. Individual personal training in accord with Catholic ideas of womanhood was stressed.[19]

Shortly after 1850 the growth of the American high school encouraged the parallel development of Catholic parish or diocesan high schools as an extension of the parochial elementary schools. More than 200 were established before 1900. They were probably similar to other high schools except for their religious objectives and instructions.

Near the close of the century Jewish groups in New York set up a few Yeshibah schools for the study of Jewish law. They have been described as Talmudian academies.[20] It seems clear that the first of these schools were orthodox in the extreme. Shortly after the start of the twentieth century Yeshibah students demanded a broader program of studies, which would include Jewish language and culture but also English language, history, general studies, and public speaking. To reinforce their demands they went on strike in 1906. As a result, the Yeshibah schools were soon reorganized along more liberal lines.

The final group of secondary schools to be considered is an important group of private-enterprise schools. Mechanic's schools were especially important for a time after 1830. These served the growing demands of industry at a time when the old apprenticeship systems were breaking down. Their approach was often criticized for being "all words and no practice," however, and somewhat later in the nineteenth century they gave way to the well-known technical institutes, such as Pratt, Drexel, Cooper Union, Haskell, Hampton, and Tuskegee. The last three of these made notable contributions to racial as well as industrial adjustments. Hampton and Tuskegee were especially helpful in preparing Negroes for the trades, and Haskell served a similar function for the American Indian.

Higher Education

Two quite distinct types of independent colleges were prominent in the late eighteenth and early nineteenth centuries. First, there was the "Harvard type," that is, the venerable schools of colonial

---

[19] *Ibid.*, p. 53.   [20] Drake, *op. cit.*, p. 280.

days and a few more of similar pattern. Then there were hundreds of newly established, strongly denominational schools. The latter were often frontier institutions aptly described as "log-cabin" colleges. Each type has its own interesting story and development.

After the Revolution, the new states sought control over the existing independent colleges. The famous Dartmouth College case went to the Supreme Court of the United States in 1819. Daniel Webster argued for Dartmouth, and Justice Marshall's opinion was that the state of New Hampshire acted unconstitutionally in attempting to reorganize Dartmouth under state control. Dartmouth's charter as an independent institution was held inviolable. This decision was widely heralded as a landmark in the preservation of academic liberties.

The Dartmouth decision stimulated the establishing of both public and independent schools. When the states failed in their attempts to take over the existing institutions, they set about establishing their own. States in which there were few or no higher institutions of learning had not, of course, awaited this development. The way was cleared also for the churches and other interests to open new schools with some assurance that they would remain independent.

The older, more established institutions escaped direct control by the state, but they were markedly affected by political and social developments. They rapidly lost any lingering denominational characteristics affecting their operation. Schools like Harvard either showed the way for most new developments which characterized the state schools or lost little time in following them.

Harvard, Brown, and Cornell were probably preceded only by the University of Virginia in developing an elective system to replace the prescribed classical curriculum, and Harvard's leadership was undoubtedly responsible for the wider adoption of the change. Harvard established the first law school (1817). King's College (Columbia), Harvard, Dartmouth, and Yale successively established medical schools before 1811. When even the new state schools were held back by conservative influences, independent institutions such as Johns Hopkins (1876), the Catholic University of America, the University of Chicago, and Clark were founded to pioneer in graduate education and research. Harvard and Yale were not slow to follow this trend, either.

Oberlin and Mount Holyoke showed the way in coeducation and

education for women. Cornell was among the first institutions to set up agricultural and mechanical arts programs under the Morrill Act of 1862. Again Harvard (1847) and Yale (1852) were first among the established schools to develop technical schools along the lines of the Rensselaer Polytechnic Institute (1824) at Troy, New York.

The period under discussion brought about a complete change in student life from the extreme conservatism, supervision, and severe discipline of colonial times to college life and activities as they are known today. Although such developments are beyond the scope of this introductory discussion, it may be noted that independent institutions were among the first to organize student clubs, honorary and social fraternities, athletics, student publications, student government, and alumni societies.

The nineteenth-century denominational college was a peculiarly American frontier development. As the frontier moved west there was keen competition among religious denominations to be first in "higher" education. Protestants feared the expanding influence of the Jesuits in higher education, and neither Protestants nor Catholics wished to leave the field to the secular schools. One source reports the establishing of 516 colleges in 16 states before the Civil War ended, of which only 104 remain today.[21] The same source reports one denomination as stating that it "has 3 universities, 26 colleges, 17 junior colleges and 4 academies but that it had closed 174 colleges and 149 academies."[22] Competition, poor location, lack of support, a shortage of qualified faculty, and the rise of public institutions were contributing factors. Certainly a high mortality rate was characteristic of these institutions.

In other ways these institutions may be sharply contrasted with the older church-related colleges. Many grew out of academies and, it seems safe to say, often were never more than academies except in name. Most served only a local area and had but a small enrollment. Control was firmly in the hands of the clergy. The purpose for many was avowedly evangelical, disciplinary, and vocational (training of ministers) rather than scholarly.

Catholics, Presbyterians, Episcopalians, Congregationalists, Lu-

---

[21] Gould Wickey, "Church and Education — Protestant," in Walter S. Monroe (ed.), *Encyclopedia of Educational Research* (revised edition) (New York: The Macmillan Co., 1950), p. 209.
[22] *Ibid.*

therans, the German and Dutch Reformed, and perhaps one or two other denominations had a long history of serious concern for higher education; now, at least as many more denominations entered the competition. The Baptists and the Methodists were particularly active in founding new colleges during this period.

The failure of Catholics to establish American colleges before the Revolution has been noted. In the new nation the lot of Catholics improved — politically, socially, and economically — and immigration swelled their numbers. It is difficult to determine the exact dates at which they founded their first colleges, however, since almost all began as elementary and secondary schools or seminaries and only gradually added college departments. Georgetown, the first permanent college and in many ways the model for others, is usually dated from 1789, but it may have begun with the Newtown school in 1677 or with Indian schools even earlier.[23] St. Mary's College in Baltimore, chartered by the state of Maryland in 1805, began as a seminary for the training of candidates for the priesthood from Georgetown. Secondary and college students were first admitted as a move to avert financial failure of the seminary. In 1852 the Sulpicians were able to close the college and again restrict their efforts to the training of priests. By 1850 Catholics founded 10 permanent colleges; 32 others failed for reasons not unlike those which caused the failure of other new colleges of the period. From 1850 to 1899 152 colleges for men were founded and slightly less than 30 percent, or 45, of these survived.[24]

The objectives of the first Catholic colleges, according to several authors, were the same as those of other early colleges. They sought "to produce the complete Christian character."[25] They were committed, among other things, to preparing young men to undertake studies for the priesthood and to serving as a center for missionary activities. Like the better non-Catholic institutions, their central purpose gradually changed from that of forming good Church members to that of educating members of the Church in the best intellectual tradition. Because the Catholic schools were founded later than comparable non-Catholic schools, this change in central

---

[23] Power, op. cit., p. 29.

[24] Ibid., pp. 46–47.

[25] Ibid., p. 35, quoting Sebastian A. Erbacher, Catholic Higher Education for Men in the United States, 1850–1866 (Washington, D. C.: Catholic University of America Press, 1931), p. 65.

function and objective did not come until later in the nineteenth century. When it did, there was a noticeable decline in the mortality rate of Catholic colleges.

Every Catholic college passed through a formative period in which it was more a preparatory school than a full-fledged college. Some found it necessary to teach the basic elements of reading and writing. At Notre Dame's "manual labor" school the student learned any of a number of common trades. Commercial or "business education" courses were common. None of these was regarded as truly "higher" education, however. The tradition of the classical education was strong; and after about 1835 Georgetown, always a leader in the early development of Catholic education, was able to offer a respectable college-level course. St. Louis University is reported as making "considerable progress" in this direction between 1832 and 1855. Notre Dame's "precollegiate" period was 1842 to about 1855.

In the last half of the century the college program of Catholic institutions required six or seven years of study and still included much of the present high school's program of studies. It was not until about 1890 that a four-year college program known as the St. Louis Plan began to gain ground. This plan, introduced by the Jesuits, was essentially the pattern followed in non-Catholic colleges of the time.

By the time any number of the Catholic schools achieved the status of true colleges the curriculum of the better non-Catholic schools was changing from the original prescriptive, classical pattern. Practical and scientific elements were being introduced. The Catholic college studies appear to have been relatively little affected by these trends until the present century, however. The basic orientation was that of mental discipline in the classical tradition.[26] In 1887 the University of Detroit, for example, offered a classical course patterned on that of Georgetown, in which the "ancient classics hold the first place as the most efficient instrument of mental discipline."[27] In addition there was religious instruction, mental and moral philosophy, astronomy and mathematics, history, literature, and natural sciences. Practical courses, especially commercial ones, had been introduced but they were placed at the elementary or secondary level and were not considered part of higher education.

---

[26] Ibid., p. 53.
[27] Ibid., p. 79, citing the Detroit College Catalog for 1887, p. 9.

About this same time, however, other Catholic schools began to introduce a curriculum more like that of the non-Catholic colleges. At Notre Dame, for example, the catalog for 1887 recognized that study of ancient languages and pure science is "not in itself sufficient for a liberal education." A program was announced which would "provide for a more than ordinarily thorough acquaintance with the English language and with English and American literature."[28]

With respect to the methods of the early Catholic colleges, Power suggests that there is no reason to believe that they were any different than in the non-Catholic colleges. There was probably heavy reliance upon repetition and a great deal of time spent in recitation and the explaining of the texts. One feature of the time was that instructors, more like tutors actually, advanced with their students each year. This had been known in some Jesuit schools since 1548 and was fairly standard Jesuit practice after 1599.[29] The Jesuit tradition of a personal and scholarly example for students was apparently also highly regarded.

The Jesuits were emulated at Georgetown even before they assumed control in 1806, and Georgetown was an example for other Catholic colleges. Bishop Carroll, the founder of Georgetown, had urged teachers to use persuasion and other ways of motivating students which "act on their understanding and affections rather than excite their fears."[30]

The authors have a special interest in education for teachers, and Chapter II notes the beginnings of teacher education in the academies. The first institution devoted entirely to the preparation of teachers was established by Samuel Read Hall in 1823, and was called a seminary after similar German schools. The teacher-training schools which followed, both public and independent, preferred the French term "normal," meaning "model."

While the separate normal school developed primarily under public auspices, the churches were acutely interested in training teachers for their schools. Wickey states that the church-related and other independent schools were the principal agencies for training teachers until after 1880. Although he notes that 40 percent of the

[28] *Ibid.*, p. 83.

[29] *Ibid.*, p. 72.

[30] *Ibid.*, p. 74, quoting from John M. Daley, S.J., "Georgetown College: The First Fifty Years' (unpublished doctoral dissertation, Georgetown University, 1953), p. 75.

normal school students were in private institutions as late as 1897, he is probably including students in the normal departments of academies in this estimate.[31]

The Catholic teaching orders traditionally trained their own members in a period of a year or more called the "novitiate." The Third Plenary Council of Baltimore in 1884 took note of the normal school movement and urged religious communities to give their members an even longer training period. Most complied as rapidly as possible.

Near the end of the nineteenth century, an independent institution which was to have great influence in the education of teachers opened its doors in New York City. This was Teachers College, Columbia University (TC). From the beginning the aim of Teachers College was graduate study which would place teaching on a par with professions such as law and medicine. The faculty of this institution was world renowned, including such historically prominent names as John Dewey, Edward L. Thorndike, Fred Engelhardt, Nick Engelhardt, Paul Monroe, Frank McMurry, William Heard Kilpatrick, and William C. Bagley. The graduates of Teachers College went to positions of educational leadership in every part of the United States and many foreign countries.

THE TWENTIETH CENTURY

In this century the right of independent responsible groups to provide educational opportunities has been firmly established. The contributions of independent schools are widely recognized and appreciated, and only sporadically challenged. One index of their acceptance is provided by the number of students whom independent institutions serve. There has been a gradual, steady increase in the percentage of the school-age population who attend independent elementary and secondary schools. The growth of our public school system on these levels has been spectacular in this century; but the independent schools, particularly religious schools, have multiplied and expanded even more rapidly (see Figs. 1 and 4, Chap. II). In 1899–1900 slightly more than 8 percent of the elementary and secondary school students were in independent schools.[32] For 1961–

---

[31] Wickey, op. cit., p. 210.

[32] Fred F. Beach and Robert F. Will, The State and Non-Public Schools, U. S. Department of Health, Education, and Welfare, Misc. No. 28, 1958, Table 1, p. 2.

1962 the figure was between 16 and 17 percent.[33] In recent years
Catholic schools have accounted for about 85 percent of the independent school enrollment.[34]

Attempts to receive financial as well as moral support for independent schools from the government have generally failed. Some
of the verbal and legal skirmishes between the supporters and foes of
independent schools are summarized in other chapters. The federal
government's role in education is delineated in Chapter III. The
rights and responsibilities of the family, church, and state in education are discussed in Chapter V, and issues and trends in American
education are identified in Chapter VI. In this section accomplishments and trends among independent schools at the several educational levels will briefly be reviewed.

The percentage of students who are in independent schools varies
markedly from state to state. Rhode Island, for example, has nearly
30 percent in independent schools; and New York, New Jersey,
New Hampshire, Wisconsin, Illinois, and Massachusetts over 20
percent. At the other extreme are a group of states, including
Arkansas, North Carolina, South Carolina, and Utah with all but
1 or 2 percent in the public schools.

Enrollment in independent colleges and universities kept pace
with and almost exactly matched that of public institutions for about
25 years between 1925 and 1950. Recently, with rapidly increasing
total enrollments and higher operational costs, the balance has
shifted to favor the public institutions. In 1960 public institutions
enrolled about 65 percent of all college and university students.

Elementary and Secondary Church-Related Schools

By far the majority of the independent schools at these levels are
Catholic. As a result, the enrollment in Catholic schools has risen
steadily in every decade since 1900, has more than doubled since 1945
alone, and now stands at nearly 5½ million. Of these students slightly
more than 4½ million are in elementary schools; the remainder, in
secondary. Approximately 3¾ million more Catholic children who

---

[33] "1962–63 Enrollment Estimates," N.E.A. Journal, Vol. 51, No. 7, October, 1962,
p. 4.

[34] Official Catholic Directory for 1962 estimated the 1961–1962 Catholic enrollment
at nearly 5½ million; the N.E.A. estimate of all independent school enrollments for
the same year was 6½ million.

attend public schools receive regular religious instruction during released time or after school.[35]

By and large Catholic elementary schools are diocesan efforts, controlled by the bishop with an advisory board and a priest-superintendent. Parish priests are the nominal and responsible heads. Usually, the actual educational direction of the school is delegated to a member of the religious order providing instructional personnel for the school. Often this is the superior of the group.

A smaller group of elementary and secondary schools is conducted by various teaching orders of the Church, independent of the parish and diocesan organization. In 1961–1962 only 453 independent elementary schools were reported in comparison with 10,177 parish schools. There were 869 high schools independent of the parish or diocese and 1566 parish or diocesan high schools.[36]

In contrast to the Catholic position, Protestant groups generally prefer to patronize the public elementary and secondary schools. Initially, this was probably because the public schools were regarded as Protestant, although not narrowly denominational. The Catholic school movement gained its impetus as a reaction against control of the public schools by Protestant societies and their use of Protestant-oriented materials. Most Protestant groups today would be well satisfied if the public schools would present merely a factual account of the place of religion in American history and culture.

Nearly all major Protestant denominations abandoned their efforts to maintain extensive separate school systems during the nineteenth century. As previously noted, however, a second wave of German immigrants led to the expansion of Lutheran schools just around 1900. From a peak of about 2500, these schools declined to about 1500 by 1936. All but 300 to 400 of these belonged to the Missouri Synod, the most conservative of the Lutheran groups. The decrease of elementary schools among other Lutheran groups has been variously attributed to the lack of need for "German" schools as the members became Americanized, inadequate financial support by laity who failed to appreciate the importance of Christian training, and attacks by the intolerant and prejudiced during the wave of hysteria against things German which accompanied World War I.

---

[35] *Official Catholic Directory for 1962* (New York: P. J. Kenedy & Sons, 1962), General Summary, p. 1 (following Part II, p. 1319).
[36] *Ibid.*

The Missouri Synod has more than held its own in the past 25 years. In fact, both elementary and secondary school enrollments have more than doubled in this time. In 1960 the United States enrollment figure was nearly 150,000 in almost 1300 elementary schools and about 8700 in 19 secondary schools.[37]

The Missouri Synod's strength lies in its loyalty to the Word of God and the historic Confessions of the Reformation. Its objective is the thorough indoctrination of its members in the teachings of the Bible and the Confessions for the perpetuation of this body of doctrine and belief. This commitment has led to higher education in colleges and seminaries for its pastors and teachers and secondary and elementary schools for its lay members.

The Lutheran Church — Wisconsin Synod in 1962 reported 225 elementary schools with 24,250 students and 11 high schools, three of them academies preparing students for the seminary, with an enrollment of 2792.[38] During the same year fifty-three congregations of the American Lutheran Church also operated elementary schools which enrolled 5520 students. The American Lutheran Church had one secondary school with an enrollment of 240.[39]

The Seventh Day Adventists and the Mennonites are also zealous in their efforts to propagate a distinctive doctrine, and both groups have recently stepped up their efforts to maintain their own schools. The Adventists, with about 1050 elementary schools[40] and perhaps 30,000 students,[41] are second only to the Lutherans among non-Catholic denominations in their efforts to control this phase of education. The Mennonites had 18 elementary schools, with an enrollment of 2500 in 1950, and some increase since that time may be expected.[42]

The Christian Reformed Church has attempted to maintain schools because of its theological views. Parents take vows when their child is baptized which imply that they are responsible for

---

[37] The Lutheran Church — Missouri Synod, *1960 Statistical Yearbook* (St. Louis, Mo.: Concordia Publishing House, 1961), p. 281.

[38] Private communication from Adolph Fehlouer, Executive Secretary, Board of Education, Lutheran Church — Wisconsin Synod, December, 1962.

[39] Private communication from D. A. Vetter, Consultant for Lutheran Schools, Department of Parish Education, the American Lutheran Church, November, 1962.

[40] A projection from 22,333 in 880 schools reported by Edwin H. Rian, *Christianity and American Education* (San Antonio: The Naylor Co., 1949), p. 208.

[41] *Ibid.*, p. 209.

[42] *Ibid.*, p. 209.

the child's education. The Christian Reformed schools are not really operated by the Church but by committees of these parents.[43]

The Christian Reformed have maintained less than 200 schools in recent years, about 110 in 1950.[44] The enrollment in these schools has been rather large, however, almost equal to that of the much more numerous Adventists' schools. Other elementary and secondary schools, perhaps several hundred, are scattered among the many remaining Protestant groups.

The Sunday school was the almost universal answer of the Protestant groups to the closing of the parochial schools in the nineteenth century. Many difficulties have accompanied the efforts to make the Sunday school effective in religious instruction. As a rule, there have been too few dedicated and adequately trained teachers. The time is short. Until recently curriculum plans and materials were not very adequate. Today new curricula and materials notable for both educational excellence and theological content are being introduced in many churches.

Sunday schools have been widely supplemented by vacation schools, and by weekday religious instruction at times when the children could be released from public schools. Weekday study of religion spread rapidly and was a nationwide, though not universal practice by 1940. In several court cases the legality of released time for the study of religion in church buildings has been established, although the use of school facilities for such instruction has been held unconstitutional.

Another Protestant contribution of the past few years has been the many nursery schools and kindergartens affiliated with local churches. This is usually a project of the individual church rather than a denominational effort. The experiences offered in these schools are quite similar to those offered in public kindergartens.

The Jewish people have strongly supported education. As a group, they have supported the public schools since the early 1900's. In recent years the establishment of independent Jewish all-day schools has been encouraged by new Jewish immigration from Europe, especially since the conditions which forced this immigration have increased Jewish determination to preserve their cultural unity. Immi-

---

[43] D. Campbell Wyckoff, "The Protestant Day School," *School and Society*, 82:98–101, October 1, 1955, p. 99.

[44] Ryan, *op. cit.*, p. 208.

gration is only one factor in the tremendous growth of the Jewish schools, of course, having the greatest influence in the intensely Jewish neighborhoods of New York City. The general religious revival in America and the emerging character of the public schools in some locations have played a part also. Most Jewish schools are administered by American-born Jews, and the students are largely second- or even third-generation Americans.

Recently, the education editor for the North American Newspaper Alliance, Benjamin Fine, estimated the number of students in 268 Jewish day schools as 50,000. In 1935 there were only 16 schools, and of these 15 were in New York City with one in Baltimore.[45] In 1962 about half of these 268 schools, including 53 secondary schools, were in the New York area; the rest, widely scattered. New Jewish schools were being established at the rate of about ten each year.

The majority of the Jewish all-day schools are maintained by Orthodox groups and are committed to Jewish learning and the traditional ways of Jewish life. Students typically spend half a day in strictly Jewish or religious study and the other half of each day in a program similar to that of the public schools, although a few more liberal schools alternate periods of Jewish and general studies throughout the day. Jewish schools vary also with respect to using Yiddish, Hebrew, or English as the medium of instruction and in the emphasis given to Jewish nationalism or to harmonizing American culture and Jewish values. Every effort is made to achieve excellence in the complete secular course of study, in addition to the Jewish or religious instruction. They seek the best available teachers, materials, and equipment and have small classes and a full school day. Their students have earned an enviable reputation in collegiate work.

Another approach to the study of Jewish culture, law, and religion is represented by an extensive system of supplementary schools meeting daily after public school hours and on Sunday. In some sections of the country a very high percentage of Jewish children has been reported in dual school attendance.

The Roman Catholic school teachers have traditionally been members of religious orders. There are several hundred teacher-training communities for women and others for men. A recent rapid increase

---

[45] Joseph Kaminetsky, "Evaluating the Program and Effectiveness of the All-Day Jewish School," *Jewish Education*, 27:39–49, Winter, 1962, p. 39.

in enrollment has led to the use of more and more Catholic lay teachers. There are more persons entering religious teaching orders than ever before, but the demand for teachers is increasing still faster. In 1961 nearly a third of the total number of teachers in Catholic schools at all levels were lay people, 57,515 out of a total of 175,806.[46] In just one year, 1960–1961, the number of lay teachers in these schools jumped 4631, while the number of religious teachers increased only 2498. In other words, nearly two thirds of the new teachers of that year were lay persons. Furthermore, in an era of rising costs it has been increasingly difficult for Catholic schools, as well as other independent schools, to compete financially for the services of laymen with suitable training and conviction.

The Lutherans employ both men and women graduated from synodal teachers' colleges and Lutherans trained in other institutions. Men are used almost exclusively in the high schools and many have the status of ministers. Other denominations recruit teachers from among those of their faith who have been trained in public institutions.

Only five states require that teachers of independent schools be licensed or certified as are public school teachers. Most independent high schools seek accreditation of the same type granted public secondary schools, however, and highly qualified teachers are a prerequisite for approval by state and regional agencies.

The instructional methods and the program of secular studies in schools operated under religious auspices are similar to those found in the public schools of the same communities. A somewhat greater emphasis upon the academic in these schools, as compared with public schools, is partly the result of tradition, partly the effect of a resistance to what is regarded as soft pedagogy, and partly the consequence of the strain which vocational or avocational studies place upon the independent school's limited financial resources.

In the independent schools, as in the public, newer approaches can be found side by side with time-honored methods. There is both an earnest effort to use the findings of the new psychology and a tendency toward the conservative in method and toward the encouragement of conformity.

The general similarity of the offerings in Catholic and public

---

[46] Official Catholic Directory for 1962, General Summary, p. 2 (following Part II, p. 1319).

schools is indicated by the fact that 91.2 percent of Catholic secondary schools were accredited by some standardizing agency in 1950.[47] Reporters of the Protestant and Jewish schools have commented on the fact that the secular program in their schools also approximates that of the public schools.

The Nondenominational "Private" Schools

A relatively small but unusually influential group of Americans attend about 1000 schools which are supported and sometimes endowed by the well-to-do. They are commonly called "private" or "prep" schools. These are usually nondenominational and serve the interests of their select clientele. The best known schools of this type are the direct descendants of nineteenth-century independent academies, but are now devoted to preparing their students for the exclusive Eastern colleges.

Because of their college-preparatory orientation, the curriculum of these schools offers a larger proportion of languages and mathematics than does the curriculum of the average public high school. Little attention is given to vocational subjects. Ordinarily teachers in these schools are exceptionally well prepared in their field. Although they often do not have training in education or psychology, they have the advantage of small classes and students who are quick to learn. The most important difference of all is the background of the students. Since many come from prominent families, many become prominent themselves. Traxler suggests that the chances for a boy in one of these prep schools to become one of our nation's future leaders are a hundred times greater than they are for a boy in the public school.[48]

"Country day schools" have been established to serve those parents who want their children to attend a prep school but wish to avoid having them board away from home. Otherwise these schools have much the same characteristics as other prep schools. The best of such schools have attempted to maintain the atmosphere of culture associated with the boarding schools. Typically, they are located near metropolitan centers and their students commute daily.

What is the value of a prep school education? In recent years there

---

[47] Frederick G. Hochwalt, "Church and Education — Catholic," in Walter S. Monroe (ed.), *Encyclopedia of Educational Research*, p. 205.

[48] Arthur E. Traxler, "The Independent School, Yesterday, Today, and Tomorrow," *School and Society*, 56:506–510, November 28, 1942, p. 507.

has been evidence that the students of these schools do better on standardized examinations of achievement than do public school graduates. On the other hand, it has also been shown at Princeton and Harvard that public school graduates of equal ability do better than graduates of the exclusive schools. In interpreting this seemingly contradictory evidence of the success of the independent schools it should be remembered that public school graduates attending Princeton and Harvard are more exceptional for the public schools than prep-school graduates attending these institutions are for their alma maters. A related explanation, advanced by Davis and Frederikson,[49] is that the public school graduates are more highly motivated to achieve than are the private school graduates, who have in a sense a secure and enviable social status.[50]

Independent nondenominational schools on the elementary level are notable primarily for pioneering experimental programs, usually as a reaction to conventional school practices. The experimental elementary school of John Dewey at the University of Chicago is a prime example. It was the first and most famous of the "progressive" schools. Dewey's school, started in 1894, emphasized social activity and, for content, the study of occupations — of the household, of the community, and of their larger cultural and historical settings. Reading, writing, and number work were developed through related activities. The Chicago school of Colonel Francis W. Parker, which was founded in 1901, incorporated many of Dewey's ideas. Colonel Parker insisted that the child himself be the center and focus of education.

After Dewey, other schools of similar type sprang up. Fairhope in Alabama started as such an elementary school in 1907. Today it encompasses all grades from nursery to college. At Fairhope students are encouraged to live naturally in a stimulating environment. They are not pushed toward learning and maturity. Another example was the Hessian Hills School, near New York City, where teachers, parents, and pupils cooperated in running the school. Activity of all kinds in the service of children's immediate needs was a prominent method of learning there. A current revival of interest in the edu-

[49] Julius A. Davis and Norman Frederikson, "Public and Private School Graduates in College," *The Journal of Teacher Education*, Vol. VI, No. 1, March, 1955, pp. 18–22.

[50] William Marshall French, *American Secondary Education* (New York: Odyssey Press, 1957), p. 267.

cational theory of Maria Montessori (1870–1950), a noted Italian educator, has already led to the establishment of several American schools to demonstrate and promote her methods and materials for capitalizing on the natural activities of children.

The children's school, established in New York City in 1916, was an extreme example of Progressivism, one which helped to give the movement its laissez-faire reputation. The founder and director of this school, Margaret Naumberg, was influenced by Freud's psychological theories. She thought Dewey's social approach placed too many restrictions on children's freedom to develop their own individuality.[51]

A rather large number of elementary schools are now conducted on college campuses as part of the teacher-training program. They are variously called demonstration schools, training schools, laboratory schools, or experimental schools. Such schools are designed to be models of the best in theory and practice. As such, they have contributed to the improvement of education both in the preparation of teachers and through systematic research in teaching and learning.

The "prep" schools have been marked by progressive and experimental tendencies also. Of the thirty high schools chosen to participate in the Eight Year Study of the Progressive Education Association, during the 1930's and 1940's, sixteen were independent schools. In these schools, as in their elementary counterparts, the importance of natural interests and freedom of development have been emphasized. The teacher has been regarded as a guide in student activities rather than a master. Scientific study and experimentation have been encouraged. The same schools have pioneered in home-school cooperation. Today, some of these schools are extremely conservative in method and curriculum while others are markedly liberal. Despite differences of this kind, the independent, nondenominational schools remain predominantly "prep" or college-preparatory schools.

Independent Vocational Schools

The information necessary to give a complete picture of the contributions of independent schools of less than college grade is not

[51] John S. Brubacher, A History of the Problems of Education (New York: McGraw-Hill Book Co., 1947), pp. 414–415.

available for either denominational or nondenominational agencies. The preceding presentation is particularly inadequate with respect to schools with a primarily vocational aim. The Catholic figures already presented do not include, for example, over 45,000 candidates for the priesthood enrolled in seminaries or 36,000 student nurses. Other religious groups are engaged in these and other types of vocational education.

Millions of students are enrolled in the numerous trade and commercial schools. In 1956–1957 the National Association and Council of Business Schools alone estimated their enrollment as about 500,000. There are also art, design, and drafting schools; barber, beauty culture, charm, and dermatology schools; broadcasting and dramatics schools; trade, industrial, and vocational schools; massage and physical-therapy schools; jewelry and watch-repairing schools; and many, many others.

Almost anything academic or vocational can now be studied by correspondence. In 1954 there were an estimated 1½ million correspondence students, all but about 175,000 in independent institutions.[52] In 1955, 700,000 new students enrolled in 421 independent home-study schools, more than entered college the same year.[53]

The Independents in Higher Education

In this century American higher education has come into its own. Americans believe that a college education is essential for individual success, and they think the American brand of college education best. Only rarely do we look to Europe for cultural or scientific leadership. We are confident that the savants and researchers of our own great universities will provide the wisdom and knowledge for a fuller, more secure life.

The independent schools continue as influential partners in higher education. The venerable independent universities of the nineteenth century have attained positions of prestige and leadership which are unrivaled. Among the schools of engineering and technology none are more highly respected than the Massachusetts, the Carnegie, the California, and the Illinois Institutes of Technology. Teacher education is closely related to the educational efforts of the various reli-

[52] Helen Allian and Homer Kempfer, "New Developments in Correspondence Education," *Adult Education*, Vol. 4 (1954), pp. 76–85.
[53] National Home Study Council, *Private Home Study Schools in the United States* (The Council, 1956).

gious groups, and substantial numbers of new teachers, probably 50,000 a year, graduate from independent schools.[54]

As in the past, the independent institutions of higher learning outnumber the public but they no longer enroll as high a proportion of American students as they once did. From an equal share in enrollment for some twenty-five years prior to 1950, the private schools have slipped until today they have the short end of a 40–60 split of our four million degree-seeking students. The tax-supported institutions have found it easier to accommodate rising enrollments without tuition increases. As a result, the enrollment balance in recent years has shifted inevitably to the public schools. It is not difficult to foresee the state institutions claiming 70 or even 80 percent of the total enrollment in a few years.

More institutions have broken or loosened ties with founding denominations. The first step is for laymen to assume control from the clergy. Then courses in ethics and the Bible are offered merely as general education or an aid to character building and are not even remotely evangelical. The naturalism of the avowedly secular school prevails. They are, in short, scarcely distinguishable from nondenominational universities, colleges, or junior colleges. In commenting on Protestant schools the vice-president of a Presbyterian university[55] has lamented the general lack of (1) an integrated and unified Christian philosophy of education among Protestant colleges and (2) textbooks with a Christian view of the world.

Among the Protestant denominations we find notable exceptions to the foregoing trends in colleges of the Missouri Synod Lutherans, the Christian Reformed Church, the Seventh-Day Adventists, and the Mennonites, the same groups that maintain significant systems of schools below the collegiate level. In 1960 the Missouri Synod Lutherans reported 6000 students in 14 colleges and seminaries.[56] Two other Lutheran Church bodies have impressive programs of higher education. The American Lutheran Church in 1962 reported 11 institutions of higher learning enrolling about 16,000 students; and in 1960 the United Lutheran Church in America had 16 colleges with 16,000 students and 13 seminaries with 1500 candidates

[54] Lindley J. Stiles, A. S. Barr, Harl R. Douglass, and Hubert H. Mills, *Teacher Education in the United States* (New York: The Ronald Press Co., 1960), p. 103.
[55] Rian, op. cit., pp. 212–214.
[56] The Lutheran Church — Missouri Synod, op. cit., p. 281.

for the ministry.[57] Both the American and the United Lutherans are completing mergers with smaller Lutheran groups which will bring additional colleges under their control. Still other Lutheran Church bodies control one or more junior or senior colleges or seminaries.

Relatively recent reports (1955) credit the Adventists with about 6000 students and 18 colleges.[58] The Christian Reformed Church operates Calvin College in Grand Rapids, Michigan. The Mennonites have several colleges. All of the Protestant colleges noted here are thoroughly Christian in control, methods, and materials. They are often given credit for developing strong and loyal congregations. The Jewish Yeshiva University is thoroughly committed to Orthodox Jewish faith and culture.

The Roman Catholic Church has the largest and most successful system of church-related colleges and universities. In 1945 there were 210 Catholic colleges and universities with under 100,000 students. Now there are 278 with 336,604 students, or 60 percent of all those attending independent college-level institutions. To these figures might be added 545 seminaries training 46,254 students for the priesthood.[59] Even more significant than the numbers is the direct control which the Catholic Church exercises over the policy and practice of these schools. The Catholics subscribe to a definite philosophy of education. In some areas of study they have textual materials which implement this philosophy. While experimentalism may appear to have gained ground in others, the overall picture of Catholic higher education is one of solidarity and achievement.

The independent and public institutions of higher education have faced many of the same problems. Both have sought a desirable balance with respect to critical issues such as: the classics and science, teaching and research, electives and prescribed courses, general and specialized education, academic and vocational studies, academic excellence and athletic prominence. A summary appraisal of the status of current thought with respect to a number of these issues reveals no great trend toward agreement over the past fifty years. Furthermore, the similarities among public and independent colleges

---

[57] George F. Harkins (ed.), *United Lutheran Church in America, 1962 Yearbook* (New York: Board of Publications, United Lutheran Church in America, 1962), p. 192.

[58] Guy E. Snavely, *The Church and the Four-Year College* (New York: Harper & Brothers, 1955), p. 136.

[59] *Official Catholic Directory for 1962*, General Summary, p. 2 (following Part II, p. 1319).

and universities with respect to tentative solutions to any problem probably outweigh the differences. Among the independents church-related institutions tend toward the conservative, while the "progressive" or experimental programs are more often found in the nondenominational schools. Thus there is probably somewhat greater diversity among independent than among public institutions with both the conservative and the more liberal views on any issue finding adherents. St. John's College, for example, has based its program squarely on the classics and their presumed disciplinary value. Bennington College, on the other hand, has experimented with making fieldwork, travel, art, and athletics an integral part of the programs which have been arranged especially for each individual student. After about ten years of experimentation with this program at Bennington, some reorganization was affected to arrange a major area of study for which general requirements were established.

American educators cherish their right to be different. One of their greatest concerns today is the preservation of free enterprise in education under conditions which make it difficult for independents to survive. For many the alternative to some form of tax support for independent schools or their students is a state monopoly in education. This is one of the issues in American education which is discussed in Chapter VI. Father Hesburgh, president of Notre Dame, gives point to the fear of a state monopoly. He relates an incident that occurred at an international educational meeting in Mexico City. When educators from everywhere seemed in agreement on an educational principle, the American delegation called for a resolution supporting the principle. The Americans, presidents of both independent and public universities, voted their approval; but no one else did. It seems the other delegations were composed of the presidents of institutions in countries without independent schools. They were not free to take any stand affecting education without political approval. Father Hesburgh believes the presidents of our public as well as our independent institutions were relatively free to act only because they have shared some of the freedom won by their independent partners.[60]

What must independent schools of college and university rank

---

[60] Reverend Theodore M. Hesburgh, "The Concerns of Private Colleges," *Unity in Diversity, Fourteenth Yearbook,* American Association of Colleges for Teacher Education, 1961, pp. 21–22.

do to merit survival? Father Hesburgh believes their merit can be shown through "quality, flexibility, and commitment." Small classes, freedom to select both students and faculty, and a dedication to teaching and scholarship can be factors in achieving higher quality. Flexibility means willingness and vision in using the freedom they wish to protect. In this way independent colleges and universities could lead the way in reform and progress. The church-related colleges and universities in particular can add new vigor and "wholeness, inspiration, and strength" to teaching and learning through a renewed commitment to "religious, spiritual, and moral beliefs and values."[61]

Summary

The American educational system is a dual one with both public and independent institutions accepted and valued. The success of our independent schools is indicated by the numbers of those who attend them, that is, approximately: 15 percent or 5 million of our 32 million elementary school students; 12 percent or 1¼ million of our 10½ million secondary school students; and 40 percent or 1½ million of our 4 million students of higher education. The independents are known also for their variety. Their freedom to be different is a strength which has made it possible for them to adapt to the academic, social, cultural, and religious needs of the groups they serve. It has also made possible experimentation and innovations which eventually benefit all schools, public as well as independent.

The colonial schools of all levels were "church-related." After the Revolution, the states of the new nation sought a system of schools for the children of all. The existing schools served special interests, usually religious ones; besides, they were too few, and poorly financed. A number of schemes to avoid full public responsibility proved unsatisfactory. Religious differences were a particularly difficult problem. The states' solution, eventually, was to establish their own schools, make school attendance compulsory, and prohibit the teaching of religion or the use of religious materials in the "public" schools.

Schools without religion were unacceptable to the Catholics and to several Protestant denominations — Lutherans of the Missouri

---

[61] *Ibid.*, p. 25.

Synod, Seventh-Day Adventists, the Christian Reformed, and the Mennonites. These groups have worked to establish their own schools, as have some Jews, usually recent immigrants or the more orthodox. Largely as a result of the Catholic effort, the new religious schools have claimed an ever increasing portion of the elementary and secondary school enrollment in this century. That portion is now 16 to 17 percent of the total and is still increasing.

There is a small, exclusive, but influential group of "prep" schools today that began as academies in the nineteenth century. The typical academy of that time was vocationally oriented. For a time they were better suited to the needs of the new nation than the older Latin grammar schools that prepared boys for the early church colleges. Eventually, most gave way to the modern high school. A few academies for boys and a few others for girls assumed the selective and cultural qualities of the great secondary schools of England. They have continued this tradition to the present time, and may be given credit for the secondary education of many eminent persons.

Eight of today's most influential universities were founded as colleges for the ministry before the Revolution. The young states lost their struggle to take over these venerable institutions, and proceeded to found their own colleges. The older schools were affected, however. They became leaders in the secular education offered by the public institutions and tended to lose their earlier religious commitment. At about the same time, a host of new colleges sprang up to advance denominational interests and train ministers for the frontier. The majority of these were short-lived; and many of the survivors, like the old church-related schools, have gradually loosened their denominational ties. The exceptions are colleges of denominations that still maintain strong elementary and secondary school programs.

Catholic higher education was firmly established in the nineteenth century. Over 55 permanent colleges were founded before 1900. Today Catholic colleges and universities have 60 percent of the enrollment in independent institutions. The evolution of the Catholic college came later but paralleled, to a point, the development of the first schools founded under Protestant auspices. Catholic schools began with an emphasis on missionary activity, later became more intellectual in the classical sense, and, near the end of the nineteenth century, broadened their curriculum to include English language and literature, and the sciences.

In every period of our history the contributions of the independent schools to commercial, industrial, and technical education have been notable. In the colonial period schools of this type were an important adjunct of the apprentice system and, in addition, offered girls some educational opportunities beyond the elementary school level. Today, the trade and commercial schools offering specific occupational training to millions of Americans are almost exclusively independent.

The independent institutions have sought teachers who are professionally qualified and who share the culture and faith of the founding group. A shortage of such doubly qualified persons has been a major and continuous problem. Catholics have relied on their several hundred teaching orders, but increased enrollments have required the employment of larger and larger numbers of lay teachers.

Professional education for lay teachers began when a "professional year" was added to the academies, an independent institution. The first normal schools for teachers were independent also, but the movement gained momentum and expanded under public auspices. The teachers' colleges which succeeded the normal schools are largely public also. Nevertheless, independent liberal arts colleges and multipurpose institutions now train about 50,000, or one third of the fully qualified teachers who are graduated each year. The majority of these find employment in the public schools.

The instructional methods and the secular program of studies of independent and public schools and colleges are similar. The larger number of both seek accreditation by the same agencies and the same standards. There are more similarities than differences also among public and independent institutions with respect to the problems they have faced and the solutions they have tried. It was suggested that greater extremes could be found among the independents. Although church-related institutions tend to the more conservative, and the nondenominational schools to the more liberal and experimental approach to some issues, both have pioneered developments that have benefited all educational efforts. Recently, the laboratory or campus schools of teacher-training institutions have been leaders in seeking and demonstrating improved methods and materials.

To merit support under modern social and economic conditions, the independent school must prove the quality of its education, the vigor of its search for progress, and the sincerity of its moral and spiritual commitments.

SELECTED READINGS

Beach, Fred F., and Will, Robert F., *The State and Nonpublic Schools* (Washington, D. C.: Office of Education, 1958).
> A comprehensive analysis of independent schools which reports on enrollments, state regulations, and relations with state departments of education.

Chamberlain, Ernest B., *The Private School in American Education* (Chicago: American Book Co., 1944).
> The report of a study of independent schools and their place in American education containing a history of independent schools along with their general characteristics and problems.

Curran, Francis X., S. J., *The Churches and the Schools* (Chicago: Loyola University Press, 1954). Chaps. I and VIII.
> Study of the rise and decline of Protestant elementary schools by a Catholic.

Dawson, Christopher, *The Crisis of Western Education* (New York: Sheed and Ward, 1961).
> Speaks out for the restoration of Christian culture in education.

Drake, William E., *The American School in Transition* (New York: Prentice-Hall, 1955).
> Educational history from the social forces point of view. Chaps. 1 and 2 deal with the colonial scene and Chap. 3 examines the impact of secularism on education. Chap. 14 is notable as a treatment of the interests, concerns and functions of religious agencies in American education.

French, William M., *American Secondary Education* (New York: Odyssey Press, 1957), Chaps. 11 & 12.
> Emphasis is placed upon the variation in non-church-related schools and evidence of their effectiveness. The background and reasons for church-related schools are suggested together with a brief description of their administration and operation.

Gummere, John F., "The Case for Private Schools," *Changing Times*, Vol. 4, No. 7 (July, 1950), pp. 37–38.
> A headmaster answers the critics of independent parent-supported schools by denying their snobbishness and emphasizing their long and honorable tradition.

Hughes, James M., *Education in America*, (Evanston: Row, Peterson & Co., 1960), Chap. 14.
> Introductory presentation of the rights, the regulation and the contribu-

tions of independent schools. Brief descriptions of parochial (Catholic, Protestant and Hebrew) and private (vocational, parent-supported, industry-supported and campus laboratory) schools.

Heely, Allan V., "The Private School in American Education," in Bereday, George Z. F., and Volpicelli, Luigi (eds.), *Public Education in America* (New York: Harper & Bros., 1958), pp. 50–61.

An evaluation of the work of independent schools in American education.

Kaminetsky, Joseph, "Evaluating the Program and Effectiveness of the All-Day Jewish School," *Jewish Education*, Vol. 27, No. 2 (Winter 1956–57), pp. 39–49.

An authoritative statement on the growth of the Hebrew day-school movement; the types of Jewish schools with their differing philosophies, problems and successes; and the characteristics of Jewish-school children and teachers.

Monroe, Walter S. (ed.), *Encyclopedia of Educational Research*, rev. ed. (New York: Macmillan Co., 1950), pp. 203–212.

Studies and findings of the development, status, contributions and problems of church-related education are presented in three articles by Catholic, Protestant, and Jewish educators.

Phenix, Philip H., *Education and the Common Good* (New York: Harper & Bros., 1961).

A Presbyterian's plan for teaching religious values in secular schools.

Pius XI, *Christian Education of Youth* (Washington, D. C.: National Catholic Welfare Conference, 1930).

Encyclical Letter on the meaning and goals of Christian education.

Power, Edward J., *A History of Catholic Higher Education in the United States* (Milwaukee: Bruce Publishing Co., 1958).

Chaps. 1 and 2 describe the Catholic heritage in higher education and the beginnings of Catholic higher education in America. Later chapters trace the developments in curriculum and method, student life and activities, administration and facilities for graduate and professional, as well as undergraduate programs.

Rian, Edwin H., *Christianity and American Education* (San Antonio: Naylor Co., 1949).

Protestant view of the history of American church-related schools at all levels, their early relations with the public school system and their present status. Appraisal of Roman Catholic educational views and achievements.

The Role of the Independent School in American Democracy (Milwaukee: Marquette University Press, 1956).

A series of addresses delivered at Marquette University's 15th annual conference on education. Some titles are: "The Historical Background of the Independent School in the United States" (Wm. Brickman), "Current Issues Facing the Independent Schools" (Sister M. Emil, I.H.M.), "Current Issues Facing Independent Colleges" (Glenn L. McConagha), and "The Partnership of the Independent and Public Schools in the Future of America" (William G. Carr). Carr's address was reprinted in the *Education Digest* for September 1956.

School and Society, Vol. 82 (October 1, 1955), pp. 98–107.

Special issue on religion in the schools includes: "The Hebrew Day School

Movement" (Joseph Kaminetsky), "American Catholic Schools Today" (John E. Wise, S. J.), "The Protestant Day School" (D. Campbell Wyckoff).

Stellhorn, A. C., "Schools of the Lutheran Church-Missouri Synod," *School and Society,* Vol. 87 (May 9, 1959), pp. 225–227.
   A statement of the educational program of this denomination that emphasizes the service of church schools to the states as well as individuals.

Traxler, Arthur E., "The Independent School, Yesterday, Today and Tomorrow," *School and Society,* Vol. 56 (November 28, 1942), pp. 506–510.
   History and status of independent schools to 1942.

Chapter V

EDUCATIONAL AGENCIES

The education of man in a general sense is the development of his whole nature. The individual himself has first responsibility for becoming what he is capable of being with the help and gifts of God. In a more restricted sense, education may denote the methods and activities of other agencies to stimulate or guide the individual's development — physical, intellectual, social, moral, and spiritual. The family, the church, and the state are our oldest, most permanent, and most generally influential institutions. In this chapter they will be viewed as the primary educational agencies, each with definite rights, responsibilities, and opportunities which will be analyzed in this chapter. All three have established schools but this is only one of their methods, only a part of their educational efforts.

Although we have a tendency to equate education with the schools, a moment's reflection will remind us of many scholars and leaders who had very little schooling, and of the vast amount we ourselves learn out of school. The neighborhood in which the child lives, his peer group, books and magazines, and radio and television will be considered here also. Although influential, these agencies are thought to have less direct responsibility in education than the family, church, and state, and so they will be termed "secondary" agencies of education.

THE FAMILY AND THE SCHOOL

In either the natural or the divine order of things the family brings the child into the world and has the responsibility and inalienable right to nourish, support, guide, and educate him. All phases of development begin in the family. For his physical needs the young child is completely dependent on his parents. The home provides the stimulation and the sheltered environment for practicing the common

111

physical skills. It is in the home that the child learns his language and forms his habits of thought. In countless interactions the family interprets his behavior and shapes his attitudes, ideals, and values. The family introduces the child to the knowledge and practice of his religion, for example, and informally builds concepts of a parent, a neighbor, a friend, an employee, etc., which may influence the child's future behavior in these roles. One psychologist, John B. Watson (cf. Chap. XIII), boasted that he could take any normal infant and train him to be anything that one might wish. There is an element of truth in this extravagent claim insofar as the early influence of the family on an individual is concerned.

The results of family education, as seen in children when they come to school, vary with the type and quality of parents and their relationships with their children. Some parents are tyrants and abuse their rights. Others evade their responsibilities in one or more areas of development by neglect or ignorance. In the home children may learn to ignore authority, fear it, or respect it. They may learn to settle differences with physical force, evasion, or arbitration. Families whose members enjoy generally wholesome relationships with each other and with the community have little difficulty in becoming good citizens. On the other hand, if the family members, especially the parents, are irresponsible, uncooperative, irreverent, or antisocial we may expect much the same from the child. An alarming proportion of "problem children" comes from families who have not even been able to remain together as a unit.

Schools are perhaps the most formal extension of the family as a child-rearing agency. The school's efforts are made more difficult by the various backgrounds of its charges. Middle-class families, for example, tend to support the school's efforts. Such families place a high value on education and reward their children for being "good" in school. Parents from lower-class groups, on the other hand, may feel that school is of little importance, and may communicate their scorn for schools and teachers to their children. Children from some social groups are actually embarrassed about doing well in school, and gain the recognition which they truly value from notable misbehavior.

The authoritarian home with its systems of rewards and punishments often leads to other problems such as insecurity, nervousness, immature behavior, and a general lack of confidence and initiative in school. Children from such homes may resent all authority and are apt to be rebellious and uncooperative, if not openly, then slyly. On the other hand, children who have experienced little or no parental control may be irresponsible, uncooperative, with a "do as I please" attitude. Occasionally they may embrace the security of the well-ordered classroom as an escape from the complete lack of direction at home. The family that avoids the extremes of either authoritarian or *laissez-faire* views gives its children the best chance for successful adjustment to school and life. In what we may call a "democratic" family climate the rights of the child to responsibility and experience in line with his maturity are cherished. There is authority in the democratic home too. The point of view makes the difference. It is one of cooperation in which the child appreciates reasons for rules and finds respect for the rights and needs of all members of the family.

Other characteristics which parents should seek for their home have been well summarized by John P. Treacy.[1] Treacy finds that good homes, educationally speaking, are those in which:

1. Family decisions and activities are influenced greatly by what is best for the children. The good of the children usually comes first.

2. Parents learn and use the fundamental facts about child growth and development. They know children.

3. Parents recognize the importance of the home in education. The school is not expected to do it all.

4. The intellectual atmosphere and physical conditions are conducive to learning. The stage is set.

5. Children are accustomed to self-sacrifice and self-discipline. They learn to work independently.

6. Parents continually evaluate their children's progress in character and personality as well as in school subjects. Then they act accordingly.

Home and school understanding and cooperation are important in the effective education of the child. Both schools and parents vary widely in the extent to which they have sought each other's help, however. Home-school interaction is perhaps easiest in smaller communities or private schools where there is more direct and immediate knowledge and control of school matters and where family

---

[1] John P. Treacy, "Good Homes Help Children Succeed," *Our Parish School Bulletin* (Menomonee Falls, Wis.: Parish Publications, 1962).

backgrounds tend to be similar. The problem is probably greater in the school systems of larger cities which must serve children of a wide variety of backgrounds. Moreover, city "systems" appear to the parent as part of a large depersonalized city government of which he has little knowledge and on which he can have little or no influence. Size of community and heterogeneity of social groups make close cooperation between home and school more difficult but not impossible. These handicaps may be overcome, at least in part, by determined and responsible leadership and effective organization.

The parent-teacher or home-school association has been an effective force for a child's education and welfare in school systems and communities of every type and size. The largest and best known of such organizations is the National Congress of Parents and Teachers. Its membership is well over 10,000,000, with local units in almost every community in the United States. From its beginnings as the National Congress of Mothers in 1897, it has emphasized cooperation between the school and the home. The purposes of the PTA, as the Congress is generally known, are:

1. To promote the welfare of children and youth in home, school, church, and community.

2. To raise the standards of home life.

3. To secure adequate laws for the care and protection of children and youth.

4. To bring the home and the school into closer relation, so that parents and teachers may cooperate intelligently in the training of the child.

5. To develop between education and the general public such united efforts as will secure for every child the highest advantages in physical, mental, social, and spiritual development.[2]

There are numerous local or independent groups with similar purposes. Catholic parent-teacher groups are usually closely associated with the activities of the National Catholic Welfare Conference, particularly through the National Council of Catholic Men and the National Council of Catholic Women.

The role of the family in education has changed as society has become more complex. Among primitive peoples the family was relatively self-contained and self-supporting. The aim of education

---

[2] National Congress of Teachers and Parents, *Jubilee History* (Chicago: The Congress, 1947), p. 12.

was to introduce children into their life roles. Imitation of parents was the usual method. As knowledge increased and life became more involved, certain individuals began to specialize in particular skills, such as toolmaking or healing, which they taught to selected young persons. Thus, the family unit began to delegate some of its rights and responsibilities for education. Today, most goods and services required by the family are produced outside. The father leaves home to travel to his job. Mother and children are not closely involved. A much larger share of the education of children and youth has been turned over to the school and other agencies. Nevertheless, the family remains as the single most important educational agent. The all-important start is made at home. In sharing their responsibilities parents still retain the right and obligation to choose the manner and type of education for their children; and they are obliged to participate to the best of their ability in the establishment, control, and support of the institutions to which they choose to entrust their children's continued education.

THE CHURCH

Christianity has dominated the civilization and culture of the Western world for nearly 2000 years. For this period the followers of Christ have had a teaching commission of divine origin. "Going into the world, preach the gospel to every creature" (Mk 16:15). Until the nineteenth century, nearly all schools were church-related. To a large extent this is still the pattern in Europe, with subsidies provided by the states. In America separate "protest" schools evolved because of the predominantly sectarian flavor of the early public schools. (Cf. Chapters II and III.)

The Catholic Church holds that her divine command to teach cannot be countermanded by any earthly power. A 1958 statement of the Bishops of the United States makes this point and adds:

But it is also true that in the natural order the Church's right to exist and to teach has its roots in man's freedom, an essential attribute of his nature, the sanctity and inviolability of which has long been recognized as a fundamental of Western Civilization. If man is truly free, he is free to accept the revelation of our Lord and to embrace the society He established.[3]

[3] Administrative Board, National Catholic Welfare Conference, in the name of the Bishops of the United States, The Teaching Mission of the Catholic Church (Washington, D. C.: National Catholic Welfare Conference, 1958), p. 1.

The special concerns of the Church are supernatural and eternal rather than temporal. Spiritual development of the individual is the first obligation; but the Catholic educator, or any Christian one for that matter, reasons "that since man is dependent on God for his existence and all his possessions, whether material, spiritual, or supernatural, it is clear that God must enter into every phase of his life activities."[4]

The point here is that the responsibility of the Church for spiritual matters cannot be isolated since it is so interwoven with man's total behavior and development. Similar logic is used by secular educators to argue that they must be concerned with the "whole child" since intellectual progress is interwoven with other aspects of development or is, in fact, inseparable. Sister Mary Janet, S.C., explains the Catholic Church's position further:

> If the process of education, then, is to fulfill its function of developing the whole person, a principle which has universal approval, the Catholic educator considers the task incompletely performed unless knowledge of God and our duties to Him are included in the educational program. Schools consider it their duty to aid parents in every other phase of the development of children — in matters of health, of home life, of leisure pursuits, as well as in intellectual skills and habits. The duty of the school also includes the development of the spiritual life, which cannot be accomplished without religion, which is its source.
> It can never be forgotten that this logic is not merely Catholic; it is Christian, and was the philosophy of the founders of this Christian nation. . . .[5]

The official Roman Catholic position on the rights and responsibilities of the Church, the family, and the state in education was stated in the *Encyclical on Christian Education of Youth* by Pope Pius XI.[6] According to Pope Pius XI, the family has the primal right and obligation to educate, both in the natural and supernatural order. Nevertheless, the family does not have all the means for providing for either the temporal or spiritual well-being of the child. The state is the means by which the ability of the family to provide for temporal needs is extended. The Church is supreme in supernatural matters.

---

[4] Sister Mary Janet, S.C., *Catholic Secondary Education: A National Survey* (Department of Education, National Catholic Welfare Conference, 1949), p. 9.

[5] *Ibid.*, pp. 9–10.

[6] Pius XI, *The Christian Education of Youth* (New York: The America Press, 1936).

Lutherans, who support the second largest group of church-related schools in America, entertain views similar to the Catholic with respect to relations between the family and state. The Lutheran belief is that among formal educational institutions the Lutheran school is most similar to the ideal of the Christian family as an educational agency.[7]

Churches recognize the rights and obligations of both the family and the state in education and seek cooperation rather than conflict in areas of overlapping jurisdiction. An example of such overlap occurs in the operation of parochial schools. The obligation and right of the state to supervise and inspect the provisions for the temporal well-being of children in church-related schools is recognized and accepted. At the same time, churches also are obliged to safeguard the education of their children in other than their own schools, particularly with respect to religious and moral instruction, but generally in all matters because of the essential unity of development.

THE STATE

The third primary agency of education is the state or civil government. In our society, government is established to "secure the rights" of the people and "promote the public welfare." In the Catholic view the right and obligation of states to promote education as an essential element of the temporal well-being of its citizens is conferred by God as well as by civil law.

> Accordingly in the matter of education, it is the right, or to speak more correctly, it is the duty of the State to protect in its legislation, the prior rights, already described, of the family as regards the Christian education of its offspring, and consequently also to respect the supernatural rights of the Church in this same realm of Christian education.
> It also belongs to the State to protect the rights of the child itself when the parents are found wanting either physically or morally.[8]

It is also clear that the state does not have the right to usurp the rights and duties of the family or of the church in education but to insure the opportunity of family and church to exercise their rights and aid them in the discharge of their duties.

---

[7] A. C. Stellhorn, *Lutheran Schools: A Manual of Information on the Schools of the Lutheran Church — Missouri Synod* (St. Louis: Lutheran Church — Missouri Synod Board of Parish Education), quoted by William Marshall French, *American Secondary Education* (New York: The Odyssey Press, 1957), p. 284.
[8] Pius XI, *op. cit.*, p. 14.

To provide for the public welfare the state takes measures to see that its citizens have the necessary preparation to fulfill their civic duties and obligations. This may require the state to provide physical, intellectual, and moral training — whatever is necessary for the common good. If experience with army draftees, for example, shows them to be in unsatisfactory physical condition to serve their country, it is the duty of government to plan and execute programs which will lead to better physical development. Clearly, social skills are necessary for the duties of citizenship. It is strikingly evident in our time that the public welfare depends also upon the intellectual and moral excellence of its citizens.

A belief in the dignity of the individual also obliges governments to promote his well-being and optimum development. This effort is certainly a moral obligation of any state which exists to further the welfare of its subjects. It is a right and duty clearly implied in our Constitution as well. To put it more strongly, it is the duty of our government to insist that every individual be given full opportunities for development of his potentialities, as an individual, as well as for the common good. Such insistence does not mean, as we have emphasized, that the state, rather than the family or the church, should provide all the opportunities for an individual. It means merely that the government should see that they are available to him.

There has never been complete agreement as to the role of the public school, as the state's most universal and formal educational effort. Some believe the school should concern itself only with intellectual development, leaving the responsibility for other educational matters to someone else. Such persons decry medical and psychological services, activity and adjustment programs, and courses designed to meet nonacademic needs, for example, driver education. On the other hand, there is wide agreement on several points which appear in opposition to this view: (1) as an agent of society, the public school should attempt to fulfill any state responsibility for education that is not being met by others; (2) the schools can do most of the things that the state needs to do educationally more cheaply, quicker, and more effectively than other institutions of the state; and (3) it is impossible to develop one aspect of the student without simultaneously attending to other aspects of development.

The public school's share of the total responsibility of the state for education is not, then, altogether clear. As a result, we find considerable variation among different states and a good deal of controversy on this point in the literature. The interrelationship and interdependence of all forms of development appears an especially strong argument for a rather full involvement of the schools with respect to all forms of development, though all need not be given equal emphasis. Public schools are handicapped, however, in that the essential religious aspects of development cannot be part of their "whole child" approach to development.

OTHER SECONDARY AGENCIES

Among other educational agencies, which we may consider secondary, are those associated with the neighborhood in which the child lives, his peer group, and the communications industries — books, magazines, radio, movies, and television. Although such agencies probably have less direct responsibility for the education of children and youth, each has a moral obligation to be a positive influence, furthering rather than obstructing progress toward worthwhile goals. This obligation is grave. Indeed, whenever the family, church, and state are apathetic toward their educational responsibilities, what we here term secondary agencies may have the greater influence.

The Neighborhood and the School

Neighborhoods differ radically in their effect on children. Each locality has its own generally accepted ideas of what children are like and how they should be treated; and in each, children and youth react with their own interpretation of how to behave toward adults and society. Differences among neighborhoods arise from the physical setting, the habits and character of the adults, the traditions, the institutions and events — all interacting.

Simply consider physical factors, such as space and facilities for living. Space is necessary for privacy and developing independence. There must be places where children can practice and experiment with adult roles. They need room to exercise their expanding physical powers — for running, jumping, and throwing. Rural areas, villages, and suburbs have such space. In contrast, urban areas are often so crowded that there is no possibility of privacy or play. The only "outdoors" may be hallways, alleys, and busy streets.

The physical surroundings are important in the education of the child. To an outsider, there is limited variety in the country or small town. Houses appear similar. The few small businesses seem much alike. One field or patch of woods strikes us much like any other. In the city, on the other hand, even the school route of the child may pass stores, taverns, gas stations, and factories. On his way to school the city child may cross busy streets, ride on buses, and explore alleys. At other times he enjoys well-planned and equipped play areas and occasional trips to the zoo or the theater.

The child finds variety beneath the surface sameness of the country or small town, however, as he explores every path, bush, fence, and gully, every doorway, corner, and piece of junk for his imaginative play. His knowledge of a whole, somewhat independent, community may be exceedingly thorough and detailed. The city child may know the area immediately surrounding his home well, but many of his contacts are fleeting and superficial. No two children react alike to any physical environment, of course, but in general we might say that in the city a child's knowledge of his environment tends to be broader than that of the small-town or farm child but more casual and perhaps not as thorough.

What adult examples or models are available to the child in his community? What is the pattern of adult-child relationships? Such things make a difference! We may consider several examples, but we must remember the great variation among individuals in their reaction to seemingly identical childhood circumstances. Some of our greatest leaders had few advantages in youth, and every fine community has known a few children whose later lives were a great disappointment.

If we look at the small towns again, we find many that are relatively self-sufficient in their economic and social life, with most of the adults finding employment near home. There are only a few types of jobs of course. Children are tolerated or even welcomed. They are generally free to watch and question adults in both their working and leisure moments. As the children grow older, they lend a hand in most activities, growing naturally into the life of the community. The adults all know each other and have similar views, values, and goals. There are the exceptions — the shiftless, the profane, the dishonest, and the incompetent — but these "bad examples" are well known; and their relations to the children and youth of the community are continually under the watchful eyes of family and friends.

To a large extent officials — teachers, policemen, playground leaders, scout leaders, etc. — have replaced parents as adult models and supervisors for children in suburbia. The examples provided by these "outside" adults are usually excellent. Both families and supervisors tend to feel, however, that children with the advantages which these enjoy can be depended upon to do the right thing with a minimum of supervision. Discipline is easy and tolerant. As with children and youth everywhere, a few always fail to use their freedom wisely. As they grow older, they may roam freely to parts of the city where they are unknown and unsupervised. There are always bad examples to be found under these conditions. Smoking, gambling, sex activities, and questionable ways of raising money are often incorporated into their way of life. These youths may become quite expert in their double lives, presenting the best of fronts at home.

In heavily populated slums or "blighted," "underprivileged," or "disadvantaged" areas of the city there are other problems. As previously noted, some families have small apartments, or perhaps just a single room with no possibility of indoor play or privacy for children. Indoors, children are in contact with every aspect of adult life, and the adults are often frustrated and short-tempered. The children are forced to get out, but outside there are only dark hallways and alleys, crowded streets, dingy taverns and shops. Sometimes there are very real physical dangers. A junior high school principal found, for example, that the biggest problem of the majority of the girls he surveyed was to get from the street into their tenement apartment without being molested in the hallway.[9]

The adults in authority outside, policemen for example, may further curtail and restrict youth activities, breaking up street games and dispersing loiterers. The only adults who have time for children may provide the worst examples. National and racial differences are heightened by enforced intimacy and competition for the essentials of life. It is a small wonder that many youngsters see themselves at odds with the world, and tend to band together for protection. Then, for something to do, they explore and raid in secrecy or in open defiance of adult rules.

---

[9] James B. Conant, *Slums and Suburbs* (New York: McGraw-Hill Book Co., 1961), p. 19.

There are blighted areas, of course, where police and other responsible adults try to find play areas for children and exercise understanding in the enforcement of rules. When adults are seen as friends, children need not war with them.

Schools are, of course, profoundly affected by the nature of the community they serve. A concept of the school which has emerged during the present century would make it "a teacher of community living to children" and a "center of community life and action for people of all ages and classes."[10]

A historically earlier view of the school was that it should limit itself to teaching essential intellectual skills. A large part of present-day controversy over the schools is caused by disagreement as to the extent schools should depart from their traditional position in assuming more responsibility for the total education of children and becoming an integral part of community life.

The problem of the role of the school in the community has many facets which cannot be adequately illustrated here. One should, however, have some appreciation of the contrasts among communities as they affect the school. The talk of raising academic standards and encouraging real scholarship, for example, has one meaning in middle- and upper-class communities and another in areas where even the adults have never learned to read and write.

Conant, in contrasting schools of slums and suburbs, notes the wide differences in provisions for youth guidance. Among his observations on suburban schools we find:

> The main problem in wealthy suburban schools is to guide the parent whose college ambitions outrun his child's abilities toward a realistic picture of the kind of college his child is suited for.
> Expert guidance must begin very early in the suburban schools in this process of educating both parent and child in the realities of college admission.[11]

When Conant turns to recommendations for the large city slums, on the other hand, he finds:

> Social dynamite is building up in our large cities in the form of unemployed out-of-school youth, especially in the Negro slums. We need accurate and frank information neighborhood by neighborhood.
> The schools should be given the responsibility for educational and

---

[10] Robert J. Havighurst and Bernice L. Neugarten, *Society and Education* (Boston: Allyn and Bacon, 1957), p. 211.
[11] Conant, *op. cit.*, p. 144.

vocational guidance of youth after they leave school until age 21. This will require more money.[12]

Aleda Druding's description of the significance of community characteristics is even more dramatic. She writes of an area in north central Philadelphia, a neighborhood of "substandard, three-story, absentee-owned multiple family dwellings." In this "depressed and culturally impoverished" section of Philadelphia, the elementary school teacher expects:

> That children may come to kindergarten without knowing their own names. "Big Boy" or "Brother" is the only name they have heard at home.
> That medical and dental checks will show hundreds of children who have never brushed their teeth or bathed regularly. Mother has never shown them how or encouraged them to brush or wash.
> That many children — perhaps most — have vocabularies so limited that they are unable to speak in sentences. "Huh?" "Out!" "Go on." "Shush!" plus a number of curse words may be their entire repertoire.
> That many children will fall asleep in class because they find it difficult to sleep at night in the noisy room they share with three or four other children and adults.
> That emotional problems are not unusual. One little girl, for example, will not go near the lavatory because she saw a dead woman's body in the bathroom her family shares with the rest of their building.
> That the experiences children have had are so limited that stories in their primers will not make sense to them. The majority of these children — and many of the parents — have not been farther from their tenement homes than twenty-five blocks. They have not seen motion pictures, eaten in a restaurant, or ridden in a bus; they have never lived in a situation where a mother and a father work together to rear a family. Of course, they do not identify with the middle-class Dicks and Janes in the typical reading books.[13]

Under conditions such as some of those we have been describing, the schools have had to establish closer relations with the community. In part the problem is obviously one of adult education. Reading is the foremost problem for both children and adults. In most homes there are no reading materials and nothing is read by anyone. Extra help must often be provided children and adults after school. In Philadelphia school-community coordinating teams have been established, with some team members chosen from the community itself.

---

[12] *Ibid.*, p. 146.
[13] Aleda Druding, "Stirrings in the Big Cities: Philadelphia," *N.E.A. Journal*, Vol. 51, No. 2, February, 1962, p. 48.

Such a person may have no special qualifications other than that of being able to go into parents' homes and cajoling or shaming them into helping.

On another front, many urban communities have been trying to provide facilities and supervision for the leisure hours of youngsters through youth organizations. These are discussed in the next section under the topic of peer groups. There are also public recreation facilities in many communities — for example, libraries, museums, parks, beaches, and playgrounds. Commercial enterprises include skating rinks, amusement parks, bowling alleys, pool halls, and soda shops or drugstores. Youth centers are sometimes organized by parents. These are all of importance as meeting places for the younger members of our society, even though no instruction is provided, or perhaps because little direct teaching is attempted. Here the peer culture, to be reviewed in the next section, can operate.

The Peer Group

Peer groups are same-age groups of youngsters who feel alike and act together. A succession of such groups influences almost everyone from early childhood through adolescence. When neighborhood children begin to play together, a peer culture, apart from that dominated by adults. begins to develop. At first children's needs are for activity and exploration, for exercise of the body and the imagination. Age mates can best provide these, for children's interests and energy set them apart from their elders. Consider the Wild West, cartoon, and slapstick-comedy content of our children's television world. This is one aspect of their culture which seldom appeals to parents. Clearly, children are drawn together by needs and enthusiasms for many things and activities which are only tolerated by adults, often with ill-concealed distaste.

The peer group becomes even more important and potent in middle childhood and preadolescence, when youngsters are given more physical freedom by adults. Boys and girls now have roles in the family, but everyone expects them to make their way among their age mates as well. Generally, children are eager to succeed with their peers but they are well aware also of the importance which adults attach to "social adjustment."

As children attempt to live more independently of the family, experiences with peer groups help and are essential in a number of ways. Frequently, these experiences help in: (1) coming to terms with the codes and values of others; (2) developing attitudes and skills for social participation; and (3) developing expectations with respect to future adult roles.

Children first learn a code and develop a conscience under the influence of the family and the church. How can they maintain their integrity in a society made up of individuals who vary in these important ways? Each person must learn this by experience. One does not have to give up his values, but he does have to learn how to conduct himself in ways acceptable to others as well as himself. Havighurst[14] suggests that the rules of childhood games are a most important factor in learning this lesson. Such rules are suggestive of adult laws, and in their making and revision children find the means of regulating group behavior in ways fair and acceptable to all.

In the peer group the child learns other skills which enable him to interest, win the respect of, and find a place among equals without recourse to adult authority. His experience in this — success or failure, pleasure or frustration — may condition his attitudes toward future social participation and cooperation.

In their mutual activities children find the social roles in which they can gain respect, admiration, or at least toleration. There are many such roles in child society. In addition to leaders, we find judges, planners, gossips, entertainers, slaves, scapegoats, and many others. Some roles which are most unattractive from the adult point of view may be a source of real satisfaction and security to the child. His place in various groups at different times is by no means always the same or unchangeable, but all in all these groups provide a proving ground for roles which he may find in later life. Role experimentation has its vocational aspects also. Age mates can encourage or discourage, through respect or ridicule, the boy who tentatively chooses the role of policeman, teacher, or ballplayer, and the girl who sees herself as a dancer, singer, secretary, or nurse.

In preadolescence youngsters seek to shake off adult supervision of their activities. There is a strict self-imposed segregation of the sexes at this age, perhaps stemming from the boys' strong need to identify with masculine roles and values. For boys this is the age of the play "gang." Such gangs are rather closely knit with definite

---

[14] Robert J. Havighurst, *Human Development and Education* (New York: Longmans, Green and Co., 1953), p. 54.

leadership. A desire for adventure and excitement and the rising need for independence combine to make many gangs at least semidelinquent by adult standards. Most do not totally reject adult standards but put up at least a token resistance to convention by getting dirty, cursing, smoking, and pilfering. The character of the gang's activities is actually a product of the social environment in which it is found. The more delinquent gang of this age level usually occurs in socially deprived areas where truancy, theft, fighting, and similar activities are not nearly so uncommon or shocking as they are in middle-class society. The strict allegiance to the code which gangs may demand of their members is well known. We expect, for example, that one member will lie in order to protect another from punishment.

Girls seldom form gangs with formal organization and leadership. Instead they tend to form "cliques" of friends chosen along social-class lines. Clique members plan together and act alike and together and tend to be snobbish in their relations with nonclique members.

The preadolescent gangs and cliques give way in time to adolescent crowds, or social groups made up of both sexes. There is excitement and adventure, as well as worry, for boys and girls as they learn to get along together in the crowd. Here the adolescent gets help for two of his most pressing problems: (1) achieving more adult relationships with others of similar age regardless of sex, and (2) learning adult social skills. The crowd provides a laboratory for social skills where no one ridicules because all are novices and experimenters.

The crowd, like earlier cliques and gangs, demands conformity from its members. Again the directions in which these group pressures force youngsters may vary greatly and are influenced by the social setting. In the last analysis these boys and girls may be learning to behave like the adults they know best.

As adolescents grow older the crowds form and re-form. They tend more and more to be limited to those of similar interests and standards. Finally they may dissolve altogether as members develop vocational interests and begin serious career preparations.

A serious social problem arises when the period of adolescence is prolonged because large numbers of young people are neither employed nor going to school. When this happens, there is a tendency for older adolescents to reorganize as gangs, which may become delinquent. Sociologists see this happening more frequently as a result of the mechanization of agriculture and industry, and mass migrations to our larger cities. Some of these cities have thousands of youths who have nothing to do but gather on street corners and look for excitement. These groups are described by Conant as "social dynamite."[15]

For nearly fifty years adults have been seeking to organize children and youth in order to harness the potential power of the peer group for worthy ends. The first youth organizations under adult supervision appeared in the cities. Religious groups found the Young Men's Christian Association (YMCA), the Young Women's Christian Association (YWCA), the Young Men's Hebrew Association (YMHA), and the Catholic Youth Organization (CYO), as well as many lesser known organizations. Other adults have sponsored such movements as the Scouts, Campfire Girls, Junior Achievement, and Junior Optimists. Similar organizations were slower to develop in rural areas, but now we have the 4-H groups, the Future Farmers of America, the Future Homemakers, and the Junior Grange. Schools have many interest clubs also.

The adult leaders of these organizations hope that the organization spirit and code will become part of the behavior pattern of the peer group. Guidance during the years of social experimentation is provided; and worthwhile achievement, as well as adventure, is encouraged by systems of ranks and awards.

Underprivileged urban areas have the more definitely welfare-oriented settlement houses, boys' clubs, and girls' clubs. Usually these have been established by middle- or upper-class benefactors, seeking merely to get children off the streets and give them something to do in order to reduce delinquency.

The summer camp is an important adjunct of many youth organizations. Recently, community recreation departments and school systems have begun to offer organized camping experiences also. The camps provide educational activities and promote social and character development during vacation periods.

Local governments frequently lend a hand with recreation programs, and parents may help teen-agers organize their own youth centers. A city near the authors' home has had great success in getting teen-age boys off the streets by simply offering them an old street car barn as a place to work on "hot rods." The barn is jammed

---

[15] Conant, op. cit., p. 146.

each night by boys who are repairing, remodeling, or polishing old cars. Many others just come to talk. This and other experiments with youth suggest at least one important lesson. Boys and girls who can be helped to develop a socially acceptable hobby, a compelling interest in athletics, hot rods, electronics, sewing, painting, or even postage stamps, are less apt to get into trouble.

Mass Media

Children give more time to watching television, listening to the radio, going to the movies, and reading than to any other activity except school. All the popular media offer information, of course. They also tend to make the whole nation more uniform in everything from speech to home furnishings. Equally important educationally are the vivid portrayals of adult conflict and conduct in various life situations.

The extent to which children pattern their own behavior after that shown or described to them is unknown. We would expect that a daily fare of television with 19 acts of violence or threats of violence per hour[16] would leave some impressions on the emotions or attitudes of young viewers. Studies of the long-term effects of movies in the 1930's suggest, however, that it is extremely difficult to predict the effects on individual viewers.[17] Any effect may be expected to vary greatly with the individual's personality and the situation in which he lives. At the very least, we do know that time spent on Westerns, mysteries, and crime shows or stories is taken from that available for body-building sports, good literature, or the truly educational radio and television programs. There are excellent programs in the kindergarten tradition for young children. Television in particular can offer youth thrilling experiences with famous personalities, life in other parts of the world, advances in science, and the best of art and literature. As parents and educators, our problem is to utilize the potential of the mass media for education.

Television has replaced movies to some extent as a major mass medium. In the day of their greatest popularity movies probably had the same effects on moviegoers as television does today on viewers. Actors and actresses were aped by children and youth around the world. An example of the influence of the movies on attitudes was

16 Havighurst and Neugarten, op. cit., p. 152.
17 Ibid., p. 151.

seen in their use to help mobilize public opinion against our enemies in World War II. More recently they have helped build anti-Communist attitudes.

Children's recreational reading is another factor in providing knowledge about the world and in forming ideas and suggesting forms of behavior. Today there are pleasurable and profitable books written especially for each different age level. These and children's classics are available in neighborhood and school libraries and in economical paperbacks on the newsstands. But by far the most popular and widely distributed of all reading materials for children are the "comics."

There is something in the comic-strip format which has a strong appeal for all ages. They are read by almost all elementary school children, and one study showed that over 44 percent of the enlisted men in World War II also read them regularly.[18] The comic-book approach has been used by schools and churches to present educational material. On the newsstand we find comic books with historical and scientific content, and others featuring acceptable animal characters like Bugs Bunny and Donald Duck. Public ire has been aroused, however, by the "crime," "horror," and "sex" comics. Widespread objections to the worst of these led the publishing industry to set up standards which have been fairly effective in improving the quality of comic books and quieting public outcry. With the advent of television, comic books seem to have passed their peak of popularity.

Although children and youth also read newspapers, the influence of these is probably relatively minor in comparison with the other communication media which have been considered here.

We have noted the positive effects of self-censorship in the comic-book industry. Similar attempts to raise the standards of other communication media have not been entirely satisfactory. Many movies, magazines, and books which are readily available to youngsters remain just within the laws against pornography, and are unacceptable to parents and religious groups.

Mass media in general tend to make people more alike in almost every way. Responsible persons must work for improved offerings and at the same time help children and youth to choose the best of

[18] H. W. Zorbough, ed., "The Comics as an Educational Medium," *Journal of Educational Sociology*, 18:193–255, 1944, p. 154.

what is currently available if we are to avoid a common mediocrity or worse. Parents and teachers have been able to help by:

1. Becoming familiar with the children's favorite reading materials and programs;

2. Pointing to values and inviting discussions which will help youngsters discriminate the worthy from the unworthy;

3. Inviting attention to worthwhile programs that children or youth may not know about, widening their range of interests;

4. Encouraging discussion of problems arising from the use of mass media in parent-teacher and other adult groups;

5. Expressing support for publications and programs which meet good standards and protesting those which do not by writing to those responsible.

Summary

Family, church, and state share the responsibility for the education of children and youth. Each has not only established schools but also influences development in countless other ways. Each has certain rights and responsibilities under natural, moral, divine, or civil law. The family lays the foundation, but seeks and must have the aid of the church for spiritual development and of the state for temporal needs to insure the proper care and upbringing of children.

One aspect of development cannot actually be isolated from another except for emphasis. We always deal with the "whole child." For this reason a church stresses intellectual, physical, and social, as well as spiritual development in its own schools, and is obliged to check the spiritual and moral influences affecting those of her children who are in public schools. The state, in turn, should aid and encourage the family and church in their efforts and must insist upon proper provisions for the temporal welfare of children as well as training which will prepare them to fulfill their obligations as citizens.

The child's well-being and development is also profoundly affected by influences associated with the neighborhood in which he lives, the peer groups to which he belongs, and the mass media of communication. Neighborhoods may have poor or excellent physical qualities. They may provide meager or profuse and worthwhile educational experiences. Adults may offer understanding and intelligent guidance; but, on the other hand, they may merely tolerate, neglect, or actively oppress children. They may be worthy models or bad examples. All these factors interact to "teach" youngsters, to shape their attitudes and behavior.

Urban and suburban living do not provide for the close contact between the adults and the children of a community which characterizes daily life in rural areas and villages. In the cities, the slums and suburbs are in sharp contrast with respect to conditions for child welfare and education. Schools in all areas are departing from their traditional preoccupation with intellectual development, and are becoming more intimately involved in teaching community living and in providing resources for community improvement.

A child's age mates provide a "second world," peopled with equals struggling with similar problems of living and learning. The peer groups of this second world are a potent force in teaching group living and in shaping the child's concept of himself and his future. In these groups, children and youth find mutual support as they grow more independent of the family. In return the group demands a high degree of conformity from its members. The directions in which peer groups urge their members, and the reactions of these members, depend on the character of the individuals, and the social conditions under which the group is formed. Delinquent gangs usually arise in economically depressed, culturally inadequate neighborhoods. Many clubs are sponsored by adults who seek to shape the group spirit and turn its educational force to desirable ends.

Watching television, listening to the radio, going to the movies, and reading are activities which occupy a very large part of children's time. One result is that children and youth everywhere become more alike and more like the characters portrayed. Individuals vary greatly in how they are affected by what they read, hear, or watch; but there can be no doubt that media which command so much attention should be worthwhile educationally and meet high moral standards. What is needed is not merely censorship, but positive efforts to utilize the proven potential of mass media for educational purposes.

The adult which the child becomes is a product of his own nature and efforts; the efforts of his family, church, and state; the schools which these provide; the influences of neighborhood, peer groups, and mass media; and many lesser factors which can not be given separate attention here.

SELECTED READINGS

Bossard, James H., and Boll, Eleanor, The Sociology of Child Development (New York: Harper & Bros., 1960).
An exceptionally comprehensive treatment of family influences with an excellent treatment of peer relations (VII) and of the larger social setting for child development (VIII).

Conant, James B., Slums and Suburbs (New York: McGraw-Hill Book Co., 1961).
A report on the differences between have and have-not schools which emphasizes the "social dynamite" which is building up in big city ghettos.

Davis, W. Allison, and Havighurst, Robert J., Father of the Man: How Your Child Gets His Personality (Boston: Houghton Mifflin Co., 1947).
A popular account of social-class differences in child-rearing practices and some of their consequences. Excellent descriptions of child socialization.

Druding, Aleda, "Stirrings in the Big Cities: Philadelphia," NEA Journal, Vol. 51, No. 2 (February, 1962), pp. 47–51.
The second of a continuing series of articles focusing on the problems of America's largest cities.

"Education and the Disadvantaged American," NEA Journal, Vol. 51, No. 4 (April, 1962), pp. 8–12.
Reviews the challenge and asks for public support of needed changes in school programs. Condensed from a pamphlet of the Educational Policies Commission of the NEA and the American Association of School Administrators.

Havighurst, Robert J., and Neugarten, Bernice L., Society and Education (Boston: Allyn and Bacon, 1957).
Cultural differences among social classes are examined in Chaps. 1 and 2; Peer-group influences are treated in Chap. 5; and Chap. 17 explores differences in the expectations of community groups and the school.

Hollingshead, August B., Elmtown's Youth (New York: John Wiley & Sons, 1949), Chaps. 8–12.
How different social classes in a small midwestern town are treated in and out of school and how they respond.

Martin, William E., and Stendler, Celia Burns, Child Behavior and Development, rev. ed. (New York: Harcourt, Brace & Co., 1959).
Study of the family, school, peer group and community (physical setting, churches and media of communication). Reinforces the treatment of corresponding topics in the present chapter.

Myers, Alonzo F., and Williams, Clarence O., Education in a Democracy, 4 ed. (New York: Prentice-Hall, 1954), pp. 128–146.
Presents a general discussion of the various non-school agencies which influence the educational growth of boys and girls and analyzes several views regarding the proper functions of the school.

Newcomb, M. Theodore, "Student Peer-Group Influence," in Nevitt, Sanford (ed.), The American College (New York: John Wiley & Sons, 1962), Chap. 13.
A review of studies of the way college students influence each other and each other's education.

Pius XI, *Christian Education of Youth* (Washington, D. C.: National Catholic Welfare Conference, 1930).

Encyclical Letter which clarifies the Roman Catholic position on the roles of family, church and state in education.

Redden, John D., and Ryan, Francis A. *A Catholic Philosophy of Education*, rev. ed. (Milwaukee: Bruce Publishing Company, 1956). Chap. IV.

Explanation of the Catholic view of the rights, duties, and functions of the several educational agencies and discusses related questions and issues.

Robbins, Florence Greenhoe, *Educational Sociology* (New York: Henry Holt & Co., 1953).

Chap. IX presents the effects of mass media of communication on children and analyzes the questions of what to do about it by means of a dramatization of a child-study group discussion. Chaps. VII and VIII present discussions of the role of peer groups and of religion in child living.

Schramm, Wilbur, "Mass Media and Educational Policy," in National Society for the Study of Education, *Social Forces Influencing American Education*, Sixtieth Yearbook, Part II (Chicago: Univ. of Chicago Press, 1961), pp. 203–229.

Discussion of the relationship of schools to newspapers and television which includes an examination of the effects of television on children and a plea for the constructive use of mass media by the schools.

———— "Television in the Life of the Child — Implications for the School," in *New Teaching Aids for the American Classroom* (Stanford, Calif.: Institute for Communications Research, Stanford University, 1960), pp. 50–70.

Points out that the typical child spends one-sixth of his waking hours watching television and discusses the implications of this fact for the child's educability and for the use of television in schools.

Tinnelly, Joseph T., C. M., "The Right to Educate — The Role of Parents, Church, State," *National Catholic Education Association Bulletin*, Vol. 60, No. 1 (August, 1958), pp. 35–46.

Statement on the respective rights of parents, the church and the state in the education of children. Precedents are found in both civil and canon law.

Chapter VI

ISSUES IN AMERICAN
EDUCATION

The modern educational scene, especially in America, is marked by heated controversy. This is recognized by professional and lay people alike. This chapter will attempt to portray some of the issues affecting education at the level of practice. Certainly, these practical issues ultimately are rooted in ideological differences in viewpoints. But they are much further removed from basic philosophical assumptions than are the issues to be discussed in Chapter XI. These latter issues are usually the concern of "teachers of teachers," whereas the former are threshed out in the public forum by layman and educator alike. The issues discussed in this chapter are: the role of the federal government in education, the subject of education, segregation, and democracy in the classroom.

THE FEDERAL GOVERNMENT IN EDUCATION[1]

The issue of federal involvement in education is uniquely American. In almost every other country in the world, including our neighbors in North and South America, the federal government plays a significant role both through financial aid and legal control. And it is only recently that federal aid to education became an issue in the United States, since in the past most people considered the support and control of schools a state and local function. Actually the federal constitution makes no specific reference to education, although the Supreme Court frequently has been called upon to make decisions affecting the schools. Here it is worth noting that the majority of Supreme Court decisions having a direct bearing on

[1] See also Chap. III, the section on "The Federal Government and Education," p. 61.

education have been rendered within the past twenty-five years. Most often, cases involving education have become "federal" because some other constitutional consideration was involved, such as freedom of speech or religion or the use of public funds for independent school costs.

In spite of the fact that there are no absolute legal restrictions regarding federal involvement in education and regardless of the many instances in which the federal government has taken a hand in education ("Land Grant" Acts, G.I. and Korean Bills), many people still are convinced that the federal government should be kept out of education. This opposition is especially strong when federal funds are solicited for private school children. Taxpayers' leagues, chambers of commerce, editorial comments, and the like launch intensive campaigns to defeat any such legislation. Voices raised in its favor include those of such powerful professional organizations as the National Education Association and its many subdivisions. Perhaps a listing of some of the reasons often proffered for and against this particular aspect of federal involvement, financial aid, will give the student sufficient insight into other phases of the same problem.

Arguments Offered Against Federal Aid to Education

1. The basic argument against federal aid to education rests upon the conviction that education is not a federal but a local and state function. It is argued that such a view is the only one in harmony with the "American tradition." Each colony founded educational institutions and supported them from local funds. In fact, most of the earliest educational foundations were sponsored, financed, and controlled by religious organizations. After all, was it not the desire to flee the evils of centralized government that brought the early colonists to this land?

The advocates of this principle of local autonomy generally will admit that some economic advantage might flow from federal aid to local communities, such as improved teachers' salaries, more modern plants, and equal opportunity for all youth. But these are regarded as of lesser value than the cherished freedom rooted in local autonomy. Some even argue that both the federal and state governments already have transgressed too far into the sacred territory of individual liberty.

2. An analysis of the "corporate mind" of the founding fathers clearly reveals that they favored Thoreau's dictum that he who "governs least, governs best." Had they wanted the federal government to be an educator they would have stated or at least suggested it in the Constitution [this argument, of course, involves interpretation of the "intent" of the founding fathers, indeed a highly controversial consideration].

3. The opponents of federal aid wish to remind the seekers of easy money that they will have to pay the bill in the long run, for the federal government will wring the money from every citizen. If the government pours several billion dollars into educational aid, the federal "take" from the individual paycheck will be proportionately larger. In addition to each dollar spent in aid to the schools, there will be a relatively large "handling charge." The Internal Revenue Service collection expense, the accounting and distribution costs, all will reduce the purchasing power of the federal "contribution" to local education. Had the same amount of money been collected and distributed locally, these surcharges might have been eliminated or the equivalent amount been used more efficiently for the improvement of the local school systems.

4. Many of the proponents of federal aid argue that local autonomy can be preserved. The opponents maintain that "federal aid without federal control" is impossible. A close scrutiny of federal aid programs in other countries will reveal that local autonomy exists only in name. Not only is central control of education found in totalitarian countries, but also in the great democracies of France and Scandinavia. Even in our own country the federal government exercises supervision of basic requirements and standards over any welfare funds, educational or otherwise.

5. One of the gravest fears of those opposing federal involvement in education is that it might lead to a federal system of education. As mentioned above in discussing the principle of local autonomy, such a state of affairs is in itself undesirable. But, since education is the most powerful weapon used in the control of men's minds, all forces should be mustered to keep schools completely independent of the central government. If the schools remain free they can thwart any attempts at thought control. On the other hand, if a central authority controls education, "brainwashing" might easily be pawned off on the people in the name of "good educational practice." As evidence they note that even the states have gone too far in their interference with the freedom of local schools. In order to receive aid in some states, the local school must teach certain courses, hire certain kinds of teachers, use specified accounting procedures, and keep the children in school for a designated number of days. Therefore all freedom-loving citizens not only must fight to halt interference in local matters but must set about regaining the freedom they already have lost.

6. One of the strengths of the traditional American school system lies in the fact that each community has been able to meet the basic needs of its children and youth. For example, schools in predominantly rural areas have usually provided an agricultural curriculum for the future farmers of the area. A school in a predominantly professional section of a large metropolitan area might devote its major educational efforts to a college-preparatory program. Such is not the case in countries where the federal government is involved in education. In France, for example, all elementary and secondary schools have the same curriculum whether they are located in Paris or Auxonne. No adjustments are made to local needs. Thus to keep education as a servant of the community only the local school authorities and the citizens of the area can determine what constitutes a good education for their children.

7. Federal aid to education, its opponents claim, is merely another phase of the "creeping socialism" which has begun to gnaw at the roots of our capitalistic democracy. Anyone who believes in the free-enterprise system must not be "taken in" by the Trojan horse of federal aid. Federal aid programs inaugurated as emergency measures during the great depression of the 1930's have become "permanent fixtures" under other names. Since it is considered unmannerly to bite the hand that's feeding you, never accept anything from the "big brother" in Washington! Better to have a little less in the way of school facilities, etc., but keep one's freedom of choice.

8. Some very practical considerations suggested against federal aid to education are to be found in the evils arising from federal bureaucracy. For example, the red tape involved in the handling of federal funds results in such frustration that the additional income is not worth the trouble. Similarly, it may take the local authorities only a year to accomplish what it takes the federal government three years to do. Recent scandals involving favoritism and theft in the handling of federal funds should give one pause before pouring money into those "leaky channels."

In summary, the opponents of federal aid assert that the term "aid" is a misnomer used to delude the people. None of the arguments forwarded by its proponents really help improve education in general, and most communities stand to lose more than they can gain.

Arguments Offered for Federal Aid to Education

Thirty-five years ago, it was difficult to find teachers and administrators who favored federal aid. Today, the number is quite large, and neutral observers feel that the majority of administrators and citizens favor it. The passage of federal aid bills indicates that the majority of the members of Congress favors some kind of aid. But the arguments against federal aid listed above are formidable and might seem to demolish any reasons given in its favor. However, the following arguments set forth by the proponents of federal aid are no less convincing.

1. The strongest point in favor of federal aid is derived from the demo-cratic principle of equality of opportunity. All national surveys of education in the United States show that the variations in educational facilities are so great that the situation constitutes a national scandal. For example, the less wealthy states pour a greater percentage of their tax funds into education than do the wealthy states. Yet their school plants are inferior, teachers' salaries are much lower, and books and equipment are in short supply. These less wealthy states cannot be charged with lack of concern for good education, because they have actually spent proportionately more money on education than states with superior educational opportunity. The local and state sources of revenue have been tapped to the utmost, and there remains but one source, the federal treasury.

2. Another argument closely allied to equality of opportunity might be stated in terms of "equality of responsibility." Our national economy has become so complex that the interdependence of municipal, state, and federal governments is as obvious as the nose on one's face. Because of this interdependence, education can no longer be viewed as a local function — it must become a national responsibility. The import of this new idea might be explained in terms of "duty and right": every citizen has a duty to support education throughout the nation, and not merely in his own community or state. As a corollary, every child has a right to all the benefits of education even if his own community or state cannot provide them. Thus all people of the nation must be taxed so that all children can receive the benefits of a good education.

Some proponents of this new "duty-right" relationship extend its application to the world community. The program of Fundamental Education sponsored by UNESCO is the first step in the direction of eliciting the support of the wealthier nations in educating the masses of the underprivileged nations. Projects in Fundamental Education have been launched in Africa, the Near East, and Latin America. These educational programs should some day become the responsi-bility of the pooled resources of all the nations of the world. But the first step in this direction should consist in a federal aid program to equalize educational opportunity in the United States.

3. Those favoring federal aid assert that the "bugaboo" of federal control has been magnified way out of proportion. Simply because federal support has been followed by national regimentation in some countries, it does not necessarily follow that such will be the case in the United States. Granted, some modicum of control is necessary; but certainly no more control than is now exerted upon the schools by pressure groups and the state government. Federal aids in the past have not resulted in unreasonable federal controls. The Smith-Hughes and Morrill Acts have not been accompanied by serious limitations on the freedom of those profiting by the aid. The assistance given to veterans of World War II and the Korean War had no "strings attached" except that the student enroll in an approved school.

In addition to these instances of aid without control in the United States, one might point to Canada and England as examples of countries giving direct assistance to local schools while exercising very little control over the school's curriculum, objectives, and teaching methods. Thus, if the proper safeguards are incorporated into any federal aid bill, there should be no fear of federal interference in matters of local concern.

4. Some proponents of federal aid not only do not fear federal control, but actually are convinced that a certain amount of it is essential. They point to the highly efficient educational systems of Russia and France, which are founded upon the principle that education is a federal function. If the United States is to maintain its position of international leadership, there must, they argue, be some national standard for minimal educational requirements. The segments of the country which are unable to meet these basic requirements should be brought up to the national standard by direct assistance from the federal treasury.

This particular argument views both federal aid and federal control as good in themselves, and essential to establishing a first-rate educational system. The history of education is replete with examples, both ancient and modern, indicating that education fared best under the guidance of a central authority. In the Roman Empire, the Eternal City was the center of educational policy, and the schools of the empire were patterned after those of Rome. When the central authority of the empire faltered and each far-flung province did as it pleased education declined, bringing on the Dark Ages. In the Spanish, German, French, and British empires of later days, basic educational standards were set up by the central government in the motherland. These standards brought stability to the educational scene and assured the people of the empire that their schools would be recognized outside their own province or territory.

Certainly, it is argued, no one should object to *minimum* national standards. If some communities or schools wish to go beyond these minimal standards, no educator or the federal government would object. In fact, the central government might even offer incentives to those schools wishing to experiment with advanced techniques and materials.

5. A very practical argument given in favor of federal aid to education is derived from the mobile nature of the American people. Such was not the case in most periods of our national history. With the exception of the era of westward movement, most people tended to stay in their own communities or states.

Today, large elements of the population might be classified as the "floating masses." These people might descend upon a certain area like the proverbial locusts and make the existing school systems wholly inadequate. Yet the local school authorities cannot subsidize such large numbers of children, nor can they secure funds from the communities or states from which these people emigrated. The only legitimate and practicable source of aid for this large floating population is the federal government, for certainly no one will say that these people have no right to an education. Most of them were forced to move for reason of employment, health, or the chance to better their way of living.

6. The present tax base for education, it is argued, is not only inadequate to support a good educational system but also is unjust. In most areas the tax on property is the main source of school revenue. If you ask any property owner to show you his tax bill, you will find that a large portion of the property taxes he pays is used for educational purposes.

Furthermore, as new schools are needed and teachers' salaries are raised to meet competition from business and industry, property taxes are becoming so exorbitant that it is cheaper to rent an apartment than to own a small home. Yet the federal government collects 75 percent of all taxes collected in the country whereas the local and state governments collect only 25 percent. Actually, the schools are supported by those units of government which have the smallest share of tax money, and a large majority of the American people (those who do not own property) contribute little or nothing to the support of education. Thus there remains only one way to arrive at a just tax base for education: to tap the source which takes the largest portion of the tax dollar. Obviously, the "culprit" is the federal government with its income-tax revenue, tariffs, luxury taxes, gasoline taxes, or anything you can mention. The hand that takes the biggest piece of the pie should in justice distribute it according to the same principles of justice.

Again, the "floating population" comes into the picture. Generally, this element of the population does not own property. As a result, they pay little or nothing to the support of the schools their children attend. Since they move around so much, the local and state governments cannot "pin them down" long enough to tax them. But the federal government can always tap them through the federal withholding-tax system, regardless of the place of residence. Only by this means can these people be made to pay their fair share of the bill for school support.

7. One final argument for some kind of federal aid to (and control of) education arises from recent attacks on American public education. The public image of American education is not good. One of the reasons cited for this derogatory view of public education is that there are no standards which apply throughout the country. Each community does as it wishes; pressure groups can unseat a school superintendent at will; one community or district has a good school, qualified teachers, and ample supplies, whereas the neighboring community falls short in these respects. Actually, there is no "typical American school." The same problem arises when one attempts to describe the American school to those in Europe or Asia — there is no standard or norm for classification.

A writer in an Eastern state attacks American public education *in general*. Really, he should attack education in his community or state (or in the East) since the public schools in some Midwestern cities or states are not at all like those in New York City or in Boston, Massachusetts. A foreigner visits a segregated colored school in Arlington, Virginia, and concludes that *all* schools with colored children in them are the same. The recommendation is that the only way to rectify the image of the American public school is to bring all schools up to a certain standard through the means of federal aid and minimal federal control.

The issue of federal aid to education is sufficiently controversial when only the public schools are involved; but it becomes explosive whenever any reference is made to tax support for independent schools. A decade or two ago not much was said about using tax funds for children in these schools. Many practical reasons have caused the injection of this issue into the arena of educational controversy. Perhaps one important cause stems from the increased financial burden placed upon those parents who support both public and private education. Others believe that if independent schools are forced to close their doors, there will remain no agency strong enough to withstand the modern trend toward "statism." But the majority of educators and voters still oppose the use of any tax funds for independent schools of any type. A listing of representative arguments "pro and con" for public support of independent schools might be of interest in relation to the larger problem of federal aid to public schools.[2]

Arguments Offered Against Public Support of Independent Schools

1. Since most of the independent schools of the country are owned and operated by religious groups, any aid to them is unconstitutional. This conclusion is based on the interpretation of the First Amendment to the United States Constitution, which asserts that "Congress shall make no law respecting an establishment of religion." Thus any aid given to private schools, most of which are religious, would constitute a direct violation of the First Amendment, since the government would be aiding religion. The Supreme Court decision in the McCollum Case is cited as proof of the unconstitutionality of any aid given religious groups. In this instance, religious instruction was being given on public school premises during the regular school day. The majority opinion of the Court states: "The operation of the state's compulsory education system thus assists and is integrated with the program of religious instruction carried on by separate religious sects. Pupils compelled by law to go to school for secular education are released in part from their legal duty upon the condition that they attend the religious classes. This is beyond all question a utilization of the tax-established and tax-supported public school system to aid religious groups to spread their faith. And it falls squarely under the ban of the First Amendment."

   Surely, say the opponents of public financial support to independent schools, there can be no doubt about the interpretation of the above statement!

2. If governmental agencies were to give tax aid to independent schools, they would be fostering a type of competition between the public and independent schools which would lead to the weakening or even the destruction of the public school system. In fact, they argue, this has happened in many instances when an independent (usually parochial) school has been established in areas or communities where there are scarcely enough pupils to fill one school. Because of religious or prestige factors, the parents withdrew their children from the public schools and enrolled them in the independent school. In such instances, the public school often was left with an insufficient number of pupils to carry out an efficient educational program. It is to be noted that in these cases the independent school succeeded in weakening or destroying the public school without the assistance of public tax

[2] See Chapter IV for a more thorough description of the role of independent schools in American education.

funds. How much more havoc would be wreaked upon the public schools if tax support were given to independent schools! A rash of new school openings would plague a large number of school districts in the country. Many public school plants, especially in rural or sparsely populated areas, would be duplicated by an independent school, despite the fact that the existing plant was adequate to handle all the pupils of the area.

In addition, parochial schools would have a definite advantage over the public institutions because of the "contributed services" of the religious teachers. In some instances the teacher in a public school is paid a salary many times larger than that received by a member of a religious order. All the money saved in this way could be spent on teaching materials, school services, and the school plant. Within a short time the independent school would be so superior to the public schools that the majority of parents would prefer to send their children to the independent school, regardless of religious affiliation.

As evidence for this stand, some European countries are pointed to as illustrations. Holland and Belgium give financial support to all independent schools provided they meet minimum educational standards laid down by the Ministers of Education. It is reported that some of the religious schools have become quite superior to the public schools. Consequently the position and prestige of the public schools is gradually waning. In England, where equal public support is given to privately owned and operated schools, the position of these schools is such that most parents prefer to send their children to them. Only the "poor" attend state schools. In some regions of Canada where tax funds are used for independent schools, no public schools are available.

3. The Zorach Case of 1952 mentions that public schools may cooperate with churches in arranging released-time programs for religious instruction. This decision even goes so far as to state that "We are a religious people whose institutions presuppose a Supreme Being. . . . When the state encourages religious instruction or cooperates with religious authorities by adjusting the schedule of public events to sectarian needs, it follows the best of our traditions. . . ." To interpret this statement of the Supreme Court to imply that it is legal for independent schools to receive tax funds certainly involves very elastic use of language. Even if it does not violate the exact letter of the law, the use of public funds for independent schools would constitute a breach of the traditional "separation of church and state." If the independent schools, most of which are religious, would receive public tax monies, the next step would be governmental support for many other religious enterprises such as youth organizations, church libraries, and dining and recreational facilities. Offer the hand, and you are likely to lose the whole arm!

A further complication of such a state of affairs would lie in the reciprocal entanglement of the church in state affairs, and in control of the churches by the state. In the long run, the churches would only be hurting themselves by inviting both indirect and direct control by governmental agencies. And the state would be opening its doors to insoluble problems of church-state relations. Therefore even if it is not *absolutely* illegal for public funds to be used for independent and parochial schools, it certainly is unwise.

4. As a refutation of the argument (given by those seeking public funds) that an injustice is perpetrated upon parents who send their children to private schools, the following reasons are given:

   a) Tuition-free public schools are open to all the children of all the people. If a parent chooses to send his children to other schools (as he may) the financial responsibility is his. If no facilities were made available to all people, they might demand support of the independent school.

   b) Many people without children pay for the support of public schools through direct and indirect taxes. Yet no one claims that they are discriminated against. Therefore, when a parent sends his child to an independent school for prestige, or out of religious conviction, he cannot cry out against the injustice of paying for public school support since all the people must support public education whether they have children in school or not.

5. A few opponents of using tax funds for independent schools base their position on the undesirability of having independent schools at all. They contend that a democratic nation needs some unifying experience for all citizens. In a "melting-pot" country such as the United States, the only agency which can effect this unity is the school. Therefore all children should attend public schools, for independent (especially parochial) schools serve as divisive rather than unifying forces.

Arguments Offered for Public Support of Independent Schools

1. The most fundamental argument used by the protagonists of public aid to independent schools is based upon the principle of distributive justice. In educational practice, this principle implies that every child receive an equal amount of the tax money spent for educational purposes. Thus, whether the child attends a public or independent school he has a right, in justice, to that portion of the per capita allowance to be spent on *purely* educational (not religious) activities. In other words, school plant, books, and teaching materials (not including catechisms, etc.), teacher's salaries (not including those of the catechism teachers), school bus rides, and school health services right-

fully should be paid for by tax funds, and only those aspects of the school program that are specifically religious in nature should be financed by the churches.

Fundamentally, it is the individual pupil (or his parent) who claims the right to tax aid, not the churches or the private corporation operating the school.

2. The unconstitutionality of using tax money for private schools is not universally accepted by experts in the field of constitutional law. A. E. Sutherland, professor of Constitutional Law at Harvard University, is of the opinion that since education relates to the "general welfare," there would be nothing unconstitutional about using tax funds for the specifically *educational* activities of independent schools. Certainly no one should deny that supplying books, buildings, and teachers for the education of a significantly large portion of the nation's children is for the "general welfare" of the nation.

In areas other than education such as health and welfare, tax money has been used to assist sectarian and private service institutions. Hospitals, welfare agencies, and overseas relief agencies all have received money from governmental sources. Again, the "general-welfare" aspects of their programs warrant the financial assistance regardless of religious affiliation.

3. Some proponents of aid to independent schools believe that the refusal on the part of governmental agencies to assist these schools *practically* abrogates the parent's right to choose the type of school he wishes his child to attend. Supreme Court decisions have made it very clear that the parent has the *first right* in the education of his children. In both the 1923 (*Meyer* vs. *Nebraska*) and the 1925 (Oregon Case) decisions, the Court specifically affirmed that the state could not demand that parents send their children to one type of school or refuse to allow parents to insist that their children learn certain subjects. But if the government withdraws all support from the schools which parents choose for their children, it is in effect denying their basic right simply because the double financial burden will eventually force the schools which receive no tax support to wither away.

When most of the independent schools have been eliminated, freedom of choice in education will be an unattainable ideal. In reality, this situation already has developed in some parts of the country where religious schools have been forced to close doors because parents cannot bear the double burden of supporting both public and parochial schools.

4. A contention sometimes made by religious leaders in their efforts to show the discriminatory aspect of refusing tax aid to religious schools relates to the "sectarian bias" of the public school. In some sections

of the country the public schools are sectarian, though not avowedly so. The King James version of the Bible is the official book of prayer, and many of the courses (especially the humanities) are shot through with sectarianism. In other sections of the country, the religion of secularism has supplanted the Judeo-Christian frame of reference. This new religion of secularism enthrones other gods such as "democracy" and "cooperativeness," and fosters a code of ethics derived from the "new" theology. In these instances the public schools are just as sectarian and just as biased as any parochial school. Why discriminate against a school simply because it espouses a traditional religion rather than the "new religion?"

5. That the independent schools will steadily decrease in numbers and influence unless some public financial support is given them is admitted by both sides. A grave fear expressed by the leadership of the independent schools concerns the possibility of a state monopoly in education. Many educators believe that a monopoly in education is just as undesirable as one in business or industry. In some respects, a monopoly in education is much more dangerous than one in industry, because education is concerned with the search for and spread of ideas and truth. If an all-powerful government decides to indoctrinate all the children of all the people in any one "ism" the easiest avenue of achieving conformity is through a state school system. If there are no independent schools to voice their objection, there will be little opportunity to counteract the biased view set forth by the state-controlled system. Illustrations of this undesirable situation are within the memory span of this generation — Nazi Germany, Fascist Italy, and Communist Russia.

Even in these United States, the land of "free enterprise," the government is rapidly attaining a monopoly in higher education (college and university). To illustrate, in California 83 percent of all college students are in state schools; in Michigan, 79 percent; in Wisconsin, 69 percent. If the present trend continues in this country, 80 percent of all college and university students will be in state schools by 1970. Under present conditions, the disappearance of the independent school is inevitable. Is this what the nation wants? Do the people wish to have no choice of schools for their children? Are we consistent when we urge the federal government to break a monopoly in the oil or automotive industry but erect one in education? Will not freedom in education find its surest guarantee in a balanced public-private structure?

As is to be expected, the solutions suggested by the advocates of public support for independent schools are many and varied. Some propose that tax rebates or exemptions be granted to parents whose children attend independent schools. Others suggest that direct aid be paid to the individual student to be used in a school of his choice as was done under the "G.I. Bill." Still others feel that all schools should share equally in all aid granted for purely educational purposes. Others believe that aid for the "fringe benefits" such as health and food services, transportation, textbooks, and housing would be sufficient to relieve the plight of the independent school. But, for the purposes of this discussion, the means are not as important as the principles!

WHO SHOULD BE EDUCATED?

The reader might wonder whether there is an issue involved in this question. Have not the American people dedicated their educational system to the principle of universal, compulsory education? Is not free schooling available to all children and youth of this country? Obviously, a democracy needs a literate electorate if it is going to function properly. Future citizens need certain basic skills such as reading, writing, computing, and speaking. Minimal knowledge and understanding of the fundamental areas of human inquiry such as science, citizenship, history, and literature are essential prerequisites for the modern adult.

But the amount of time needed for achieving these goals has not been clearly determined. European children seem to meet all of these requirements in eight years of schooling. In fact, it is admitted by American visitors abroad that the average European elementary school graduate is superior to our high school graduates in the areas mentioned. Therefore, it has been suggested that compulsory education in the United States should terminate with our present junior high school curriculum (ninth grade), and only those with ability and the desire for advanced education be permitted to go beyond that point. Those who leave school at the completion of the junior high curriculum should be offered the opportunity of taking technical training in trade schools or on the job. The problem becomes more acute when one considers the vastly increased enrollments of recent years (see Chap. II).

In opposition to this view of limiting advanced education to the able students, one finds a large number of American educational leaders calling for more compulsory schooling, as well as encouragement for more students to attend colleges and graduate school. For example, the 1947 report of the President's Commission on Higher

Education envisages a four-year college enrollment made up of 32 percent of the youth of college age. Also, at least 50 percent of our youth should attend two years of junior college, i.e., through the fourteenth grade. All of the students of high school age, except mentally defectives, should attend high school for four years.[3]

It is evident, then, that there is no agreement among educators or others concerning the amount of advanced education American youth should receive, even though all agree that at least eight years of compulsory elementary education is necessary for all in a democracy. On the one hand some contend that only the gifted (top 15 to 20 percent) should be educated beyond the junior high school level. Others insist that the great majority of youth should be given free education through the junior college years and nearly half should reach graduate-school level. The issue is discussed heatedly by professional educators and other citizens alike. Some of the reasoning behind the quarrel follows.

Reasons Given for Limiting Advanced Education to the Gifted

1. Those who favor a limitation of the number of youth admitted to the secondary schools and colleges do not infer that other youth should not receive further schooling. But, they say, it should be nonacademic in nature and should involve preparation for the skilled jobs. This type of postelementary training is offered by all European countries, and to some extent by the United States in the trade and technical institutes provided at public expense or by industrial firms. Thus, when they speak of limiting the number of students attending high school and college, reference is made to academic schools and colleges. Most of the advocates of "education for the gifted" are not shirking their responsibility for giving every American child the opportunity of attending an institution that will prepare him for his life's work. But, they add, only the talented should attend "educational" institutions; the others should attend "training" schools.

   The case for limiting advanced education to the academically gifted is not new to the American people. The Constitution speaks of "equality" in the sense of a basic legal equality; nevertheless, none of the founding fathers was so unrealistic as to deny the existence of individual differences. Jefferson himself insisted upon the "natural aristocracy" that existed among men. Also, he considered this "hierarchy of talent" a most desirable situation and one which might produce desired results in a democracy. It is to be noted that Jefferson

[3] President's Commission on Higher Education, *Higher Education for American Democracy*, Vol. I (New York: Harper & Brothers, 1947), p. 41.

speaks of an aristocracy of virtue or talent, not an aristocracy of birth.[4] Chapter VII traces the Platonic origin of this view and shows its influence in ancient, medieval, and modern educational schemes. In fact, many consider it such an obvious "reality of nature" for there to be a wide range of intellectual talent that they ask how anyone could ever recommend anything but putting a limit on the amount of time spent in education.

Basically, then, the key argument used by those opposing the admission of large percentages of our youth to advanced education lies in their view of "human nature." Individual differences are a reality, and academic aptitude is the determining factor in admission to advanced education. This principle is taken for granted in all other walks of life. For example, the major leagues give every player a chance to prove himself, but if he does not have the ability he is just not kept in the fold; industry recognizes the ability (or lack thereof) in its selection of top executives and lower level administrators; democratic governments do not deceive themselves by assuming that all are equally fit to rule, though all have equality before the law.

2. It was mentioned above that Jefferson and the founding fathers believed that the success of democracy depends upon an educated electorate. Those who favor limiting advanced education to the gifted have no quarrel with this basic premise. They contend that if the lower schools eliminate all the "frills" and nonsense, nine or ten years of schooling should give the vast majority of our youth the necessary skills and knowledge to insure their effectiveness as citizens in a democracy. If the lower grades would concentrate on the "communication and computation" skills and Grades 5 to 10 do a thorough job in introducing the social studies, science, and humanities, there should be no need for more formal schooling to insure an educated electorate.

There is even less need for advanced formal schooling for the majority of our citizens today because of the increased (and improved) mass media of education. Television, to mention only one, offers an avenue of advanced informal education available to practically every man, woman, and child in the country. At present it is chiefly a means of entertainment; but it gradually is becoming more educational. In addition to the educational TV channels, many of the commercial stations are offering excellent programs in all fields of learning. It is not uncommon for an adult to master a foreign language within a few years by faithfully "attending" (in his living-room easy chair) one of the many TV classes. People with an interest in modern science can tune in to a "Continental classroom" and receive some of the nation's best instruction given at their own educational level.

[4] See Jefferson's letter to John Adams of October 28, 1813, in L. J. Cappon, *The Adams-Jefferson Letters*, Vol. II (Chapel Hill: University of North Carolina Press, 1959), p. 388.

In large urban centers, there is no dearth of courses offered by evening classes in the local public school, the YMCA, the churches and many other privately owned and operated educational institutions. Many small communities offer similar opportunities though they are usually more limited in scope. This kind of education is more desirable than more compulsory schooling for youngsters, since the adult enrolling in the course usually has the motivation necessary to carry him to true learning.

3. Some educators and students of society see grave social consequences in giving too much formal education to too many people. For example, some youths feel that because they have had twelve to sixteen years of formal schooling, certain types of work are "beneath their dignity." In many instances, these young people do not have the ability to handle the type of work for which they think they are qualified simply because they have been in a school building for a certain number of years. Many of these youth, "educated beyond their intelligence," refuse to recognize their limitations and are unwilling to "start at the bottom." Instead of accepting their limitations, they rebel against employers and society in general. Had they been trained as technicians or skilled laborers, social unrest would not have resulted because of the false impression they were given of their abilities.

Vocational guidance counselors point to the present imbalance between the wages of the "white-collar" workers and the skilled and semiskilled artisans. In some parts of the country the average salary of the white-collar worker is less than half that of the factory worker. A plumber with ten years of schooling may be making five dollars an hour whereas a graduate of a business course in a college with sixteen years of education may be earning only two and a half dollars an hour. Thus an oversupply may develop in certain fields and shortages in others, simply because too many people are getting too much formal schooling. As far as the social consequences are concerned, too much schooling is just as fraught with danger as too little.

4. Chapters II and IV have pointed up the overwhelming numbers of students now enrolled in public and private schools. With increased enrollments, the teacher shortage has worsened. In the face of these "hard facts" is it not unrealistic and foolhardy to consider "expanding educational opportunity" as the President's Commission has suggested? Would it not be more sensible to limit the number of students entering senior high schools and colleges, using a combination of ability and personal motivation as the criteria for selection, in preference to accepting more students than can be educated properly? The practice of accepting anyone who seeks admission, or what is even worse, requiring attendance, can only lower the standards of our educational institutions. In general, such standards already are too low compared with those of Europe and our chief competitor, Russia. Just herding

more students into our classrooms will never insure a good education. On the contrary, it will weaken the whole educational edifice.

5. A very practical argument against compulsory education beyond the tenth grade is derived from the experience of the classroom teachers. The presence of low-ability students in senior high school and college classes is a most frustrating experience for the teacher. These students are simply unable to grasp anything beyond the introductory or elementary level in the sciences, social sciences, the humanities, and mathematics. It is a complete waste of teacher time to attempt to teach them anything more. Not only are they unable to learn any difficult material, these students are also frequently responsible for the many disciplinary problems of the modern school. Since the material is beyond their grasp, they soon become disinterested and begin causing serious trouble. The student who wants to learn is hampered in his efforts by the presence of the relatively large number of dullards and troublemakers. In smaller high schools, where sectioning according to ability and interest is not feasible, the entire situation becomes "miseducative" — the good student suffers and the poor student is beyond assistance.

6. Finally, those who oppose advanced compulsory education argue that those who want it can get it since there are no prejudicial laws to thwart advanced study. Therefore, it seems senseless to make advanced education (even senior high school) compulsory.

Reasons Given for Education for All American Youth

The ideal of educating a relatively large percentage of youth beyond the elementary level is an American innovation. As some of the succeeding chapters will show, the concept of universal education, even at the elementary level, is largely a product of the nineteenth century. At no time in history did any country try to educate all the children of all the people. And when modern nations, both democratic and nondemocratic, adopted the principle of universal education, it was applied only at the level of fundamental education. Schooling at the secondary level was limited to the upper 10 to 15 percent of the population. Such was not the case in the United States. Some of the reasons given for educating the children of all the people are theoretical, others are practical. Some are refutations of the arguments listed by those who favor education beyond the ninth or tenth grades only for the gifted.

1. Perhaps the most basic argument given in favor of expanded educational opportunity is derived from the most recent (revised) view of

democracy (see Chap. IX). The implications of this view are that equality involves more than a simple legal status; each child or youth has as much right to free education as any other child; an intellectual elite claiming special privileges in the field of education is just as undemocratic as an "elite of blood or money or social status" claiming certain rights or privileges not granted to others. Therefore, to deny anyone the opportunities of advanced education because he is not from the intellectual elite is undemocratic.

2. The great influence which psychological "environmentalism" has on educational leaders in the United States is often mentioned as a theoretical reason for making advanced education available to all students. In simple terms (perhaps oversimplified), advocating environmentalism implies, among other things, that the environment is the most important factor in determining one's mental potential. It is claimed that research studies have demonstrated that the intelligence level of children can be significantly raised by placing them in improved home and school conditions. Thus, if the intellectual level of the population is to be raised, more education is the surest means of achieving this goal. If the present generation of children receive a better education, they in turn, as parents, will improve the environment of their homes; their children will be more receptive of the educational opportunities afforded them; and this type of ascending spiral will insure the intellectual and cultural progress of the people. The evolutionary bases of this argument are apparent, and relate directly to the basic premise of the environmentalists.

3. Because of the vast extension of knowledge, the success of modern democracy demands more than nine or ten years of compulsory education. No longer can it be maintained that mastery of the basic skills of "communication and computation" plus an "introduction" to the social and natural sciences and the humanities are adequate for the purpose of producing an enlightened electorate. "Enlightenment" for modern democracy demands much more than elementary education. The traditional subjects of the school, most especially the natural and social sciences, have undergone such radical changes and have expanded so greatly that several additional years of schooling will not suffice to close the gap.

In addition to the enlarged body of knowledge the school is expected to give its clientele, many of the educative functions, formerly assumed by the home and other agencies, now have been delegated to the school. Health and physical education, social activities, and driver training, to mention only a few formerly taken care of by the home or community, have been placed in the lap of the educational system.

Modern schools are "community schools" where pupils work together to solve the problems of their local, state, national, and international communities. They not only learn how to read and write, but they learn how to get along with one another through group activities. Field trips and excursions acquaint the student with his own local environment and that of his state and nation. Pupils learn to "live democracy" in the schools so they have a meaningful conception of that term based on experience as well as "book learning." All these activities take time — much more time than was needed by the traditional school to achieve its very limited goals.

4. The greatly increased demand for leaders and "experts" in the modern, complex democracy places another demand upon the schools not expected of them in pre-World War I days. Prior to the modern era of social democracy a relatively small number of "born leaders" was able to handle most of the leadership functions in government, business, and community agencies. Today a vastly expanded industrial economy, a highly technical and complex governmental structure at the federal, state, and large metropolitan levels, and extensive community services of all kinds make it imperative that new sources of leadership be sought. Obviously, the conception of leadership itself must be broadened to include anyone who plays a contributing role to the solution of problems in our complex society.

Thus, in addition to the many types of leaders in politics, the "expert" in every field is now viewed as a very important leader in his own field: those who arbitrate disputes between the factions in industry and community affairs; those who gather information relative to some problem to be solved. Certainly, the school is equipped best for this task of leadership training since it has within its walls the potential leaders of the next generation. But more time is needed to accomplish this task, for admittedly it is a slow process. If eight or ten years are needed for mastery of basic skills and achievement of an introductory understanding of the fundamental areas of human knowledge, at least two to four additional years are needed for the school to prepare its clientele for the enlarged responsibilities of leadership.

5. A very practical reason for keeping all youth in school for twelve or fourteen years is based on purely socioeconomic conditions of modern America. In the first place, business and industry cannot absorb such large numbers of unskilled and immature youth. Several generations ago there were many jobs in agriculture, forestry, and retailing — to mention only a few — which could be handled by teen-agers. Such is not the case today and both organized labor and management do not want such a large number of young people flooding the labor market.

Nor is there any work for these youngsters around the home as was the case several generations ago. Juvenile delinquency would certainly increase significantly if such large numbers of young people were not forced to attend high school. Undoubtedly their presence in the schools gives some difficulties to teachers, administrators, and other students. But it is certainly the lesser of two evils, for their youthful energies can be channeled in a constructive and recreational direction rather than in a destructive one. If these students are not interested in "academic subjects," other courses are provided for them of a very useful nature. In reality, most of our large high schools already provide such opportunities: coeducational cooking, homemaking, hobby classes, recreational art and music, leatherwork, basket weaving, and the like. All of these courses will prepare the student who is not "academically inclined" to live a fuller and richer life as a parent and citizen. Certainly these are worthy goals for the school and such courses are interesting for a "captive" group of students.

SEGREGATION IN THE SCHOOLS

The issue of racial segregation in the schools is only one aspect of a many-faceted problem. Instances of other types of segregation exist not only in education, but in other areas of human relations as well. For example, some residential communities will not accept Jews, nonwhites, or people of low income; some civic or social clubs, fraternities, sororities, and similar organizations are open only to certain professional or educational groups; in prisons, the perpetrators of certain types of offenses are not admitted to the various associations of "respectable criminals." All of these majority-minority problems are of great interest and importance for the student of society and education. But the limitations of space make it mandatory that this discussion be limited to segregation in education.

Many schools have practiced segregation throughout the history of American education. Southern and Northern public and private schools have prohibited the nonwhite races from attending some schools; some professional schools (medicine, dentistry, and law) have quotas for each religious and racial group; some school systems insist that not more than 25 percent of their teachers may be Catholic; some school districts will not hire atheists. Of all the areas of discrimination and segregation, the one that raises the most "emotive dust" undoubtedly involves racial differences. In spite of Supreme Court decisions, the opposing sides are still battling over the corpse. Following are some of the arguments offered for and against segregated schools.

Prosegregationist Arguments

1. One of the basic legal arguments given by the segregationist is that

education is a state and local function. Consequently, the federal government and the federal courts have no jurisdiction over the educational policies and practices of the states. If the people of the state believe that the common good is served best by operating segregated schools, it is their prerogative to do so. If the citizens of another state wish to foster integrated schools, they can legislate in that direction.

2. An argument closely allied to this one maintains that the principles of traditional American individualism are violated by federally enforced integration. They cite early Supreme Court decisions such as the famed "Oregon Case," which clearly states that the parent has the first right to educate. "The fundamental theory of liberty upon which all governments in this Union repose excludes any general power of the state to standardize its children by forcing them to accept instruction from public teachers only. The child is not the mere creature of the state; those who nurture him and direct his destiny have the right coupled with the high duty to recognize and prepare him for additional obligations."

Only when the parent does not educate his child properly can the government interfere. Certainly, the government cannot prove that the parent is not educating his child properly simply because he is not sending him to an integrated school. If the government proves that certain segregated schools do not meet the basic standards of a good education, the obligation lies in bringing those particular schools up to par. Thus, if the schools for colored children are inferior to those for white children, improve the schools for the colored. It does not logically follow that integration is the means for improving these schools. On the contrary, integration in most instances can only lower the educational standards of all schools by mixing the inferior with the superior students.

3. Some segregationists argue that basic differences among men have and always will exist. These very differences constitute the biological and sociological foundations of segregation. To legislate against segregation is to legislate against nature itself. The natural tendency for people to differ from others caused segregation of all kinds to become the accepted custom in some areas. In some countries or areas, segregation is more than a custom, it is an integral part of a way of life.

4. Some oppose integration on the grounds that true integration can come only from the free and genuine acceptance of the persons involved. For example, the Irish and German immigrants had very little difficulty becoming "one" in the "melting pot" of the New World simply because the basic differences between these two groups were insignificant. After one generation, the language barrier was removed and, for all practical purposes, the two people had everything in common. Such is not the case in integration of whites and nonwhites.

One or two generations will not erase the color line between the races. In fact, cross breeding only results in offspring acceptable to neither race.

On the basis of this argument segregationists maintain that legislation can never bring about true integration. Rather, it must come about from the free and uncoerced (and often very gradual) intermingling of the peoples involved. "Legislated integration" can bring nothing but chaos, suffering, and humiliation to all involved. Thus, both on pragmatic grounds (the bad consequences) and on philosophical principles, enforced desegregation is unacceptable.

5. Lurking beneath the surface of the arguments listed above is the basic belief that the nonwhite races are inferior to the white. Those maintaining the inferiority of nonwhites cite the results of intelligence tests, job success, and school achievement to prove their point.

Following the same general lines of reasoning, many argue that this innate inferiority and the inclination to evil are demonstrated by the proportionately larger number of Negroes involved in all types of crimes and misdemeanors. Similarly, these innate weaknesses are shown in the Negro's neglect of personal property, lethargic job performance, and inability to hold down any position of responsibility.

6. In areas where segregation is strongest, the greatest, though often unexpressed, fear is that school integration eventually will result in interracial marriages. The very thought of interracial marriages is so repugnant to many people who otherwise might not oppose integration that they stage a battle royal on even minor points. Thus, the issue of "where one sits on a bus" would seem to be quite remote from the problem of interracial marriage, but it is felt that capitulation in such minor matters will open the floodgates to all kinds of intermingling of the races and eventually will result in interracial marriages.

But why must marriage between the races be avoided at all costs? Simply because the nonwhite races are inferior, as mentioned above. Any mixing of the races will result in the deterioration of the white (ruling) race. Unless we want Western culture to slip back to near barbarism, the purity of the white race must be kept intact.

7. Some opponents of integration are convinced that if the nonwhite races are given equal rights and privileges they will soon take over the whole world by sheer force of numbers. Then the whites who are responsible for the present high level of our civilization will be deprived of the very products of their own diligence and intelligence. As evidence for this stand, the recent events in Africa usually are cited. All of the benefits of civilization that the new African nations have are the direct results of the efforts of the white colonial powers. Were it not for the white man the African tribes would still be in the

stone age. But as soon as the colored take over, the whites are deprived of their rightful holdings and often driven from their own homes by the cruel and inhuman persecution of the new masters.

Arguments for Integration

The zest with which integrationists fight for their point of view varies a great deal from person to person. Some contend that racial integration must be effected in the public schools with one fell swoop. Others, believing that integration is fundamentally right, feel that a gradual change from segregated to desegregated schools will result in a really permanent union. Similarly, the methods used to effect integration vary from the use of physical force to mild persuasion. Many of the reasons for insisting upon integration are held in common by most antisegregationists.

1. Probably the most fundamental argument offered against segregation is derived from the basic equality of all men. There are two main sources of proof for this position: (a) The Judeo-Christian belief that all human beings are the children of God and possess the same fundamental nature. No one race, nationality or social class is fundamentally superior to another. Differences among the races and other groups are accidental, not essential. (b) Even if one does not accept the Judeo-Christian view of the common Fatherhood of God, all men still are *biologically* equal. Here again, the differences among the races, nationalities, and other groups of human beings are accidental, not essential. Most evolutionary theories favor the belief that *homo sapiens* is derived from one common ancestor in the animal kingdom rather than a variety. Trait differences among the different varieties of men are usually accounted for in terms of environmental factors. Consequently, the segregationists' contention that certain races are inferior is tenable neither on theological nor empirical grounds.

   To argue that the colored race is inferior because average scores on intelligence tests are significantly lower for the colored proves nothing. These tests were "standardized" on middle-class white populations and test the intellectual maturity (verbal ability) of that group (or any other group of the same socioeconomic levels). Thus the colored pupils in a nonsegregated school and from the higher socioeconomic groups tend to have higher intelligence quotients than their poorer segregated brethren from the lower classes. The same holds true, moreover, for the different classes of white children. Their success on standardized tests varies according to environment rather than any innate inferiority or superiority.

   Similarly, one must reject the argument that the colored race is criminally inclined. Statistics show that the incidence of juvenile delinquency and adult crime is higher among the "poor whites" than among upper middle-class whites; less crime and delinquency is found in the "better-class" colored than in the lower classes. Obviously, "blood" is not the primary causal factor in crime and delinquency, for otherwise all members of a certain race would be delinquents and all members of another race would be law-abiding citizens.

2. In addition to the fundamental equality which would apply in any political-social structure (monarchy or aristocracy) further grounds for equal treatment for all races is derived from democratic principles. American democracy, in particular, is based on the premise that *all* men possess a *fundamental* equality which cannot be denied them. Since segregation upon racial grounds violates this basic principle, it must be abolished in the United States.

"To separate (children) from others of similar age and qualifications solely because of their race generates a feeling of inferiority. . . . We conclude that in the field of public education the doctrine of 'separate but equal' has no place. Separate educational facilities are inherently unequal. . . . Segregation is a denial of the equal protection of the laws."[5] The psychosociological aspects of this decision are far-reaching, for the whole complex of emotions, attitudes, and ideals becomes involved. Segregation generates divisive and undemocratic attitudes; those discriminated against build up feelings of resentment toward their would-be persecutors; violence and rebellion replace logic and law. Therefore, the only sensible way of solving the problem consists in granting equal rights to all people of all races.

3. The Supreme Court mentions the "separate but equal" principle that obtained prior to the 1954 decision. The opponents of segregation offer great masses of evidence showing that the "equal facilities" were far from equal. In general, schools for the colored had inferior buildings, less qualified teachers, and vastly substandard library facilities. In practically every community where the schools were compared on a per-pupil cost basis, larger amounts were spent on the schools for whites. Even if the facilities had been equal, as measured by "buildings and books," the schools for colored would still be viewed as inferior because of the exclusive character of the schools for whites. Thus, no matter what physical arrangements are established, all segregational practices place some pupils in an inferior status. Such practices violate the spirit of the Constitution if not the letter of the law.

4. At a time when the United States is in a position of world leadership, any discriminatory practices weaken its prestige. How can the United States' delegate to the United Nations insist upon the basic human rights clauses in the UN Charter when his own people violate

---

[5] See 1954 Supreme Court decision in *Brown* vs. *Board of Education of Topeka*, 348 U. S. 483.

these very principles? How can our civil servants in charge of aid to underdeveloped countries (especially in Africa) preach the advantages of democracy when a large minority of African descent is not granted equal rights in education, employment, and the use of the franchise? It behooves the United States to clean its own doorstep before preaching cleanliness to other nations.

5. In terms of dollars and cents, segregation is more costly than integration. In many areas, especially where population is sparse, the maintenance of separate schools for colored and white duplicates facilities unnecessarily. Often there are scarcely enough pupils in some of these areas to populate one school, much less two. In some sections of large cities, segregation prohibits the maximum use of existing school plants, and often forces school administrators to construct new schools which would not be needed if existing schools were operated at maximum capacity. In addition to the expense of school construction and maintenance, the cost of staffing a dual system is well nigh prohibitive if school boards are to employ qualified teachers. Such fiscal policies will eventually result in lowered educational standards for all groups.

6. The segregationist contention that integration in the schools will result in interracial marriages is probably correct. In probably every country where the mingling of the races has been accepted such has been the result. But, the integrationist asks, what evidence do you have that an "inferior" race has been produced by the "mixing of the blood"? In reality there is no "pure race" in the world! Every existing race at some time or other in human history has been fused with other stock. Only by employing arbitrary and artificial definitions of "inferior" can one demonstrate that the amalgam of two or more races resulted in an inferior species. On the contrary, examples of too much inbreeding in humans or animals definitely produces physically inferior species.

7. The fear of some segregationists that the colored race will eventually "take over" if they are granted equal rights in education and other areas can be used as an argument in favor of integration. Now is the time, the integrationists maintain, for the whites to accept their colored brothers into their schools, their places of business and entertainment, and their homes. Since the colored account for only 10 percent of the total population, they can be absorbed very easily into the white race. Within a relatively few generations there will be only one race in America and there will be no fear of one race dominating the other. Although this solution might appear distasteful, or even repugnant, to some people of today, it certainly is more desirable than a struggle between the races which conceivably might end in the destruction of the white race.

DEMOCRACY IN THE SCHOOLS

In Chapter XI, the philosophical issues involved in the meaning of democracy are discussed. Our concern at this time is with the practical application of one's view of democracy to school administration and classroom activities. In regard to democracy in the classroom, the most frequently discussed issue is discipline. When teachers are asked to indicate the problem they consider most important in their teaching, that of discipline has a greater frequency than any other (including salaries). Granted, there are many disciplinary problems in the school. "What makes discipline an issue, and how is it related to democracy in the schools?" The answer lies in the trend among modern educators who insist that the school be a miniature democracy; that each classroom should be managed democratically; that school children should be free to express themselves; and that teachers are not rulers.[6]

Obviously such a view of the school calls for a radical revision of one's approach to school discipline. Following are some of the characteristics of the new and of traditional approaches to school discipline.

The "New School" of Discipline

1. At the outset, the advocates of democracy in the school exhort the teacher to divest himself of all "authoritarian" methods, beliefs, and attitudes concerning the role of the teacher in maintaining order in the class. Such an outlook is basically miseducative, and hinders rather than helps the learning process. In general, they contend, teacher authority is not the source of discipline.

2. In a democracy, the authority rests with the people; in a democratic classroom, the authority rests with all involved in the learning process, teacher and students. Consequently discipline may be defined as the cooperative effort of students and teacher working on a real problem. A student has disciplined himself when he can work in harmony with the other members of the group; a disciplined classroom is one characterized by purposeful activity on the part of the class. Note that this new conception of discipline does not mean that students should be dashing around doing as they please. An essential characteristic of a disciplined class is orderliness. But orderliness does not mean that students must be silent, line up in a straight row, speak only when asked to do so by the teacher, and subdue all natural inclinations. On

[6] See Chap. X, pp. 240 f, 247, 252, 260, 263.

the other hand, if students are working at their own level on projects of real interest to them, very few disciplinary problems will arise.

3. Since the whole class, rather than the teacher, is responsible for discipline, group pressure should be the most effective means for getting the recalcitrant pupils to cooperate. The desire of all people to "belong" or to be accepted by their peers is sufficiently strong to restore the harmonious functioning of the class. A wise teacher will utilize this natural drive to lead students to democratic discipline. Only in extreme cases will it be necessary for a teacher to resort to external authority to settle disciplinary problems that arise in the classroom.

4. The conception of "democratic discipline" demands a new approach to rules and regulations affecting the students. To be truly democratic all rules of conduct or behavior must be derived from the consensus of the ruled. Administrators and teachers who truly believe in democracy will see to it that the students themselves are involved in the making of the rules by which they will be governed. Further, the adults must recognize that such participation by students is not to be considered a privilege but a right.

Psychologically, the students are more likely to abide by rules they have made; if they break these rules they are violating their own authority. Thus the usual challenge to an external authority is removed, and youth is not as apt to rebel just for the sake of showing the adult world that he is hostile to external authority. Basically, then, the students are "set free" to solve their problems with the help of an expert, the teacher. By talking problems over with teachers and administrators, students learn respect for the rights of others and soon become effective members of the social groups of which they are a part.

The advocates of this democratic methodology warn teachers that children must be trained gradually for democratic freedom. It is unwise, and even dangerous, to "turn over the discipline of the class to a group of students who have been accustomed to authoritarian control. Generally, they will not know how to handle their new-found freedom, and anarchy will reign instead of order. Problems cannot be solved in the midst of bedlam. On the other hand, a class that has been schooled in the methods of democratic discipline from kindergarten on can be trusted with their own discipline. In very few cases will such a class need more than the guidance of the teacher."[7]

5. Psychologists feel that harsh, authoritarian discipline warps the personalities of youth. If a youngster has been subjected to harsh disciplinary action, he usually reacts by performing socially destructive

---

[7] See G. V. Sheviakov and F. Redl, Discipline for Today's Children (Washington, D. C.: Association for Supervision and Curriculum Development, N.E.A., 1944), 1956, passim.

162162162162 THE AMERICAN SCHOOL SYSTEM

acts. Authoritarianism begets hostility! He will find ways of getting revenge on adult society which, he feels, has been cruel to him. He will "take it out" on his peers or, oftentimes, on children weaker than himself. Even if the offender does not go to the extreme of doing physical harm to others, he seldom becomes a constructive, productive member of the social organism.

Since all empirical evidence points to the futility of authoritarian discipline, teachers and administrators of youth should abandon it once and for all. Perhaps the traditional educator might be excused for his advocacy of strict discipline, because he knows no better; but there can be no justification for such an approach in the modern age of science and democracy.

6. The proponents of the new approach to discipline generally seek the causes of misbehavior in the environment rather than in the ill will of the students. To illustrate, Burton locates disciplinary problems in: (1) surplus energy, (2) physical discomfort, (3) outdated curriculum and methods, (4) the desire to be noticed, and (5) serious personality disturbance. In the first category he lists such actions as whispering and humming, minor "horseplay," teasing, scribbling on desks or blackboard, throwing things around the room, writing notes, and "acting up." Restlessness, inattention, eating, drinking, coughing, and sleeping are usually due to the physical condition of the students. Poor curriculum, teaching methods, and classroom management cause lack of interest and concentration, absences and tardiness, and loitering. The student's natural desire to be noticed accounts for bragging, impertinence, showing off, "wisecracking," bluffing, and "playing tricks" on fellow students and teacher. The last category includes the serious forms of misdemeanor such as fighting, drinking, smoking, hysteria, overaggressiveness, and other acts usually associated with delinquency.[8] The recommended solution to such problems consists in finding the causes of the misbehavior; if the cause is removed, the problem will disappear. Some disciplinary cases must be handled by trained psychiatrists, others can be solved by improving the classroom atmosphere or changing the curriculum.

7. In general, the new school takes a dim view of punishment as a means of achieving good discipline. Punishment, they claim, always has been ineffective and should be rejected simply because it doesn't achieve the goal of "good behavior." In addition to being undemocratic and productive of hostility and neurosis, punishment can never achieve the positive results that modern psychology and psychiatry have demonstrated to be valid and productive of socially acceptable behavior. Psychologically, the only one profiting from punishment is the neurotic teacher who relieves his or her own frustrations by punishing an inferior.

[8] W. H. Burton, The Guidance of Learning Activities (New York: Appleton-Century-Crofts, 1952), p. 715.

The "Old School" of Discipline

Through the public press, critics of "educationists" among religious leaders, military men, and community leaders are calling for a return to the old school of discipline. The motivation for the outcry against "progressive school discipline" varies from critic to critic. The points that follow might be acceptable to one believer in the old school, but not to another. They simply are representative of the criticisms commonly heard today.

1. A very fundamental argument presented in defense of teacher-centered discipline is derived from the traditional conception of authority. This view, loosely stated, looks upon the teacher as a representative of the parents. Consequently, he has the same authority over the child during the school day as the parent has when the child is at home. No law has questioned the parent's right to discipline his children as the situation demands, provided the parent remains within the bounds of humane discipline. The teacher, acting in loco parentis, has similar authority over the class, and cannot relinquish it to the group. For this reason, a court of law will hold the teacher responsible for injuries and damage to individuals or property if the teacher has not used all prudent means to keep such order in the class as is necessary to prevent injury or damage. The court does not point to the students and hold them responsible on the grounds that they hold authority in a democratic class. Thus, both legally and in "reality," final authority in the class rests with the school or the teacher, despite what the starry-eyed idealist might conjure up in the name of democracy.

   For the supernaturalist, any conception of authority must include an admission of the authority of a Supreme Being. Ultimately, all authority is derived from God, and the teacher's authority is no exception to this general rule. Thus, when a pupil obeys the teacher as one legitimate authority he is obeying God; when the teacher sets forth reasonable rules and regulations within his proper domain, the student is bound in conscience to abide by them.

2. The child or youth, because of his very nature, must be disciplined by the authority of teachers and other adults. This conclusion is based on the premise that youngsters are inclined to evil, and need firm discipline to keep them out of trouble. Those who hold this view do not contend that all types of misbehavior are evil or sinful in themselves. Throwing spitballs, whispering, and "cutting up" are not intrinsically sinful; nevertheless, they reflect the youthful indisposition toward law and order. Thus, even in these minor matters, the pupil must be controlled by the firm hand of teacher authority. The sooner the child learns that he must follow the rules laid down by his elders, the easier life will be for him.

Does it follow that the child should be given no freedom? Certainly not! The teacher must be mindful of the child's rights, and when the child has complied with the basic rules of order and completed the required work in proper fashion he should be given the opportunity to pursue his own special interests (provided they do not disrupt the rest of the class). Further, after the child has understood that the proper teacher-pupil relationship is one of superior to inferior, the incidence of misbehavior will be greatly reduced. When the proper respect for authority has been developed within the child's mind he will become truly "free," for he has learned to control the inordinate desires of self-will. This self-control is necessary for adult life as well as for school life. The free man is one who lives by reason, not by impulse. The disciplined person is one who knows his rights but also respects those of legitimate authority. He is a "conformist" in areas of human endeavor where conformity is necessary, a nonconformist in others.

3. An understanding of the value of obedience is a necessary by-product of a good education. The proper attitude toward obedience is stressed by all educators in the Judeo-Christian tradition. Both the Old and New Testaments emphasize the necessity of obedience to God's Commandments. If obedience is necessary in the Kingdom of God, likewise it is an essential element of any social structure. The father of the family must insist on filial compliance to his will; the teacher, in loco parentis, has the same right and duty; the state and the church can expect obedience to directives in their respective spheres. Perhaps more than one half of man's waking hours are spent in carrying out the orders of his superiors in the family, in business or industry, in the state or the church. The person who has not been disciplined will constantly be at odds with all elements of his social environment. His success in this life and the life hereafter will be greatly hampered by his lack of discipline.

The goal of all group discipline is not discipline for its own sake but self-discipline. Thus any disciplinary techniques which do not bring about self-discipline have not succeeded in achieving their goal, and such methods have been miseducative. On this point, the advocates of the new and old schools of discipline agree!

4. In recent years, acts of violence and even criminal behavior have become more frequent among pupils of junior and senior high school age. Although the school is not blamed for all the trouble, many law-enforcement officers, social workers, and clergymen feel that it has contributed to the rise of delinquency. Many teachers believe that the child can do no wrong; some of these teachers, having been schooled in deterministic psychology, say that the child is not responsible for his actions; some administrators will not back the teachers who "discipline" pupils; even parents object to their children receiving punish-

ment of any kind. Under such circumstances, the youngster is convinced that he can "get away with anything," and the transfer from unchecked school misbehavior to out-of-school delinquency is an easy step. Because of the magnitude of the problem of delinquency, and because of the belief that the school must "teach discipline" as well as subjects, some states and communities have reintroduced corporal punishment for certain types of offenses. New York City has segregated its "tough kids" into schools run by "disciplinarians." Many teachers again are using the adage "spare the rod and spoil the child." Many observers are convinced that there will be a gradual return to the discipline of the old school. This does not mean that there should be a return to the inhumane beatings of early colonial days; but punishment and many other techniques of the preprogressive era will be used to restore order and the proper respect for authority.

5. Some modern psychologists believe that youth not only needs but wants the guidance of a firm (not harsh or cruel) disciplinarian. Such feelings may not be expressed overtly by children and teen-agers, but are often betrayed by indirect statements and actions.

A nationwide survey, reported in *This Week* Sunday magazine recently, showed that there was great personal and social maladjustment among youth who had as much freedom as they wished. On the other hand, those young people who had experienced the firm (but loving) discipline of parents and teachers were more secure and better adjusted than their "free" peers. Apparently, those who had learned respect for authority had also learned that happiness in life can be achieved only when one has acquired the proper balance between freedom and obedience, between society and self, between conformity and free expression.[9]

6. Generally speaking, most educators have abandoned the naïvely naturalistic doctrine of Rousseau regarding discipline and punishment. Modern living is too complex and dangerous to leave all behavior to chance. Even the pragmatist recognizes the futility of such an educational pattern. No "practical person" believes the child should be given no orders, or that nothing should be prohibited. Necessity may be a good teacher but the lesson may come too late. Too, the punishment coming from the natural consequences of an act may be much more severe and harmful than the preventative punishment administered by a parent or teacher. Thus, the *laissez-faire* discipline of the schools of the 1920's and 1930's has brought about its own undoing. The child of those decades was not prepared for the realities of later life in the world of business and labor, and the youth of the 1940's was not prepared for the discipline and rigors of military life.

[9] A. Walters, *Persons and Personality* (New York: Appleton-Century-Crofts, 1953), p. 109.

Implications for School Administration

The principles enunciated in regard to the two points of view on classroom discipline also apply to the general administration of the school. The traditional conception of the job of the school administrator viewed him as the representative of the authority of the school board. Practically speaking, each administrator exercised his authority quite autonomously. If the community and the school board did not agree with his policies, practices, and ideology, his contract was not renewed. But so long as he held the post of administrator, the authority over teachers and students rested in his hands.

At times, administrative authority was abused; more frequently it was used with the presumed good of the teachers, students, and community in mind; usually the authority was exercised through a definite chain of command or hierarchical structure. The chain of command was "from the top down," with the superintendent passing on directives to the principals and supervisors who in turn passed them on to teachers and students.

The "new" conception of democratic authority views the school administrator as the "implementor" of the policies determined by the people at the "grass-roots" level. In other words, all authority and policy-making regarding the school rests with the people. Thus all segments of the community, parents, students, teachers, and community leaders should participate in the formulation of all basic policies affecting education. The job of the school administrator is to carry out these democratically founded directives; the administrator does not make the policies — he puts them into practice. His training as an expert in school administration aids him in the setting up of the machinery for carrying out the will of the people. The chain of command is reversed in this new approach; the authority rests with the people rather than with the administrator; the administrator carries out the will of the community rather than his own policies or plans. Of course, as a member of the community each administrator has as much right as any other citizen in a democratic society to assist in the formulation of policy.

In summary, it might be pointed out that the key issue between the new and the old schools of discipline and control lies in the relationship between the teaching-learning process and the conception of truth (both moral and speculative). Since truth is relative for the new educator, he cannot "lead his students to truth" as the traditional teacher might do. The traditionalist believes there are some fundamental immutable truths which the teacher supposedly knows. It is his job to see to it that the student acquires these truths. To do so involves the use of authority and discipline. But the teacher of the "new order" and the students are co-workers in the quest for solutions to life's problems (not truths). This cooperative activity calls for democracy in the classroom.[10]

THE ROLE OF THE SCHOOL IN AMERICAN SOCIETY

Throughout the history of education one will note that the main purpose of the school in any society has been quite limited. The school's job was viewed by most ancient, medieval, and modern nations as limited to supplying the type of training or education which no other agency could give.[11] Primarily, the school was supposed to concern itself with the development of the students' mind. As Chapter X relates, the school has varied its curriculum and methods in the course of time, but the concern for mental development has dominated its activities.

The first major departure from this view was witnessed in twentieth-century America. The development of the "whole child" became the slogan of the new education. Whereas traditional education had confined itself primarily to academic activities designed to develop "minds," the new education proposed to develop all phases of pupil growth — mental, physical, social, aesthetic, and moral. Gradually, this broadened objective was translated in terms of "adjustment."

The trend to make "life adjustment"[12] the major goal of the American school advanced rapidly during the first four decades of the twentieth century. But recently, when the Soviet Union moved ahead of the United States in the field of space technology, many interested in education began a concerted attack on the schools for their failure to produce scholars. "Life-adjustment education" became the target of their verbal shafts. Life adjustment, they claimed,

---

[10] See Chapter XI, sections on the nature of democracy and the meaning of truth.
[11] See Chapter V.
[12] The term "life-adjustment education" was not used to designate the type of education referred to above until after World War II. But its "philosophy" was developed much earlier.

had replaced the study of mathematics, science, history, and language. Every attack was met with a counterattack; for every educator clamoring for a return to the "solid subjects," there was one shouting for the "education of the whole child." Name-calling became a favorite pastime; "reactionary," "educationist," "medievalist," "anti-intellectualist," "socialist," and "communist" were labels commonly used. Perhaps a short summary of the two extreme positions will assist the student to discern the basic differences between the warring factions.

Life-Adjustment Education

The Commission on Life Adjustment formulated the following definition of life adjustment in its 1948 statement: "Life Adjustment Education is designed to equip all American youth to live democratically with satisfaction to themselves and profit to society as home members, workers, and citizens."[13] Although it is concerned especially with a sizable portion of youth of high school age whose needs and interests are less well served by our schools than are the objectives of preparation for either a skilled occupation or higher education, it does stop there. Thus, it is worth noting that *all* American youth are in need of this kind of education. The college-bound student may need some additional work to prepare him for college, but the life-adjustment core is designed to realize the fundamental goal of the schools of elementary and secondary level. This new statement includes those earlier goals recommended by the Commission, such as: (1) ethical and moral living, (2) worthy use of leisure time, (3) health and safety, (4) consumer education, and (5) self-realization.

According to the Commission, any school desiring to meet the standards of life-adjustment education must have the following characteristics:

1. The curriculum should contain common learning experiences based upon the real-life problems of the students rather than upon the traditional subject matter organization. In terms of curricular offering, this means that the only "required subject" will be the common learnings or "core studies." Two types of core programs are found in many schools: English-social studies and science-mathematics. The English-social studies core replaces separate subjects such as geography,

13 Commission on Life Adjustment For Every Youth, *Life Adjustment for Every Youth* (Washington, D. C.: Superintendent of Documents, 1948), p. 4 ff.

history, civics, sociology, economics, spelling, composition, and English. The content of these subjects is not treated in a logical or chronological order as was done formerly. Rather, the class draws whatever information is needed from these subject-matter areas to solve the problem at hand. Since most of the problems students select are contemporary ones, the most up-to-date resources will be in greatest demand. For example, if the students are studying the Cuban or Algerian problem, they will draw heavily on modern geography, economics, politics, world history, and sociology. An occasional glance might be cast in the direction of premodern aspects of these subjects. Spelling, grammar, and composition will be learned as the student expresses himself orally and in writing.

The science-mathematics core likewise uses student problems as the starting point for study. Once a problem has been defined, the student begins his search for solutions by turning to the scientific sources he will need to solve the problem. In other words, he will not take the sciences and mathematics as separate subjects but will draw from all the science-mathematics fields as the demands of the problem call for information and knowledge from each.

2. A characteristic of the life-adjustment program flowing directly from the first one requires that direct experience be the basis of the learning process. Field trips to business and industry, the study of plant and animal life in its natural habitat, and practicing democracy in the school should replace verbal instruction in these areas. Whenever possible the student should "learn by doing" rather than by instruction from the teacher. The suggestion is that most of traditional formal instruction by the teacher and books be replaced by student activity. Books and teachers will remain "sources for learning," but not the primary ones; the students' own direct experiences will be central.[14]

3. The school with life adjustment as its goal should seek to enroll and retain all children and youth through the twelfth grade. With a problem-centered curriculum and experience-centered learning, this goal should be relatively easy to attain. The traditional school had little holding power simply because its curriculum and teaching methods were designed for the few (gifted), not for all. If a student is not only permitted but encouraged to pursue studies of interest to him or if he is working on problems that have meaning for him, he will remain in school.

4. The life-adjustment school should develop in its clientele a respect for individual worth and personality. This goal can be achieved in group work, where the student cooperates with others in solving common problems. Such group interaction will enable the student to learn to respect the rights and feelings of others. Each student will

[14] See Chapter X, pp. 241 f, 245, 247, 252, 257 f; Chapter XVI, p. 396 f.

realize that the major portion of his waking hours will be spent working with others. He will learn that individuality is limited by the necessity of reaching some agreement on goals to be achieved and means of achieving them. In fine, he will be able to strike a proper balance between individual freedom and the public good.

5. The school of life adjustment will provide for democratic living in all phases of the school's operation. Each classroom should reflect the best in democratic planning and procedure, with both students and teacher involved; the entire school will be democratically run with administrators, teachers, parents, and community representatives participating. If the classroom is not a miniature democracy, the student will never "experience" true democratic behavior; if the entire school is not democratically operated, it can never be the school of democracy. In practice, this characteristic implies that the teacher will not appear before the class as the authority "dispensing truth and order" but will guide the students in their selection of problems to be studied and solved. The discipline of the class will be as described above in the brief summary of the new approach to discipline. School administrators will not forge ahead without consulting the views and following the recommendations of all in the community. Rather, they will "administer the will of the people."

6. Evaluation of pupil success in the school will be in terms of desirable changes in pupil behavior and growth. In general, this characteristic involves the abandonment of all traditional marking and grading systems which pit one student against the other. Thus both the dull and bright pupil will be considered successful if they have demonstrated improved social behavior and more efficient use of problem-solving techniques. If no growth or improvement has taken place the student is considered unsuccessful regardless of his store of factual knowledge. This new approach to achievement is reflected in the practice used in core or common learning classes of grading the student satisfactory or unsatisfactory, or simply by a parent-teacher conference informing the parents regarding their child's growth.

These two grades represent the composite of the traditional letter or number grades plus all the other factors mentioned. Under these circumstances it is possible for a student in the eighth grade to receive an unsatisfactory mark even though he has mastered all the subject matter eighth graders are supposed to know (by traditional standards). Perhaps he showed no improvement over the preceding year. Perhaps he did not cooperate with his classmates in solving common problems. Such behavior is sufficient grounds for considering the student's growth as unsatisfactory.

7. Another characteristic of the life-adjustment school is the large number of elective subjects available in addition to the common learnings

designed for all. Every student should be able to select subjects that meet his needs and interests. The college-bound student should be able to elect advanced mathematics, humanities, science, and social-science courses. The vocational subjects should be available for the terminal student. Fine arts, crafts, and hobby experiences should be offered to satisfy the special talents and interests of students. No one subject-matter area should be considered superior to the other.

Obviously, any school attempting to satisfy all these criteria of life-adjustment education must have a comprehensive guidance program. Standardized testing programs to determine the interests and abilities of students are a necessity. Individual and group counseling are essential to provide an interpretation of these tests to the students and assist them in their choice of school activities. Occupational information must be kept up to date and available to all. Continuous follow-up of all students is essential to determine whether the school is actually meeting the needs of its clientele.

Those favoring the life-adjustment education do not hesitate to warn the public of the additional amount of financial resources that must be made available to the schools if they are to achieve the goals of this kind of education. All the special services called for will require additional classrooms, educational materials, library facilities, and teachers. If the school is to meet all the needs of all the students, financial resources must be nearly doubled. The traditional school could operate with a limited number of classrooms and teachers for the basic subjects. Library holdings did not have to include "everything under the sun," but could be limited to those books having a direct bearing on the subject matter taught. Some guidance services were needed, but "academic counseling" was considered the only proper function of the school. Vocational and personal guidance was conceived to be the responsibility of the family and social agencies. Thus the traditional school could function well with a small financial outlay. But the school for life adjustment cannot.

One misconception that the advocates of life adjustment wish to eradicate is that the school should assist the student to adjust to the status quo. Such is not the case! Most advocates of life adjustment believe that the school should be the vanguard of social changes. The very rejection of the traditional subjects as the core of learning activities implies a repudiation of the conservative leanings of the traditional school. Thus, from the point of view of life-adjustment education, the school should not be the reflector and conserver of the beliefs and values of society, but should serve as the catalyst of the social order. The school should strive to instill in youth the desire for social change; social betterment, the welfare of all people should be placed above individual welfare and freedom; social democracy should be preferred to individualistic (capitalistic) democracy; democracy itself should be viewed as an evolving dynamic process rather than a static form of government. Life adjustment then, is not to be equated with social lethargy or quietism, but with peaceful social renewal and reconstruction.[15]

Intellectualism in Education[16]

Those favoring a return to the traditional goals of the school (intellectual development and/or mastery of subject matter) do not believe that the school should produce maladjusted children. On the contrary, they want their children to be well adjusted, good citizens of their democratic country, and productive workers and leaders. But they contend that the primary responsibility for life adjustment and social change rests with the home and other non-school agencies. Some of the fundamental arguments for this view follow.

1. Each agency in society must fulfill its obligation to that society according to its unique nature. Thus the family by its very nature is the agency responsible for propagating the humankind and meeting the needs of physical, moral, and spiritual care during infancy and early childhood. But the complexities of all civilized societies make demands upon their members which cannot be satisfied by the parents. In general, parents are not equipped to direct the more advanced intellectual training of the child. Another agency, the school, was erected by civilized societies to meet this need. The school is not usurping the basic parental right to educate the offspring, but is simply supplying the type of education the parents generally cannot offer.

Moreover, the task of developing the mental powers of the child and supplying the knowledge essential to their progress must be handled systematically step by step throughout the years of formal schooling. Such is not the case for many objectives of life-adjustment education, most of which are within the province of the home, the community, the church, and other agencies. Therefore, the school, by its very nature and purpose, should confine itself mainly to the intellectual development of its clientele through teaching the fundamental disciplines: mathematics, the sciences (social and natural), and the humanities. If the school attempts to be all things to all men, it must necessarily weaken its own position by inflating its goals beyond its proper function.

15 See T. Brameld, *Toward a Reconstructed Philosophy of Education* (New York: Dryden Press, 1956), Chap. I.

16 For a more detailed account of intellectualism and its historical and philosophical roots, see Chapter IX.

2. If the goal of the school is limited to intellectual development and mastery of the basic disciplines, obviously not all students can profit from its curriculum to the same degree. Thus beyond the level of fundamental education (usually eighth grade) only a relatively small number should be admitted to the advanced levels of academic schooling. Those who do not possess the mental capacity to profit from formal education in the academic areas should be steered into vocational education.

Not all opponents of life-adjustment education are against having vocational training in the same school *building*; but they do insist that such adjustments to the system of universal compulsory education beyond elementary school are a necessity because of the current demands of an industrial society. Within those schools offering both the academic and vocational curricula, the academic is to be considered the true educational activity; the vocational is to be viewed as "training" for a job in business and industry. The hierarchy of functions must always be kept in mind!

3. Life-adjustment education, say its opponents, is an outgrowth of the progressive movement. The emphasis on students' problems, needs, and interests promoted by the progressivists resulted in the neglect or complete disregard of *systematic* formation in the basic academic disciplines. The weaknesses of the problem-centered approach were apparent as early as World War II and became more obvious when the United States fell behind Russia in launching space satellites. American schools, it was charged, had been too solicitous with producing well-adjusted people and were not producing scholars. On the other hand, the Russian schools concentrated on rigorous academic discipline and were consequently able to produce intellectually disciplined scholars, especially in the mathematical and scientific fields.

4. The advocates of mental discipline do not defend all the techniques of traditional education nor do they deny that much that was done in the traditional school was miseducative. To illustrate, they too frown upon rote memorization without understanding; they disclaim the educational value of the parrotlike regurgitation of what the teacher says; they question the educational value of those activities which discourage independent thinking. Nevertheless, they insist that systematic treatment of the basic disciplines is essential to their true understanding. The occasional acquaintance with these disciplines in connection with the solution of a contemporary problem will not assure the student of mastery in any subject-matter area. "He will know a little bit about many things but not much about anything." Such an approach to knowledge is not the foundation for true scholarship, even though it might be of use for the devotee of "parlor discussions."

5. In response to the statement that the academic subjects are available on an elective basis to students who have an interest in them, the proponents of the intellectual discipline assert that too many of our youth will avoid the difficult subjects. Because of the high-income level of many American families, children have been pampered to such an extent that they shrink from any activity which requires concentrated systematic effort. The school itself has contributed to this attitude by allowing students to earn high school credit in driver training, swimming, coeducational cooking, flycasting, and the like. The only way to bring the students, especially the talented ones, to utilize their capacities is to require all to take academic disciplines. In this manner many a student who feared certain subjects because of their difficulty, may find that he has a special interest and talent for them. If youngsters are permitted to avoid such subjects, much of the potential for scholarship will go undeveloped or even unnoticed. It is because the school has failed to develop the intellectual powers of its clientele that the charge of "anti-intellectualism" has been laid at its door. In fact, it is argued, once the parents realize what their children are missing by not taking a heavy academic diet, they demand for their children a return to the solid subjects which they themselves had in their student days. The softness of the life-adjustment program has sounded its own death knell.

6. Finally, the intellectualist disagrees with those who believe that the school should be the vanguard of social change. The role of the school in this very important matter should be neither "conservative nor revolutionary." If the school is faithful to its goal of giving the students a basic knowledge and understanding of the important academic disciplines and developing the powers of critical thought, it has fulfilled its duty to society. The task of changing the social order or conserving the *status quo* should rightfully be performed by the adult population of the nation. Thus, a teacher favoring a change from capitalistic democracy to social democracy has every right to be active in political organizations designed to bring about such changes. But he has no right to use the school as a proselytizing agency to further his own social and economic philosophy. If he is a mathematics, science, or language teacher, then the discussion of such topics is out of his field. If he is a social-science teacher, he must present his view as one of several alternatives on the topic. At any rate, he should never be permitted to indoctrinate the immature mind of the student with his own views on controversial matters.

It is worth noting that many of the early progressives held the same view as the intellectualists in regard to the school's role in the social order. A. V. Sayers, for example, urges the school to develop a "critical intelligence" in the student which will enable him to inaugurate needed social change when he becomes a member of adult society.

Summary

From the foregoing discussion of the conflicting views affecting American public and private education it is evident that there is no easy solution to the problems of federal aid to education, segregation in the schools, the purpose of the school in the social order, democracy in the schools, and who should be educated. The student may have weighed the pros and cons of each side of the issues and decided upon his own creed in each instance. The formation of a creed on such issues is essential, for no teacher can remain neutral about them. Although he might not place himself in either of the camps that represent the extremes, he will most certainly lean more to one side than the other. With more study and experience the student may someday change his creed, but that decision, too, will be opposed by many teachers and administrators.

A salutary lesson the student might learn from this chapter, then, is that any point of view on these very crucial issues in American education will find "worthy opponents." Therefore, the student's own creed must be based upon sound reasoning and adequate evidence lest he be easily swayed by specious arguments.

SELECTED READINGS

Blum, Virgil C., *Freedom of Choice in Education* (New York: Macmillan Co., 1958).
>One of the most comprehensive treatments of the rights of those attending independent schools to a just share of public funds for the support of their schools.

Burkhart, J., "The Dangers of Federal Aid to Education," *School and Society,* Vol. 82 (September 17, 1955), pp. 83–84.
>Lists the major disadvantages of federal aid to both public and independent schools.

Carpenter, W. W., and Capps, A. G., "The Case for Federal Support," *School Executive,* Vol. 75 (December, 1955), pp. 43–46.
>A defense of the thesis that the arguments for federal aid to public education far outweigh the arguments against such aid.

Cash, W. J., *The Mind of the South* (New York: Doubleday-Anchor Books, 1954).
>A thorough analysis of the beliefs and attitudes of Southerners concerning the equality of the races and the attendant educational problems arising from such beliefs and attitudes.

Conant, James B., *The American High School Today* (New York: McGraw-Hill Book Co., 1959).
>A report based on the results of a nationwide survey of the American

high school today. The author discusses many of the issues mentioned
in this chapter and suggests solutions to these problems.

Cressman, G. R., and Benda, Harold W., *Public Education in America* 2 ed.
(New York: Appleton-Century-Crofts, 1961), Chaps. I, IV, XVII.
These chapters point to issues involving federal aid, democracy in edu-
cation, and problems involving church-state relations.

Ehlers, H., and Lee, Gordon C., *Crucial Issues in Education* (New York:
Henry Holt & Co., 1959), Introduction and Chapters 5–8.
Provides a good selection of short statements, pro and con, on the issues
of federal aid, segregation, the purpose of education, and the education
of the gifted.

Morris, V., "Grass-roots-ism and the Public Schools," *School and Society*,
Vol. 85 (June 22, 1957), pp. 217–219.
A report on public opinion regarding the schools.

Rose, Arnold, *The Negro in America* (Boston: Beacon Press, 1956).
A thorough sociological analysis of the position of the Negro in America.

Scott, C. W., Hill, C. M., Burns, H. W., *The Great Debate* (Englewood
Cliffs, New Jersey: Prentice-Hall, 1959), Chaps. 2 and 5.
Chapter 2 has one section devoted to the issue of adjustment vs. knowledge as it relates to the role of the school in society. Chapter 5 gives the
pros and cons of selective education for the gifted.

Wright, J. C., "A Life Adjustment Program," *School Life*, Vol. 29, No. 6
(March, 1947), pp. 16–18.
A description and defense of a life-adjustment program in action.

Part II

THE ROLE OF PHILOSOPHY
IN EDUCATION

Chapter VII

PRE-CHRISTIAN EDUCATION

Many people unfamiliar with education today believe that present ideas, programs, and practices are of relatively recent origin. Such, however, is not the case. In fact, the Greek philosopher Plato (427?–347 B.C.) is probably the most important educational theorist in the entire history of education in the Western hemisphere. Some educational theorists even maintain that John Dewey (1859–1952) was the first thinker who successfully challenged the Platonic conception of education, which is based on the idea of intellectual classes.[1] Plato's belief that youth should be educated according to their intellectual ability has dominated the thinking of educators for twenty centuries. The curriculum content changed from time to time; methods of teaching changed now and then; but the "ideal education" of this remarkable man, Plato, still pervades the thinking of the majority of educational leaders in the Western world. (Education in the United States is the only major exception.)

It must be remembered that Plato lived at a time when Athenian democracy with its highly individualistic structure was crumbling before the forces of the well-organized and disciplined monarchies and aristocracies. Therefore, he concluded that only those who were "intellectually fit" should be entrusted with governing the state. These potential rulers were to be selected from all socioeconomic groups during their early years in school. The criteria used were: love of and interest in knowledge for its own sake; the ability to think in universal terms so as to see the interrelations between things; self-control; success in resisting evil; honesty; quickness in learning difficult material; physical strength and skill; and good citizenship.

---

[1] Undoubtedly, there are some similarities between Dewey's and Plato's recommendations for educational policy and practice. The basic differences between these outstanding philosophers are noted in Chapter X.

With such rigid qualifications, it is only natural that the vast majority of pupils fell by the educational wayside very early. But those who passed these tests were to be given the type of education which leads to the highest level of wisdom and justice and devotion to the common good (or the welfare of the state).

It is interesting to note that Plato believed that intellectual capacity was a divine gift; he likened highly intellectual people to vessels made of gold whereas the lower classes (guardians, soldiers) were compared to silver, and craftsmen (workers) to brass and iron. However, there was no reason why a "silver" parent could not have a "golden" son or vice versa. Therefore he felt that class distinctions based on intellectual prowess are both natural and good. They are based on "facts of nature" and the recognition of human value. There also is a recognition by Plato of the "equality of educational opportunity" so much in vogue today, for he insisted that the demands of justice entitled the children of poor parents to an education in keeping with their intellectual capacities, whether these be great or small.

To achieve the best results, the state should offer free public education where all may have an equal chance to demonstrate their abilities and limitations. He felt the classification according to ability should be completed before the twentieth year. But once the potential leaders had been selected, the state should spare no expense in the development of these elite for wholehearted and disinterested devotion to the common good. Although intelligence is the first prerequisite, it must be accompanied by the widest knowledge of men and their affairs, a spirit of service, and a subordination of personal gain.

In many respects, Plato advocates a very radical form of democracy, and modern critics often overlook his advocacy of "equal opportunity in education." They picture Plato as recommending that nearsighted, "ivory-tower" philosophers should rule the world. Not so! He wanted "intelligent, practical" rulers, and though he recognized that the perfect ruler was an ideal to be sought, he felt that the proper kind of education could bring one very near to this ideal. Historians of education also point out that Plato's specific recommendations for educational policy and practices never were implemented in any educational system. Rather each educational system interpreted Plato's ideas to fit its own educational goal.

His plan for education, the most important business in a man's life, includes recommendations for curriculum content. For Plato, the most important phase of education is in the nursery (how "modern" this idea is). Play activities should dominate the education of the child until he is ten years old. This important stage makes full use of environment designed to develop the proper attitude toward life. Children must be given broad opportunity for the free expression of any natural interest they might have in the arts, not as a matter of formal training but as play and use of the imagination. They might do needlework, painting, ceramics, and carving to develop a sense of form, propriety, order, and love for the beautiful. Stories of wisdom, courage, bravery, and fidelity should be told the children in order to place before them the best examples of these great human virtues. Stories as well as examples of drunkenness, crime, ugliness, and teaching should be kept from children. Even those great Greek classics extant at Plato's time should be expurgated so that children's minds and hearts might not be contaminated.

When formal instruction begins at ten years of age, the arts, especially music and literature, still are the center of the curriculum. But now the elements of good form, refinement, and excellence are presented very systematically. Also at this time, mathematics is introduced into the school program, for the purpose of developing unity, symmetry, and logical coherence into the thinking of the student. Plato also felt that physical education should be an essential part of the formal schooling, for students would become soft and effeminate unless there existed an adequate physical-culture program to insure the balance between firm muscles and grace, strength and delicacy.

Another very "democratic" feature of Plato's aristocratic educational program was that there must be no distinctions of sex. Women are to have the same privileges and opportunities as men in education, government, the professions, and athletics. In fact, he advocated that the state care for the children of women active in politics and other fields requiring full-time work.

As mentioned above, the selection of pupils for the different classes would take place at or about the age of twenty. After the ten years of the formal education which began at age ten, teachers should be able to decide which pupils had the ability to rule, which ones were qualified to become guardians (soldiers), and finally those who were to serve as craftsmen, professional people, and workers. The elite (future rulers) took a five-year liberal-arts course composed of music, arithmetic, plane and solid geometry, and astronomy designed chiefly to develop the powers of abstract thought. Then they proceeded to the study of dialectics (philosophy) as the culmination of their education for leadership. The guardians were given ten years of training for military service consisting of gymnastics, tactics, and also courses designed to foster devotion to the state. The lowest class — the professionals, tradesmen, and workers — were trained through an on-the-job apprentice program very similar to that used in the guilds of the Middle Ages, and somewhat comparable to the long-standing European apprentice-training program.

   To many readers, the most intriguing part of Plato's educational theory is the comparison of his ideas with existing educational patterns. Of course, such comparison is fraught with danger because of the great changes that have taken place in the social structure of the civilized world. But there are some features general enough to allow for comparison.

   a) Plato's plan begins with early training (in the nursery school) of the imagination under the influence of wholesome art, environment, and example.

   b) Beyond training in the basic skills given in the first five years of formal education, the emphasis was on development of "reasoning power" (creative thinking) rather than mere information.

   c) Education for leadership is dominated by intrinsic values (knowledge and beauty for their own sake) rather than instrumental values (utility).

   d) Great stress is laid upon education for the "good life" (ethical values) as well as upon physical education ("a sound mind in a sound body").

   e) The state has the first right and obligation in education: it must select the "gifted" from all socioeconomic ranks, and train and transfer leadership.

   f) Education is the most important and exalted function of the state since through it the common good can best be served.

   Following these rather broad outlines of the Platonic ideal in education, the similarity to medieval and humanistic education (see Chaps. VIII and IX) is easily noted. However, one would not expect to find any present-day national system of education striving for the same ideal. Yet students of comparative education feel that, with some modification due to cultural changes, most European systems always have been and still are Platonic in character.

The French system is usually presented as the best example of modern Platonism in education. The nursery schools devote themselves to the development of imagination through free play activities. The first formal education given in compulsory primary schools does not have as its goal the "conveying of information," as so many Americans believe. On the contrary, like Plato, French educators are convinced that information or factual knowledge is secondary to the goal of developing the intellectual powers of the pupils by "training," "enriching," and "broadening." Therefore, the primary school's ideal is not to teach many subjects, but to teach well and thoroughly what it does teach. They prefer solid knowledge to superficial opinion, and a few perfected skills to many half-learned ones.

Those of us who have visited France will attest to the fact that the French primary school does come very near this ancient Platonic ideal. Eighty-five percent of the people have had no education beyond the primary school (eight years), yet a casual conversation usually becomes an intellectual exercise. Many an American serviceman who was a college graduate found the French primary school graduate to be his equal in mastery of basic language and number skills, intellectual acumen, and curiosity and aesthetic taste. Probably Plato would recognize the goals of the French primary schools as a modernized version of his own stated goals for the first stage of formal education.

As Plato recommended, French educators effect a rather drastic weeding-out process at the end of the primary school period, since only about 15 percent of the pupils are admitted to the level of secondary education. Admission to this level is based upon rigorous examination to determine the student's knowledge of the *culture generale* and his abstract intellectual power.[2] Although the classical subjects have given way to more modern ones in the French secondary schools, the purpose of both the old and the new curricula is

---

[2] Since 1957 students can be admitted to secondary educational institutions upon the recommendation of their primary teachers. But "borderline" cases must take the qualifying examinations.

to develop the intellectual powers of the country's future leaders. For example, in a boys' secondary school, all the students take courses in classical and/or modern foreign languages, history, literature, and the sciences. In the final year, all take advanced mathematics and philosophy. Clearly these are not "fresh-air" courses, but involve rigid intellectual discipline. The demands upon the French student's intellectual ability in the secondary school generally exceed that in the typical American college. And only after the French student has successfully completed his secondary school curriculum can he apply for admission to French universities.

Thus, as in Plato's ideal *Republic*, only the intellectual elite will reach the top of the educational ladder. The vast majority of pupils will be disqualified by their lack of intellectual ability at the end of the primary school. Even some of the 15 percent admitted to the secondary level are eliminated during the seven-year course. Finally, the "cream of the intellectual crop" receives the highest training for leadership and service to the country in France's universities.

Another aspect of similarity is found in Plato's recommendation that education be a state function controlled by the central government. So too in France, educational policy and control emanate from Paris. All of the educational regions are directly responsible to the Minister of Education. This central control is so efficient that one particular item of the system is identical in the whole of France. Even in the private schools programs are identical to those of the state schools with the exception of religious instruction, for these schools are also under the control of the Minister of Education. The only aspect of the French education adapted to local needs is in the area of technical training (apprenticeships, etc.).

Yet another facet of the Platonic ideal is found in the French national system, namely, selection of the gifted from all socioeconomic levels. At least in theory, every French child is entitled to as much free education as his intellectual powers warrant. The French state considers it an obligation to subsidize any academically talented child in the hope that this child will use his talents for the good of the state in some position of leadership or professional service.

The passing of more than two thousand years has not dimmed the Platonic ideal. This fact is even more significant when one realizes that Spain, Italy, and the Latin American countries have educational systems which are similar in most respects to the French pattern. Furthermore, the vast colonial empire which France formerly controlled has adopted basically the same system. Even after independence was gained by the French colonies, the intellectualistic educational programs for leadership were still retained. Also a study of the educational systems of Germany and the Slavic and Scandinavian countries will reveal great similarity to the Platonic ideal. In all of these countries education is a state function, though not as centralized as in France. Education beyond the primary school is reserved for the selected few who demonstrate outstanding intellectual powers. Only these gifted students will receive advanced education, in preparation for leadership in the state and the exalted professions of medicine and law.

What may be even more astounding is the modified application of the Platonic ideal in those countries where egalitarianism is the watchword. Modern Soviet Russia presents the best picture of Plato's aristocratic system in a presumably egalitarian society. Just as Plato recommended, all children are under the tutelage of the state from infancy until they leave school. Since the 1958–1959 Khrushchev reform, all must attend school for eight years, after which they enroll in a combined work-school program for three years. Only the exceptionally gifted students are excused from the combined work-school program. They immediately begin specialized education in preparation for university entrance. Those who complete the three-year work schools are also entitled to a university education if they can meet the exceptionally high entrance requirements. If they are not qualified for university work they may attend one of the many different kinds of technical institutes, which prepare them chiefly for those jobs demanded by industry and mechanized agriculture.

The main point in this short summary of the modern Russian educational system is not to compare the actual curricular patterns, but to illustrate that in Russia only the most gifted are to be selected and educated by the state at no expense to the individual, and that this intellectual elite is to be trained for service to the state in positions of political and scientific leadership. Such a position involves an admission on the part of the Soviet leaders that all men are not equal and that life in a classless society has not brought about the "leveling-off" process so basic to Marxist environmentalism.

But one need not go so far afield to find signs of a somewhat modified return to the Platonic ideal in education. In Chapter X it is mentioned that American education constitutes the first large-scale experiment in universal education at the secondary level. The philosophy of John Dewey is presented as the first thoroughgoing anti-Platonism in education. But during the past decade the number of voices raised in the educational ranks for a return to educational elitism has sharply increased. Whereas during the 1920's, 1930's, and 1940's educational curricula were geared to the "average" student, and expansive specialized remedial programs were established for the retarded, now there are many elementary and secondary schools putting special emphasis (and funds) on the education of the gifted. The cry has been raised that our graduates of secondary schools and higher educational institutions cannot compete with those of European countries (especially Russia); the gifted have been neglected and submerged in the "masses"; let us educate our gifted, at government expense, for service to America in positions of leadership in government and the learned professions. Certain in-service courses, summer institutes, and government sponsored and financed workshops have devoted their entire time and manpower to the education of the gifted.[3] Colleges and universities with bulging enrollments no longer enroll a "representative sample" of the population, but warn prospective students that they must have the proper intellectual and academic qualifications before they can be admitted.

Certainly the American college curriculum is a far cry from that recommended by Plato. Nevertheless, the belief that the general school system should be supported and controlled by the state, and the lower levels used to select the "intellectual elite" who will be trained for service to the state is ideologically Platonic. Also, as Plato maintained, it is generally held that men are born unequal at least in intellectual talent, and that the educational program should be constructed upon this "reality of nature."

Many educators favoring programs for the gifted may not concede that the programs they are recommending bear any similarity to the Platonic ideal. However, a close scrutiny of some gifted-student programs will reflect modernized adaptations of the great philosopher's ideals. For example, one of America's well-known ex-

---

[3] The National Defense Education Act is an example of the increased concern the federal government has shown for education of the intellectual elite.

perimental schools begins the process of identifying the academically talented students (the top of 15 to 20 percent) at the seventh-grade level. But even before this grade level, teachers are requested to spot the bright pupils and be prepared to recommend them for special programs. Standardized tests of intelligence, achievement, and other areas are coupled with school grades and teachers' judgments regarding the students' intellectual, emotional, and social maturity.

For a student to be classified as gifted at this school, his scores on intelligence tests should indicate that he has exceptional ability (IQ of 125 or above). His scores on standardized achievement tests should be in the upper 10 percent of the class. Each of the academic areas uses the results of the subtests to ferret out the gifted in the respective subject area. For example, the English and social-studies departments are more concerned with the students' "verbal" abilities; the mathematics and science departments expect outstanding ability in quantitative reasoning. Further selection is effected in the gifted group by distinguishing the "very able" from the "very most able," with the latter group being afforded special opportunities for placement in very advanced courses.

Once the intellectually elite have been identified they are placed in honors classes in those subject-matter areas where they have demonstrated outstanding ability. These honors classes do not contain any "average" or below-average students. Such enforced segregation enables the gifted students and their teachers to move ahead very rapidly and probe very deeply into the subject matter. The gifted student is challenged by the presence of other able students and is not held back by the slow and average learner. Every opportunity is afforded him to forge ahead as rapidly as he can. For example, an eighth grader can begin with algebra, then complete plane and solid geometry, then take advanced algebra, trigonometry, and some logic, and, in his twelfth year, take calculus and analytics.

Because of the rapid pace at which some of the students progress, college-level courses are offered in English, European and American history, mathematics, biology, physics, chemistry, and modern languages. These courses stress more than mere *memoriter* materials. Besides learning the "facts," students develop more abstract concepts and generalizations. The ability to organize and integrate the matter within the subject area and with other related subjects is stressed. Such advanced abilities are developed by penetrating discussions as well as lengthy and difficult term papers and essays. The various aspects of deductive and inductive reasoning, critical thinking, and problem-solving play an important role in all the honors classes. Seminars encourage the students to carry on independent research and study in special areas, sometimes over a long period of time. Small groups of students work together on projects without the help of the teacher, thus preparing themselves for leadership in their own areas of specialization and in civic affairs.

Finally, the program stresses the value of learning for its own sake. Great prestige is accorded academic achievement. No longer is a boy considered effeminate if he is an outstanding student in English or modern languages. Scholarship brings more prestige than athletic achievement or juvenile notoriety. Student attitude toward high achievement is positive rather than derogatory. The same attitude seems to have been "caught" by the community itself: the gifted need special consideration, for upon them will come the leaders of the next generation.[4]

What is "Platonic" about this program? Note that early identification of the gifted is most important so that, just as Plato recommended, the future leaders and scholars might be given separate educational consideration. After these gifted have been identified they become a "privileged class," deserving of the best and most advanced educational program the state can offer. Furthermore, these elite are not to be hindered in their progress toward intellectual and moral excellence by those of low or average ability. Segregation of the gifted, then, becomes a general educational principle based on the "nature of human nature." Some human beings possess greater intellectual gifts than others, and these youth have a right to greater consideration, with an attendant responsibility for greater service to the country in the areas of civic and professional leadership.

But the reader might ask: "Do not all educational philosophies advocate special consideration for the gifted?" The answer is: "Definitely not!" As indicated in Chapter X, the philosophers of the "new education," especially John Dewey and his followers, are emphatically opposed to the elitism of Plato and those educational philosophies based upon Plato's theories. In opposition to this elitism, the advocates of the new education propose a more egali-

---

[4] A more detailed report on this program can be obtained from the Superintendent's Office, Evanston Township Schools, Evanston, Ill.

tarian approach. In general they believe that if all people are given the same educational opportunities the great difference in individuals will gradually disappear. Therefore they affirm that those who have special talents should not be segregated from the regular classes, but adaptations for these individual differences should be made within each class. If pupils of all ability levels are found within the same class, no one shall deem himself superior to others. In this way the egalitarian ideal can be maintained; the pupil with special talents will use them for the good of the class; the low-ability student will learn much from his more fortunate fellow pupil; the general level of intelligence will gradually be raised and, as some maintain, gross, individual differences will eventually disappear.

In conclusion one might say that most educational theorists may be divided into two categories, the Platonic and anti-Platonic, in their views on education of the gifted. Practically all educators up to the twentieth century can be classified as favoring Plato's view. Since the beginning of the twentieth century most educators in the more conservative or traditional camp still favor the approach of the great Greek philosopher (whether they use his name or not), whereas those in the liberal or progressive movement in education are steadfastly opposed to the Platonic view. Even after the advent of the "hot and cold wars" of the twentieth century which have forced American schools to become more "academic," the advocates of the new education have held out against segregation of the gifted.

It is granted by most educational historians that Aristotle made few changes in the Platonic scheme of education. True, Aristotle's general philosophy represents a major break with Platonism. But such is not the case in educational theory. On the other hand, Roman education, though it was greatly influenced by Platonic educational theory, was basically different from it in several respects. Rome's role in the history of ideas is most evident in the areas of law, administration, and practical achievements such as architecture and engineering. Even more important, however, is the role the Romans played in spreading civilization in the Western world. Their achievements in this respect are very much like those of Europe of the eighteenth and nineteenth centuries in civilizing the newly discovered American continents.

The main characteristic differentiating Roman from Greek edu-

cation was its practical bent. The Romans did not believe in culti-
vating literature for its own sake. Grammar, rhetoric, and logic were
studied to prepare one for political life and not because they developed the intellectual powers of the student or because they were
worthwhile in themselves. The study of ethics was very popular
because it taught people how to live the "good life."

The elementary school years of Roman children were devoted to
the mastery of the basic skills, reading, writing, and simple computation. Such training usually required six years and served as the
basic prerequisite for the secondary school (grammar school). The
basic content of the curriculum of the secondary school was language
structure and literature. This simple pattern later developed into
the well-known *trivium* of grammar, rhetoric, and logic. In the
course of time, the trivium was supplemented by the *quadrivium*:
astronomy, arithmetic, geometry, and music.

Although, at first glance, these subjects might appear very im-
practical or theoretical, especially at the secondary level, the Romans
definitely taught them for very practical reasons. Arithmetic and
geometry were designed for carrying on business and simple surveying and measuring. Astronomy was studied because it enabled the
student to determine the location of days, months, and years in
constructing calendars. Music was intended to develop the student's
understanding of poetry, which in turn was meant to enhance his
oratorical style. Roman schools of higher education had the same
practical approach as the lower educational institutions since their
courses were devoted chiefly to medicine, law, architecture, and
mechanics. Because of this pragmatic bent, Roman education bears
great resemblance to the American pattern.

To illustrate this similarity further, one need not go beyond the
the works of the great Roman orator, Quintilian, who lived in the
first century after Christ. First, he believed that most pupils had
adequate native ability to learn, and if they failed to do so it was
because of the lack of skill on the part of the teacher. Second, the
teacher was directed to study the needs, tastes, and mental capacities
of the students and adjust his teaching to them. Third, the natural
motivation of play should be used to the fullest extent in the education of young children. To implement this theory large ivory letters
were used as playthings so that learning the alphabet would be
pleasant for the pupils. Fourth, good example given by teachers

and found in literature should incite the pupil to good behavior as well as to good oratorical style. Fifth, corporal punishment was not for pupils but for animals and slaves. In fact, Quintilian maintained, if students were given adequate time for recreation and play, most would be quite willing to study, and punishment would be unnecessary. Furthermore, he felt many graces could be used to learn subject matter as well as to develop good character traits in youth. Finally, he favored instruction in classrooms of public schools over private schools or tutorial instruction given at home, for he felt the advantages of instruction given in groups outweighed its disadvantages. Even in classes with many students, he argued that the pupil must do his own reading, writing, thinking, and studying, and that the presence of other students challenged him to doing better work. He also felt that the bad example given by some pupils in school was not as bad, and certainly no worse, than that given by many parents at home.

Quintilian's emphasis on the school's responsibility for teaching the pupil "how to live the good life" also bears great similarity to the modern American school's goal of "living democracy" in the classroom. Both objectives give education a strong ethical purpose, essentially differentiating it from Greek and humanistic education with the development of intellectual powers as the main purpose. This pragmatic objective of developing "good men" and "good citizens" was very evident in the American schools of the 1930's, 1940's, and 1950's. It was argued by the American advocates of this old Roman goal that the school should assume its share of this task, formerly left to the home and church, and seriously devote its time to teaching people how to live the good life in a democratic society.

Because of this new outlook many schools, both public and private, introduced citizenship courses designed to prepare the student for worthy home and community membership. About 1945 "life-adjustment" courses were introduced into most schools at the junior high school level.[5] Courses covering home decoration and maintenance flourished. Cooking, sewing, practical arts and crafts, and preparation for marriage and family life became an important

---

[5] See "Prosser Resolution" of Committee on Vocational Education, June 1, 1945, in J. D. Hull, *A Primer of Life Adjustment Education* (Chicago: American Technical Society, 1949).

part of the high school program. Credit was given for such courses on the same basis as for the traditional subjects of mathematics, languages, sciences, and history. Even these academic subjects were given a practical slant. Teachers emphasized the great value that mathematics would have in making a family budget, computing the interest on a new stove, car, or house; a knowledge of science would enable the student to understand the complicated products of science found in home and the community; correct language usage in the mother tongue in studying a foreign language would enhance the student's job opportunities as well as his leisure-time activities. History and other "social-studies" courses were designed to help the student solve contemporary social problems rather than to master the subject-matter content of history, political science, geography, economics, and sociology.

A cursory glance at the college and university curricula of twentieth-century America also bears out the same similarity. The students, and often the professors, usually ask: "How useful is this course?" "Will it enable me to get a job after I leave college?" "Why should I spend four years in college when I can make just as much money without college attendance?" Because of this concern for the "bread-and-butter" aspect of postsecondary school education, even the "liberal-arts" courses have resorted to motivating students by emphasizing the practical value of the content. Such comments as these were common: "You will be able to enjoy literature in your leisure time." "Industry wants college graduates who have a broad educational background." "The United States Foreign Service and the United Nations prefer employees who are fluent in a foreign language." These and similar statements suggest the strong pragmatic emphasis in all phases of contemporary American higher education.

Perhaps another reason for the similarity in the educational outlook of the Roman and American people might be found in the similarity of the political role both play in their respective civilizations. Rome represented an amalgamation of all the cultures of the time. Upon her shoulders rested the political leadership of the civilized world. There was great demand for technical know-how. Great wealth and a strong desire to maintain and even raise the standard of living prodded citizens to follow those pursuits that "paid off" well. Great amounts of money and resources had to be spent to defend the empire from military attack. So, too, in the

America of the twentieth century one finds the same conditions. American culture is an amalgamation of European (and even Asiatic) cultures which resulted from immigation. Because of American success in the world wars of the first half of the twentieth century, political leadership in the Western world has become her lot. There exists a great demand for technical knowledge and skill both at home and abroad. The natural resources of the American continent and the industriousness of the people have brought about unprecedented heights in the standard of living, and an insatiable desire for the material benefits that a technological civilization offers. The military threat from without has forced the American people to spend great amounts of money and resources for the defense of their own way of life and that of their allies. It is no small wonder, then, that both Roman and American education have a very "practical" orientation.

Will the decline of American culture follow a pattern similar to that of the decline and fall of Rome? The answer to this most provocative question is left to the "students of society" and the history of the centuries to come.

Summary

Modern education in the Western world is greatly indebted to the educators of the Greek and Roman world. The Greek emphasis upon the "things of the mind" was especially prominent in the theologically oriented education of the predominantly Christian centuries. Although the Romans did not completely divorce their educational goals from the intellectual ideals of the Greeks, the practical concerns of building and governing an empire called for a more utilitarian educational system designed to prepare civil servants, engineers, lawyers, and architects.

These twin goals of intellectual development and preparation for a job have been quite evident in American education. At one time or another one might have been more influential in the development of American education. The most recent trend seems to be in the direction of greater emphasis on scholarship (intellectual development), especially in mathematics and the sciences. Perhaps, then, after fifty years of pragmatic education, the American school is once again becoming Platonic.

SELECTED READINGS

Butts, R. F., *A Cultural History of Western Education*, 2 ed. (New York: McGraw-Hill Book Co., 1955), Chaps. II–IV.
These chapters delve into the social and intellectual foundations of Greek and Roman education.
Cole, Luella, *A History of Education* (New York: Rinehart Co., 1950), Chaps. II–IV.
A most interesting account of Greek and Roman education with many examples of the actual practices, curricula, and physical conditions of the schools of ancient times.
Good, H. G., *A History of Western Education*, 2 ed. (New York: Macmillan Co., 1960), Chaps. II and III.
Gives the highlights of educational events in the era of Greek and Roman education.
Kane, W. T., *History of Education*, rev. ed. (Chicago: Loyola University Press, 1954), Chaps. III and IV.
A good summary of the achievements of Greek and Roman educational theory and practice.
Marrou, H. I., *A History of Education in Antiquity* (New York: Sheed & Ward, 1956), Part I, Chap. VI; Part II, Chaps. I–XI; Part III, Chaps. I–VIII.
A thorough study of the educational principles and practices of Greek and Roman schools.
McCormick, P. J., and Cassidy, F. P., *History of Education* (Washington, D. C.: Catholic Education Press, 1946), Chaps. VII and VIII.
Detailed account of the historical foundations of Greco-Roman educational institutions.
Uhlich, Robert, *History of Educational Thought* (New York: American Book Co., 1950), pp. 1–89.
A most penetrating and understanding analysis of the philosophical foundations of Greek and Roman education by an admirer of classical education.

Chapter VIII

CHRISTIAN EDUCATION

It has been suggested that the two major events in the history of ideas since the beginning of recorded history are the appearance of Christianity and Communism. Indeed, Greek and Roman cultural achievements constituted an important landmark along the road of human history. Likewise, the religious beliefs of the Hebrews were most significant in molding the mind of civilized man. But these influences were either absorbed or overwhelmed by Christianity to such an extent that their main effect on Western culture came through Christianity. That Christianity dominated the culture of the Western world during the first nineteen centuries of our era is a matter of record. And that Communism seems to be the first major threat to Christian culture is recognized by Christian thinkers. It is to the educational contributions of this Christian culture that this chapter is devoted.

EARLY CHRISTIAN EDUCATION

Obviously there was no complete break in the continuity of education because of the appearance of Christianity. Eras of education flow into one another with modifications, rejections, and assimilation of ideals and practices put to the service of a new ideology. Many of the evils and ills of the old culture made fertile soil for sowing the seed of Christian life. The immorality attributed to pagan gods and corruption in high places motivated many of the educated class of pagans to look elsewhere for an ideological haven.

As noted in Chapter VII, the Greeks placed their major educational emphasis on the "things of the mind" and Roman education was geared to the practical jobs of governing and building. However, it must be kept in mind that this generalization about the "intellectuality and practicality" of Greek and Roman education respectively does not infer that the Greeks had no "practical" concerns and the Romans no "intellectual" concerns. On the contrary, the Greeks firmly believed that their educational programs should "produce results" in ordering the individual's personal life and the life of the community. Similarly, the Romans did not divorce their practical tasks from the ethical-metaphysical bases from which they were derived. Because of disillusionment with these goals, many noble-minded people gave up everything to join the early Christians. It is not difficult to understand why the early Christian educator rejected practically everything that these older cultures stood for and concentrated on the life of the spirit. In fact, Jesus Christ Himself started from the very opposite pole of the Greek and Roman thinkers. He rejected self-reliance on reason, physical strength, political power, and wealth in favor of man's reliance on the grace and paternal care of one Supreme Being. This God was not a frivolous and sensuous being like the anthropomorphic gods of the Greeks and Romans, but the all-perfect Creator of all existence, natural and supernatural. Also, Christ went far beyond the rather cold, legalistic system of moral and ritual prescriptions of the Old Testament based on the fear of an all-just, all-powerful, and at times revengeful God. He portrayed God as a loving Father, the true parent of all men. The concept of the brotherhood of all men flowed directly from this new interpretation of "God the Father — man the son" relationship. Thus all men achieved a basic equality before God, regardless of their birth or station in life.

That such a reinterpretation of the relationship of the Deity to man would have great appeal to the lower classes is obvious. But, strangely enough, many of the educated and upper-class pagans were attracted by the doctrines of brotherhood, charity, self-denial, and "otherworldliness." But the cultured Roman and Greek encountered great difficulty in accepting the paradox of an almighty God submitting to the humiliating death by crucifixion — the "folly of the cross." What could be more degrading than for a God to assume human form and then die the ignominious death of the cross at the hands of mere men? In spite of this real difficulty the educated converts from paganism were attracted by the many anti-Greek and anti-Roman features of the new faith. But the cultural heritage of the civilized world could not be shed like a cloak. Thus, early in the Christian era, the leaders were divided into two groups. One group felt that Greek and Roman culture contained much that was in harmony with Christian theology. Furthermore, the philosophy of the ancient cultures was not only a reflection of man's eternal search for truth but actually had discovered and propounded many truths acceptable to the new creed. If these truths could serve as a foundation for a Christian philosophy of life, they should be utilized to the utmost.

In opposition to the first position, members of the other group of Christian leaders were convinced that the Greco-Roman culture and Christian living were mutually exclusive. They viewed philosophy as the outgrowth of human pride based on man's reliance of his own rational powers. They considered the Greek and Roman way of life as internally bound up with the search for wealth and sensual pleasure. As evidence for this view they pointed to the literature of the heathen culture, which not only sanctioned immorality and atrocity but veritably placed it on a pedestal as a model for youth.

In the medieval Church the Franciscan friars again led a movement for a return to the simple life of poverty, self-denial, and distrust of the purely intellectual and cultural. They placed the emphasis on the love of God rather than on knowledge of Him. The ensuing battle between voluntarism and intellectualism bears great similarity to the struggle between the early Christian protagonists of Greek and Roman culture and those who wished to divest themselves entirely of that heritage.

This basic difference in regard to the proximate goal of education will be evident throughout the rest of this chapter. Stated in modern terms, each side seeks to defend the intellectualist or voluntarist emphasis regarding the main features of the educational program. One group maintains that the goal of the Christian school is to develop the intellectual powers of the students and give them a basic knowledge and understanding of the important subjects, including religion, sciences, social sciences, mathematics, the humanities, and languages. Note, the emphasis is on knowledge and understanding as the prime responsibility of the school toward its clientele. The implementation of this knowledge for living a good Christian life is not considered the school's major responsibility, although it is a partner in the enterprise. The church, the home, and other agencies must see to it that the student "lives what he learns." In this view of the role of the Christian school, the function of formal education is limited to man's knowing powers, and the training of man's will is of secondary importance. Within this limited area, they feel the school can do a more thorough job. They can assess the finished product (the student) on the basis of what he knows and thus judge the success of their teaching. If the students have mastered the basic disciplines (as measured by tests), the school has achieved its major goal.

In opposition to the intellectualist position, some Christian educators have asserted that the proximate aim of the school is to develop in the student the habits of good Christian living. The advocates of this point of view say that knowledge and understanding is one of the goals of the Christian school but not the most important one: Christian living is of prime importance. That means the school will be considered successful only if its attempts to get the student to live the full Christian life have been achieved. To attain this goal the school will have to develop those attitudes, appreciations, and habits — as well as knowledge and understanding — which will enable the student to be a practical Christian. The practical Christian is one who attends church regularly and "lives the liturgy" as a Christian businessman, laborer, or professional; he is a good citizen of his community, state, nation, and the world; he is a worthy parent.[1]

In many respects the modern conditions influencing the rise of the "Christian living" movement are similar to those of ancient Christianity: (1) The home has lost much of its influence over the life of the children, the paganizing influence of the modern world on the home has disrupted the family control over the children. Modern means of transportation and media of communication are paganizing the minds of youth to such an extent that the school must assume the responsibility for insuring proper beginnings in Christian living. (2) Civic life has been so secularized in recent years that Christian principles no longer influence human relations. Witness the breakdown of public morality as evidenced by corrupt practice in high office, widespread divorce, juvenile delinquency, racial conflict, and international distrust. The best means for counteracting such evils is by "living" Christian principles in the school rather than just "learning about" them. (3) Modern industry has

---

[1] For expression of these points of view see: Kevin O'Brien, *The Proximate Aim of Education* (Milwaukee: The Bruce Publishing Co., 1958), and V. E. Smith, *The School Examined* (Milwaukee: The Bruce Publishing Co., 1960).

dehumanized man, almost equating him with the machine. The Christian view of labor must be instilled in youth so that as a future laborer he will bring Christ back into the workaday world. The schools must strive to achieve this goal, since the working parent is, in most instances, a product of secularistic technology. But the school cannot change this view of labor simply by talking about it. All school labors and activities must exemplify the principles of Christian living, thus enabling the student to influence the world of work and business when he becomes a part of it.

So, in many respects, the problems facing Christian education today involve its leaders in the same dilemma as the early Christian thinkers: should education concern itself primarily with the development of Christian living or should intellectual development be its goal? If one is emphasized or preferred as the proximate aim of education, then the other assumes a minor role, and so the conflict which began in the first centuries of the Church concerning the role that secular (pagan) learning should play in the Christian school is still with us (and probably always will be).

To return to the topic of this chapter, during the first three centuries of the Christian era there was no formal structure for educating members of the Church. Since no recognition was granted by the Roman empire to the Christian religion, it was impossible to establish institutions for learning. Most of the teaching at this time consisted in preaching the Gospels and giving religious instructions to those who wished to join the Christian Church. The catechumenal schools were formed in order to meet the latter needs, as all Christians had to be instructed in the basic doctrines of the Church before they could be baptized. The bishops, priests, and deacons served as the teachers in these schools; and as the number of converts grew, candidates for the priesthood and even laymen were added to the catechumenal staffs.

The students in these schools were divided into groups: (1) those who expressed an interest in learning about the Christian faith, and (2) those who had received instruction in the doctrine of the Church and were seeking baptism. The instruction for the first group might be compared to modern "inquiry classes," and were not designed to probe the depth of the Christian religion. Rather, the emphasis was placed on simple explanations of Christian doctrine, a statement of the basic requirements of fasts, attendance at services, moral directives, and an explanation of the liturgy of the Church. The second group, those preparing for baptism, received much more thorough training in these areas, and also had to prove their worthiness during a relatively long probationary period.

None of the catechumenal schools were concerned with the teaching of reading, writing, and other school subjects of the day. If the Christians received any instruction in these areas it was acquired in the state schools. Since the majority of the Christians were from the lower classes, who could neither read nor write, all teaching and testing were done orally.

In general, the very informal structure of the catechumenal school allowed it to achieve its major objective, the preparation of converts for baptism. As the demand arose for apologists in the early Church, more formalized educational institutions arose. These catechetical schools, as they were called, were usually located in the bishop's see city. In addition to teaching the doctrines of the Christian religion, the catechetical schools eventually gave instruction in history, literature, philosophy, and natural sciences. The inclusion of these subjects was necessitated by the pressing demand for a rebuttal of attacks made by pagan thinkers on the beliefs of the Christians. It was from these schools that the great leaders of the early Christian Church came. Any student of ancient history will have heard of the catechetical schools of Alexandria, Caesarea, Antioch, Edessa, Carthage, and Jerusalem. The names of Origen, Clement of Alexandria, Gregory Thaumaturgus, Justin Martyr, St. Cyril, St. Basil, and other "Fathers of the Church" are generally associated with these famous schools.

A point of interest in the educational proposals of the Fathers of the Church with application to modern times lies in their stated preference for Christian schools rather than public schools. St. John Chrysostom, for instance, agreed that parents might permit their children to attend public schools if they were certain the teachers would concern themselves with the religious and moral training of the children. But if the parents might have no guarantee that the virtue of their children would be safeguarded, they "ought not to send their children where they will learn vice before they learn science, and where in acquiring learning of very small value they will lose what is far more precious, their integrity of soul." He believed that there were only two alternatives: "a liberal education which you may get by sending your children to public schools, or the salvation of their souls" which can be assured only by sending them to the Christian schools. He added, however, that if a liberal education can be integrated with the educational enterprise of saving the child's soul, it should be done. But if a choice must be made between a liberal education and a Christian education, the latter is to be preferred.[2]

The modern Christian educator might interpret St. John Chrysostom's directive to mean that the only true liberal education is a Christian education. Hence, if an incompatibility ever arises between the two, the "liberal" aspect must be eliminated in favor of the "Christian."

Because of a revival of paganism (secularism) in the modern world some Christian churches, chiefly Lutheran and Catholic, have been faced with the same dilemma. The answer to the dilemma was stated very clearly in the encyclical on Christian education of youth by Pope Pius XI: ". . . It is clear that there can be no true education which is not wholly directed to man's last end" (salvation) and parents should "above all refuse to send them [their children] to those schools in which there is danger of imbibing the deadly poison of impiety." ". . . the so-called 'neutral' or 'lay' school, from which religion is excluded, is contrary to the fundamental principles of education."[3]

One great educator of this period, often neglected by modern "Christian realists," deserves special mention. Because of his adherence to Platonic Idealism, St. Augustine does not have a large following among those modern Christian philosophers who consider St. Thomas Aquinas their guide. But all Christians recognize his greatness in the areas of ascetical theology, exegesis, and dogmatic theology.

As a pagan youth he received an excellent education in the liberal arts, and became a brilliant teacher in both Africa and Italy. At the age of thirty-three, he became an ardent Christian and applied all his extraordinary talent to the salvation of souls. His well-known writings, The City of God, Confessions, Retractions, De Magistro, Catechizing the Uninstructed, and Christian Doctrine contain the elements of a unitary philosophy and practice for education. As an

---

[2] Gaume (ed.), St. John Chrysostom, Vol. 1, p. 115 ff.
[3] Five Great Encyclicals (New York: The Paulist Press, 1939), pp. 39, 46, 60.

experienced teacher, he was well equipped to discuss the many-faceted aspects of education. For example, he delved into many topics that are now treated in courses such as educational psychology, philosophy of education, and even educational methods. He discussed, for example, the nature of man, the role of the senses in learning, the nature and place of memory in learning, the thinking process, authority and discipline in education. His advice to the teachers of catechumens is surprisingly up to date. He admonished those teachers to center all their teaching around one basic concept; he insisted that the instruction be adjusted to the individual differences of the pupils; he deemphasized rote memorization; he advised teachers of the importance of attending to pupil's physical comfort, building instruction around his interests, and keeping him active; he warned teachers not to try to cover too much subject matter, but rather achieve great depth in treating the important ideas; he held that an exclusive appeal to the intellect is inadequate — emotions, attitudes, and ideals must be brought into play and cultivated.[4]

St. Augustine, unlike the great Tertullian, was firmly convinced that much secular knowledge — especially rhetoric, literature, and philosophy — could be used by the Christian teacher to further the spiritual development of his pupils: "Moreover, if those who are called philosophers, and especially the Platonists have said what is true and in harmony with our Faith, we are not to shrink from it but to claim it for our own use. . . . In the same way all branches of heathen learning have not only false and superstitious fancies . . . but they contain also liberal instruction which is better adapted to the use of truth, and some most excellent precepts of morality; and some truths in regard even to the worship of God are found among them."[5]

If one were to place St. Augustine in one of the two camps of Christian education mentioned above, he most certainly would favor those proposing "Christian living" as the proximate aim of education. His use of secular learning is to promote the Christian life within the soul, not to develop the intellectual powers of the students. Whatever secular learning is employed is made subservient

---

[4] See St. Augustine, "On Catechizing the Uninstructed," passim, Works of St. Augustine, M. Dods (ed.) (Edinburgh: T. T. Clark, 1873), pp. 265–335.
[5] St. Augustine, "On Christian Doctrine," op. cit., pp. 75 and 76.

to the goal of developing Christian virtues rather than intellectual virtues.

A final aspect of Augustinian educational theory, based upon his view of knowledge, is found in some modern Christian (especially Protestant) theories of teaching. St. Augustine conceived the role of the teacher to be one of assisting the student to find truth and knowledge within himself. He insisted that the student did not learn from the teacher in the strict sense. Rather, the teacher used words or symbols which incite the pupil to find such referents within himself. Basically then, teaching is a process of helping the student develop his selfhood.

As the Church became recognized by the civil authority and most of the peoples of the civilized world joined the Church, the need for a defense of Christian doctrines waned. With little or no demand for apologists, the schools gradually disappeared around the eighth century A.D. Many educators believe that if these higher-level schools had been redesigned to meet the needs of the changing times, the Dark Ages would not have been so dark. The tradition of scholarship, erudition, and outstanding teaching was established, and might have been redirected to serve the Church and society. The gradual weakening and eventual disappearance of these schools should serve as an example of what can happen to any educational structure which does not rise to meet the challenges of the times. Obviously, the weakening of the catechetical schools cannot be given all the blame for the Dark Ages. Waves of barbarians swept over Europe; Greco-Roman culture was crumbling; and, as Father Kane maintains, the Church's hierarchy and clergy did not support needed educational reform.[6]

But the passing of the early Christian schools did not mean the death of early Christian ideals. Many historians have pointed up the influence of Christ's teaching on subsequent centuries. Certainly, the great stream of Christian mysticism, both Catholic and Protestant, had its origin in early Christian education and opened avenues of fruitful contemplation on the meaning of self-realization and self-fulfillment.[7] Perhaps the very simplicity of society in early Christian times did not call for penetrating analysis of the relation of the in-

---

[6] See W. Kane, S.J., *History of Education* (Chicago: Loyola University Press, 1954), p. 76.

[7] See Rom 15:2–12: recognition given to "individuality."

dividual to society. Similarly not much by way of social reforms came from the early Christian schools. But the social implications of Christ's teachings in the early centuries actually did result in "revolutionary" doctrines. Even though the doctrine of the "Fatherhood of God and brotherhood of man" did not eliminate the practices of slavery so common at the time, St. Paul admonished that "Masters be just and fair, knowing that you too have a master in heaven" (Col 5:1) and "Masters, act in the same way toward them and forbear threatening, knowing that both you and they have a Master in heaven and that with him there is no respect of persons" (Eph 6:9). Whether a more forceful stand by the early Christian schools might have eliminated slavery is a controversial subject among historians; nevertheless, these schools did abolish it in theory by insisting on the equality of all men before God. No distinction was made between slave and freeman in the early Church. In fact, some slaves rose to the ranks of episcopal leadership, and they and their fellow bishops were the champions of man's freedom of conscience against the powerful Roman state.

Another problem, that of the political organization of the state which the modern Christian considers quite important, was not given a prominent place in early Christian education. But some modern Christian thinkers (with the advantage of historical hindsight) have pointed up the predominantly democratic character of Christ's teachings as they apply to the political sphere. Again, the basic equality of the sons of God is proposed as the fundamental principle of all good government. Consequently, any dictatorial or totalitarian rule is considered un-Christian because it violates the free nature of the individuals subject to that rule.[8] The fact that the revival of democratic ideals in the sixteenth and seventeenth centuries has its origin in Christian as well as Deistic thought seems to suggest that the seeds of political democracy can grow within the Christian context even though no explicitly democratic principles were taught by the early Christian educators. But some social doctrines taught and practiced in the early Christian schools do have a message for modern times. One social doctrine fostered by the early schools is exemplified in the Christian practice of sharing the

---

[8] J. Maritain, Man and the State (Chicago: University of Chicago Press, 1951). One interpretation given to Maritain's thesis in this book is the compatibility of the Christian and democratic "faiths."

goods of this earth with one's less fortunate fellowman. St. Paul's Epistle to the Corinthians (1 Cor 10:24) admonishes: "Let none seek his own profit, but his neighbor's." Similarly he warns the rich "to do good, to be rich in good works, to give easily, to communicate to others" (1 Tm 6:7, 18). Although the experiment of giving all one's wealth and property to the community fund was short-lived, the fundamental assumption that all material goods belonged to God has its social effects. The earthly possessor of these goods was merely their dispenser, and it behooved him to share these "temporary holdings" with the brethren. A perusal of a work on the lives of the saints will show that every one of them took this counsel very seriously. Even though many of these great saints possessed great wealth, they lived very frugal lives and considered it their Christian duty to minister to the poor, the sick, the widowed, and the orphaned. Many, like St. Francis of Assisi, gave all their possessions to the poor, much to the dismay of their families and friends. Even to this day, in spite of the selfishness of some individual Christians, all of the Christian churches have been in the forefront of the many movements and organizations to help the underprivileged. It is a gross oversimplification to explain away this basic Christian belief by saying, as some opponents do, that this is a means of "buying converts."

One more ancient Christian ideal with implications for the modern world concerns discriminatory beliefs and practices. Africans, Indians, Orientals, as well as Greeks and Romans were not only accepted in the Church but considered equal.[9] Undoubtedly some Christians of the times did not abide by this precept and even attempted to base discriminatory practices on a biblical foundation, just as they do today. But certainly the advocates of discrimination cannot point to the life of Christ in seeking grounds for these beliefs. He not only mingled with people regarded as inferior, such as the Samaritans, but He actually eulogized the "Good Samaritan" in the parable. All of Christ's words and works as well as the practices of the Christian schools constitute practical and theoretical refutations of discrimination on the basis of racial or national origin, class status, creed, or color.

No student of history would ever claim that this noble ideal of

---

[9] With God "there is no respect for persons" (Eph 6:9). See also Eph 2:14–22; Acts 2.

the *basic* equality of men has been preached and defended by all Christians. Down through the centuries of the Christian era one Christian sect has persecuted another; Christians of the same sect have regarded certain members as "inferior" because of color or race; Christians have set up economic boycotts of non-Christians; much innocent blood has flowed in wars of an allegedly religious origin. Because Christians do not always practice what they preach, the noble ideal of Christian equality may become tarnished; but a constantly recurring renewal of the profession of faith in the Fatherhood of God and the fundamental brotherhood of man restores luster to this ideal both in theory and practice.

As mentioned above, the Christian schools of the first four centuries after Christ had as their major objective the teaching and/or defense of the Christian religion. The schools of the Roman Empire were the major sources of education in the basic skill subjects, the humanities, and other branches of secular learning. Basically, there was overt or covert hostility between the two. Yet the Christian community was too poor to sponsor schools of its own to conduct both secular and religious instruction. Consequently, ancient times cannot be compared to the efforts on the part of religious sects during the nineteenth and twentieth centuries to operate their own schools because of the same basic disagreement with secular education.

When the American Catholic bishops and some Protestant leaders decided that the best place to give a religious education was in a religious school, they were able to call upon a laity with some financial resources. Such resources were not available among fourth-century Christians. Furthermore, because of the lowly origin of most early Christians, and the prevailing anti-intellectualism among them, there was a limited source of intellectual leadership. The influence of the catechetical schools was too negative or defensive ("apologetic") to compensate for the dearth of intellectual power. Major dissensions among Christians began to divide and weaken them as early as the beginning of the fourth century.

Thus when the Roman Empire and its culture began to decline, there was no strong Christian educative force to step into the vacuum created by this decadence. The Dark Ages of Christian education parallel the Dark Ages of secular education.[10] Just how "dark"

---

[10] The two centuries before and after Charlemagne usually make up the "Dark Ages," roughly, from the sixth to the tenth centuries.

these four centuries were is debatable. Some historians believe that the twentieth century, in spite of all its scientific achievements, is in some respects just as dark. The two great wars, the political and social upheaval in the Orient and Africa, and the rise of Nazism, Fascism, and Communism are certainly not manifestations of any great "light." "Man's inhumanity toward man" has never been more pronounced than in the twentieth century. "Scientific enlightenment" has created means of torture and destruction far more cruel than anything imagined by the feudal lords of the ages of darkness. Even the prospect of a life of peace and happiness after death has been plucked from the hearts of many modern men. But the final decision as to the relative degree of "darkness" of the modern era versus the Dark Ages is left to future historians. If the leaders of the world do not succeed in solving the problems of "coexistence and existence," there may be no twenty-first-century historians.

To return from speculative comparisons to the realities of education during the Dark Ages, one is impressed by the efforts on the part of educators and rulers to bring light back to the world. One must remember that the deterioration of Roman education left the monasteries with the task of educating youth. The schools conducted in the monasteries, called monastic schools, were relatively small in number and had a very limited curriculum. Their main purpose was to train the monks themselves to read, write, and sing. These schools were able to admit only a small number of the Christian youth of the time. Actually their limited influence served more to conserve the knowledge of the past than to push forward the frontiers of new knowledge. Not only did the monks preserve Christian and classical learning but they kept alive the advanced methods of tilling the soil, cattle raising, and agricultural management. The best known modern descendants of the monastic schools are the Benedictine schools which still incorporate many of the ideals for the training of Christian youth in their twentieth-century monasteries and convents.

The cathedral schools which existed before the monastic schools also had a very limited objective, the education of the clergy. These schools were maintained in the residence or the cathedral of the bishop. Their curriculum consisted of Scripture and theology, with philosophy, the classics, and mathematics added later. But neither the monastic nor cathedral schools were concerned with the education of the laity. And what little education was given in the parish schools did not give the lay ruler the liberal education necessary for enlightened leadership. Herein seems to lie the heart of the problem of the revival of learning in the Dark Ages. Formal education was given only to the monks and clergy. The lay rulers were not educated at all since most of them could neither read nor write. It is no small wonder, then, that the rulers did not promote the cause of education. The governing of their domains reflected a complete ignorance of the fundamental principles of good government which were expounded by the great Greek and Roman thinkers.

A notable exception to unenlightened lay leadership during the Dark Ages is found in the Emperor Charlemagne, who began his rule in 768. Even though he was unable to read when he became emperor, his insistence upon culture and education was immediately felt. It took him only a few years to remove practically all of the most serious military threats to the kingdom, leaving him time to study and inaugurate needed domestic reforms. His general "house-cleaning" reached into the domain of the feudal lords, the monasteries, and the higher and lower secular clergy. Christian historians are the first to admit all of these areas needed more than a "white-washing" — they needed a thorough overhauling.[11] Each feudal lord wanted a completely free hand in managing his own affairs (often for his own enrichment). Abbots and bishops were temporal rulers, their clergy and monks were their ministers of temporal affairs rather than of religious and cultural matters.

To bring back "things of the mind and spirit," Charlemagne gathered scholars from Europe and the British Isles under the direction of Alcuin of York. Aachen (Aix-la-Chapelle) became the headquarters for this famous school which served as a center for the education of both lay and clerical leaders. Although this educational foundation did not succeed in dispelling the darkness, it produced the spark which enkindled the fire of medieval learning.

Another apparent weakness of the educational institutions was the lack of coordination and communication among them. Each one was isolated in some small principality, and bore the provincial characteristics of the area. An attempt was made in the later centuries of the Dark Ages to remedy the situation among the monastic schools, and great good seems to have resulted from centralizing

---

[11] See W. T. Kane, S.J., *History of Education*, rev. ed., Chaps. VI and VII.

many of the monasteries under the directorship of Cluny. Many educational historians believe that the united efforts of the monasteries not only brought new zeal to Christian living but also was instrumental in reforming the existing feudal institutions. Had Charlemagne found a coordinated educational effort such as the Cluny system early in his reign, he might have been able to change the cultural face of Europe even more extensively than he did. In fact, the organized efforts of the monastic schools were responsible for many reforms envisaged by Charlemagne. Their example and their teaching prodded masters to apply the original Christian principles of basic human equality and justice in their treatment of the serfs; knighthood became associated with Christian charity and brotherly love rather than with the superiority of the sword and lance; the interprincipality defense of travelers replaced the robbery, violence, and murder formerly carried on by each feudal state.

In addition to the influence of Charlemagne's educational reforms and the systematic reorganization of the monastic schools, one other light in the Dark Ages bears mention. The return of classical learning through the "back door" of Moorish Spain, so to speak, lent great impetus to the revival of learning. As mentioned earlier in this chapter, there was among Christians a general disapproval of classical pagan learning. The reasons for this distrust are quite understandable, especially to us who are able to employ "historical hindsight." But one of the most adverse consequences of the general mistrust of classical learning was the large gap it left in the liberal education of Christian leaders. More specifically, Aristotle's realism was not considered as a possible integrative system for Christian and pagan thought. The Christian thinkers of the first centuries of the Church had found Platonism more congenial to Christian beliefs because of spiritual tones of Plato's doctrines. Aristotle, on the other hand, was viewed as a materialist because of his emphasis on the external world as the source of human knowledge.

But, one might ask, what role did the Spanish Moors and Jews play in the revival of Classical learning, especially since the Moors belonged to the Mohammedan religion? Actually, Mohammedanism began as an anti-intellectual movement and for the majority of its adherents it remained such. In spite of this orientation to an emotional (subjective) spiritualism, a small group of Mohammedan scholars devoted their time and efforts to the study of philosophy and science. Two renowned philosopher-scientists Avicenna (eleventh century) and Averroës (twelfth century) vitalized the study of Aristotelian philosophy. It was chiefly through the influence of Averroës that the Spanish Christians recognized the value of Aristotle's work. Similarly, the study of the sciences, especially as applied in medicine, was reintroduced to the anemic intellectual climate of Western Europe. In fact, practically all of the noted men of science in those days received their training from the Moorish doctors. Even though the achievements of these medieval physicians cannot be compared to those of modern medicine, the work they did was quite scientific. They attempted to cull what was scientifically worthwhile from the homespun remedies and superstitious beliefs and construct a respectable body of medical principles and practices. More important, however, for the purposes of education, was their insistence on the use of scientific method (crude as it was) to solve problems of the physical universe.

The three main forces, then, shedding light upon the Dark Ages and setting the Western world back on the path to great intellectual achievements were: (1) the educational, social, and political reforms of Charlemagne; (2) the efforts of the monasteries to conserve the cultural achievements and treasures of the civilized world; (3) the return to the West of Aristotelian realism and the scientific outlook via Moorish Spain.

THE SCHOLASTIC PERIOD — THE "GOLDEN AGE" OF CHRISTIAN EDUCATION[12]

As noted above, the early Christian schools were designed primarily to teach religion, and instruction in secular subjects was obtained in the public schools of the empire. The monastic and cathedral schools of the Dark Ages primarily served the educational needs of the clergy and monks, tending to deemphasize secular learning. The schools of the Middle Ages, on the other hand, sought to integrate all learning through the disciplines of Christian theology and philosophy. It was the achievement of this goal that has merited for this period the title of the Golden Age of Christian education.

In addition to the Eastern learning acquired from the Moham-

---

[12] This period of glory usually includes the twelfth, thirteenth, and fourteenth centuries. William of Ockham, who died in 1349, is considered the last of the great Scholastics.

medans and Jews of Spain, the Western world profited greatly from the intermingling of culture effected by the Crusades. The revival of the study of law, brought about the demand for "law and order" to replace the anarchy of the Dark Ages, sent leaders on a search for Roman law manuscripts and other legal documents. The need for the construction of new churches and public buildings revived interest in the study of architecture. In general, the times were ripe for a revival of learning in all areas of human endeavor.

Another revitalizing influence of this time is found in the newly formed religious orders — the Franciscans, Dominicans, Carmelites, Servites, and Augustinians. Prior to their founding, the Benedictine Order had carried the major portion of the burden of Christian education. The new orders vied with one another in their attempts to convert the heathen or heretic, dispense charity, and promote intellectual pursuits. The members of these orders often became associated with the many different kinds of schools that were beginning to spring up all over the Western world. They taught in diocesan and cathedral schools, parish schools of chant, guild schools, city (public), and private schools. But the best known work of the religious orders was done in the great universities which had their beginnings in the twelfth and thirteenth centuries.

As one might expect, the universities came into existence as an advanced extension of an already existing school, such as the cathedral school. Among the universities are numbered such names as Salerno, Bologna, Paris, Oxford, Cambridge, Salamanca, Toulouse, Naples, Padua, Montpelier, and many others. In many instances, those universities built upon the existing language (trivium) and mathematics (quadrivium) subjects found in the cathedral school. Thus, grammar, dialectic, and rhetoric (trivium), and arithmetic, music, geometry, and astronomy (quadrivium) supplied the liberal education needed for admission into the professional schools of law, theology, and medicine. This medieval belief that a liberal education must precede professional education is still espoused by all modern European educational systems and by the majority of educators in the New World. Granted the subjects composing the liberal curriculum have changed, a liberal education is still the prerequisite for a professional education.

The close relationship of the religious orders and the great medieval universities did much to foster the revival of learning among both the clergy and laity. If one can trust the enrollment figures given by teachers in these great universities, their influence must have been most extensive. For example, some claim that Paris and Oxford had nearly 40,000 students. Even if 4000 is a more accurate figure, this represents a very large enrollment considering the size of the population, the absence of compulsory education at lower levels, and the low educational condition of the Dark Ages just past. Certainly the graduates of these universities must have acted as a leaven to the intellectual life of the Western world.

Many great scholars were associated with these medieval universities, but only a few can be mentioned in this chapter. Perhaps the most influential of them all, as far as Christian education is concerned, was St. Thomas Aquinas (1225–1274). This great theologian is not remembered primarily for his contributions to educational theory and practice. Rather, his contribution to education was indirect in the sense that he gave to the intellectual life of the Christian world of his time an integrative system for all knowledge — theological, philosophical, and practical. In fact, his teachings served as a guide for the solution of the most important problems involving politics, economics, and ethics — as well as metaphysics and religion. This does not imply that St. Thomas gives all the answers to all questions. It means rather that his teachings are a perennial source for guidance, for quickening the spirit, and for coming to grips with new questions as they arise. St. Thomas was not a system-builder. He was rather a Christian theologian who discovered in the philosophical principles of the Greeks, especially Aristotle, a basic soundness and source of truth. Viewing them in the light of Christian faith, he gave them fresh meaning and genius. St. Thomas' originality lay in his successful synthesis of Christian theology with the rational structure of Greek thought, in particular that of Aristotle and the Neoplatonists. Aristotle's formal (deductive) logic became the tool of theological reasoning, making of theology a coherent system; his metaphysical principles were reexamined and, infused with elements taken from the Neoplatonists and submitted to the light of faith, were applied to theology and questions of man's being and nature, his ethical principles and political theory served to give Christian morality and political action a rational basis. The mention of a few of the basic changes made by St. Thomas in Aristotle's philosophy might serve to show the Christianizing influence of St.

Thomas on the philosophy of the great Greek thinker. Inspired by Scripture (cf. Ex 3:15) St. Thomas elevated the Greek metaphysics of essence, common to Plato and Aristotle, to the level of a metaphysics of being, thus preparing the way for a genuine act of creation and a concept of God who is at once First Mover and personal Creator and Lord. Aristotle believed that the universe necessarily existed from all eternity; St. Thomas admitted the possibility of the existence of the universe from all eternity but rejected it as "fact" because Revelation speaks of creation in time. Again, Aristotle is ambiguous in his teaching on the human soul, in all probability holding a theory of immortality only for mind. St. Thomas taught that each human soul was a unique, individual spiritual entity created by God and meant to vivify matter in the composite being man. Thus the immortality of the mind clamored for the resurrection of the body. In fine, never before in the history of philosophy or education had any thinker organized knowledge of all kinds in such a manner that the complete gamut of natural and supernatural experience was encompassed.

Although St. Thomas was commissioned by his order to organize and administer courses of study, he did not do much philosophizing about education in the modern sense of the term. In fact, it was not until the twentieth century that Thomists became vitally interested in ferreting out the educational implications of the great medieval thinker's system. Some of the most significant of these, for purposes of this chapter, are:

1. The primacy of the intellect in educational endeavors. The ultimate aim of education is the same as the ultimate goal of man's existence, the attainment of the Beatific Vision. But the proximate aim of education (as schooling) is the enlightenment of the intellect. This process is essential since man accepts through his will what he sees as a "good" with his intellect. Man, by his very nature, desires with his will that which is good. It seems, then, that the most important job of the school is to give the student a thorough knowledge and understanding of his religion and all other disciplines, for thereby the student will know the truth. Only then can the human person make right choices.

2. Sense knowledge as the starting point for all human knowledge. St. Thomas agrees with the principle that the student is the one who learns — the teacher cannot do this for him. But if all learning is based on what is outside (in the sense that it is not innate) the

role of the teacher, textbooks, and other educational materials must be viewed as most important. Since the mind of man, at birth, is a *tabula rasa*, it is the responsibility of the teacher to make sure that the student learns the truth rather than falsehood. From the outset, it must be guaranteed that the pupil will acquire the true knowledge of God, of the physical universe and of himself. The learning of these basic truths cannot be left to chance acquisition on the part of the learner — they must be provided for in the curricular offerings.

Certainly, St. Thomas does not exclude the possibility of a student's acquiring knowledge independently of formal instructions. As a scholar, he himself had acquired a great deal of knowledge in this fashion and he certainly would want each student, young and old, to discover for himself as much knowledge as his abilities would allow. But teachers and textbooks can simplify the process.

3. Each person is free in his choice of alternative courses of action. This principle is viewed as an essential aspect of the moral order whether it be applied in the school or in the larger society. Thus each pupil is free insofar as he is not compelled by internal or external forces in deciding how he shall act. Each pupil, then, is responsible for his own behavior and must bear the consequences of his bad behavior and be rewarded here (or hereafter) for his good behavior.

This doctrine of freedom is, of course, modified by the Christian notion of the fall of man with its attendant darkening of the intellect and weakening of the will. But the rational powers of man, aided by grace, are such that he is capable of overcoming the inordinate drives of emotion and appetite. Within this context, freedom and discipline are correlatives, not opposites. One cannot be had without the other.

4. The essential unity of man's dual nature. Although man is composed of body and soul, the learning process cannot be depicted as being the function of one and not the other. Therefore, the "person" learns, not his mind or his body as the case may be. Some kinds of learning may be described as predominantly physical whereas others involve more mental activity; nevertheless, it is the *man* who knows, not his senses or his intellect.

To harmonize this statement with No. 1 above which posits the primacy of intellect, it is necessary to grasp the interrelationships of soul and body and to see the hierarchical structure of the elements entering into the human person. For St. Thomas the lower exists for the sake of the higher. This means that the body is for the sake of the soul. The *living body*, in fact, is an *ensouled* body, and our senses accordingly partake, to some degree, in the work of the intellect, the soul's highest faculty. Thus, the educational endeavor is *ordered* ultimately to the perfection of man's highest power, his intellect.

The application of this principle to the school curriculum accounts for the "hierarchy of subjects" found in institutions operated on Thomistic principles. The intellectual disciplines are at the top of the preferred list, with "skill subjects" and physical education at the bottom.

There are other aspects of Thomistic philosophy that have bearing on educational theory and practice. Obviously, this brief historical summary cannot discuss all of these. But the few listed above should give the reader a key to an understanding which can be treated with greater depth in a course in philosophy of education.

Many Christians, both Catholic and Protestant, are under the impression that St. Thomas had no "worthy opponent" in his time. Such is not the case! In keeping with modern publicity principles, "equal time" will be granted to the opposition. The major opposition to St. Thomas' views came from the scholars of the Franciscan Order, St. Bonaventure, Roger Bacon, Duns Scotus, William of Ockham, and other thirteenth- and fourteenth-century thinkers. Of these, Duns Scotus is probably the most brilliant dialectician and is considered by many modern non-Thomistic philosophers as the shining philosophical light of the Scholastic period. Charles S. Peirce, the American pragmatist, classified himself as a Scotistic Realist in metaphysics. Other modern philosophers have admired the great analytic skill of Scotus. Of course, the teachings of Scotus have been rather consistently espoused by the thinkers of the Franciscan Order up to the present time. One of Scotus' doctrines, with direct bearing on education, might be stated in terms of "the primacy of the will." Whereas the Thomist insists that enlightenment of the intellect must precede making choices (willing), the Scotist insists that training of the will takes precedence over enlightenment of the intellect. Thus, the love of God and faith in God are more important and must precede the intellectual knowledge of His existence. Educationally, the implication is that "living the Christian life" should be the proximate aim of the school rather than the development of the intellectual powers. The proximate aim of the school, then, should be the "development of Christian living." When a student leaves the school he should be living the Christian life as fully as his capabilities allow. The product will be judged first and foremost "on how good a Christian he is," rather than "how much he knows." Thus the aim of philosophy (and education) according to the Franciscan school is not so much the *understanding* of things but the consummation of faith and love. Scotus put very little trust in unaided reason. Certitude can be derived only from faith. Thomas Plassmann, O.F.M., states this position very succinctly:

> When all educational precepts, theories, and programs have had their say, it will be seen that the one immovable incubus which retards human endeavor in its search after true culture and refinement is original sin; that the only effective means to overcome this evil is found in the mysteries of the Incarnation and Redemption.[13]

Following St. Francis of Assisi, these educators believe that training the will of the student to love and serve God is the primary function of the school curriculum and all school activities. Obedience to God, motivated by the love of God, is more important than any knowledge the school can offer its clientele. Does it follow that the Scotist gives no place in the school to the intellectual disciplines? Certainly not! But intellectual development plays a subsidiary role in the educational process; it, too, is to serve the aim of making the student a good Christian.

This difference of opinion between the Thomists and Scotists represents another instance of the basic conflict in Christian education mentioned in the early pages of this chapter. Early Christian educators distrusted knowledge for its own sake because of its pagan origin. But some medieval educators felt that knowledge was of secondary importance and should serve a role auxiliary to that of Christian living. Today's Christian educators find themselves in the same quandary for reasons very similar to those given by the early Christian. But why should the problem arise in the medieval period which admittedly was intellectualistic? Perhaps it was grounded on the fear that too great an emphasis on the intellectual powers of man might foster dangerous forms of intellectual pride and "superiority feelings." Perhaps many of the teachers and scholars of those days actually did despise the ignorant in spite of the fact that he was living as a good Christian. Perhaps it was a reinterpretation of the well-known biblical question, "What does it profit a man . . . ?" Surely many Christians asked the question, "What is more important, to have great knowledge or to love God and neighbor?"

To return to Scotus and Franciscan education one might cite

    13 T. Plassmann, O.F.M., *End and Aim of Franciscan Education* (Milwaukee: The Bruce Publishing Co., 1929), p. 4.

another educational effect of their views. Because of the emphasis on will (action) the direct or activity method of teaching was used extensively in their teaching in the mission schools. The schools of the California Indian missions designed series of "object lessons" in Christian living. The school schedule was centered around Christian religious practices. The practical arts, such as weaving, masonry, pottery-making, architecture, and agriculture were integrated into the Christian life of the school. In many respects, this approach to teaching contains all the essential elements of the activity methods developed much later by Pestalozzi, Montessori, and the leaders of the American progressive-education movements. True, the progressives substituted democratic living for Christian living, but the belief that "living is learning" is common to both. Further, the important role given to the "practical arts" in the educational program is common to both the progressive and early Franciscan schools.

A final point stressed in Franciscan education concerns the role of the teacher in the educative process. The teacher must exemplify all the virtues of the true Christian life. Kindness, forbearance, and love are key traits for successful teaching. Severity is a last resort, to be employed only when kindness and gentleness have failed completely. Thus the most important qualification for teaching is not knowledge, but character. Surely, knowledge is one of the qualifications for teaching but not the most important. Again this same view of the teacher's role is advocated by the Pestalozzian and progressive schools. The teacher communicates more by his example than by the precepts and knowledge he offers to his students. He must "live Christianity or democracy" with the students: only then can they understand the true meaning of these ways of life.

Much more might be written about the intellectual struggle between the Thomists and the Scotists of the Middle Ages. But one will find that the immediate intellectual descendants of these great thinkers really add nothing to the expansion or clarification of their systems. On the contrary, their disputes centered around quite inane topics within the system. Soon the followers of both systems became so notorious for their quibbling that the term "Scholastic" became a synonym for sterile argumentation. But the very existence of these great differences in philosophical opinion should dispel, once and for all, the false notion often held by some modern "liberals," that the Middle Ages were characterized by absolute conformity. In fact, at the zenith of its development, the medieval period displayed a latitude which is most surprising. The controversies based upon free speculation in the twelfth to fourteenth centuries refute any charge of orthodoxy imposed "from above."

It is not to be denied, however, that the medieval universities and those associated with them were so exclusively intellectualistic in their activities that many important areas of human endeavor were neglected. Practically all Christian historians of the period recognize the glory of this period but also detect in the overemphasis on dialectic and metaphysics the seed of its own decay. As Father Kane puts it, "The middle ages learned the lesson which we today are learning over again — that to unbalance education is to destroy it."[14]

There was, however, in the medieval period, one major attempt to bring balance to the higher learning of the time. As mentioned earlier in this chapter, the Spanish Moors and Jews had reintroduced the study of the natural sciences to the Western World and two great medieval scholars, St. Albert the Great (a Dominican) and Roger Bacon (a Franciscan), put forth great efforts to bring about a revival and reform in these fields. This was an area in which the universities and the religious orders might have developed new scholarly interest to bolster up the declining vitality of the schools. St. Albert led the way for he studied and wrote in the fields of astronomy, physics, botany, chemistry, and geography. Especially in the area of physical geography he pushed forward the frontiers of knowledge. Roger Bacon was even more a scientist in the modern sense of the word, for his formulation of scientific method based upon observations of measurable phenomena might be considered the prelude to modern inductive sciences. Some of his special studies included the refraction of light, the basic chemical principles of explosives, and observations of the motion of the earth and heavenly bodies for correction of the calendar. But he was also a firm advocate of applied science in the modern sense of the term. His suggestions for the harnessing of power sound like twentieth-century science fiction. Basing his predictions on empirical principles, he spoke of self-powered ships, automobiles, and airplanes. Over and above the specific contributions he made to empirical science, one might cite as his greatest achievement the development of the "scientific attitude." For in the domain of the natural sciences he insisted that

---

[14] W. Kane, S.J., *History of Education*, rev. ed., p. 106.

observation must be the starting point; reliance on authority, custom, and the opinion of those not trained in science is fatal. However, Bacon insisted that all scientific knowledge should be directed toward the understanding of Sacred Scripture which he conceived to be the ultimate goal of all knowledge-seeking. As one Scholastic historian suggested, the followers of these two great men "argued themselves out of their jobs." This is the story of the rise and decline of the Golden Age of Christian education.

One point often causing consternation to the modern student in his study of medieval education is the apparent lack of well-organized systems of elementary and secondary schools. From the twentieth-century American and European point of view, some success in elementary and secondary schools is considered essential for university entrance. Thus one must have a certain number of units in English (or the native tongue), science, mathematics, and history to be admitted to a college or university. In medieval times, however, the only requirement for admission was a writing and speaking knowledge of Latin (and sometimes Greek). Mastery of these languages could be obtained in the local parish schools, the cathedral and private schools, or by self-instruction. When the applicant had demonstrated his knowledge of the classical languages, he was not expected to produce a diploma of graduation from a secondary school or give evidence that he had received sufficient "credits" in the basic areas of learning. Even by our standards of today, this university entrance requirement may have been more exacting than it appears at first glance. In fact, some modern institutions of higher learning say: "Give us a student who can read his own language well, think critically in that language, and express himself clearly, orally, and in writing and we shall make a scholar of him."

It must also be remembered that in medieval times, the classical languages were the essential tools of scholarship. No scholarly works were written in the vernacular. Texts in law, medicine, theology, and philosophy were all written in Latin and Greek. Furthermore, any student possessing the intelligence necessary to master these difficult languages was bright enough to delve into the subject matter written in those languages. This medieval emphasis on verbal ability as the criterion of intelligence is found in modern intelligence tests (or college aptitude tests as they are sometimes called). The reader will recall from his experience in taking such tests that, even in the content areas, these examinations were primarily a measure of "verbal intelligence." Similarly, the modern college or university curriculum cannot be handled without possessing a very advanced degree of verbal ability. Many beginning students in American colleges and universities fall by the wayside, not for a lack of native ability, but because of basic weaknesses in verbal factors. So perhaps the entrance requirements of medieval universities were not essentially much different from those of American universities.

A summary of the educational achievements of the Golden Age of Christian education might include the following points: (1) The revival of Greek learning introduced by the Moorish scholars reached its peak in the educational activities of the Middle Ages. (2) Although the major scholarly emphasis was placed on philosophy and theology, the Middle Ages witnessed renewed interest in medicine, law, mathematics, and the natural sciences. (3) The medieval universities, especially Paris and Bologna, set the pattern for the administrative and academic structure found in modern times. (4) The religious orders made educational pursuits a very important aspect of their total programs. (5) The renewed interest in higher learning was reflected in major improvements in the lower schools. (6) The pursuit of secular knowledge was not considered hostile to theological studies or to "Christian living."

SELECTED READINGS

Cole, Luella, A *History of Education* (New York: Rinehart, 1950), Chaps. V–VII.
A very excellent description of the practices found in early Christian schools.

Dods, M. (ed.), *Works of St. Augustine* (Edinburgh: T. T. Clark Ltd., 1873).
The student is urged to read the educational treatises of St. Augustine mentioned in this chapter, especially *De Magistro*, about the teacher.

Drane, Mother Francis Raphael, O.P., *Christian Schools and Scholars* (New York: Benziger Bros., 1924).
A very detailed account of the contributions of Christian scholars to educational theory and practice.

Good, H. G., *A History of Western Education*, 2 ed. (New York: The Macmillan Company, 1960), Chaps. IV and V.
An understanding yet critical review of education during the eras when Christian thought dominated the civilized world.

Kane, William, S.J., *History of Education*, rev. ed. (Chicago: Loyola University Press, 1954), Chaps. V–X.
Covers the period of Christian education in the earlier Middle Ages, the monastic schools, and the period of the medieval universities.

Kevane, Eugene, "St. Thomas and Education," *Catholic University of America Bulletin*, Vol. 28, No. 4, April, 1961, pp. 1, 2, 6–8.

An interesting and original analysis of St. Thomas' view of education applied to university education of today.

Marique, P. J., *History of Christian Education*, Vol. I (New York: Fordham University Press, 1924).

A comprehensive survey of the achievements of Christian education with an emphasis on the historical and philosophical foundations of Christian education.

McCormick, P., and Cassidy, F. P., *History of Education* (Washington, D. C.: Catholic Education Press, 1946), Part II.

A historical account of the chief events and personages in Christian education.

O'Brien, Kevin, *The Proximate Aim of Education* (Milwaukee: The Bruce Publishing Co., 1958).

A study of the proper and immediate end of education. A defense of the view that the immediate end of education is Christian perfection rather than intellectual development.

Smith, Vincent E., *The School Examined* (Milwaukee: The Bruce Publishing Co., 1961).

A defense of the view that the proper and immediate goal of the school is perfection of the intellect. Also suggests a curriculum that will insure the maximum development of the intellect according to Thomistic principles.

Ulich, R., *History of Educational Thought* (New York: American Book Co., 1950), pp. 61–102.

Treats of the views of Jesus of Nazareth, the ancient Church Fathers, and the thinkers of the medieval Church in relation to the aims, content, and methods of education.

Wade, Francis C., S.J., "St. Thomas Aquinas and Teaching," *Some Philosophers on Education* (Milwaukee: Marquette University Press, 1956), pp. 67–86.

An application of the basic principles of Thomism to the teaching-learning process.

Chapter IX

THE HUMANISTIC TRADITION
IN EDUCATION

Humanism has been the inspiration for one of the most persistent patterns of Western education. The educational beliefs of Plato, Aristotle, and the medievalists might be considered the foundation of humanism. The term "humanism," as it is used in educational circles, refers to the school's endeavor to develop in its clientele those characteristics of man which differentiate him from brute animals.[1] Starting from the definition of man as a *rational animal*, humanists point out that it is "reason" that distinguishes man from all other forms of animal life (including the primates). Consequently, any educational program which emphasizes the development of man's rational powers as the pervasive aim of education might fit into the category of humanism, broadly defined. Whether the curriculum be the traditional seven liberal arts, the classics, or the modern intellectual diet of science, mathematics, and languages, the humanistic ideal might still be the motivating principle.

For the purposes of this chapter the humanistic outlook on education will be viewed from three different approaches: the humanism of the Renaissance classicists (fifteenth to seventeenth centuries); Christian humanism of the sixteenth to eighteenth centuries; neohumanism of the twentieth century.

HUMANISM OF THE RENAISSANCE

The decline of medieval education with its theocentric ideals was followed by a return to the classical literature of the Greeks

---

[1] In general, humanism includes any view in which interest in human welfare is central. During the Renaissance it took the form of a rejection of religious studies. In the nineteenth century it took the form of a "worship of humanity." Literary humanism, an American movement, consists in the protest against vocationalism in the schools and advocates a return to the "humanities."

and Romans as the heart of the educational program. These literary works were considered as exemplars of the achievements of the human mind by Renaissance scholars. These great works were studied for their historical and informational content, but especially for their form of expression. Thus, the classical humanists would select those literary masterpieces of poetry, drama, oratory, and philosophy that they considered worthy of imitation by the student.

This return to and imitation of the form and style of the ancient authors effected a major change in the approach to the study of the language of the educated. Up to this time, Latin had been the language of the Church, the professions, and the schools. It was a "living language." Naturally, as is true of any living language, Latin had undergone some drastic changes since the days of Caesar and Cicero, and the humanists set about to correct the many "errors and corruptions" of medieval Latin. The ideal humanistic scholar and student was one who could duplicate the style of the literary greats of the Greeks and Romans. Such a drastic change had the twin effects of killing Latin as a living language and placing a premium on the rote memorization of the masterpieces of classical literature. Certainly, Cicero's and Virgil's works were among the most perfect in Latin and were, therefore, to be mastered by anyone who wished to be considered "educated." Similarly, classical Greek had to be mastered thoroughly since so many of the best literary products of the human mind were written in Greek by men such as Homer and Demosthenes. In addition to enabling the student to read the ancient classics, the study of Latin and Greek came to be regarded as the best form of mental training a student could have.

The educational influence of this early imitative humanistic development did not terminate with the passing of the Renaissance. In fact, our grandparents were expected to pursue much the same goals in both their high school and college programs. During the last decades of the nineteenth and the first decade of the twentieth century, the study of the Greek and Latin languages and classical literature still constituted the core of the best secondary schools and college curricula. The classical scholar was still looked upon as the person of greatest prestige on the academic staff. The mastery of Latin and/or Greek was the criterion for selection of the gifted. The intellectual development of the future statesman, doctor, or lawyer, it was argued, was assured by the study of classical languages and literature, for they exemplified the outstanding achievements of rational man.

Some of the great names of the early humanism are Petrarch, Erasmus, Chrysolaras, Dante, and Montaigne. In educational circles men like Vergerius, Vittorino, Castiglione, Vives, Thomas Elyot, Roger Ascham and Bude promoted the cause of humanism. Although some of these scholars, for example, Dante, wrote their great literary masterpieces in the vernacular, nonetheless they drew heavily upon the Greek and Roman classics for their themes, and to some extent for their literary style. In general, they were very critical of the medieval scholar's emphasis on formal disputations and futile arguments. The hierarchy and lower clergy were ridiculed in the many satirical writings of the humanists. Rabelais' *Gargantua and Pantagruel* is characteristic of the attitude of many humanists not only toward the ignorance and superstition of the times but also toward the religious beliefs and practices of the Christian faith.

It is evident, then, that the humanists did not stay aloof from theological concerns. In reality, many became deeply embroiled in the religious conflicts of the Reformation. Some joined the religious revolutionaries, whereas others remained loyal to the Pope. But, as Christopher Dawson suggests, it was the common bond of humanism that preserved the unity of Western culture in spite of profound theological differences between the two groups.[2]

CHRISTIAN HUMANISM

Although most of the humanists of the Renaissance were Christians, theological concerns did not play the most significant role in their educational schemes. Their insistence upon the return to the pagan Greek and Roman classics embodied a mild scorn for the theocentric education of the early Christian and medieval periods. Some educators, however, felt that the classics could be integrated into a truly Christian education. Among the proponents of this latter position are the educators of the Protestant Reformation and the Catholic Counter Reformation.

One of the first moves of the Reformation was directed toward weakening the control of the Catholic Church in education, so that the human spirit might develop "unhampered" by the Church. In

[2] Christopher Dawson, *The Crisis of Western Education* (New York: Sheed and Ward, 1961), p. 38 ff.

fact, when the Treaty of Augsburg gave each monarch the right to determine the religious affiliation of his entire region, he also received the authority and responsibility for education. Because of this political move Europe saw its first state-controlled education since the disintegration of the Roman Empire in the early centuries of the Christian era. But it was not until the middle of the sixteenth century that the first free public school system was founded (in Württemberg, Germany). Although religion was taught in these schools, the schools themselves were completely removed from ecclesiastical jurisdiction.

The influence of humanism in the schools of the Reformation is quite apparent. For example, Melanchthon, Luther's most noted educator, believed that the children should begin learning Latin words as soon as they started to read their own language. The Latin works of Cato and Donatus should serve as beginning texts for the youngsters. After they could read they were introduced to fables and other Latin selections which they were expected to master and from which they would learn the intricacies of Latin grammar. After the pupils had mastered Latin grammar, they read the works of Cicero, Virgil, and Ovid. At this stage the student was expected to speak and write in the pure Latin style of the classics. Instruction in morality and religion, however, was the aim of all teaching, even that derived from the classics.

In spite of the religious and moral tone of the instruction, the emphasis in Melanchthon's program was almost exclusively on verbal skills developed by the mastery of the classics. Because of this emphasis on linguistic training, a student usually entered the university without any knowledge of mathematics and science. But the lack of preparation in these subjects did not retard the student significantly because the university placed a premium on a classical education.

A significant result of the Protestant humanistic view of education was the lasting influence it had on the secondary schools on the continent for the next several centuries. The sixteenth-century Sturm Gymnasium (high school) became the prototype. The mother tongue was used only with the very young and then to teach the catechism. For the rest the curriculum was mainly Greek, Latin, rhetoric, public speaking, prose, poetry, drama, and composition (in Latin, of course). The students always had to speak and write Latin!

But not just any kind of Latin; in most instances, it had to be the Latin of Cicero. Music, mathematics, and astronomy were given some time, but these too were studied in the classical languages, not the vernacular.

The Reformation in the British Isles witnessed a similar humanistic evolution in education. The curriculum of the typical English school of the times contained Latin and Greek grammar and composition, translations and explanations of Cicero, Livy, Homer, Xenephon, and similar classics, and the Greek and Latin Bible. Translations were to be made from Greek into Latin and vice versa, not simply from the classical languages into English. Students were called upon, without advance warning, to give extemporaneous talks in Latin and Greek before all the students and faculty assembled for meals. Again, the style used by the student was to be that of Cicero or Demosthenes, not the student's own. Even during recreation periods, monitors saw to it that students communicated in Latin rather than English.

As in the continental schools religious and moral training was integrated with the humanistic (classical) curriculum. At times it might be difficult to determine whether the classical curriculum was designed to foster Christian virtue or the religious training to embellish the humanistic one. But there is no doubt that the time spent on the humanistic content far outweighed that spent on religious or moral training. Also there seems to be little doubt that the form of Christian humanism developed in the England of the Reformation was transplanted to the American colonies and dominated most secondary schools to the twentieth century (with some modification especially in regard to the use of the vernacular). Again, as in Protestant Germany, the humanistic studies constituted the cultural link with the education of the Western world.

Another very influential form of Christian humanism may be found in the Catholic educational developments of the Counter Reformation. Although the educational reforms of the Counter Reformation came from several sources, only the most significant one can be treated in this chapter. There seem to be little doubt that St. Ignatius of Loyola (1491–1556) and the members of his Society, the Jesuits, effected the greatest educational reforms in the Catholic Church of the times.

A significant aspect of the Jesuit educational program for youth was its largely humanistic content. It is true that many schools of the times had this content because of the influence of the Renaissance. But it was not merely an accident of the times that the classics became an integral part of the program in the Jesuit schools. St. Ignatius himself devoted one chapter of the Constitutions of his Society to the educational principles to be employed in Jesuit schools. These principles, based on Ignatius' own educational experiences as a mature student, represent a deliberate attempt to unite the literary humanistic studies to the intellectual and spiritual values of the Catholic Middle Ages.

Three decades after his death his followers began work on the document which eventually would be the master plan for Jesuit education. This plan, the *Ratio Studiorum* (Plan of Studies) which was the Jesuit code of liberal education, embodies the general principles laid down in the Constitutions as well as the experience of a half century of educational work on the part of the members of the Society. A committee of six Jesuit educators from all over the world began work on the *Ratio*. Their tentative plan was submitted to the Jesuit teachers in all their schools for criticism and comment. When the *Ratio* appeared in final form in 1599 it contained the best educational thinking (of any organized group of school administrators and teachers) the world had yet seen. Furthermore the direct influence of the *Ratio* was to be felt everywhere in the world, for the majority of the political leaders and professional men were trained in Jesuit schools (there were over 200,000 students in Jesuit colleges and universities and of course many more in the lower schools at the end of the seventeenth century).

The curriculum recommended in the *Ratio* makes the study of Latin grammar and literature the core of the studies in the lower schools. About two thirds of class time was spent on Cicero and other Latin readings. The primary objective of these studies was to write and speak excellent classical Latin; the secondary objective was to develop the intellectual powers of the student for clear and critical thinking. The humanistic curriculum, it was believed, would achieve best these two objectives.

The *Ratio* was the first educational plan to employ the graded system somewhat as we know it today. Students could progress from grade to grade at their own rate, but usually the five grades required seven years for completion. A glimpse at the important features of the curriculum for the first five grades (which compare to the modern European secondary level) gives evidence of its rigor and humanistic content.

First Grade (Lower Grammar)
1. Elementary Latin and Greek grammar
2. Easy selections from Cicero and a few other Latin authors

Second Grade (Middle Grammar)
1. Intermediate Latin and Greek grammar
2. Latin readings: Cicero's *Letters*, Caesar, and Ovid's simplest poems
3. Greek readings: Aesop's *Fables*, Lucian's *Dialogues*, and the writings of Cebes, one of Socrates' pupils

Third Grade (Upper Grammar)
1. Advanced Latin and Greek grammar
2. Complete mastery of required Latin readings: Cicero's more difficult *Letters* and his treatises *On Friendship* and *Old Age* and easier selections from Ovid and Virgil
3. Greek readings: St. John Chrysostom, Aesop, etc.

Fourth Grade (Humanities)
1. Command of the Latin language; knowledge of history, etc., by study of "great books"; introduction to rhetoric
2. Latin readings: Cicero, Caesar, Livy, Horace and Sallust for *style* and *content*
3. Greek readings; St. Basil the Great, St. Gregory Nazienzen, St. John Chrysostom, Plato, Plutarch and Homer

Fifth Grade (Rhetoric)
1. Eloquence or perfect style in writing and speaking Latin is the goal of this last grade of the lower school
2. Latin readings: any selections, but chiefly Cicero, known for their style and beauty
3. Greek readings: selections from Plato, Aristotle, Homer, Pindar, Thucydides, etc., also known for their style and beauty[3]

Certainly this is not a curriculum designed for intellectual "light-weights."

---

[3] See T. Hughes, *Loyola and the Educational System of the Jesuits* (New York: Scribner's, 1912).

As mentioned above, the humanistic (classical, literary) content accounted for two thirds of the curriculum. In addition the students studied world history, some science and mathematics, catechism, and the Bible (in Latin and Greek). The students spent about twenty-five hours in class; religious exercises and physical education were compulsory.

The Jesuit schools were characterized by centralized administration, and in this respect modern public and private high schools have followed their lead. For example, one person was at the head of the school whose duties were much the same as those of the principal of today. One person was responsible for the discipline of the school — somewhat as the assistant principal in the modern school. The principal (or prefect of studies) exercised a supervisory function over the faculty and after making classroom visitations discussed instructional problems with the staff. The *Ratio* served as a guide for all schools, much as the "curriculum guides" do for modern systems. In most respects the Jesuit system was the most perfect educational system the world had seen.

Another characteristic of the Jesuit system likening it to modern education was its planned program of teacher education. Prior to the Jesuit system the selection and training of teachers had been quite haphazard. Now, for the first time, certain characteristics were demanded in the future teachers of the Society. They had to possess:

1. High mental ability (well above average)
2. A thorough and complete liberal or general education
3. Devoted interest in youth
4. The ability to work with the administrators of the school
5. Mastery of teaching skills and creativity in new teaching situations.
6. High moral character

Any student who aspired to be a teacher had to pass all of the examinations at all grades of the lower school with distinction. In addition, he had to demonstrate his ability to express himself clearly, forcefully, and persuasively before his peers and examiners. Upon completion of the lower schools, the candidate for the Society entered the novitiate which was devoted almost exclusively to spiritual formation. After completing his university studies, the student began his special training as a teacher. This training contained work in pedagogy, observation of experienced teachers, and finally practice teaching under the direction of the prefect of studies (principal). After several years of full-time teaching, many pursued theological studies and became priests. Many of the priests, however, returned to full-time teaching or administrative duties either in the lower schools or universities of the Society.

In the lower schools, each teacher taught all the subjects to the class (the "self-contained" classroom, in modern parlance) and stayed with the class throughout their entire five-grade program. Each teacher was to devote his entire time to his students and in preparation for his classes. He was assigned no pastoral or other outside duties which might hamper his teaching efficiency. Teaching was a full-time job.

Likewise, in Jesuit schools, being a student was a full-time occupation. Those students who could not afford to pay tuition were granted scholarships so they would not be distracted by the activities derived from outside work. Attendance at classes was compulsory and taking notes on all that was said by the teacher was considered necessary. Class attendance and note-taking were essential because of the teaching method used, the *prelection*. According to one interpretation, the prelection method called first for the teacher reading a selection from Cicero or some other classical author. An explanation and analysis of the passage followed the reading. This second step, in which the students participated, entailed taking notes on the grammatical structure of the passage as well as on any other background information the teacher might give about the historical setting of the passage.

Attendance at the lectures and note-taking also were necessary since students later would be expected to participate in class discussions and disputations on the matter covered in the lecture and explanation periods. Thus it was to the student's advantage to be diligent in getting whatever the teacher presented so that his own compositions and oral reports might be in perfect Latin.[4]

Whatever modern evaluation is made of Jesuit education at that time, be it by friend or foe, all will admit that it was the best education offered during the Counter Reformation. Likewise, no one

---

[4] For a more detailed explanation of the teaching-learning techniques of Jesuit schools, see E. A. Fitzpatrick, *St. Ignatius and the Ratio Studiorum* (New York: McGraw-Hill Co., 1905).

will deny its systematic, thorough, and comprehensive character — such traits are emulated by modern educational systems.

Another lesson the modern world has learned from the educators of both the Reformation and Counter Reformation is the influence of education on all areas of life, political and spiritual. Both saw in education a weapon more powerful than the pulpit in molding the minds of youth. The school is viewed as the central agency for building the intellect, character, and attitudes of the future statesmen and leaders. Capture the minds of youth for a cause and the cause is won. Give youth an ideal and they will sacrifice, even life, to realize the ideal! Certainly educators prior to the Reformation recognized the power of the school as a political and spiritual weapon, but they did not approach it through the avenues of free and universal education.

NEO-HUMANISM

As mentioned in the early paragraphs of this chapter, the humanistic approach to education predominated educational thinking prior to the twentieth century. Even though modifications were made by curricular changes such as replacing the classical languages with the modern and a heavier concentration on mathematics and science, the twin goals of intellectual development and mental discipline remained. Thus when speaking of neo-humanism the student should not expect to find the identical school subjects and teaching methods as obtained in the humanistic schools of the sixteenth and seventeenth centuries. Also, the new humanistic school has not escaped completely the influence of the naturalism and progressivism described in the next chapter. Similarly, the findings of scientific psychology have affected both the educational theory and practice of neo-humanism. In some instances it may be extremely difficult to determine whether any specific educational institution, public or private, possesses a humanistic orientation or not. In other instances a school might be quite obviously humanistic. Those who attended high schools designed primarily as "college prep" schools are the products of a more or less neo-humanistic approach. Most liberal arts colleges and the science, letters, and arts divisions in large universities have the humanistic orientation. The large comprehensive high school in urban areas may have several "tracks," one humanistic, one vocational, and one general. In such schools the humanistic "track" is roughly equivalent to the college-preparatory program. In fact, the most recent trend in secondary education constitutes somewhat of a return to the traditional goals of education (or more correctly) many secondary schools remained quite humanistic in spite of the onslaught of the "new education" discussed in the next chapter.

This persistency of humanistic education in the United States is not accidental, for just when the progressive and naturalistic movements were getting under way, Irving Babbitt (1865–1933) was leading the campaign for the education of the mind. According to Babbitt and his followers, the ideal education consists in the study of the outstanding literary works of the civilized world. These great works constitute the "essentials" of any curriculum worthy of the name, education. Other activities and courses should be classified as "training" or recreation, not education. Under these headings Babbitt would list physical education, all vocational education (including shop, home economics, etc.), clubs, assemblies, and the like.

Another influential wing of neo-humanism in American education is led by Mortimer Adler and Robert M. Hutchins. For them, reason is the faculty that differentiates man from all other forms of life. Therefore any education worthy of the name will concentrate on the development of man's rational powers rather than the physical or social aspects of human life. The development of these functions should be the concern of other agencies such as the family and the state.

Thomas Molnar, a professor of literature, expresses the same view when he expresses the belief that the "task of (true education) is and always will be the perfecting of the intellect and the acquisition of genuine culture."[5] Similar views are held by many scholars whose names the student will encounter in the course of his college career, A. J. Nock, Norman Foerster, Stringfellow Barr, T. S. Eliot, Paul E. More, Douglas Bush, and a host of others.

Yet another source of the humanistic revival might be found in Christian schools. In such schools, the "road back" toward humanism was not particularly long because most of them had not digressed markedly from the traditional humanistic goals of education. Many

---

[5] Thomas Molnar, The Future of Education (New York: Fleet Publ. Co., 1961), p. 144.

of the spokesmen for the Christian schools restate a modernized version of the traditional position to protect the Christian schools from the inroads of the naturalistic and "progressive" ideologies in education. Jacques Maritain, by his work, *Education at the Crossroads*, has played a major role in defending the humanistic ideal for Christian schools.

Vincent E. Smith, following Maritain's lead, is much more specific in his statement of the place of the humanistic ideal within the Catholic school. He states "that all institutions within the Church have for their aim to make man good; but the aim most proper to the school is to make man good intellectually. In this respect, a Catholic school differs from a Catholic hospital or a Catholic newspaper or a Catholic cell within a labor union. All of these agencies aim to make man good; all of them aim at character building. But the aim specific to the school is to make man good in his intellect."[6] He makes this humanistic position most clear when he considers some of the nonteaching functions such as health education and character education which the school has been forced to assume. He adds, "In doing so, however, the school should recognize that, because of temporary social circumstance, it must become more than a teaching institution; the school should likewise work toward the correction of these circumstances. For as a matter of present-day practice, moral principles can be learned at home; but fully organized knowledge, because it requires systematic and a correspondingly specialized time which normally parents cannot afford, will usually be acquired only in the classroom or in work related to the classroom."[7]

It is worth noting at this juncture what Vincent Smith considers "perfectly teachable" and therefore the school's task to teach. That knowledge "worth having for its own sake" which "perfects the intellect is the responsibility of the teacher." He insists that practical knowledge of the "how-to-do-it" type is not the concern of the school. Consequently the liberal studies (as opposed to vocational) should constitute the heart of the true educational program.[8] Although the "liberal studies" are not treated at the same level in high school as they are in college, they should, nevertheless, be covered

---

[6] V. E. Smith, *The School Examined* (Milwaukee: The Bruce Publishing Co., 1961), p. 34.

[7] *Ibid.*, p. 35.

[8] *Ibid.*, p. 72ff.

somewhere along the continuum of the educational program. Thus Smith contends that logic, mathematics, the natural (or physical) sciences, ethics (or moral science), metaphysics, and Christian doctrine constitute the basic "teachable subjects or basic disciplines."[9]

These basic disciplines contain subject matter "worth knowing"; in other words the purpose of teaching these subjects is that the student perfect his intellect by knowing them. The teacher's primary concern is *not* with the use the student will make of this knowledge, for the knowledge is worth possessing simply because it is knowledge. To illustrate, the religion teacher's *primary obligation* is to see to it that his students *know* their religion. It is the responsibility of the home and the church to see to it that they *practice* their religion.

The reader might wonder why Vincent Smith and others who are classified as neo-humanists do not insist upon the same curriculum as the classical humanists. In the classical humanists' curriculum, two thirds of the time was devoted to classical Greek and Roman literature and grammar. But in Smith's proposal, no such prescription can be found. This situation emphasizes a point made earlier in this chapter in classifying "humanists," namely, even though the curricular content may change, the basic purpose of the school as an educational institution does not change. That knowledge which perfects or develops the intellect or mind and is worth knowing for its own sake is the school's first responsibility. Jacques Maritain's educational program is not identical to that of Vincent Smith nor does Christopher Dawson in *The Crisis of Western Education* advocate the same curriculum as R. M. Hutchins or Mortimer Adler. But they do view the primary purpose of the school in the same humanistic light. Similarly, J. F. Mulligan, S.J., an advocate of modern humanistic education in Jesuit schools, contends that any true humanistic education must go well beyond the study of the best literary works of the civilized world; it must be adapted to "places, times, and persons." Consequently, the sciences must be considered an integral part of a truly liberal education.[10]

Yet another strong voice for the new humanism is found in the

[9] *Ibid.*, Chaps. IV to IX.
[10] J. F. Mulligan, S.J., "Jesuit Education and the Natural Sciences," *Jesuit Education Quarterly*, XXI No. 4, March, 1959, 209–222. George E. Ganss, S.J., expresses essentially the same view in *St. Ignatius' Idea of a Jesuit University* (Milwaukee: Marquette University Press, 1954), Chap. IX.

works of the critics of "progressive" education. In general, most of the critics are products of a traditional school with its basically humanistic approach to the curriculum and teaching methods. They express intense dissatisfaction with what they consider the diluted pragmatic educational curriculum of the modern elementary and secondary schools. More specifically their criticism is leveled at John Dewey, the outstanding philosopher of the progressive education movement. They decry the anti-intellectualism of the schools, a curriculum geared to the needs and interests of the pupils, the activity-centered classes, the emphasis on vocational and physical education, the presence of coeducational cooking, fly casting, and the like as an integral part of the school program.

Most of all, however, they deplore the gradual elimination by progressive educators of formal courses in English grammar and composition, history, geography, classical and foreign languages, science, mathematics, and literature. These basic subjects which, they believe, contain knowledge worth knowing and best suited to develop the intellectual powers of the pupils, have been replaced by diluted "core" courses covering broad areas as social studies and English and contain no systematic treatment of any body of knowledge. The student (or group of students) is free to draw upon any of the "traditional subjects" that might assist him in some project in which he might be interested. Within such an educational structure, it is argued, the student can only emerge an intellectual midget wholly unprepared for leadership in the world of scholarship, government, the professions, or business.

In fine, they believe the nation's schools should be purged of the progressive educators who have completely destroyed all true education. An immediate return to the study of the basic subjects is imperative, they contend, if the United States is not to become a second-rate power (intellectually). The educational systems of Russia and other foreign countries are proffered as examples of nations that have forged ahead rapidly because of their insistence upon the students' mastery of the basic skills and knowledge.

The literature representative of this latter neo-humanistic movement is voluminous especially during the past decade. Some of the best-known works are Arthur E. Bestor's *Educational Wastelands*, Albert Lynd's *Quackery in the Public Schools*, Mortimer Smith's *And Madly Teach*, John Keats's *Schools Without Scholars*, and the many publications of the Council for Basic Education. Many of the nation's most popular magazines have run articles on the evils of "progressive education" concurrent with the demand for a return to the "traditional education."

Many of the "Issues" chapters in this book treat of the fundamental conflict between the progressive and humanistic schools of thought. At the time of this writing, the issue is far from being settled. Perhaps this generation will not witness the final solution of the problem. But one fact is evident, the neo-humanistic influence on the schools is being felt at all educational levels from elementary schools through colleges; every future teacher must understand the fundamental problem involved and be prepared to "take sides."

Summary

Humanism in education is as old as formal education itself. Its foundations are rooted in the educational patterns of ancient Greece and Rome. Even during the dominance of Christian education (sixth to fourteenth centuries) it was kept alive in the use made of the classics by some of the Christian schools. The Renaissance witnessed a virile revival of the classical learning which was later incorporated into the educational patterns of the Reformation and Counter Reformation. With some modifications for time and place, the humanistic ideal controlled education until the last decade of the nineteenth century. The first few decades of the twentieth century ushered in the innovations of the new education with its naturalistic and progressive theories and practices. But, by the end of World War II, the counterrevolution of neo-humanism was well under way; in the 1960's the gradual ascendance of neo-humanism is evident throughout the American educational picture.

SELECTED READINGS

Beck, R. H., "The Social and Educational Philosophy of New Humanism and New Conservatism," *Proceedings* (Lawrence, Kansas: Phil. of Ed. Society, 1960), pp. 93–104.
  Surveys the latest developments in the camp of the neo-humanists. Gives a representative list of the important names among the leaders of this movement.
Bestor, Arthur E., Jr., *Educational Wastelands* (Urbana: University of Illinois Press, 1953), Chap. 2.

A polemic treatise highly critical of progressive education. Calls for a return to the "solid subjects" of the traditional school.

Dawson, Christopher, *The Crisis of Western Education* (New York: Sheed & Ward, 1961).
A statement of principles underlying the humanistic tradition in Western education. Shows how these principles have been abandoned by the modern educational systems of the Western world and recommends a return to a cultural unity based on spiritual principles.

Fitzpatrick, E. A., *St. Ignatius and the Ratio Studiorum* (New York: McGraw-Hill Book Co., 1905).
An analytical study of the *Ratio Studiorum*. Also contains descriptions of the practices based upon the recommendations of the *Ratio*.

Ganss, George E., *St. Ignatius' Idea of a Jesuit University* (Milwaukee: Marquette University Press, 1954), Chaps. 8–10 and Appendix II and III.
A most scholarly treatise on the principles which should govern Jesuit institutions of higher learning in the modern world. Defends the view that the proper aim of the Jesuit university is both intellectual and moral.

Good, H. G., *A History of Western Education* (New York: The Macmillan Company, 1960), Chaps. VI–VIII.
A survey of the significant events and the contribution of important educators to humanistic educational theory and practice.

Hughes, T., *Loyola and the Educational System of the Jesuits* (New York: Charles Scribner's Sons, 1912).
A comprehensive study of the ideals and practices of Jesuit education during the past three centuries.

Hutchins, R. M., *No Friendly Voice* (Chicago: University of Chicago Press, 1936).
A restatement of the humanistic position coupled with a statement of the fallacies of modern education in America.

Hutchins, R. M., *The Conflict in Education* (New York: Harper & Bros., 1953).
Points up the basic theoretical and practical differences between neo-humanism and progressivism.

Hutchins, R. M., *The University of Utopia* (Chicago: University of Chicago Press, 1953).
A description of the ideal form of higher education in harmony with the philosophy of humanism and Aristotelian realism.

Kane, William, S.J., *History of Education*, rev. ed. (Chicago: Loyola University Press, 1954), Chaps. X–XII.
Covers the humanistic period in educational history pointing up both the strengths and weaknesses of this educational philosophy.

Keats, John, *Schools Without Scholars* (Boston: Houghton Mifflin Co., 1958), Chaps. 1 and 5.
A colorful attack on progressive education and a call for a return to the intellectual goals of the traditional school.

Lynd, Albert, *Quackery in the Public Schools* (New York: Little, Brown & Co., 1950), Chap. X.
An attack on the "educationists" of American education and their educational program.

Maritain, J., *Education at the Crossroads* (New Haven: Yale University Press, 1943).

A statement of the Christian humanistic position by one of the best known contemporary Scholastic philosophers.

Molnar, Thomas, *The Future of Education* (New York: Fleet Publishing Co., 1961), Chaps. 1 and 4.

Shows where the author feels the modern American school has failed to serve its major function, i.e., developing the intellectual powers of its clientele.

Smith, Mortimer, *And Madly Teach* (Chicago: Henry Regnery Co., 1949).

A criticism of the American public school teachers for knowing "how to teach," but not knowing "what to teach."

Smith, Vincent E., *The School Examined* (Milwaukee: The Bruce Publishing Co., 1961).

A defense of intellectualism in education. Also contains a blueprint for the ideal curriculum of the Catholic school.

Chapter X

THE NEW EDUCATION

The term "new education" has been applied to those educational practices, policies and philosophical beliefs which gained wide popularity in the late nineteenth and early twentieth centuries. The succeeding pages will show the origin and development of this educational movement from its European beginnings to its flowering in America. In its early stages, the new education was mainly revolutionary in character since much in it was directed *against* traditional educational practices and beliefs. At this early stage, one finds many of the 'lunatic fringe" practices which brought ill-fame to the movement.

The second phase of development is characterized by the construction of a theoretical framework for the movement. This framework represents a fusion of the findings of empirical psychology and sociology with the pragmatic philosophy of John Dewey. During this second phase (the 1930's and 1940's) the new education reached its point of greatest influence.

The third phase of the movement, that of decline, began during, or shortly after, World War II. But its demise as an educational force did not destroy completely its influence. Even though the last two decades of the twentieth century have witnessed a return to the intellectualism of traditional education, many of the beliefs and practices of the new education have been retained.

ORIGINS OF THE "NEW" EDUCATION

There have always been some rumblings of revolt in education, but most historians of education agree that no change in educational theory has been as radical as that inaugurated in twentieth-century

America. Although the names of John Dewey and the progressivists are usually associated with this revolt against traditionalism, it began more than a hundred years before Dewey's time. One of the greatest influences upon the "new" education was J. J. Rousseau's (1712–1778) naturalism, found in his famous work, *Emile*. As Professor Robert Ulich of Harvard suggests, one probably could not find any philosopher whose "half-truths" had so much influence on the lives of men as Rousseau.[1] Because of this great influence, recognized by friend and foe alike, it might be well to summarize Rousseau's educational beliefs.

Rousseau maintains that education plays the most important role in life, since man is born in a state of natural goodness and the only way he can be corrupted is by improper training. As long as man lives in harmony with nature and in response to his natural developmental tendencies, he will be well educated. It is when educators try to disrupt this natural development by superimposing "unnatural" norms of behavior, chiefly those of adult society, that the whole educational process becomes miseducative. "Everything is good as it comes from the Author of Nature; but everything degenerates in the hands of man . . . he will have nothing as Nature made it, not even man; like a saddle horse, man must be trained for man's service — he must be made over according to his fancy, like a tree in his garden."[2] To avoid miseducating children, Rousseau gives very specific recommendations for each stage of development.

1. *From birth to age five.* At this stage the mother is the teacher who should follow the natural growth pattern of the infant. She should encourage activity on the part of the child; without overtasking his strength, the child should be hardened to the common adversities of nature such as hunger, thirst, climate, and fatigue; the open air and nature are the best mediums for education at this stage.

2. *From five to twelve.* At this stage, the chief responsibility of the educator is to keep the child from being exposed to error and vice, for if he is not exposed to evil he will not commit any wrong;

---

[1] R. Ulich, *History of Educational Thought* (New York: American Book Co., 1950), p. 211.
[2] J. J. Rousseau, *Emile* (W. H. Payne, trans.) (New York: Appleton, 1896), p. 4.

as in the first stage, strong emphasis should be placed on developing physical fitness; the primary materials of education should be "things" rather than oral or written explanation of things; the method of observation is the primary teaching-learning method; reading might be introduced in the last year of this stage.

3. *From twelve to fifteen.* At this stage the child's learning should arise from his natural curiosity to discover things around him; geography and natural science consist in the study of his neighborhood rather than the study of books on these subjects (Mark Twain's Huck Finn and Tom Sawyer would please Rousseau); he should begin learning a useful trade at this time so that he may support himself and his family in later life.

4. *From fifteen to twenty.* At this stage the pupil is exposed to the first formal education; that is, he studies systematically the subjects usually taught in school. Also at this stage in his development he is introduced to the religions of the world so that he can select one to his own liking. He is also introduced to sex education at this time, for Rousseau felt he was not ready for it at an earlier age. Education for family life constituted the final step in the educational process.[3]

Certain of Rousseau's recommendations are found at the root of the new education: great emphasis was placed on the study of the child himself, his natural needs, abilities, desires, likes, and dislikes; all education should have a practical or useful goal; all instruction should be adapted to the developmental level of the child; the norms for school behavior should be based on child behavior rather than adult behavior.

Rousseau was not the kind of man to put his own educational theories into practice (as is often the case with many original thinkers). Among those who attempted to apply his theories, Henry Pestalozzi (1746–1827) is probably the most important and best known. One of the dominant motivating forces of this devout Christian was his ardent desire to help the poor people about him. In order to achieve this end he tried various professions including teaching, a career which began with the education of his own child.

---

[3] See J. J. Rousseau, *op. cit.*, pp. 240–258.

With some modification he tried to apply the principles advocated in *Emile* to his child's education. He then decided to try this "natural approach" with a group of poor children whom he welcomed to his mortgaged farm home. They were given practically no formal education, but instead worked in the fields and in the farm home. However, Pestalozzi was always among them, discussing the objects with which they were working. Within a few months these street urchins showed such marked improvement that Pestalozzi was able to appeal for outside support for his project. When he received this support he unrealistically accepted more pupils than he could handle (about eighty). With this large group he was unable to continue his close personal contact with the children, resulting after five years in the failure of the project.

After this failure he devoted the next two decades to earning a living and writing. Much of his literary work was published, enabling him to disseminate his educational theories. His big opportunity came when the Swiss government financed an experiment in the education of the orphans of the Swiss revolt at Stanz. But the relative success of this experiment was short-lived because of another war. He then began teaching a class of preschool children (seven years old and younger) with whom he had great success. Then followed the first public recognition from educational authorities. Pestalozzi had used no textbooks or recitations and did not maintain rigid order in his classes. Yet, when his students were examined by the educational authorities, they had not only surpassed pupils of other schools in "letters, spelling, and reading" but also had distinguished themselves in creative writing, art, and mathematics.

Shortly after this recognition, Pestalozzi was joined by three young men who shared his educational views and were of great assistance in establishing the first well-organized "Pestalozzi school." Educators came from all over the world to observe the "natural methods" of teaching employed in the school. All were amazed by the relaxed, informal atmosphere, the absence of formal recitations, and the negligible amount of "memoriter learning." Yet these pupils learned "traditional subject matter" very well. But as before, the popularity of the school increased its enrollment beyond Pestalozzi's administrative ability[4] and after twenty years the school closed for the last time. Pestalozzi died, broken in spirit and body, a year later.

---

[4] His last school at Yverdon had 200 pupils and 20 teachers.

Pestalozzi was dead, but his ideas had just begun to live. His experiments had indicated that subject matter can be learned in ways which children enjoy; it is most natural for children to want to learn as much as possible about the world in which they live; children actually enjoy difficult tasks as long as they are meaningful to them; more learning takes place in a pleasant relaxed atmosphere than in one fraught with tension; class size becomes an important factor in the application of the newer methods; the Pestalozzian system can function within the Judeo-Christian religious context even though this system had its origin in Rousseau's naïve naturalism.[5]

An ardent disciple of Pestalozzi's methodology was the philosopher-psychologist, John Frederick Herbart (1776–1841). While a tutor in Switzerland, he visited Pestalozzi's experimental school and was immediately converted to his ideas and methods. Unlike Pestalozzi, however, he gave an intellectual and scientific structure to these ideas and actually put them into practice in a campus laboratory school. He also delivered lectures on pedagogy at the Universities of Königsberg and Göttingen, which lent great prestige to his educational work as well as the motivation necessary to construct a systematic theory of education.

Probably the greatest contribution to modern education made by Herbart was his insistence upon the primary role of scientific psychology in the study and application of the teaching-learning processes. Even though his psychological doctrines might not be in harmony with all the findings of modern empirical psychology, his belief that psychology should be the guide to educational practice is generally accepted among modern educators. Also, he was the first to recommend the use of the lesson plan, based on the principles of psychology, for assuring the proper use of teaching methods in presenting subject matter to students. His theory of lesson planning, still found in many "methods" texts, contains the following steps:

1. *Preparation.* This consists in recalling to the students' minds anything they might already know, from previous experience and study, about the material they are about to learn. In this phase extensive use is made of audio-visual materials that will arouse their interest.

2. *Presentation.* This consists in using specific experiences to achieve understanding of the general ideas to be learned. The student

---

[5] See Chapter XII, p. 308 ff and Chapter XIV.

knows the material only when he has extracted these general ideas from the manifold of direct experiences and observation.

3. *Association.* This involves the correlation of the facts and ideas learned with others already known to the student.

4. *Systematization* (*application*). This consists in producing a unitary knowledge in the mind of the student, enabling him to apply the knowledge acquired in the first three phases of the learning. Many of the texts in "methods of teaching" have used the above adaptations of the Herbartian approach, calling it the "inductive-deductive" teaching-learning method.[6]

Herbart's theory of lesson planning is closely interwoven with his doctrine of interest. In this respect he disagreed with Rousseau's doctrine of natural interest, which was manifested by the student's desire to study those areas for which he has a "natural liking." Herbart felt student interest should be aroused by the teacher and the subject matter, thus encouraging the student to broaden his knowledge far beyond his natural inclinations. This accounts for much of the use of audio-visual aids, field trips, and other forms of extrinsic motivation prevalent in today's schools.

A final point worth mentioning in relating Herbart to modern American education is his break with the traditional belief that the primary goal of the school is intellectual development. Rather, he contended that "character education" was the primary aim of the school. Thus he believed that a well-rounded education will teach people how to live the "good life."[7] Although he believed that knowledge must precede action, he asserted that the school must see to it that action really follows. The traditional school concerned itself primarily with the transmission of knowledge, leaving to other agencies, such as the community and church, the application of the knowledge to personal and social living.

To summarize: Herbart contributed to the development of the new education a systematic theory of lesson planning based on psychological principles, the fundamental role of scientific psychology in guiding educational practice, the belief that extrinsic motivation is just as important in promoting learning as intrinsic motivation,

---

[6] J. F. Herbart, *The Science of Education* (Boston: D. C. Heath & Co., 1895).

[7] J. F. Herbart, *Outlines of Educational Doctrine* (New York: Macmillan Co., 1901), p. 7.

and the conviction that the school must be concerned with "living" as well as "knowing."

Another educator, Frederick Froebel (1782–1852), well known for his introduction of the kindergarten into education, has had great influence on the "new" education. Like other pioneers of educational reforms of his day, he attempted to integrate scientific knowledge and philosophical beliefs with the Christian way of life.

Like Pestalozzi, Froebel tried several professions before deciding to become a teacher. Also like Pestalozzi, he was convinced that it was possible to discover and formulate some general scientific principles for guiding the teaching-learning process. The first of these principles, stated negatively, admonishes the teacher not to interfere with the natural unfolding of the child's development. In other words, the teacher should be a guide and helper, not a director or dictator insisting upon adult behavior and standards. Positively stated, the child's education must emanate from self-activity generated as a response to the child's natural environment.

Froebel's second basic principle is that all activity of the child, both in school and out, should reflect and contribute to the natural unity and harmony of his personality. This principle presupposes the organic unity of the child's nature, prohibiting that type of education which does not develop the "whole child." Thus, the school must be concerned with the physical, moral, spiritual, and emotional development of the child as well as his intellectual or mental development. It is only when the teacher recognizes this principle that the pupil can manifest "creative self-activity."

A third principle asserts that social participation is essential to good education, for this brings about that unity in society essential to an organic universe. Thus it is just as important for all members of a class to work in harmony as it is for the different parts of the human body to function together. The school, therefore, must be the training ground for citizenship, a function traditionally reserved to nonschool agencies. This principle is in harmony with and complements the second insofar as it extends the idea of unity to society. This conviction, that the school should foster the ideals of unity in society, is prevalent in the "new" education.

A fourth principle in Froebel's theories which has greatly influenced modern education might be stated as the "primacy of infancy."

Preschool education, to Froebel, was just as important as any of the other stages. Actually, he demonstrated by his labors in founding kindergartens that the preschool level was most important. It is in these early years that the child's habits, attitudes, interests — his whole personality — are formed. For this reason he insisted that the environment of the young child should be ideal in order that the child's first experiences might be good. The teacher should be a model of piety, patience, and everything wholesome. It is at the preschool stage that the child must be launched on the sea of creativity. Since play is the most natural activity of children, it should be utilized to develop the inner creativity of the child. Froebel's own choice of the word *kindergarten* reflects this basic idea — the preschool class should be like a garden where the plants are allowed to grow and develop, with help from the gardener, just as their nature demands. To encourage this natural growth through play activities, Froebel developed sets of games and objects, some of which are still used in the kindergarten. An interesting aspect of these objects and the activities in which they were used was the ever present goal of attempting to achieve some unity (second principle). Thus, when the child used cubes, cylinders, or sticks his goal was to make something complete in itself, such as a building. Similarly, geometrical objects were cut in pieces, and again the purpose of the game was to rebuild the pieces into a unified whole.

An inspection of these four principles and the activities derived from them reveals their close interrelatedness. Thus Froebel was faithful to his own principle of unity, and for this reason many educational historians feel that his beliefs represent the first expression of a "systematic" theory of education to be proposed up to his time. He had been successful in harmonizing his philosophical, theological, and scientific beliefs in an educational program extending from the nursery school to higher education.

To summarize, Froebel's major contributions to modern education are: (1) his insistence upon self-activity as the key to learning; (2) the importance of early childhood education in the development of the personality of the child; (3) education must concern itself with the "whole child," not merely his intellectual potentialities; (4) all education should have a central, integrating purpose perceptible to the child at his own level; (5) preparation for life in society should begin in early childhood.

Although there are many other European educational reformers such as Basedow, Rosmini, De La Salle, Montessori, and Spencer, space can be devoted only to the last two mentioned.

The work of Dr. Maria Montessori (1869–1952) deserves special attention because of the recently revived interest in her educational principles and practices. It is also worth noting that she is the only woman mentioned in connection with the educational movements traced in this book. Classifying her in the "new" school of educational theorists seems to be most appropriate since, for the most part, she rejects the educational methods and materials of the traditionalist.

Perhaps the most significant of the points aligning her with the "new" school of educational thought lies in the importance she placed on pupil freedom. The pupil should not be subjected to the teacher's will but should be given the opportunity to develop his talents with the teacher's assistance. Furthermore, the pupil should gradually develop complete independence in his learning activities and only seek the teacher's assistance when necessary. However, like the progressives, she realized that absolute freedom in the classroom is impossible. The realities of social life demand self-discipline and self-restraint on the part of all involved in the educational process. But she did reject the repressive discipline found in most schools of the times.

The second characteristic of the Montessori system, a corollary of the first, which places it in opposition to traditionalism, is her insistence upon adapting all educational activities to the individuality of the pupil. By demanding small classes, she argues for allowing each child to progress at his own developmental rate, using materials and subjects which interest him most. In this respect, she reiterates the belief of the progressive school that individualized instruction is the best mode of teaching at all educational levels. Yet another aspect of her theories reflecting the newer trends in education was her reliance upon material designed to train the senses and develop perception and practical skills. Manipulation of blocks, cylinders, geometric figures, and the like replaced verbal descriptions of the same processes. "Learning by doing" was the rule for learning both manual and social skills.

One final characteristic of the Montessori scheme bearing a significant resemblance to that proposed by the "new" education relates to the role that child psychology plays in determining the content and method of education. Her view might be summed up in the statement: "Understand the child and you know the curriculum and method of education."[8]

Like Pestalozzi and Froebel, Spencer (1820–1903) opposed the traditional humanistic studies because, he said, they did not prepare the pupil for "complete living." Since the classical curriculum prevalent in the schools at that time had no practical bearing on the present or future life of most children, he felt it should be abandoned in favor of a more realistic one. As guides to the new curriculum, Spencer proposed the five types of activities necessary to prepare the child for "complete living." First in importance are the activities with direct bearing upon self-preservation. In the modern curriculum, these activities are found in health and physical education courses and in certain phases of science courses, especially biology. Second are those studies which enable the student to support himself and his family. In the modern curriculum these activities usually are found in vocational education departments — wood and metal shop, printing, mechanics, woodworking, sewing and cooking, commercial and business training, etc. The third category includes those courses and activities which aid the student to become a good parent. Most modern schools have courses, or units within courses, on home and family life, child care, marriage preparation and similar topics. The fourth area of study recommended by Spencer concerns itself with civic and economic competence and is very evident in the modern school. Besides those courses specifically devoted to education for citizenship and economics, one finds these areas integrated with history, geography, science, and even literature. Finally, the school must not neglect to educate the child for the worthy use of leisure time. The "fine arts" (music, painting, drawing, sculpture, dancing, and dramatics), sports and games, "reading for enjoyment," and the like are all found in the modern school.[9]

It must be kept in mind that at the time Spencer proposed these objectives for the schools the humanistic curriculum, limited chiefly to "intellectual activities," was still the only one found in schools.

---

[8] See Mortimer E. Standing, *Maria Montessori, Her Life and Work* (Fresno, Calif.: Academy Library Guild, 1959). Also, Nancy McCormick Rambusch, *Learning How to Learn* (Baltimore: Helicon Press, 1962).

[9] Herbert Spencer, *Education: Intellectual, Moral and Physical* (New York: D. Appleton Co., 1866), pp. 14, 16, 18, and 29.

Therefore he recognized the magnitude of the task and admitted the school could not do a "complete" job in all of these areas. Nevertheless he felt the school must give some attention to all of them (in the order of importance listed). But forty years after Spencer's death nearly every elementary and high school of any size in the United States had incorporated all of these areas in the curriculum.

It is also worth noting that the Commission on Reorganization of Secondary Education, in the well-known *Cardinal Principles of Secondary Education* published in 1918, incorporated Spencer's objectives in the seven basic purposes of secondary education: health, command of the fundamental processes (reading, writing, computing, spelling), worthy home membership, vocation, civic education, worthy use of leisure time, and ethical character. Also, the Educational Policies Commission of the N.E.A. has utilized Spencer's thought in its statement of educational objectives. Note how his five basic areas are interwoven into the following statement of *The Purposes of Education in American Democracy:*[10]

1. THE OBJECTIVES OF SELF-REALIZATION

The Inquiring Mind. The educated person has an appetite for learning.
Speech. The educated person can speak the mother tongue clearly.
Reading. The educated person reads the mother tongue efficiently.
Writing. The educated person writes the mother tongue effectively.
Number. The educated person solves his problems of counting and calculating.
Sight and Hearing. The educated person is skilled in listening and observing.
Health Knowledge. The educated person understands the basic facts concerning health and disease.
Health Habits. The educated person protects his own health and that of his dependents.
Public Health. The educated person works to improve the health of the community.
Recreation. The educated person is participant and spectator in many sports and other pastimes.
Intellectual Interests. The educated person has mental resources for the use of leisure.
Aesthetic Interests. The educated person appreciates beauty.
Character. The educated person gives responsible direction to his own life.

---

[10] Educational Policies Commission, N.E.A., *The Purposes of Education in American Democracy* (Washington, D. C.: N.E.A., 1938).

2. THE OBJECTIVES OF HUMAN RELATIONSHIPS

Respect for Humanity. The educated person puts human relationships first.

Friendships. The educated person enjoys a rich, sincere, and varied social life.

Cooperation. The educated person can work and play with others.

Courtesy. The educated person observes the amenities of social behavior.

Appreciation of the Home. The educated person appreciates the family as a social institution.

Homemaking. The educated person is skilled in homemaking.

Democracy in the Home. The educated person maintains democratic family relationships.

3. THE OBJECTIVES OF ECONOMIC EFFICIENCY

Work. The educated producer knows the satisfaction of good workmanship.

Occupational Information. The educated producer understands the requirements and opportunities for various jobs.

Occupational Choice. The educated producer has selected his occupation.

Occupational Efficiency. The educated producer succeeds in his chosen vocation.

Occupational Adjustment. The educated producer maintains and improves his efficiency.

Occupational Appreciation. The educated producer appreciates the social value of his work.

Personal Economics. The educated consumer plans the economics of his own life.

Consumer Judgment. The educated consumer develops standards for guiding his expenditures.

Efficiency in Buying. The educated consumer is an informed and skillful buyer.

Consumer Protection. The educated consumer takes appropriate measures to safeguard his interests.

4. THE OBJECTIVES OF CIVIC RESPONSIBILITY

Social Justice. The educated citizen is sensitive to the disparities of human circumstance.

Social Activity. The educated citizen acts to correct unsatisfactory conditions.

Social Understanding. The educated citizen seeks to understand social structures and social processes.

Critical Judgment. The educated citizen has defenses against propaganda.

Tolerance. The educated citizen respects honest differences of opinion.

Conservation. The educated citizen has a regard for the nation's resources.

Social Applications of Science. The educated citizen measures scientific advance by its contribution to the general welfare.

World Citizenship. The educated citizen is a cooperating member of the world community.

Law Observance. The educated citizen respects the law.

Economic Literacy. The educated citizen is economically literate.

Political Citizenship. The educated citizen accepts his civic duties.

Devotion to Democracy. The educated citizen acts upon an unswerving loyalty to democratic ideals.

Certainly, these objectives assign to the school the task of educating the whole person.

Another very influential organization in American education, the National Association of Secondary School Principals, restates Spencer's thought in terms of *The Imperative Needs of Youth:*[11]

1. All youth need to develop salable skills and those understandings and attitudes that make the worker an intelligent and productive participant in economic life. To this end, most youth need supervised work experience as well as education in the skills and knowledge of their occupations.
2. All youth need to develop and maintain good health and physical fitness.
3. All youth need to understand the rights and duties of the citizens of a democratic society, and to be diligent and competent in the performance of their obligations as members of the community and citizens of the state and nation and of the world.
4. All youth need to understand the significance of the family for the individual and society and the conditions conducive to successful family life.
5. All youth need to know how to purchase and use goods and services intelligently, understanding both the values received by the consumer and the economic consequences of their acts.
6. All youth need to understand the methods of science, the influence of science on human life, and the main scientific facts concerning the nature of the world and of man.
7. All youth need opportunities to develop their capacities to appreciate beauty in literature, art, music, and nature.
8. All youth need to be able to use their leisure time well and to

---

[11] Bulletin of the National Association of Secondary-School Principals, *The Imperative Needs of Youth of Secondary School Age* (Washington, D. C.: N.E.A., March, 1947), Vol. 31, No. 145.

budget it wisely, balancing activities that yield satisfactions to the individual with those that are socially useful.

9. All youth need to develop respect for other persons, to grow in their insight into ethical values and principles, and to be able to live and work cooperatively with others.

10. All youth need to grow in their ability to think rationally, to express their thoughts clearly, and to read and listen with understanding.

Later publications concerned with educational goals have not veered from these Spencerian ideals to any significant degree.

PROGRESSIVE EDUCATION

Although the educational reformers mentioned thus far were Europeans, their recommendations were never incorporated into the national systems of European countries. It was left to educators in the New World to apply the proposals to private and public education. One American educator, Superintendent Francis W. Parker (1837–1902), a Civil War colonel, had observed the experimental schools of Europe and tried to introduce many of their practices into the schools of Quincy, Massachusetts. In contrast to the "assign-study-recite" pattern used in teaching the classics and basic subjects, Parker built the school's activities around the pupils' interests and needs. This approach, he felt, motivated the students to learn more about the world around them and how to cope with it than they learned from the unrealistic, classical fare prevalent in the schools.

Like Pestalozzi, he incurred the wrath of many people in the community for substituting frills, fads, and play activities for the "solid subjects." Also, people objected to the permissive atmosphere in Parker's classrooms which, they felt, failed to discipline the pupils in habits of obedience and respect. Consequently, Parker's activities were "investigated" by the State Board of Education, but he was exonerated when it was determined that the Quincy children surpassed the achievement level of the majority of pupils in the state. Many visitors came to observe the "Quincy experiment," just as they had done in the Pestalozzi and Froebel schools. This success led Parker to dare to bring his ideas to teachers in training. Cook County Normal School in Chicago offered him this opportunity. The same initial opposition greeted him at Chicago, but recognition of his work soon followed.

Because of his work at Quincy, Chicago, and other places, Parker is regarded as the father of progressive education. Following his example, many public and private school educators immediately took up the fight against traditional education. In their zeal to abolish anything that smacked of traditionalism many of the more extreme progressives "threw out the baby with the wash" and seized upon everything that was new, simply because it was new. Thus, though many of their ideas and practices were a result of psychological experimentation, the untrained and overzealous often turned classrooms into "do as you please" recreation centers. This latter is the type of progressive education usually referred to when ridicule is intended.

Almost twenty years after Parker's death the leaders of the progressive movement formed an organization later called the Progressive Education Association. But, contrary to popular opinion, progressive education never dominated the schools (public or private) of this country, though its influence was felt in practically every type of school. This influence was effected by the teacher-training institutions, which had many advocates of progressive education on their staffs.[12]

Before Parker died, John Dewey (1859–1952) had been attracted to his very practical approach to education. And it was Dewey who added the philosophical structure which gave direction to the often-unrelated ideas and practices of the progressive movement. To be sure, Dewey disagreed with many of the practices, especially the more extreme, but the general trends in progressive education were akin to his own pragmatic philosophy. Although one cannot delve into the intricacies of Dewey's philosophy in this chapter, it might be well to list a few salient features of his educational outlook.

One of the most widely used teaching-learning methods of the modern school, problem-solving, is Dewey's brainchild. This method, which has no prototype in the history of education, is based on Dewey's analysis of "how we think." Dewey maintained that every act of reflective thought consists of the following steps: (1) a felt difficulty (problem); (2) the location and definition of the problem; (3) suggestions for possible solutions to the problem; (4) reasoning about the bearing of the suggestions in order to select one for testing; (5) observation and experimentation leading to the rejection or acceptance of the suggested solution to the problem.[13]

---

[12] See Chapter XIII, p. 391 ff.
[13] John Dewey, *How We Think* (Boston: D. C. Heath Co., 1910), p. 72.

Many a reader not far removed from his elementary and high school days might remember the application of the method in a social-studies or science class. The teacher creates an atmosphere of freedom, encouraging the students to state their own problems or express their interests and needs rather than follow a set pattern of subject-matter mastery. Careful guidance is given by the teacher to assist the pupils in selecting a problem that might both challenge the student and fit his experience. This process may take several class periods, and only then is the pupil ready to state the problem. Generally the brilliant student states the problem and is ready to proceed to the next step within a short time; but the less gifted students need much help from the teacher since the problems, needs, and desires of young people are often not consciously perceived by them. The teacher guides them to a rejection of irrelevant facts and issues, as well as leads them to pertinent information which will aid them in stating and comprehending their problems.

The next phase of student activity on the problem involves the reduction of the whole problem into simpler subproblems or units. The student's own experiences and related information and ideas are brought to bear on these subproblems. To achieve this goal, he must know how to locate source material and collect whatever information is needed from it in a systematic way. In gathering this information the student is constantly reminded of the main problem lest he wander off on numerous tangents not directly related to the main goal of his study.

After the problem has been clearly stated and much information and experience applied to it, the student begins formulating tentative solutions. These tentative solutions (or hypotheses) are not supposed to be merely "wild" guesses, but must be based on study and reflection. And it is only after critical scrutiny of the many suggested solutions that the student is to select one for testing. This step presumes that the student has arranged the various possible solutions in order of probable worth; if this procedure has not been followed, the teacher urges it upon students.

After the student has selected what seems to be the best proposal for a solution to the problem it is "put to the test of experience." Open-mindedness is encouraged; free discussion among students and teacher takes place; what one student fails to notice, another presents to the class; all experimental evidence related to the suggested solution is proffered; any experimental tests of similar hypotheses are brought to light. Finally, on the basis of all these factors, the solution is accepted or rejected. However, even after this rather lengthy procedure, an accepted solution is always subject to revision when new evidence becomes available.

Certainly the method of problem-solving is radically different from traditional teaching methods. First, it is based on pupil-centered activity as opposed to the teacher-centered methods of the past. The teacher functions as a guide and helper rather than as a director. Second, the problems, interests, needs, and desires of the pupils play an important role in the selection of the materials to be studied by the class or individuals in the class. In the traditional school the selection of subject matter to be learned was wholly in the hands of the teacher, whereas in the problem-solving approach the teacher guides pupils in their search for that subject matter which will aid them in solving their problems. Third, the teacher is not conceived as the "dispenser of truth," but rather as one who motivates students to search for their own truth.

The application of Dewey's method has implications beyond the realm of teaching method. Perhaps it might be best to allow Dewey to speak for himself on these points. A good summary of his fundamental position is found in his *Pedagogic Creed*:[14]

I BELIEVE THAT

— the only true education comes through the stimulation of the child's powers and by the demands of the social situations in which he finds himself. Through these demands he is stimulated to act as a member of a unity, to emerge from his original narrowness of action on feeling, and to conceive of himself from the standpoint of the welfare of the group to which he belongs (p. 3).

— this educational process has two sides — one psychological and one sociological — and that neither can be subordinated to the other, or neglected, without evil results following. One of these two sides, the psychological, is the basis. The child's own instincts and powers furnish the material and give the starting-point for all education. Save as the efforts of the educator connect with some activity which the child is carrying on of his own initiative independent of the educator, education becomes reduced to pressure from without. . . . Without insight into the psychological structure and activities of the individual, the educative

14 John Dewey, *My Pedagogic Creed* (Washington, D. C.: Progressive Education Association, 1929).

process will, therefore, be haphazard and arbitrary . . . it will result in friction or disintegration or arrest of the child's nature (p. 4).

— . . . The child has his own instincts and tendencies but we do not know what these mean until one can translate them into their social equivalents (p. 4).

— . . . In order to know what a power really is we must know what its end or use or function is, and this we cannot know save as we conceive of the individual as active in social relationships. But, on the other hand, the only possible adjustment which we can give to the child under existing conditions is that which arises through putting him in complete possession of all his power. With the advent of democracy and modern industrial conditions, it is impossible to foretell definitely, just what civilization will be twenty years from now. Hence it is impossible to prepare the child for any precise set of conditions. To prepare him for the future life means to give him command of himself . . . (p. 5).

— education, therefore, must begin with a psychological insight into the child's capacities, interests and habits. It must be controlled at every point by reference to these same considerations. . . . They must be translated into terms of their social equivalents — into terms of what they are capable of in the way of social service (p. 6).

— education, therefore, is a process of living and not a preparation for future living.

— the school must represent present life — life as real and vital to the child as that which he carries on in the home, in the neighborhood, or on the playground (p. 6).

— much of present (traditional) education fails because it neglects this fundamental principle of the school as a form of community life. It conceives of the school as a place where certain information is to be given, where certain lessons are to be learned. . . . As a result they do not become a part of the life experience of the child and so are not truly educative.

— moral education centers upon this conception of the school as a mode of social life, that the best and deepest moral training is precisely that which one gets through having to enter into proper relationships with others in a unity of work and thought.

— . . . the teacher is not in the school to impose certain ideas or to form certain habits in the child, but is there as a member of the community to select the influences which shall affect the child and to assist him in properly responding to these influences.

— the discipline of the school should proceed from the life of the school as a whole and not directly from the teacher (p. 8).

— all questions of the grading of the child and his promotion should be determined by reference to the same standard. Examinations are of use only in so far as they test the child's fitness for social life and reveal the place of which he can be of most service and where he can be the most help.

— the true center of correlation on the school subjects is not science nor literature, nor history, nor geography, but the child's own social activities (p. 9).

— they [cooking, sewing, manual training, etc.] are not special studies . . . rather that they represent, as types, fundamental forms of social activity (p. 10).

— the study of science is educational only in so far as it brings out the materials and processes which make social life what it is.

— there is, therefore, no succession of studies in the ideal school curriculum. If education is life, all life has, from the outset a scientific aspect, an aspect of art and culture and an aspect of communication. It cannot, therefore, be true that the proper studies for one grade are mere reading and writing and that at a later grade reading or literature or science, may be introduced. The progress is not in the succession of studies, but in the development of new attitudes towards and new interests in, experience (pp. 10 and 11).

— education must be conceived as a continuing reconstruction of experience; that the process and the goal of education are one and the same thing.

— to set up any end outside education, as furnishing its goal and standard, is to deprive the educational process of much of its meaning. . . .

— the question of method is ultimately reducible to the question of the order of development of the child's powers and interests.

— the active side precedes the passive in the development of the child-nature (p. 12).

— ideas (intellectual and rational processes) also result from action and devolve for the sake of the better control of action (p. 13).

— interests are the signs and symptoms of growing power.

— these interests are to be observed as showing the state of development which the child has reached.

— they prophesy the stage upon which he is about to enter.

— only through the continual and sympathetic observation of childhood interests can the adult enter into the child's life and see what he is ready for, and upon what material he could work most readily and fruitfully.

— these interests are neither to be humored nor repressed (p. 14).

— education is the fundamental method of social progress and reform.

— education is the regulation of the process of coming to share in the social consciousness and that the adjustment of individual activity on the basis of this social consciousness is the only sure method of social reconstruction (p. 15).

— the art (teaching) of thus giving shape to human powers and adapting them to social service is the supreme art . . . no insight, sympathy, tact, executive power, is too great for such service (p. 16).

— the teacher is engaged not simply in the training of individuals, but in the formation of proper social life.

— every teacher should realize the dignity of his calling; that he is a social servant set apart for the maintenance of proper social order and the securing of the right social growth (p. 17).

Dewey's later writings clarified and expanded upon these basic beliefs, but many educational philosophers maintain that the *Pedagogic Creed* contains the essential principles of his philosophy of education. Also, it can safely be affirmed that Dewey had (and still has) more disciples than any other American thinker. Within a very short time the teachers' colleges and colleges of education within the universities were staffed with Dewey's followers. This fact accounts for the rapid spread of the influence of the "new" education. Never before in the history of education has any assortment of new educational ideas and practices received such widespread acceptance within twenty years. Even educators who opposed Dewey's basic philosophical assumptions were quick to recognize and utilize those ideas and practices which were psychologically sound and not contrary to their own philosophical beliefs.[15]

It might be well to mention several of Dewey's best known disciples. For example, W. H. Kilpatrick is considered the "interpreter" of the philosophy of Dewey. He applied the activity principle to graduate school classes and also developed the project method of

[15] See Msgr. George Johnson, *Progressive Education and the Activity Curriculum in the Light of Catholic Principles* (Washington, D. C.: N.C.W.C., 1940 and 1941). Also H. H. Horne, *The Democratic Philosophy of Education* (New York: Macmillan, 1932). Sr. Mary Raby, *A Critical Study of the New Education* (Washington, D. C.: Catholic Education Press, 1944).

teaching so widely used in elementary and secondary schools today. The heart of the project method lies in its emphasis on activity in a natural setting. From this activity principle Kilpatrick developed his whole educational outlook in regard to the following points. First, the teacher must start with the growing child and help him live as a child (not as a miniature adult). The child will naturally increase his involvement in the social life around him until he becomes an effective, participating member of the social whole. Second, all learning must arise from the interests and needs of the pupils rather than from the demands of the examinations, recitations, or texts. The old curriculum consisting of lessons and subjects planned in advance by the teacher must give way to "actual living" planned jointly by the teacher and pupils. Third, the pupils must be taught to think for themselves and make decisions in this rapidly changing world rather than learning about the past. Only then will they be able to cope with new problems as they arise in the physical and social universe.[16]

A close inspection of Kilpatrick's view will reveal that it contains the basic elements of Dewey's *Pedagogic Creed*.

Another well-known disciple of Dewey, albeit a critical one, Boyd H. Bode, was a popularizer of Dewey's conception of democracy. Following Dewey's lead, he maintained that people can no longer be satisfied with the traditional beliefs and practices of democracy, but must constantly reexamine and reconstruct its meaning. The former meaning of the term, he said, implied a set of political principles and practices and carried no necessary implications with respect to economic, ethical, religious, or social beliefs. In this respect it differs from some of the modern "isms," such as Communism, which permeate all aspects of life. Bode therefore recommends in his book, *Democracy As a Way of Life*, a process of living which would pervade political life, religious beliefs and practices, family and social life, and, above all, the life of the school. The school, then, must be a place where pupils spend their time, not merely to learn, but to "live the democratic life."

The effect of Dewey's and Bode's recommendation for a democratic school can be noted in many classrooms. There is a much more

---

[16] See W. H. Kilpatrick, *Foundation of Method* (New York: Macmillan, 1925), and "The Case for Progressive Education," *N.E.A. Journal*, Vol. 30 (November, 1941), pp. 231–232.

permissive atmosphere; the initiation, progression, and evolution of
learning is a result of teacher and student activity; students participate in some phases of determining the norms of behavior for the
school; student councils are given responsible roles in school
government.[17]

Dewey had (and still has) hosts of other disciples using many
labels such as experimentalists, progressivists, instrumentalists, prag-
matists, and reconstructionists. Other educational theorists have accepted some of Dewey's beliefs but rejected others. However, even
at the height of his popularity Dewey's views had much opposition
from realists, idealists, essentialists, and humanists.[18] Many of the
beliefs of the opposition will be presented in the chapters on "issues"
or may be found in texts on educational philosophy.

A relatively recent school of educational thought mentioned above,
and claiming some kinship to Dewey's philosophy, has attracted
much attention, and has had great influence on educational practices. These thinkers, the reconstructionists, have devoted much more
effort to an analysis of social and cultural forces in education than
did the early philosophers of the "new" education. Their beginnings
are usually located in the days of the great depression of the 1930's.
The social and economic problems of those trying years prompted
these theorists to place the major emphasis of their reform on the
role the school should play in "reconstructing" the social order.

In most respects, these reformers object to the political and social
neutrality of the schools. They object to the traditionalists' belief
that the school's role in society is to teach the basic skills, conserving and transmitting the essential elements of the cultural heritage to the student in the form of organized subject matter (literature, history, civics, science, and mathematics). They also object
to the tenet of some traditionalists who assert that the school should
"reflect" the cultural traditions in a most conservative way, and above
all that the school should never serve as the agency for social change.
Thus, the reconstructionist is opposed to any form of conservatism.

However, they go further and assert that the early progressivists'
view was not thoroughgoing enough for our present world of tur-
moil. The progressive school sought to build "critical intelligence"

---

[17] See Chapter VI for more about the issue of democracy and education.
[18] Consult C. Good, *Dictionary of Education* (New York: McGraw Hill Book Co.,
1959) for brief descriptions of these "schools" of educational philosophy.

in the student by having him concentrate on the method of problem-solving. This method would "transfer" to adult life, and the mature adult might then take his place in society and decide to "reconstruct it." But the school itself would avoid any form of indoctrination! At most, then, the school should develop a methodology for modifying the social order, according to the progressivists, but should never be the vanguard of any one "ism." The reconstructionist accepts this progressive approach as the first step, but insists that educators must agree on some social-political goals and then proceed to achieve these goals through the agency of the school.

The first basic change needed to reconstruct society must be made in regard to policy-making for the school. To effect a real change, all school policies must have their origin in the representation of all those involved in the educative process. Therefore:

1. School boards must represent all the people, not merely the upper and middle classes; they must be a true cross section of the entire community.

2. Teachers, administrators, students, and educational experts must be allowed to participate in making those decisions affecting the implementation of the general policies formulated by the school board. In this manner, the needs and interests of all those concerned in the educative process will be met to the greatest possible degree of satisfaction.

3. The federal government, as the representative of all the people in all the states, must assume major responsibility for the support and direction of the educational enterprise.

4. Federal aid and direction must be granted to all those agencies playing a subsidiary role to education, such as health, welfare, recreation, and natural resources, to assure their availability to all the people.

5. Federal ownership or control (again as the representative of all the people) should be granted in all those areas of production, such as steel and automotive industry which affect all the people.

6. The individualistic, competitive spirit of the early American economy must be replaced by a social-cooperative attitude. It is the task of the school to develop this new attitude toward people and the socioeconomic order.

7. The spirit of selfish nationalism must give way to the ideal of international understanding, cooperation, and help. Because of

increased intercommunication and rapid means of transportation, people must become citizens of the world rather than of any one community, state, or nation. Again, it is the school's job to develop the "new" attitudes in children.

Obviously, the above recommendations set forth by spokesmen for reconstructionism represent a rather radical departure from the views of many educators. The purpose of the school in society becomes all-inclusive in the sense that all aspects of culture and society or their reform become its proper concern. The chapter on "Philosophical Issues in Education" will treat this topic more thoroughly, but some explanation of the implication of this philosophy might be of interest at this point.

1. The most important objective of education seems to be "social efficiency." In other words, the school must develop in the student a cooperative spirit designed to make him an active member of his own and the larger social groups of the community and world. The individualistic competitive spirit of traditional education must be replaced by a willingness to work with others toward commonly agreed upon social goals.

2. The predominant teaching method will be group problem-solving. Activity, including individual projects, will be directed toward the solution of problems agreed upon by the group (teacher and pupils). The goal of this method is a "social consensus" representing the beliefs and views of all those in any way involved in the problem. Social consensus is attained whenever agreement is reached about goals, solutions, values, ways of doing things. As such, this social consensus represents truth, or at least it is as near to truth as human intelligence can arrive. Training in the method of group problem-solving ("democratic method") with its goal of consensus becomes most important in the activities carried on in the classroom, for it will transfer to the adult life of the citizen. True democratic living can be achieved only if it is begun in the primary school and practiced throughout all levels of education.

3. The curriculum of this "school for social democracy" will consist of those subject-matter areas which meet needs, demands, and interests and which solve the problems of the various groups in school. Thus the curriculum will vary from school to school, and from community to community. For example, a rural school will devote most of its time to solving problems of the soil, crop raising,

livestock, health, machinery maintenance, and the like. Whatever science, mathematics, language arts, and social studies are needed will be utilized in these practical areas. On the other hand, a school in an industrial community will concentrate on those areas designed to assist the student to find his place in an industrial community where he can work for the public good, both in industry and in the civic life of the complex urban structure. Greater stress will be placed upon industrial arts, problems of labor and management, and "social studies for community living."

4. Since the school should be a community school, the evaluation of its success and that of its students will be in terms of problem-solving ability, adaptability to new and complex social difficulties, cooperativeness and community service. A student will not be graded on the basis of mastery of subject matter, for subject matter is important only insofar as it assists the group to solve some problem. In short, the student will be evaluated chiefly on the extent to which he has developed "democratic cooperativeness."

5. Discipline, in the reconstructionist school, will be group-centered, not teacher-centered. Each social situation will suggest its own form of discipline. Again, democratic cooperativeness will be the touchstone to all school discipline. All norms of conduct for the school (and community) will be arrived at by the uncoerced democratic consensus of all involved — students, teachers, administrators, parents, and community leaders.

The reader will note a great similarity between Dewey's ideas and those of the reconstructionists. But he will find that the reconstructionists have carried many of Dewey's ideas to their extreme. Because of the many socialistic trends in modern political theory, arising from the need to solve the problems of our highly complex industrialized society, the reconstructionists have won many followers in schools of education in this country. Indeed, they are one of the major educational forces to be contended with in this age.

It was pointed out above that even though most of the ideas (ideology) of modern education had their origin in Europe, they were not applied to any great extent except in America. One of the factors which fostered these large-scale revisions in the existing educational patterns was the advent of free compulsory education for all children. As the age limit for compulsory school attendance rose, educators saw the inadequacies of some of the more traditional patterns designed chiefly for the gifted student. Thus many of the theoretical and practical views of the "educational reformers" mentioned above were mingled with the traditional beliefs and practices.

Why were late-nineteenth-century American educators so concerned with educating "all the children of all the people"? Because of the belief that popular democracy, to be successful, must of necessity have an educated electorate! Because of the great economic inequalities among the people, it was of paramount importance that this minimal education be offered to all at no expense to the recipient. Since early American education was privately supported, radical changes had to be effected in the outlook of the people. No figure in American education contributed as much to the cause of state-supported public schools as did Horace Mann (1796–1859). Because of his "progressive" thinking in these matters he is often classified as an advocate of the "new" education.

His first step in this direction was the espousal of the cause of the teacher-training institutions. These schools, he believed, should be state-supported and tuition-free so that candidates from all socioeconomic classes could secure adequate training for teaching "democracy's children." His proposal was accepted by virtually every state in the Union. Ideologically at least, Mann may be considered the father of the normal school system which for many years prepared the elementary teachers of this country.

The next logical step in his program was to insist that free state-controlled education be offered to all children of elementary school age. If free education were to be given all children, he believed it must of necessity be nonsectarian. Because of the deeply rooted sectarian biases in the New England states, Mann's solution to the problem of religion in the public schools was the simplest way out of the difficulty. Each religious denomination would be responsible for the religious education of its children, the public schools would spend their time on the "nondenominational" academic subjects. He did not want the schools to be antireligious or irreligious but "neutral." Therefore the charge that Mann advocated "godless" education is not in harmony with his own religious views. To him, there seemed to be no solution to the problem of religion in the public schools satisfactory to all the warring sects other than by excluding all sectarian teaching from the schools.

Another name worthy of mention in connection with the development of free public education is that of Henry Barnard (1811–1900). Like Mann, he also worked diligently for the establishment of normal schools and as the first United States Commissioner of Education did much to advance these two causes. He was responsible for the present policy of that office of collecting and distributing information about education. This has been of great value to public and private schools alike.

Certainly, there are many other scholars and thinkers who have contributed much to modern education. Your instructor and the suggested readings will fill in the gaps. Such sources will include many living educators and the "schools of education" they represent. It will be noted that most of these modern educators do not label themselves "progressive." The reason for not using the term is that the progressive movement came to a close with the last publication of the journal, *Progressive Education* (1957).

Summary

There is no doubt, however, that progressive education has left its permanent mark on American education. In summary, the following beliefs about education can be traced to the progressive movement and its antecedents:

1. The school should be concerned with the development of the whole child — mental, physical, emotional, and "spiritual."
2. The educational program should be based at least as to its starting point upon the needs and interests of the pupils rather than upon some predetermined classical or academic curriculum.
3. The pupils should be actively involved in the learning process rather than passively committing to memory assigned lessons.
4. Subject matter should be organized into "experience units," or at least into subject-matter units composed of those facts, principles, and activities which "naturally" belong together.
5. All schools should offer as wide an array of "practical subjects" as possible, to meet the professional and vocational needs of the students.
6. The curriculum of the secondary school should be elective, with the exception of a few subjects such as English, etc.
7. Ample opportunity should be offered in the school for the development of the creative abilities of the students. Art, music, home decorating, woodworking, dressmaking, dramatics, and the like should be cocurricular, rather than extracurricular activities.
8. Problem-solving (or one of its adaptations, such as the project) should be the dominant teaching-learning method.

9. The school should adapt its curriculum and the content of the different courses to the individual differences of the pupil. Not all the students should be expected to do the same schoolwork, even though they are in the same class or age group.

10. A permissive atmosphere should reign in the classroom, rather than the harsh authoritarian rule of the traditional school. Students should "live democracy" as the best way of learning its meaning. They should learn to work with others in the group to become able to contribute to the betterment of society.

11. Students should be given some voice in directing their own school behavior through the medium of student government, homeroom, and class officers.

12. Evaluation should be based upon relative norms (average), "growth," and adjustment.

13. Guidance of pupils by teachers and a professional staff should replace the traditional, impersonal rule of administrators.[19]

SELECTED READINGS

Beck, R. H., "Progressive Education and American Progressivism," *Teachers College Record*, Vol. 60, No. 2, November, 1958, pp. 77–89.
  The first of a series on the origins of and principles underlying American Progressivism. Shows the relation of this movement to progressivism in politics.

———— (ed.), *The 3 R's Plus* (Minneapolis: University of Minnesota Press, 1956), pp. 3–11.
  A collection of essays by representatives of the subject-matter areas taught in American schools today giving the aims, content, and recommended methods for each area.

Brameld, Theodore, *Patterns of Educational Philosophy* (New York: World Book Co., 1950), Chaps. 4–6, pp. 13–22.
  Presents the beliefs about knowledge, reality, and value of the educational philosophies of progressivism and reconstructionism. Also shows how these philosophical beliefs determine educational aims, the curriculum, and the different facets of educational practice.

Childs, John, *American Pragmatism and Education* (New York: Henry Holt & Co., 1956).
  A clear statement of the philosophy of pragmatism and its educational implications by one of John Dewey's best-known disciples.

Dewey, John, *My Pedagogic Creed* (Washington, D. C.: Progressive Education Association, 1929).
  A list of foundational beliefs on the major points of educational philosophy by America's most famous educational philosopher. Many of Dewey's later works are amplifications of the views stated in this *Creed*.

Herbart, J. F., *Outlines of Educational Doctrine* (New York: Macmillan Co., 1901).

---

[19] See *Policies and Criteria for Approval of Secondary Schools* (North Central Association of Colleges and Secondary Schools, 1959–1960).

Contains a description of a new approach to teaching which affected the concern which modern education has for methodology.

——— *The Science of Education* (Boston: D. C. Heath Co., 1895).
One of the first treatises proposing the thesis that education is a "science" operating on the same principles and practices as the other natural sciences.

Mayer, Martin, *The Schools* (New York: Harper & Bros., 1961), Chaps. 2–3.
A nontechnical description of progressive educational theory and practice pointing up its advantages and weaknesses.

Rousseau, J. J., *Emile* (W. H. Payne, trans.) (New York: D. Appleton Co., 1896).
One of the outstanding "classics" of modern education calling for an educational program based on the natural interests and needs of the child.

Spencer, Herbert, *Education: Intellectual, Moral & Physical* (New York: D. Appleton Co., 1866).
The first complete statement of naturalistic objectives of education demanding that the school be concerned with the "whole child" rather than the intellect alone.

Ulich, Robert, *History of Educational Thought* (New York: American Book Co., 1950), pp. 162–337.
A review of the philosophical contributions to the theory and practice of modern education.

Chapter XI

PHILOSOPHICAL ISSUES IN
AMERICAN EDUCATION

In Chapter VI some of the practical problems facing American education were viewed in the context of the modern educational scene. Undoubtedly there are some philosophical positions underlying the different points of view on discipline, federal aid to education, and the other issues listed. For example, if one's political philosophy tends to be very conservative, the chances are that he will be against most forms of federal aid to education. Also, if one's beliefs about the nature of man involve the notion that children are strongly drawn toward evil, he will most likely favor a rather rigid approach to classroom discipline. Consequently, none of the issues treated in this book can be completely divorced from philosophical beliefs.

The main difference, then, between the issues treated in this chapter and Chapters VI and XVIII lies in the assumption that a person's attitude toward those discussed in this chapter will be derived almost exclusively from his philosophy of life. An individual's viewpoint on those taken up in Chapters VI and XVIII will depend upon many practical considerations as well.

A note of warning might be in order. As indicated in Chapter I the opposing positions on the issues usually are presented in their more extreme forms. Obviously, there are moderate views, at least on some of the philosophical issues. Furthermore, a great deal of oversimplification will be evident in the treatment of these issues simply because a highly technical discussion of topics such as "truth," "democracy," and "freedom" is not possible (nor desirable) in an introductory text.

THE MEANING OF DEMOCRACY

Ask almost any American what he esteems most highly in the

realm of social values and he will undoubtedly answer, "Democracy." If you press your questioning and ask for a theoretical and/or operational definition of democracy, you will receive a great variety of answers. In some instances you will find that these definitions actually are contradictory. About the only characteristic you might find in common is that democracy is "good." Everybody is for it. Even the Soviet Union and its satellites describe their one-party systems (police states) as "people's democracies." Not too long ago the Nazis considered their National Socialistic regime the "highest form of a democratic state." The Italian Fascists viewed their corporate state as the ideal expression of "true democracy."

The literature on professional education is no exception to this "rule of confusion." There is scarcely an American book in the field of professional education which does not sing the praises of democracy. They all speak of the "democratic classroom," the "democratic personality," and "developing democratic attitudes," but the discerning reader is never quite sure what is meant by democracy. In fact, many educational leaders are convinced that the vagueness which surrounds the term represents a desirable situation, since it allows for a "progressive reconstruction" of the meaning and practices of democracy.[1] They argue that any static meaning given to "democracy" stultifies its growth and crystallizes its practices to the extent that it cannot meet the needs of changing times. Others, however, believe that the term should be given a definite meaning, otherwise true communication is well nigh impossible.

This text shall not be able to settle this dispute. But it might be well to point up the major view of the meaning of democracy found in educational literature, to enable the student to discern what each writer means by the term. To simplify the classification of the many definitions of democracy, they shall be lumped into two major categories: democracy as (A) *a form of government* and (B) *a way of life.*

Democracy as a Form of Government

Ancient democracy. One of the best ways to extract the true meaning of a term like democracy (which involves a set of practices) is to look

---

[1] See Boyd Bode, *Democracy as a Way of Life* (New York: Macmillan Co., 1950), and T. Brameld, *Toward a Reconstructed Philosophy of Education* (New York: Dryden Press, 1956), Chap. I.

at its application in *actual practice*. The first "democracy in action" as far as is known was found in Athens at the time of Pericles (429 B.C.). In the Athenian democracy, *all citizens* had the right and duty to belong to the main governing body called the *ecclesia*. This group selected the officials of government and the members of the courts who were directly responsible to the *ecclesia*. Since the number of citizens was relatively small (women, foreigners, and slaves were excluded), each citizen had a direct voice in the government of the state. Because of this direct participation in the government and the direct control of all officials by the citizens, Athenian democracy is often regarded as "pure" democracy. There were no "intermediaries" as found in the highly complex representative systems of today.

The tremendous influence of Plato and Aristotle on the political thought of succeeding centuries seems to have caused the complete lapse into oblivion (almost 2000 years) of the Athenian conception of democracy. Both Plato and Aristotle opposed democracy because they believed it was a system designed to allow the majority to rule for their own good rather than for the good of all. These two great philosophers taught that any government must rule for the good of all, and therefore they favored aristocracy and monarchy respectively as the best forms of government. In these two forms, the best and wisest person (or persons) would rule for the good of all.

Some students of political theory speculate that if the monarchs and rulers had lived up to the lofty ideal of ruling for the good of *all their subjects*, democracy, or the rule of the people, might not have had a revival at all. But, as history shows, not all rulers made the "common good" their chief objective. Many became despots of the worst type; the courts of kings and nobles were often centers of luxury, whereas the great majority of the people did not receive the food and care given the animals in the king's stables. In addition to this practical failure of the rulers to live up to their own ideal, several philosophical arguments were presented against the Platonic and Aristotelian conceptions of monarchy and aristocracy as the best forms of government.

The opposition roughly seems to be derived from two basic sources: (1) the deistic-naturalistic views expressed by Rousseau, Locke, Paine, and Jefferson, and (2) the theistic (Christian) views of Suarez and Bellarmine. The deistic-naturalistic outlook on life is based on the belief that man is on his own to solve his problems; therefore, all political power rests with men, and the authority given to rulers comes from the people rather than from any power above the people, such as God. Locke, for example, asserts that the whole political power of the community rests in the majority, who in turn shall designate those who will execute the laws made by the majority. As such, "representation" is adequate for designating a form of government as "democratic."[2] Both Rousseau and Paine viewed democracy as a way of administering the political structure of society. Jefferson seems to have incorporated all of these basic ideas into his broader conception including representation, governmental structure or form and political administration. It was this deistic-naturalistic formulation of democracy which served as the foundation for the early American "experiment" in democratic government.

The theistic (Christian) view of Suarez and Bellarmine, as well as the deistic position of Locke and Jefferson, rejects the doctrine that the king or ruler has any "divine right" to govern. But, they argue, it does not follow that God does not concern Himself with the temporal events of mankind. On the contrary, His authority over man remains the same regardless of the form of political structure employed. But since God usually acts through secondary causes, He has chosen to vest the authority to govern in the people themselves. It is their prerogative, then, to select those upon whom they wish to bestow this authority. Any ruler who abuses this authority can be deposed by the people. Thus no king or ruler could claim that he has a "divine right" to rule.[3]

In practice, the democratic ideals of Suarez and Bellarmine are similar to those of Locke, and might be placed under the heading of "democracy as a form of government."[4] As such, democratic action is limited to the sphere of politics and does not apply to religion, the family, or other institutions. Also, for this reason, these philosopher-theologians did not consider it inconsistent with democratic principles to have an autocratic structure in the Church, a religious order, the family, and many other types of social units.[5]

Democracy as a Way of Life

Not until the twentieth century was there any real challenge to the traditional view of democracy described above. John Dewey is usually credited with the new formulation of democracy, and he and his

---

[2] See John Locke, *Second Treatise on Civil Government* (London: Everyman's Library, 1924), p. 182.

[3] Some Protestant Christian theorists hold that same view about authority. Martin Luther, however, and most of his followers, contend that the people select the rulers and then God bestows upon those designated the power to govern.

[4] The extent to which Suarez and Bellarmine influenced Jefferson and the others who helped frame the Constitution is a controversial issue among historians. Some hold that the origin of Jefferson's views is found in deism. Others believe that many of Suarez' and Bellarmine's views are incorporated in the Constitution.

[5] The student of the history of political thought will recognize that the democratic principles expounded by Locke, Suarez, and Bellarmine are not completely novel. Their seeds can be found in the philosophical views of the Greeks as well as in those of the Scholastics. Surely, the great Scholastics and even Plato did not advocate the "divine-right" idea.

followers insist that democracy can no longer be regarded as a purely political concept. Democracy is much more, they assert, than the method or means used to arrive at governmental decision. Democracy becomes the criterion by which all kinds of behavior are judged. Thus social and economic decisions, statements of right and wrong, family and community relations, classroom management and discipline, religious doctrines and values are all viewed as acceptable or not acceptable insofar as they conform to certain "democratic characteristics." What are these characteristics?

1. *The acceptance of the belief that "truth" is a dynamic, changing concept.* This characteristic implies that there is nothing absolutely true for all times and under all circumstances.

The person accepting this view will show an active willingness to put aside any statement which he considers true and reflect upon new facts and ideas that might lead him to abandon even those beliefs which he holds most sacred. Thus the person, community, nation, or religious organizations will always be willing to make changes in their basic beliefs and practices in the light of new facts and ideas.

2. *A recognition of the relativity of all values is a basic characteristic of the new conception of democracy.* All political and social arrangements, and the norms governing them, are subject to constant revision by those who participate in or are subject to them. This means that as times and circumstances change, all our religious, moral, social, and aesthetic values will change. What is considered right or wrong today may not be considered such some years hence. The beautiful and the ugly might "exchange positions" in the generation to come. "Private property" and individualism may be social values to be esteemed in one culture but despised in another. The ethical norms expressed in the Ten Commandments may have been acceptable moral guideposts in the prescientific age, but are no longer satisfactory for life in the space age. Also, the moral directives of the world's churches must be changed to meet the needs of a new and complex society. In the words of Professor Bode: "In a democracy there is no place for absolutes."[6]

3. *Acceptance of egalitarianism is basic to democracy.* The term "egalitarianism" connotes the opposite of elitism. Elitism implies that some people are more fit to rule than others because of such factors as heredity, education, or social status. Egalitarianism implies that all people, barring the few with serious mental deficiencies (congenital or accidental) can, by proper education, be rendered equal in all phases of behavior. This involves a "leveling-off" or even a "raising-up" process whereby all will possess the basic qualifications for leadership. However, leadership itself needs a new definition to be consistent with the egalitarian outlook. Everyone is to some extent a leader. Those

6 Boyd H. Bode, *Democracy as a Way of Life*, p. 113.

who help the group determine its goals or decide what the problem at hand is about; those who seek information to assist the group in locating the problem or suggesting ways out of difficulties; those who arbitrate disputes, keep records of action, or initiate new action are all functioning as leaders. In such cooperative situations it may even be difficult to put a finger on the actual leaders, for anyone who contributes in any positive way to the deliberations or work of the group is actually functioning as a leader. In fact, the egalitarian concept of leadership is opposed to the traditional view of the leader as the "strong man" of the organization, or the father-figure, the person with power (overt or covert), the planner, or the expert.

Yet another implication of egalitarianism is found in the dictum "equality of opportunity" for all in all phases of life. For example, all children must have the opportunity to attend tuition-free schools and to profit from and experience satisfactions in such schooling. All persons should have equal opportunity to have steady employment, if they so desire, in jobs suited to their interests, desires, and abilities. All people have the same right to health services, recreational facilities, and security in old age and times of personal disaster.

4. *Certain attitudes and personality traits are characteristic of the new democracy.* This means that a kindly and humane attitude must be developed toward all people. All must be treated equally; all must have a fair share of the goods of this earth (and outer space). The findings of social psychology, mental health, and human relations research must become part of the fabric of democracy. A democratic person will get along with others and cooperate in group projects for the improvement of life on this planet. If this "democratic personality" is developed in home, school, and community, there will be less strife in labor relations, less "throat cutting" in business, and less violence in international relations. Some advocates of the "new democracy" even are convinced that it contains the elements necessary to remove war from the face of the earth.

5. *The individual should direct his thinking and subsequent action for the improvement of group living.* Every individual should be allowed and encouraged to do independent thinking, but should be encouraged to do so for the solution of common problems. Thought and action which contribute solely to the benefit or pleasure of the individual are not democratic. Rather, the individual is exhorted to use his talents and abilities for the public good. The advocates of the new democracy are radically opposed to the "rugged individualism" of early America, both on practical and philosophical grounds. Philosophically, it contradicts the principle of egalitarianism, and practically it tends to channel the goods of this earth into the hands of the few.

6. *Majority decisions represent the nearest point to "truth" that can be*

reached in solving difficulties involving decisions, policies, norms of behavior, and ideological matters. Although unanimous agreement is the ideal to be sought in matters of human behavior, the theorists of the new democracy recognize that a majority acceptance of some plan of action is sufficient for putting the plan in effect. However, they aver that the majority must respect the opinions and interests of the minority insofar as possible. This respect of the minority view represents a recognition of the relative nature of all practical decisions, policies, and ethical norms. Some day, then, the minority view may become the accepted view of the majority. Finally, this conception of democracy implies the belief that final authority in all matters involving human behavior rests with the people and not in any outside authority such as church, God, or "natural law."

Points of Agreement on the Meaning of Democracy

Certainly, there are areas where the two different views presented above have something in common: (1) For example, both agree that the method of arriving at decisions should be based on the free use of the vote. All citizens should be permitted to use this franchise to express their views on major issues. (2) Majority rule is the basis for action in a democracy, at least to the extent that it is to be preferred to minority rule. (3) *Political* equality is essential to any view of democracy. All this statement implies is that no citizen has any more political right than any other to vote or rule (the egalitarians go much further, but they do insist on political equality). (4) The government is supposed to reflect the will of the people in general rather than that of any power or interest group.

ACADEMIC FREEDOM

Very closely associated with the discussion of the preceding section on the meaning of democracy is the issue of academic freedom. This issue has become more significant in the past two decades because of the stepped-up activities of organizations considered destructive to the "American way." During World War II, for example, the "subversive activities" of both the Nazis and Communists were believed to be directed at the universities and colleges, as well as at the lower schools of our nation. During the Korean War and the decade following it, congressional committees, state legislatures, and local authorities began to scrutinize for their un-American content the doctrines taught in the nation's schools. In addition to this "official" scrutiny, many citizens have raised their voices against what is being taught in the public and private schools. This writer recalls a speech in a small midwestern community attacking faculty members in the local colleges and high schools for having "communistic leanings." He based his charges on the reading lists of the teachers which included "socialistic" books, and upon certain staff members' criticisms of the "profit system" in American industry. Further investigation on the part of the teaching staffs revealed that the charges were leveled not only against the teachers of social studies in the public institutions, but also against a large number of the parochial high school teachers and several religious-sponsored college staff members.

A perusal of the "public pulse" or "Letters to the Editor" in any newspaper will reveal that many parents are very critical of what their children are being taught. Certainly, then, the issue of academic freedom is a very real one and should be a concern of all future teachers.

So that there is some common ground for a discussion of this issue, the definition used in the *Encyclopedia of Social Science* might be used as a starting point. "Academic freedom is the freedom of the teacher or research worker in higher institutions of learning to investigate and discuss the problems of his science and to express his conclusions whether through publication or in the instruction of students without interference from political or ecclesiastical authority or from the administration officials of the institution in which he is employed, unless his methods are found by qualified bodies of his own profession to be clearly incompetent or contrary to professional ethics."

Although the definition refers specifically to college or university personnel, it might be applied to elementary and secondary school teachers as well. Granted, there is relatively little in the elementary school curriculum which might be considered controversial, nevertheless there are some topics, chiefly in the social studies, which have been the cause of difficulty. For example, some citizens have criticized teachers for being un-American and unpatriotic in their treatment of the United Nations, and other topics involving the "world community." In high school there are many more subjects for discussion which might stir up the ire of some people in the community. To mention only one, a modern biology class in high school can hardly avoid discussing "evolution," a topic which is very apt to cause controversy because of its theological implications.

Another point of clarification is needed; academic freedom does not refer to the civil or personal rights and liberties of the teacher as an American citizen. In this respect a teacher enjoys the same privileges and rights and has the same civic duties as any other citizen. Thus a teacher does not appeal to the principle of academic freedom if his civil or religious freedom has been violated; nor can he cry that his academic freedom has been violated if he has been hauled into court for a crime or felony. Certainly the job of a teacher carries with it responsibilities as well as rights. However, in spite of these legal qualifications and limitations put upon teachers, some advocate a much more liberal view of academic freedom than others. Following are some of the arguments for and against unrestricted academic freedom.

Arguments for the Liberal Interpretation of Academic Freedom

1. The restriction of academic freedom is contrary to the tenets of democracy. This statement, representing the basic argument proposed for unrestricted freedom, proposes that it is inherent in the very nature of true democracy and is guaranteed by the Constitution of the United States. Therefore, any limitations put upon the teacher's freedom (except as specified in the Constitution) are not only unwise and unjust, but basically illegal.

2. The constitutional guarantee of freedom of thought, speech, and the press should have special significance for the teacher, since his exercise of these is the surest means of convincing others, especially his students, of the value of these freedoms. A teacher who does not express the truth as he sees it, or does not allow his students to do so, is not only being unfaithful to the spirit of the Constitution but is laying himself open to the charge of intellectual dishonesty.

3. A study of the history of ideas reveals that most of the outstanding contributions in science, politics, philosophy, and even theology have been suspect in the early stages of their development. People fear the strange and the unfamiliar, and often label them as radical or revolutionary when in fact they might represent the truth. Note the opposition and ill-treatment meted out to Socrates, Moses, Christ, St. Thomas Aquinas, Galileo, and many others. All were considered radicals, disrupters of peace, corrupters of youth, or, by some people, even maniacs. Therefore, the classroom or professional publication should be the forum for open discussion of ideas at the level of the students (usually socialized medicine, evolution, and Marxism are too

difficult for discussion in lower elementary classes). Suppression of new ideas can only serve as a brake to the wheels of progress, and in the long run the new ideas will succeed in "seeping" out into the public forum.

4. The suppression of ideas through limitations on academic freedom is psychologically unsound, for it makes the "forbidden fruit" more enticing to the young mind. An open display and discussion of controversial topics will remove the dangers of the youthful flare for seeking the forbidden. Also, the student will develop the ability for critical thinking, with the result that he can sift the wheat from the chaff, a task which he must perform throughout his life.

5. Even if some members of the teaching staff espouse unpopular or erroneous political views, they are not *ipso facto* to be suspect in other areas of scholarly endeavor. Witness the large number of teachers in Communist countries who are truly competent in the various fields of science, the fine arts, literature, and even history. In these instances, the holding of a false political philosophy does not necessarily impair their scholarly and creative work in other fields.

6. Granted that unrestricted academic freedom might constitute evil to some people, it is, nevertheless, better to gamble on too much freedom than on too little. If one insists on the principle of restricting the freedom of speech and the press, he is inviting all other kinds of limitations on the basic freedoms. Whatever group assumes power will have the legal tools necessary to crush all opposition. History has shown this to be the case in the many political, religious, and social tragedies of the ages.

Arguments for Restricting the Teacher's Academic Freedom

1. The first restriction to be put on academic freedom is derived from the very nature of truth itself. Under no circumstances should a teacher be allowed to teach falsehood. The only application of academic freedom is to be found in those topics where the truth is not yet known. Consequently the civil and ecclesiastic authorities and the school administration have every right to silence a teacher when they, in conscience, believe that he is teaching falsehood.[7]

2. The teacher is an employee of the academic institution and/or community hiring him and must be willing to accept the limitations and restrictions placed upon him by his employer. For example, if a teacher is employed by a community very conservative in politics, religion, economics, and moral behavior, the teacher is obliged to treat all academic subjects from this conservative point of view. The area of social

---

[7] See below, "Nature of Truth," pp. 279–283.

studies, for example, deals with many topics which might be given a conservative or liberal interpretation, and it is the duty of the local school officials to see to it that the teacher gives an interpretation in harmony with community beliefs. Similarly, in a religious school, the teachers can be expected to give no instruction and express no views contrary to the accepted doctrines of that religion.

3. The liberal interpretation of academic freedom is very unrealistic since it presumes that students should be able to distinguish error from truth. However, elementary and high school students simply are not mature enough to make these very difficult distinctions, for even college students tend to accept the dicta of their teachers. Therefore, someone in authority must be able to put restrictions on what is taught in the schools lest the minds of youth be led into error.

4. Assuming that teachers remain "neutral" in their teaching, and that they present objectively both sides of the question, a somewhat dangerous attitude might be developed in students. Constant repetition of this noncommittal approach might lead the student to believe that there is no truth and that all knowledge is relative to time, place, and altered circumstances. The student will have no firm moorings upon which to build a set of values to guide his everyday life. Such a state of mind can only lead to insecurity and frustration. Perhaps a complete breakdown in personal integrity will result — indeed, a catastrophe for the individual and society.

5. Many of the arguments given for unrestricted academic freedom presuppose that a teacher will not propagandize un-American or antireligious doctrines. Such a presumption is simply naïve! Witness the significant number of "subversive" teachers and professors found in public and private institutions of learning. These people have used academic freedom to destroy freedom. Consequently, citizens have every right to insist that school administrators control what is being taught in the schools. Some sort of loyalty oath might be a necessary condition for employment, and the teaching of any suspect doctrines should be considered adequate grounds for dismissal.

6. Some educators, generally favoring unrestricted academic freedom as the "ideal" under normal conditions, feel that because of the imminent danger of Communist infiltration certain limits must be placed upon the teacher's freedom. The extraordinary conditions of the world today demand that unusual steps be taken to safeguard our way of life. When the Communist menace has disappeared, or at least has been thoroughly weakened, the ideal of unrestricted academic freedom can be restored to the educational institutions of this country. Until such a time "eternal vigilance is the price of survival."

THE NATURE OF TRUTH

A discussion of the nature of truth might appear a bit removed from the practical business of the school. But a glimpse at the history of education will show that traditionally the school has concerned itself with truth. The lower levels of education, elementary and secondary, purported to teach the accepted truths of the society they served. The higher levels — college, university, and graduate — sought to discover (or create) new truths.

Truly then, the school curriculum consisted of the formal organization of those truths (knowledge) in such a way that they might be learned by the pupils. Whether it was the *trivium* and *quadrivium* of classical schools, the humanistic studies of Renaissance schools, or the very broad science, mathematics, social studies, and literary curriculum of the modern school, all were viewed as truths and knowledge worth passing on to the younger generation. The curriculum organization was not considered essential, but the truths to be taught were to be contained in the curriculum regardless of the organizational patterns. One school might teach the truths of history, science, mathematics, and religion through a study of the "great books" of the world. Another might give very specialized courses in each of the content areas such as ancient history, medieval history, European history, American history, and so on for each area.

Others might prefer to teach all the "social sciences" in an integrated or "core" course which includes history, sociology, economics, geography, and political science. Similarly, physics, chemistry, biology, geology, and astronomy might be taught in a general science course. Literature, art, poetry, drama might be lumped into a humanities course.

The crucial criterion of any curriculum, then, was the extent to which it covered these truths cherished most by the society holding them. A teacher was considered successful if he communicated these truths to his students, or at least helped them find them for themselves.

The advent of the twentieth century posed the first serious challenge to this belief of the school's responsibility toward transmission of the truth to the young. This challenge consisted in giving the term "truth" an entirely different meaning.

The "New" Meaning of Truth

Throughout Chapter X it was noted that the new education was characterized by its dynamic reinterpretation of all basic educational principles and practices. Consciously (or unconsciously) the proponents of the new education gave "truth" a dynamic definition. What basic characteristics can be noted in this definition?

1. All truth is changing; there is no statement, principle, law, or theory which always was and always will be true. The origin of this new attitude toward truth developed quite naturally from the rapid change in scientific beliefs of the eighteenth and nineteenth centuries. During these centuries practically all scientific statements about the universe were rejected completely or at least called into question. The traditional beliefs about the shape and size of the earth were disproved by scientists. The origin of plant and animal life upon earth as described in the Bible was discarded in favor of the different theories of evolution. Radically new discoveries in the field of medicine displaced practically all of the foundations and principles of medical science. The new sciences of sociology and psychology challenged the most cherished beliefs about man's mental and social behavior.

This state of affairs led some thinkers to assume that all truths are relative; all aspects of reality and knowledge are in a state of constant flux. Hence, when the label of truth was attached to any statement, it was meant in a dynamic frame of reference allowing for constant revision or even complete rejection.

2. The way of arriving at truth or knowledge is limited to one approach, the scientific. Accompanying the scientific advances of the past two centuries one notes the trend among scholars and laity alike to regard "experience and science" as the sole sources of truth. The success of science in providing for the material needs and wants of people in the civilized world has done much to convince them that science can find the answers and solutions to all questions and problems. This attitude, combined with the tough-minded outlook that seeing is believing, has bolstered up the belief that experience and science can provide all the knowledge and truth man needs for his existence.

The most widely used method in modern education, problem-solving, is one of the outgrowths of this reliance on the techniques and presuppositions of the scientific age. As was noted in Chapter X, Dewey believed that man acquires all his knowledge in response to difficulties that arise around him. In other words, if there were no problematic situations, man would just "vegetate" and never acquire any knowledge at all. But when one runs into difficulties that disrupt the smooth flow of his existence, he sets out to solve the difficulty so that peace of mind can be restored. Dewey and his followers always have maintained that the method of problem-solving (see Chap. X) is an adaption of scientific method for settling the difficulties of daily living, as well as for seeking answers to questions about the physical universe. But the end result of this process is not a statement of a truth that will remain static. Rather, the knowledge gained is relative to the time, place, and altered circumstances under which the difficulty arose. And as long as the knowledge acquired solves the problem, "truth" has been achieved. Constant revision of any truth is to be expected, for "new circumstances will change old truths."

3. This dynamic view of truth and knowledge calls for major changes in the school's responsibility to the student. In the first place, the school must gradually bring the student to the realization that there are no truths or doctrines that are absolute or changeless. Second, the curriculum must reflect the basic belief that no subject matter is so sacred that it cannot be replaced by some other content more pertinent to the modern world and its problems. This is often referred to in educational jargon as "the evolving curriculum." Third, the student and his problems should dominate the activities of the school, rather than any preconceived notion of what is "right or wrong" for boys and girls to study. Fourth, teaching methods should be geared to developing in the student a method of learning that will assist him in adjusting to new situations and help him to "create" new truths as new problems arise. Fifth, the student must be unhampered by authoritarian dicta, theological beliefs, and prearranged bodies of subject matter in his search for and creation of new truths. As Kurt Lewin, the social psychologist, once said, true science can only prosper in a democratic atmosphere.

Traditional View of the Nature of Truth

Many thinkers contend that the advocates of the doctrine of changing truth have gone too far in their rejection of the classical conception of changeless or "absolute" truth. Some of the arguments proposed are:

1. It is granted that in some areas of human knowledge, such as science, the dynamic concept of truth is essential to the very nature of the subject matter. Many of the old beliefs and theories about the nature of the universe had to be discarded in the light of new scientific evidence. Even very recent findings are being questioned. The honest scientist (one faithful to the principles of his discipline) must always be willing to admit that his own discoveries and theories need constant revision or even rejection.

2. Because truth is not static in one area of human endeavor, it does not

necessarily follow that it must be the same in all others. Some truths proposed by philosophers are not the result of scientific investigation but are based on reason. For example, "every effect must have a cause"; "the universe could not have evolved from nothingness"; "justice is to be preferred to injustice"; "lying is wrong in itself," and so on, are considered true for all times and in all places. Those truths are derived from the fields of metaphysics and ethics.

Theology also is considered a domain of human knowledge presenting as immutable certain truths such as: the nature of God and His role in the lives of men, the fall of man from original innocence, the moral directives of the Ten Commandments, the place of charity in human relations. All of these truths are not derived from the empirical sciences but are based on a supernatural source.

3. The school's role, then, is quite different from that proposed by the advocates of relative truth. First, the school must develop in its students the ability to distinguish the different kinds of knowledge. They must learn to recognize an immutable truth from a changing one. They must be able to determine whether the knowledge they are acquiring is based on theological beliefs, philosophic reasoning, or scientific experiment. Even in those areas where immutable truth is to be found, some conclusions remain "controversial," and as the student progresses to higher studies these points of controversy can be presented.

In harmony with this view of the existence of both changing and changeless truths, the school curriculum will contain both elements. In a school operated on the premise that certain religious beliefs are absolutely true, these truths will be contained in the curriculum. Again, the organizational pattern is not essential but the actual content is. Thus the truths of religion might be taught in separate religious classes or they might be "integrated" in the student's reading and history classes. At the college level the basic principles of the philosophy of man, ethics, and metaphysics might be given in philosophy courses or be taught through the medium of the "Great Books." On the other hand, the sciences will be treated as areas of knowledge where change is to be expected. The student should develop an attitude of "wait and see" or "I'll change my mind when there is sufficient empirical evidence to warrant a change."

4. Certainly, not all traditionalists agree on the meaning of truth. Perhaps the most common view in Western civilization (and education) refers to a more or less abstract rationalistic concept of truth. However, several important modifications for understanding the classical Christian conception must be made. In Thomistic thought, for example, truth is found essentially in our judgments and judgments are opera-

tions of intelligence exercised by living persons. Hence, in a very real sense, one can say that man utters or makes truth, for truth is a living contact between man and reality achieved through human judgments. Thus, truth is something dynamic and vital, not a lifeless and static entity "out there." But man's judgments are true to the extent that they correspond to reality (existence); that is, they are not purely subjective preferences or creations. Also, certain truths about God and man's nature and destiny are not accepted as true solely because they have been revealed in a supernatural way but because they can be grasped by strictly demonstrative arguments.

To summarize this latter position, then, it can be asserted that some kinds of knowledge are by their very nature and origin true and immutable; others, by their very nature and origin, are subject to constant revision and change.

THE NATURE OF THE PUPIL

It is considered a truism among educators that "to know the nature of the pupil is to know the nature of education." But again, in this instance, there is a great difference of opinion among educators regarding the nature of the pupil. To simplify the discussion of the issue, the traditional and modern views will be contrasted, and no attempt will be made to point up the various differences of opinion in each of the two main camps.

The Traditional View

From ancient Greek times to the twentieth-century revolution in education, educators were in quite general agreement concerning the child's nature. Some of the main points upon which they agreed are:

1. The child is composed of mind and body, and the school's main concern is with the development of the mind. The historical surveys in Chapters XII and XIII show quite clearly that mental activities constituted the heart of the traditional curriculum. Even when an educator recommended some kind of physical education it was to serve an auxiliary role, namely, that a sound mind needed a sound body in which to dwell. So the physical activities were meant merely to strengthen the body so that the mind might be developed to its fullest extent through the academic activities. Before the twentieth century, full-blown programs in health and physical education were practically unknown, just as vocational education, homemaking, and social education were never found in schools.

2. The child is inclined to misbehave and therefore needs rather strict discipline in school. Although different schools of theology and philosophy disagreed on the extent to which the child was inclined to evil, there was basic agreement that the child's nature had to be held in check. Every reader has heard the following statements about child nature: (a) A child is inclined to be lazy; therefore the teacher must see to it that he is kept busy at all times, or, in the words of the adage, "Idleness is the devil's workshop." (b) The child is inclined to revolt against the authority of parents and teachers. Therefore strict discipline will teach him respect for his elders and authority. (c) The child will follow the path of least resistance. The school, therefore, must insist that the child take difficult subjects or it will be catering to the child's tendency to avoid hard work. (d) The "student's mind will be disciplined" by difficult subjects. The imposition of physical discipline upon the pupil will aid the process of mental discipline.

3. The child is destined for an afterlife because of the spiritual element in him, the soul. The first eighteen centuries after the birth of Christ witnessed a general acceptance of this belief about the nature of man. Consequently, all educational activities had as their *ultimate* goal the salvation of the soul of the educand. This belief accounts for the close relationship between religion and education until very recent years. Even though the various religious denominations held different beliefs about the supernatural, there was common agreement that the "things of the spirit" were more important than the things of the body. This attitude was reflected in the belief that an easy and comfortable life was not conducive to good spiritual health; life involves hardships and privations, too, and these could be used as means for drawing closer to God. Contemplation was to be preferred to practical pursuits; the "good life" was found in the things of the spirit, not in material wealth or creature comforts.

4. The belief that the child possessed a spiritual soul contained the formulation of the concept of a free will operative within that soul. Although there were many theoretical differences among Christian philosophers and theologians about free will, their directives for educational practice were almost the same. Thus the child was to be held personally responsible, and punished for any misbehavior and rewarded for his good deeds or achievements. Environmental forces were minimized, at least when reward and punishment were meted out. In fact, the belief that environment influenced child behavior is of very recent origin, with most of the research being done on the topic in the twentieth century. Even though the traditionalist insisted that teachers and parents give good example, the final responsibility for misbehavior was placed upon the pupil.

The Modern View

1. The child is not a composition of body and soul or of mind and body but an *evolving organism*. As such, he is made up of the same stuff as other organisms around him and only differs from them in degree (not in kind). Obviously, this view of man's nature found its origin in the evolutionary theories of the scientific age.

Although this belief that man is merely an evolving organism might seem far removed from educational practice, its direct influence on the school has been most significant. Its effect on the curriculum has been to divest the intellectual subjects of their prestige position and put them on a par with other school activities. Physical and vocational education are not relegated to a second-rate position for dullards but become an integral part of the school program. Homemaking, social functions, and all extracurricular activities are deemed worthy components of a good school curriculum.

Very often this same idea is expressed in the dictum that the school must develop the "whole child" — not just his mind. Fifty years ago the typical school maintained only "books and classrooms." But nowadays one finds health centers, gymnasiums, swimming pools, social centers, game rooms, clubrooms, and the like. In one sense all of these innovations had their origin in application of organic evolution to education — the school views its clientele as natural organisms to be developed, not minds to be disciplined.

2. The child is naturally good, or at worst morally neutral. This statement constitutes a denial of all the traditional beliefs about the fall of man and his inclination toward evil. The effect of this change in outlook about the moral nature of the educand has been very noticeable in the schools.

First, the school is redesigned to meet the needs, interests, and desires of pupils rather than those of the adults administering it. The "child-centered" school of the progressive era is a representative outgrowth of the belief that what a child is interested in is good. The curriculum should be built around these interests and needs.

Second, because the child is a growing organism (and growth is desirable), his own growth pattern and potential should determine what he should learn and when he should learn it. The belief of the modern educator that teaching should be adjusted to differences among learners is a direct result of this concept of "growth."

Third, discipline has an entirely different connotation. The so-called misbehavior of students is no longer regarded as the overflowing of the evil tendencies of the child, but rather as a genuinely natural and normal expression of native curiosity, youthful vitality, natural activity needs, and basic organic drives. Such manifestations are not to be thwarted but rather guided along socially acceptable modes of behavior. Discipline is viewed as a socializing process, one of adjustment and self-discipline. The teacher no longer is considered "the authority," the ruler, the purveyor of rewards and punishment, but preferably a guide and counselor in the admittedly difficult process of adjustment and self-discipline.

3. An outright denial (or practical disregard) of the supernatural element in man is characteristic of the modern outlook. The secularization of education in the Western world of the nineteenth and twentieth centuries is sufficient witness to this trend. Except in those private schools operated by religious groups, religion has been almost completely separated from education, both as to control and influence. Only a century or two ago, the belief that man's main purpose on earth was preparation for the life hereafter permeated nearly all educational institutions. Today a man's religious beliefs no longer serve as the integrating factor for all his activities. Religion is relegated to a "Sunday-morning activity," thus leaving the school completely out of the picture. The school may help the pupil prepare for a job, build good physical health, provide for good family living, learn good citizenship and the worthy use of leisure time; but it must not concern itself with "life after death." Thus for all practical purposes the pupil does not have an immortal soul.

4. The modern emphasis upon the influence of environment in human behavior has radically altered the traditional approach to free will and responsibility. Most manuals of child and adolescent psychology, guidance, and mental health direct the reader to look for the causes of misbehavior in the child's environment rather than in his free choice. If a student is stupid, belligerent, noisy, lazy, or truant, check the home, the community, or even the school environment and you will find the causes for such behavior. Also, those psychologists maintaining that hereditary factors are responsible for behavior patterns claim that the "genes" are at the root of the trouble. This same tendency can be found in those corrective agencies dealing with juvenile and adult misbehavior. Regardless of the degree of the evil, the trend seems to be to look for the cause of antisocial action in factors other than the free will of the person.

One might ask whether the traditionalist denies that man's free will is not at all affected by hereditary or environmental factors. In response, most traditionalists will aver that inherited abilities and disabilities, as well as environmental forces, can and actually do affect human behavior. But they quickly add that man has within himself the power to rise above these forces and overcome the deficiencies of heredity and environment.

Similarily, the traditionalist does not deny that physical health is important but rather that such problems are not the primary concern of the school. Nor does the traditionalist assert that all child behavior is motivated by an "evil nature." Rather, he claims that not all human behavior is naturally good or morally neutral.

CENSORSHIP

The issue of censorship in the schools has its philosophic roots in other issues discussed in this chapter. For example, one's view of the nature of man and truth certainly will affect his convictions about what should be printed or what should not be printed. For example, if one believes that no statement or set of beliefs can be held with certitude, he has no grounds for censorship. Likewise, if one believes that all youth are inclined toward evil, he cannot permit them to read books or see movies which might cater to these evil tendencies.

The fact is that some censorship has always existed in the field of education. The school itself, through its administrators and teachers, has exercised indirect censorship in the selection of textbooks and other teaching materials. Other organizations have put pressure on the schools to ban or favor certain teaching materials. The American Association of Manufacturers has always opposed texts with "socialistic" or anticapitalistic leanings. The American Legion has fought for the suppression of unpatriotic or internationalistic materials. Religious and racial groups have carried on intensive campaigns for the removal from schools of materials critical of their religious or racial creeds.

In opposition to this general practice of censorship in the schools, one finds educators who insist that all forms of censorship are undemocratic because the individual's *right* to read, see, or hear what he wishes is thereby violated. A correlative of this right consists in the individual's freedom to express himself in the various communication media without interference. The only exception admitted by the opponents of censorship is in time of war or extreme national emergency. Following are some of the main arguments for and against censorship.

Arguments for Censorship

1. A basic reason for censorship in the schools arises from the desire on

the part of teachers, administrators, and parents to protect youth from the dangers that presumably flow from exposure to ideas or images detrimental to faith, morals, and social values. Thus atheistic or secularistic literature may lure the young from the faith of their fathers. Immoral pictures and reading materials may tempt the child or adolescent "to do likewise." Strong censorship of political ideas is defended on the grounds that subversive elements might seize control of the government by conspiracy and force, in spite of majority opposition. That such conspiracy has been successful in European and Asian countries is a matter of record. Therefore a realistic program of censorship is necessary to protect our most cherished political, moral, and religious beliefs.

2. Censorship of literature and visual materials — including movies, TV, and the stage — is a special case because of the moral issues involved. The basic reason for censorship of these media of communication and their products is that some materials are patently immoral and consequently have no right to be displayed in the schools.

Another reason given for censorship of such immoral materials is based on the misuse by youth of their newly acquired freedom. The only way to keep youth from reading immoral books or seeing bad plays and movies is to prohibit the publication or showing of all such material. As evidence to bolster up this view, its advocates point out that the increase of youthful crime and delinquency parallels the increase and availability of immoral comic books, novels, movies, and TV programs. The cause of the evil must be removed before the bad effects can be controlled.

3. A theoretical argument for censorship is based on the belief that "freedom consists in the right to do as one ought rather than as one pleases." A man who is truly free follows the dictates of right reason in preference to the promptings of passion, or unguided reason.

Plato, the Stoics, St. Augustine, the Scholastics, Spinoza, Hegel, and Bergson, among others, held this view. These great thinkers argued that if truth and wisdom are known, error and vice can be detected and prohibited. Even if one holds that right and wrong have no basis except "social acceptance" and political sanction, then whatever is contrary to established (accepted) norms should be prohibited.

The essential point is that censorship has as its main goal the protection of the people from those forces which might lead them into immorality and error. As such, censorship is good for the individual and the community. It protects the individual from performing acts harmful to himself and others. It protects the community from evil influences which tend to undermine the security derived from the confidence due the government and the esteem due its institutions, traditions, and values.

This belief that only goodness, truth, and beauty have a right to exist makes censorship not only socially useful but theologically and philosophically necessary. A democratic people should construct their own code for discerning goodness, truth, and beauty, since these can flourish only if falsehood, evil, and ugliness are banned. Without this censorship, democracy will corrode from within and be too weak to resist attack from without.

4. Most advocates of censorship favor control on a sliding scale. The intellectual, physical, and moral maturity of the person will affect his reaction to the content of literary and artistic works. It is deemed safe for the scholar to read prohibited books without serious danger; the mature adult can read "sex novels" or see "adult movies" without jeopardizing his morals. But these same books and movies might prove harmful to the untrained mind or the immature child and adolescent. Therefore, the rules of censorship should be flexible enough to allow for differences in age, maturity, intellectual and educational background, and social circumstances.

5. The belief that a relatively rigid censorship code should be imposed in schools has been defended by many respected citizens, organizations, scholars and law-enforcement personnel. J. Edgar Hoover, of FBI fame, often points up the necessity of strict control over immoral and seditious publications and movies. The representatives of the churches have been almost unanimous in demanding a ban on antireligious and immoral printed matter and dramatic productions. The leaders in science and health organizations urge the suppression and removal from publication of printed matter and advertisements deemed scientifically false. Again the same basic reason proposed is that people must be protected from harm by those in authority.

Obviously, if these arguments are applied to even the adult population, how much more do they affect those of school age? Usually those who favor censorship in general favor "even more" of it in the school.

Arguments Against Censorship

1. As mentioned in the introductory paragraph to the issue of censorship, one's conception of truth determines the basic outlook on censorship. Those arguing against censorship maintain that truth is a dynamic and changing facet of human existence. As times and conditions change, so will one's knowledge and values! The only way to provide for the healthy growth of society and the individual is to allow a free exchange of facts, knowledge, and beliefs in the "marketplace of ideas." Certainly the school should represent a fertile ground for generating new ideas. Such activity is impossible if any form of censorship is exercised over the reading and "viewing" matter of the student. In truth the greater the variety and novelty in materials, the

greater the likelihood that the student will produce new and creative ideas.

2. Another philosophical argument against censorship grows out of one's conception of freedom. If knowledge and moral character are ingredients of freedom, they cannot be "legislated." All statements of truth and morality must come from the free discussion and test of ideas and practices. Only in this manner can the individual as a member of society exercise his freedom. Conformity derived from passive acceptance of the dictates of those in authority can only lead to degradation of the individual and the enslavement of the group (society). The cause of freedom is never helped by limiting freedom!

3. As noted previously, a close scrutiny of the history of ideas provides ample evidence that new ideas, both scientific and political, were suspect when they first appeared. Sixteenth- and seventeenth-century books on "democracy" were banned (and burned) because they challenged the "divine right of king's" doctrine. Many early scientific theories were considered dangerous to moral and spiritual health. Modern dictators (Hitler, Mussolini, and the Communists) "ban and burn" anything not in harmony with their dogmas.

The whole history of man's fight for freedom of choice and action points up an almost innate drive in man to make his own decisions in matters that affect himself, and to cooperate with others in making decisions that affect all. Such decision-making can be nurtured only when people are free to make choices about reading, listening, and viewing. This training must begin in the school; it cannot wait until adulthood.

4. Another grave danger lurking in all censorship proposals lies in the assumption that those in power are competent to judge the morality and political acceptability of all publications and productions. What competence, they ask, do the police have in judging the morality of a movie or book? How can the Postmaster General distinguish between art and pornography? What does the cleric know about science to make judgments about the acceptability of scientific theory? Even though such censorship is exercised in "good faith," with the good of the people in mind, it is still dictatorial. If the attitude of constant reliance on the goodness of the censor is developed in schools, how can one expect creative ideas to be forthcoming?

5. The practical arguments leveled against censorship are many and only a few can be given here:

   a) The immediate danger in any program of censorship is that the ban might fall on the good as well as on the bad. History attests to the crushing of the good with the bad in countries where the principle of censorship is accepted and enforced. Even though many despots have been the patrons of the arts and sciences, it is not wise to entrust the freedom of expression to the autocrat. Often the criterion used is not what is "good or bad" in itself, but what serves the ends of the dictators.

b) The censorship of indecent literature and movies does not guarantee good moral behavior. In fact, there is no conclusive evidence to show that there is more crime and delinquency among those who are free to read, hear, and see what they wish than among those who are not permitted to do so. There are too many other variables which enter into the picture, such as educational level and living conditions.

c) The social consequences of too much censorship are worse than those of too little. For example, revolutionary ideas and immoral designs are driven underground and become more dangerous than when they are met in the open forum. If the high school student can read of the challenge of Communism under the direction of the teacher he is not likely to be led astray by its false doctrine.

d) Youth especially is tempted by the forbidden. The psychology of this statement is demonstrated by the large number of young people who try to attend movies labeled *Adults Only*. The most practical way to counteract this tendency is to remove such activities from the category of "forbidden fruit." Their "appeal" will be gone, and most youths will pay little or no attention to them.

INDOCTRINATION

Until very recently, the question of indoctrination was not raised in education. The traditional conceptions of the nature of truth, democracy, freedom, and the foundation of child behavior presumed that some form of indoctrination was an essential component of a good educational program. Those elements of knowledge considered necessary for the supernatural way of life were taught to the pupil and he was expected to grasp their relevance. The same requirement existed in all the other branches of knowledge taught in the schools. Thus this issue is less than fifty years old, and not until the 1930's did it make any difference in the schools.

The most difficult task in treating the issue of indoctrination lies in finding some definition of the term that might be acceptable to all that use it. Webster's definition may serve as a starting point: to indoctrinate means "to instruct (in), or imbue (with), principles or doctrines." "Doctrine" means "what is held, put forth as true by a teacher, a school, or a sect." But Webster's definition is of little help when one is asked whether one favors or opposes indoctrination in the schools. Perhaps, in this case the definition is more of an issue than whether or not the school should indoctrinate. A few other definitions might set the stage for a further discussion of indoctrination.

Some years ago Bishop Shields argued that a child must have such faith in his teachers that the child will accept without question whatever the teacher passes on from the wisdom of the past. Without this acceptance the child will not be able to build his own character nor acquire the proper attitude toward others. Then no one could integrate himself with the community, and the state itself would disintegrate.[8]

John Dewey conceived of indoctrination as the conscious and systematic resort to any means within reach to convince the student that one particular set of views was right and all others wrong. Similarly, W. H. Kilpatrick labeled as indoctrination any educational endeavor designed to teach children facts, principles, or theories in such a way that these would not be questioned later on their merits in the light of new evidence. Theodore Brameld employs a variation of the Dewey-Kilpatrick definition when he asserts that indoctrination consists in any formal or informal teaching which implies that what is taught is so true and desirable that other alternatives are to be rejected as false and undesirable.[9]

Just to have some reference point, let the last definition serve as the context for listing the pros and cons of indoctrination.

Arguments for Indoctrination

1. If one believes that there are some immutable truths, then indoctrination is not only permissible but necessary. But the teacher should try to make the student intelligent about these basic beliefs so that he will accept them because of an understanding of the justifying reasons. Obviously the intellectual maturity of the student will affect the mode of indoctrination. Young children will not ask for, nor need all the reasons. But high school and college youth should be given reasons or be assisted in finding them.

---

[8] T. E. Shields, *Philosophy of Education* (Washington, D. C.: 1917), p. 265.

[9] See B. F. Pittenger, *Indoctrination for American Democracy* (New York, 1941), p. 5; I. Doughton, *Modern Public Education* (New York, 1935), p. 500; T. Brameld, "What Is Indoctrination?" *School and Society*, Vol. 35 (November 9, 1957), pp. 326–327.

2. In matters involving faith and morals, health and safety, and the common good, youth should be told the truth and the alternatives should be presented as false and unacceptable. These matters are considered too important to be left to the choice of the immature mind. The teacher would fail in his obligation to youth if he were not to indoctrinate in these basic areas. No sensible parent or teacher would fail to indoctrinate children on the dangers of poison, fire, traffic, and narcotics.

3. Present world conditions demand that students be indoctrinated in the fundamental truths of democracy, freedom, and morality. The threat of Communism is so great that one cannot gamble on the results of the idealistic and naïve premise that all views should be presented with equal zeal. The experience of the American turncoats in Korea shows that unless one indoctrinates for the "good," many will be unprepared to reject the "evil."

4. Indoctrination is not good or bad in itself; it is simply a means that can be put into good or bad use. Thus indoctrination is bad if by it one inculcates hatred, violence, and selfishness. But if one includes the development of understandings, beliefs, and loyalties with respect to the basic and abiding principles of justice and freedom, it is good. Just as is true of any other teaching method, indoctrination is "neutral," and it is the use that the teacher makes of it which vitiates or justifies it. By analogy, the lecture method of teaching in college might be said to be neutral — neither good nor bad. Its value or uselessness depends upon other factors, such as resultant learning on the part of the listener or its motivating force.

5. The use of indoctrination in the classroom does not exclude the consideration of divergent doctrines. In fact, the good teacher will attempt to bring in as many opposing views as possible and point up the error in them. Thus a teacher who indoctrinates the students in the principles of democracy will not attempt to conceal the brute fact that totalitarian views are rampant in the modern world. On the contrary these false ideas will be explained, analyzed, and evaluated in the light of democratic principles. The student should be encouraged to ask questions, pose problems, and seek answers and solutions to these difficulties. Also, since every error is intermingled with some truth, these grains of truth found in the desert of falsehood should be unearthed.

6. There are many areas of knowledge where the students might be given free exercise of their intellects (and wills) without any form of indoctrination being exercised by the teachers. Controversial topics abound where the student is merely selecting between several "goods." Does one prefer higher taxes to poor roads? What role should the federal government play in education and health? Should a public

utility be operated by the community or by a privately owned corporation? Many of the "practical issues" in education and government
do not involve absolute and immutable truth. Freedom of expression
in such areas is viewed by many as necessary for the well-being of the
individual and society.

Arguments Against Indoctrination

1. The basic argument against all forms of indoctrination is derived from
   the relativistic concept of truth. If absolute truth is unattainable, the
   teacher has no reasonable grounds for indoctrinating the students on
   any topic. The teacher's prime responsibility is to assure an equal
   hearing for all points of view since no one position has any priority
   to be heard and accepted.

2. The terms "democracy" and "indoctrination" are incompatible. The
   teacher who indoctrinates his students is unfaithful to the basic
   democratic belief of freedom to learn. This principle forces the opponent of all forms of indoctrination to "walk the tightrope" since
   he has no more right to speak for his own commitments than for
   others. The reader has, no doubt, listened to teachers who have tried
   to be "neutral" in all matters. Very often, such teachers are convinced
   that no set of beliefs is right or wrong in itself, and are being loyal
   to this belief.

3. Those who oppose indoctrination contend that enforced belief does
   not insure true commitment. The latter state of mind can be effected
   only after the student has carefully scrutinized all the alternatives. If
   he has not had the opportunity to make a thorough study of the pros
   and cons of each proposal, it cannot be said that he has made a free
   choice. He is a slave of the system rather than a believer in the system.
   Frequently, a "convert" to a religion or political philosophy is better
   than one "born into it" because his commitment is based on free
   choice after the alternatives have been studied and tested.

4. An argument often voiced against indoctrination is that the indoctri-
   nator sets himself up as God. But experience has proved that "to err
   is human." Why, then, should a teacher "play God" when, by reason
   of his human station, his lot is to err? It behooves the wise teacher to
   leave the final judgment of right and wrong to the individual, who
   in turn is responsible to God alone. The teacher's task is completed
   when all possible information and knowledge on the subject have been
   grasped and weighed by the student.

5. Indoctrination militates against one of the most significant objectives
   of education, critical thinking. A student cannot learn to do critical
   thinking if this goal is thwarted in any area. Thus, to tell the student
   he should be a critical thinker in politics and economics but not in

religion and morals is to invite disaster to his intellectual integrity. To encourage him to doubt and question the beliefs of one "ism" but not those of another is dishonest. Either he becomes a critical thinker in all areas of knowledge or none!

6. Indoctrination often results in consequences hostile to the very end for which it is used. Hence, when a student discovers that he has been given only "one side of the story," his reaction to this deception may be very violent. Often, youth will "throw out the baby with the wash" and join the opposition in preference to remaining in the fold of decent men. Note how many people who have been indoctrinated in a strict moral code will go to the opposite extreme at the slightest provocation. On the positive side, many psychologists believe that the only way to break the Communists' grip on the minds of the enslaved peoples is to show them "how the rest of the world lives." Then the fallacies of their own indoctrination program will become evident to the people; and the Communist system will crumble from within because of a lack of trust by the people. Revolution might be successful!

Summary

That one's view of the nature of man and the nature of truth is most fundamental to building a consistent philosophy of education should now be evident to the reader. Actually the problems of academic freedom and censorship will be solved in the light of basic beliefs about the nature of man and truth. Even one's concept of democracy will flow from these two main streams of philosophical knowledge.

Because of the fundamental character of these two most important issues in philosophy of education, the student is likely to be very limited in his choice of alternatives. Such is not always the case in the other issues such as federal aid, merit ratings, and unionism. In these latter two, people with differing views of man's nature may both be for or against any specific side of the issues. But such ambivalence is not possible when one must "take sides" about the nature of truth or the nature of man.

SELECTED READINGS

Bestor, Arthur, Jr., *Restoration of Learning* (New York: A. Knopf Co., 1955), Chaps. 1, 3, 10, 25, 26–29.
    Defends the traditional view of the issues in the philosophy of education discussed in this chapter.

Butler, J. D., *Four Philosophies*, rev. ed. (New York: Harper & Bros., 1957), Chaps. 9, 14, 20.
 Gives the important beliefs of the philosophies of idealism, realism, and pragmatism regarding the pupil, the objectives of education, and the educational process.
Butts, R. F., *A Cultural History of Western Education* (New York: McGraw-Hill Book Co., 1955), Chap. 17.
 Presents the foundational ideas of American education in the twentieth century. Points up the conflicting authorities in education and cross-currents in the educational program.
DeYoung, C. A., and Wynn, Richard, *American Education* (New York: McGraw-Hill Book Co., 1960), Chap. 17.
 Treats the contemporary issues in American education, e.g., religion in public education, administration and finance, objectives of elementary, secondary, and higher education.
Ehlers, H., and Lee, Gordon C., *Crucial Issues in Education* (New York: Henry Holt & Co., 1959), Chaps. 1–4.
 A collection of readings presenting both sides of the issues treated in this chapter.
Gallagher, D. A. (ed.), *Some Philosophers on Education* (Milwaukee: Marquette University Press, 1956).
 The entire volume is devoted to the philosophical issues in contemporary education.
Maritain, Jacques, *Man and the State* (Chicago: University of Chicago Press, 1951), Chap. 5.
 A Scholastic interpretation of the meaning of democracy.
Molnar, Thomas, *The Future of Education* (New York: Fleet Publishing Co., 1961), Chaps. 2, 6, and 7.
 A humanistic interpretation of the role of the school in democratic society, academic freedom, and indoctrination.
Van Dalen, D. B., and Brittell, R. W., *Looking Ahead to Teaching* (Boston: Allyn & Bacon, 1959), Chap. 12.
 A "first look" at the philosophical issues in American education.

Part III

THE ROLE OF PSYCHOLOGY
IN EDUCATION

Chapter XII

THE PSYCHOLOGY OF

TRADITIONAL EDUCATION

The study of man's activities and of himself as revealed through these activities is psychology. Modern universities offer courses dealing with man and his activities both in the departments of philosophy and psychology. What is the reason for this? Why are there two psychologies? The answer lies in the fact that man, the common subject of both scientific and philosophical psychology, can be studied in different ways. The science of psychology seeks explanations of man's activities and the subject of these activities which can be verified by observation under carefully controlled conditions, permitting precise and objective (impersonal) measurement. The philosophical psychologist, on the other hand, makes his inferences concerning man by reflecting on observations of human activities in natural, uncontrolled, and unmanipulated situations.

The reciprocal relations of the two psychologies will be examined more closely in Chapter XIII. Many of the most important psychological questions have not proved amenable to study by the methods of the scientist; others, however, have been answered by him in a precise and quantitative way impossible for the philosopher.

The scientific investigation of human activities did not develop until the mid-nineteenth century and did not significantly affect education directly until the start of the twentieth. In this chapter we will be concerned with the schools before they felt the impact of the new science, specifically with the prescientific psychological views that helped to make them what they were.

From what we have said, it is evident that the prescientific psychologists were philosophers. To trace the history of some psychological views which have profoundly influenced education, we would have to call the roll of the great philosophers whose views have been reviewed in Part II. This is not our purpose in the present chapter. All we can do is single out certain views that played a dominant role in education during the past century. We will be especially concerned with views that encouraged educational practices that we see changing with the new psychology and the new century. The "schools of thought" which will occupy us throughout the rest of this chapter are: (1) faculty psychology and formal discipline, (2) the psychology of association, (3) naturalism, and (4) the Herbartians and dynamic associationism.

These schools or views which are part of our more immediate tradition may not include all the high points of progress to that time. Some quite modern views have ancient antecedents, and the trend toward present-day theory and practice, or toward that of the future, is better described by a wavering line than a straight one. In any generation, past or present, you can find both some of the most modern views of man's nature and activities and protests against these "new" views.

FACULTY PSYCHOLOGY AND FORMAL DISCIPLINE

During the eighteenth century the so-called "faculty psychology" was quite prominent, especially in Germany and Scotland. One of the thinkers most influential in contributing to this psychological current was the German, Christian Wolff (1679–1754), whose *Rational Psychology* appeared in 1734. Wolff accepted the Cartesian idea that the soul or mind and the body of man are two distinct entities. He agreed with Leibniz (1646–1716), however, that God has attuned the mind and body of man like two clocks so that what transpires in one reflects what occurs in the other.

Wolff maintained that the mind or soul possesses active powers to represent the world to itself in two different ways, knowing and willing. The activities of knowing and willing, in turn, proceed from separate and distinct "faculties" of intellect and will. A faculty was the power of the mind to carry out a related activity. Although Wolff attempted to show how the will and intellect are interrelated, his efforts to do so were not judged very successful, with the result that, in practice, those influenced by his thought erected these two faculties as different compartments or pigeonholes into which different elements of life are channeled.[1]

Others postulated additional faculties, such as feeling, remembering, and reasoning. The nineteenth-century phrenologists were to set the all-time record in the number of faculties identified — well over 30.[2] These pseudo scientists probably entered the competition because biologically oriented theorists were suggesting that each faculty has its own place in the brain; and furthermore, if a given faculty is particularly well developed, that the corresponding area of the brain will be enlarged. The next step for the phrenologist was to find that these enlargements affected the shape of the head. Lectures and demonstrations of the diagnosis of character on the basis of bumps were extremely popular and undoubtedly contributed to public acceptance of separate mental faculties.

In applying faculty psychology to education the tendency was to treat each supposed faculty as something completely autonomous and unrelated to any other faculty thought necessary to explain the range and variety of human activity. It is easy to see that such a psychology destroys any unity in man and any influence of intellect on will, of sensation on intellection, of emotional activity on cognitive life. Of course, opponents to the faculty psychologists were quick to point out these consequences. In addition, they claimed that the advocates of this theory merely gave names to certain activities performed by men and then postulated faculties or powers to account for these activities without in any way analyzing the nature of these activities and powers.

Since the faculty psychology of German and Scottish pedagogues of the eighteenth century is sometimes associated with the teaching of Aristotle and St. Thomas Aquinas (1225–1274) that man possesses certain powers or faculties which serve as instruments in his various activities, it is important to note the great difference between the role played by the "faculties" in Aristotle and Aquinas and that played by them in these eighteenth-century theorists. For Aristotle and Aquinas the faculties of the human person are not regarded as airtight compartments or pigeonholes into which different elements of experience are stuffed. Both lay great stress on the unity of the

---

[1] F. Copleston, A History of Philosophy (Westminster, Md.: The Newman Press, 1960), Vol. VI, p. 109.

[2] Gardner Murphy, Historical Introduction to Modern Psychology (New York: Harcourt, Brace and Company, 1949), p. 56.

human being, and on the fact that it is the man who feels, senses, desires, thinks, and wills. He performs these activities by means of distinct powers or faculties, but the latter do not exist of themselves or operate independently of each other. Rather, the faculties influence each other, and they are meaningful only when seen as unified in the subject of all human activity, man himself. If eighteenth-century faculty psychology was related to these earlier views, the relationship was one of rejection or misinterpretation.

One critic of faculty psychology is remembered, oddly enough, as a proponent of the educational theory which that psychology fostered. John Locke (1632–1704) was an educational essayist of note as well as one of the British associationists whose views are presented in the next section of this chapter. Locke attributed all knowledge to impressions received through the senses, but postulated "internal senses" for acting upon the incoming impressions. These abilities of the mind were called powers, to differentiate them from faculties. The interpretation of the educational significance of powers was, however, very similar to that of faculties, even in Locke's own writing.

Formal discipline is a philosophical or educational theory based squarely on a psychology of mental powers or faculties. To a formal disciplinist the function of education is to train the faculties through suitable exercise. There have been advocates of formal discipline in every period of Western civilization since the Greeks. Quintilian, most famous of the ancient Roman teachers, advocated geometry for exercising the mind and sharpening the wits and so did John Locke, the great English essayist, in 1689. And in 1953, it was Arthur E. Bestor who wrote: ". . . schools exist to teach *something*, and . . . this something is the power to think."[3]

The formal disciplinist chooses subject matter for its exercise value. A logical extension of this point of view, and by no means an uncommon conclusion, is that the more difficult the material to be learned, the better, regardless of the specific content. The humorist Mr. Dooley said, according to Brubacher, that "it matters little what a child studies so long as he does not like it."[4]

With respect to method, the beginnings of the traditional assign-

[3] Arthur E. Bestor, *Educational Wastelands* (Urbana, Ill.: University of Illinois Press, 1953), p. 10.

[4] John S. Brubacher, *A History of the Problems of Education* (New York: McGraw-Hill Book Co., Inc., 1947), p. 140.

study-recite procedure were soon apparent. The teacher was expected to set the task, get the pupil to work, and in due time call upon him to demonstrate his success, that is, to "recite."

In their more sophisticated statements mental disciplinists even identified the age level at which each faculty, such as memory, is best trained. Suitable exercise materials were recommended for this faculty and for others. The following are typical recommendations for youth of high school age in 1890:

> . . . Thus far the use of studies on the knowledge side has been considered, but the mental power, the development of the mental faculty — that higher purpose of education — must be constantly kept in view. Properly employed, mathematics trains the abstractive and deductive powers; science the perceptive, conceptual and inductive powers; history the ethical and the higher personal emotions; literature the aesthetic and the ethical emotions; all studies exercise memory and the imagination more or less; proper school requirements cultivate right emotion and train the will; all physical training, as reading, speaking, music, drawing, exercise, give the mind power over the body and train the will.[5]

A popular text for teachers of the nineteenth century by Emerson E. White, *The Elements of Pedagogy*, also gives the impression that learning was considered to be pupil activity that developed and trained the mind.[6] This, of course, was an educator's psychology of learning. The psychologists were acquiring a status independent of philosophy by this time, but they had given little attention to how learning takes place.

In Germany Herbart had been attacking these views for some time and James's influential writing in America was hostile to them. The first scientific study of formal discipline by Thorndike and Woodworth appeared a short time later, 1903. Gates has reported that this study "shook the older convictions to the core," and that "this report created a veritable explosion of interest and relatively rapid conviction."[7]

---

[5] James H. Baker, "The High School as a Finishing-School," *Journal of Proceedings and Addresses of the National Education Association*, Vol. 29 (Washington, D. C.: National Education Association, 1890), p. 635.

[6] Emerson E. White, *The Elements of Pedagogy* (New York: American Book Company, 1886).

[7] Arthur I. Gates, "Contributions of Research to General Methods of Instruction," *The Scientific Method in Education*, National Society for the Study of Education, Thirty-Seventh Yearbook, Part II (Bloomington, Ill.: Public School Publishing Company, 1938), p. 81.

Apparently the explosion was relatively well contained within the schools of education and departments of psychology, however, for Rugg, reviewing curriculum-making by national committees of subject-matter specialists to 1926, saw "Three Decades of Mental Discipline." He castigated the continuing national committees generally and the Classical Investigation (1921–1925) in particular for their failure to utilize Thorndike's data and for resting their case on "disciplinary" values.[8] Of special significance is Rugg's evidence of the tremendous influence of the reports of these committees on shaping the school curriculum: "Both state and local, town and city systems came to base their syllabi definitely upon the recommendations of the committee."[9]

Formal discipline stood, and eventually fell, on its claims for the transfer of training. By transfer of training was meant the influence of training (learning) in one situation on what one can do in new and different situations. All educational efforts aim for transfer from the school situation to life. This is the most appealing reason for the existence of the schools. Teachers under the sway of mental discipline maintained, however, that transfer was easy to get. All one has to do is teach the subjects that train each faculty. These faculties then operate equally well with the materials of any field. A strong memory, for example, like a strong arm is generally useful. The child who trained his reason well by arduous study of classical languages and mathematics was thought to be equipped to reason cogently in any field — the world situation, his income tax, or what's wrong with education.

The transfer of training controversy has a more recent history also. The generality of transfer is one of the current issues in psychology which are discussed in Chapter XVI. Pedro Orata[10] has contributed to our understanding of this area by his comprehensive reviews of related experiments. His studies have led him to expect some form

---

8 Harold Rugg, "Three Decades of Mental Discipline: Curriculum-Making Via National Committees," *The Foundations and Techniques of Curiculum-Construction*, National Society for the Study of Education, Twenty-Sixth Yearbook, Part I (Bloomington, Ill.: Public School Publishing Company, 1926), pp. 61–62.

9 *Ibid.*, p. 64.

10 Pedro T. Orata, *The Theory of Identical Elements* (Columbus: Ohio State University Press, 1928); "Transfer of Training and Educational Pseudo-Science," *Mathematics Teacher*, 28 (May, 1935), pp. 265–269; "Recent Research Studies in Transfer of Training with Implications for the Curriculum Guidance, and Personnel Work," *Harvard Educational Review*, 11 (May, 1941), pp. 359–378.

of general transfer. More recently, Kolesnik[11] has made a similar contribution by bringing together much of the research material on transfer of training, the philosophical and theoretical as well as the experimental.

Faculty psychologists assumed a faculty whenever they found a word that suggested one. They did not actually study the mental processes. They might be given credit, however, for focusing the attention of better scientists on the study of individual differences in the ability to learn and to do different things and on the important problem of transfer.

The effects of formal discipline in education included support for several undesirable, but perennial, educational tendencies:

1. Standardizing of the curriculum around the classical subjects (considered the best for "exercise");
2. Stressing intellectual goals at the expense of those relating to the body and the emotions;
3. Neglecting vocational subjects (trained faculties were the best preparation for any vocation);
4. Neglecting practical applications or outcomes in all subjects.

The special "contributions" of formal discipline may be seen in:

1. A curriculum and methods designed to provide the maximum mental exercise in the time available;
2. An insistence upon the student's doing the work (otherwise he doesn't get the exercise);
3. Acceptance of failure as evidence that the student lacks the mental equipment to profit from further training of the faculties involved.

Although philosophy and the social sciences are usually given credit for establishing our educational aims, for a time the psychologists were to lead the way as they rejected formal discipline. As Anderson put it, "Perhaps the most revolutionary reformulation of objectives that has ever been made in education is that which has been taking place as a result of the discrediting of formal discipline at the turn of the century following the research of James, Thorndike, Woodworth, and others."[12]

---

[11] Walter B. Kolesnik, *Mental Discipline in Modern Education* (Madison: University of Wisconsin Press, 1958).

[12] Lester Anderson, "Introduction," *Learning and Instruction*, National Society for the Study of Education, Forty-Ninth Yearbook, Part I (Chicago: University of Chicago Press, 1950), p. 9.

THE PSYCHOLOGY OF ASSOCIATION

The whole movement of thought which we call the Renaissance, and the subsequent scientific revolution, was marked by man's effort to find the answers to his questions in the physical world of his experience. The mechanics as well as the inquiring spirit of Galileo were carried over into philosophy and psychology by Hobbes (1588–1679), Descartes (1569–1650), Leibniz (1646–1716), and their followers.

British philosophy from Hobbes to Hume (1711–1776) is commonly referred to as empiricism. The reason is that the chief British thinkers during this period — Hobbes, Locke, Berkeley, and Hume — all agreed on one point, that the exclusive source for all human knowledge lies in experience. Their agreement on the role of experience in knowledge, however, does not mean that they reached the same conclusions on the basis of their experience. Far from it. Yet there is in all these men a common tendency or direction relative to the nature of man and man's knowledge that reached its culmination in the psychology of association. It is this common trend that we shall examine.

For Hobbes, Locke, and Hume the objects of knowledge, what we know, are not "out there." They are not things of the physical world but our own subjective states of consciousness, variously called images, ideas, impressions, conceptions, or thoughts. Locke assumed the mind to be a blank tablet (*tabula rasa*) at birth, somewhat like a photographic plate. All that the child learns is imprinted on this plate by direct sensation of the world around him or by reflection on the data of sensation. Hume gives sensory perceptions top priority also and thinks ideas merely faint images or less lively representations or revivals of sensations previously experienced. Here we see clearly the emphasis of this school of thought on environment or the physical world as the source of all knowledge.

The associationists went further and attempted to reduce all knowledge, however complex, to the simplest images, impressions, or ideas given in previous sensations. They devised mechanistic principles or laws of association to explain how these simplest elements combined to advance knowledge to its more complex and involved stages. Later associationists — Hartley in the eighteenth century and Thomas Brown, James Mills, and Alexander Bain in the nineteenth century — were very thorough in their attempts to reduce all relationships among ideas to the association in time or space of objects or events in experience. It does seem reasonable that the idea of eggs may suggest the idea of bacon because eggs and bacon have been associated in sensory experience. Of course, eggs might suggest ham or Easter instead. So quite a number of supplementary principles were formulated by the associationists to account for the various possibilities. These referred to such factors as frequency of association, recency, liveliness, prior habits of mind, and the like. The list was quite long, in general agreement with common sense, and is generally accorded some validity by modern learning theorists. There is a danger, of course, in assuming that the whole of thought is no more than the mechanical association of simple parts derived from sensation. The uniqueness of some creative thoughts, for example, seems underestimated; and other essential factors in knowledge, such as the role of judgment, may well be overlooked.

We should note also that in the associationists' view our knowledge is strictly limited to relationships among our own ideas. We cannot really know things as they are in themselves, only as they appear to us in consciousness. The human mind becomes simply its own contents. If there is any substance underlying these contents it cannot be known, and the same is true of any supposed real causes in things.

The empiricism of the associationists was significant in the current of thought which was to lead to scientific psychology. It was significant also for theories of knowledge, suggesting that we really know and teach ideas or images only, not things of the real world. Any generality of these ideas, it would follow, is not due to nature but to psychological processes of the mind.

Locke had more direct influence on the schools than other English empiricists because of his educational essays. As we have noted, he used this influence to support formal discipline. Among other effects of associationism on educational psychology were increased attention (1) to the mental processes of the learner and (2) to his past history, as well as support for (3) conducting education in accordance with laws of learning and (4) the notion of education as a process for filling the mind of the learner with ideas.

NATURALISM

Rousseau, Pestalozzi, and Froebel were pioneers of the "new" education which was challenging the old order (compare Chap. X), but for a time their contributions were absorbed into the body of traditional education. Following the lead of the great Moravian educator and clergyman, Johann Amos Comenius (1592–1670), they promoted a "natural method" of learning through the senses. Rousseau's extreme views of the innate goodness of child nature strongly influenced Pestalozzi, the schoolman of the group, and hastened the abandonment of the oppressive forms of negative discipline which had often characterized school practice. Froebel, who was a student of Pestalozzi, led a movement for early childhood education, which was to win him recognition as the father of the modern kindergarten. He emphasized three principles: self-development (the natural unfolding of the child's total personality), activity, and social cooperation. Much of Froebel's own thinking and writing had a mystical quality, but the durability of his contributions to the kindergarten and other aspects of the "new education" (see Chap. X) is testimony to the basic soundness of his views.

Pestalozzi's efforts to understand the nature of pupils and to conduct education in accordance with the laws of nature brought him to the frontiers of a new educational psychology. Pestalozzi's approach to learning emphasized wooing the learner through the senses, step by step through experiences with concrete objects to generalizations. The laws of natural child development, as he understood them, were to guide the selection and presentation of materials and a careful grading of instruction.

To Pestalozzi, it seemed that natural growth involved the following stages: (1) vague sense impressions; (2) more distinct sense impressions, which then (3) become clear and capable of description. At this stage, when our sensations are clear and distinct and capable of being described, we do not as yet know the real character of things. This is achieved (4) when the clear images are transformed into definite ideas by which things can be defined. Then the objects known previously only by their individual traits can be classed with other objects, and the use of general or common names learned.[13]

---

[13] William Boyd, The History of Western Education (London: Adam and Charles Black, 1952), pp. 323–325. (summarizing Pestalozzi's How Gertrude Teaches Her Children).

In the transition from the stage of vague sense impressions to definite ideas education plays a large role. The teacher, because he has passed along this path, possesses the definite ideas which he hopes to instill in the child. What he must do is work upon the primitive intuitions or sense impressions (*Anschauungen*) which are the bases of all subsequent knowledge.[14] In his instruction, the teacher should widen the child's experience by presenting objects to give direct impressions. His task is next to remove the confusion necessarily involved in any primitive intuition or impression and gradually bring each successive impression to a definite idea, which is then related to the totality of previous experience. In other words, the function of the teacher is to use immediate experience as a means for leading the child to see the content of definite ideas or, inversely, to show the child the significance of individual impressions by linking them up with definite ideas.

Pestalozzi's insistence on patience on the part of the teacher, on the development of sound relationships between teacher and students, on respecting the natural ladder of learning — all this is to the good. What remains obscure in his educational views — probably because he did not trouble himself to examine his starting points — is the nature of the primitive intuitions that form the starting points of all knowledge and a tendency to confuse mere sensation with intellectual knowledge. The precise relationships between the contents of consciousness and real things are not clarified.

Pestalozzi was so successful in training teachers to use the new methods that he revitalized the schools of Prussia. He aroused attention in the United States as early as 1808, but little came of it until Edward A. Sheldon introduced his methods in the Oswego, New York, schools around 1858. Sheldon's experiment was so intriguing and so thoroughly publicized that a number of normal schools for teachers were organized to propagate the technique.

The teaching of every existing subject was modified; and some new ones, like science, were introduced on a modest scale. Besides an emphasis on observing in all subjects, the ability to communicate orally was stressed, so that students could express their observations and generalizations correctly.

In arithmetic, students passed slowly from the study of sensible objects to the manipulation of abstract symbols. Mental arithmetic

---

[14] *Ibid.*, p. 324.

became prominent (and has since been defended stoutly on the grounds of mental discipline). Geography was studied at "home" and not in texts.

In schools that were traditionally inclined the methods degenerated into just another way to collect, organize, and memorize a massive collection of facts to train the powers of the mind or to fill it with knowledge. As often as not, oral verbalism was merely substituted for the written word. The following example is from a lesson conducted by Pestalozzi to develop ideas. Imagine what happened in less skilled hands.

> Thus he would ask: "Boys, what do you see?" (He never addressed the girls.)
> Answer: "A hole in the paper."
> Pestalozzi: "Very well, say after me:
> "I see a hole in the paper.
> "I see a long hole in the paper.
> "Through the long narrow hole I see the wall.
> "I see figures on the paper.
> "I see black figures on the paper.
> "I see round black figures on the paper.
> "I see a square yellow figure on the paper.
> "By the side of the square yellow figure I see a round black one.
> "The square figure is joined to the round figure by a large black stripe, etc."[15]

The eventual contributions of the "naturalists" in the development of the new education in America were not to be denied, merely delayed. The popularity of Pestalozzi's methods as a distinct system was almost entirely confined to the elementary school and was succeeded by the influence of Herbart in America after 1890. The lingering influences on American education from 1890 to the reforms of the scientific movement have been suggested. These included: (1) wider understanding of the practical educational significance of child nature and the laws of learning, (2) the use of a greater variety of teaching aids, (3) some modification of the traditional curriculum, and (4) elimination of harsher methods of negative discipline.

THE HERBARTIANS AND DYNAMIC ASSOCIATIONISM

Johann Friedrich Herbart (1776–1841) may be credited with

---

[15] Roger De Guimps, *Pestalozzi, His Aim and Work* (New York: D. Appleton and Co., 1890), p. 181. Quoted by V. T. Thayer, *The Passing of the Recitation* (New York: D. C. Heath and Company, 1928). p. 22.

psychologizing education more completely than ever before. He was also an important figure in the history of psychology, inspiring others, like Wundt, who went on to establish psychology as an independent and experimental science. Herbart himself was influenced by Leibniz, as was Wolff. Herbart, however, was fundamentally opposed to the faculty psychology of Wolff. He was an associationist, although a rather unique one. His contributions, like those of the English school, were part of a transition from the old to the new in psychology and education. His educational interests included character education and education for a moral life. He even saw the need for providing desirable activities for children if undesirable ones are to be inhibited — a "brilliant insight far ahead of his times."[16] (Compare Chap. X.)

His role in the development of traditional educational practices, particularly assign-study-recite procedures, is clear, however, and the central concern of the present discussion.

Herbart may be described as a dynamic associationist. Like the English associationists, he believed the mind was made up of a large number of ideas or impressions built up through the medium of the senses. He differed from the English school, however, in the way he thought these ideas were related or associated in thought. Herbart denied that ideas are associated quite passively, merely because they were connected in original experience. He drew upon developments in natural science to postulate positive and negative forces, like those of magnetism, which led similar ideas to attract each other and repel ideas which were dissimilar. The similar ideas were thought to cluster and form "apperceptive masses" which would be receptive to new similar ideas passed along from the senses. These masses were thought to be passing back and forth from the realm of the conscious to that of the subconscious, according to their relationship to the ideas which occupied the consciousness (attention) at the moment.

The learning process was that of the assimilation (apperception) of new ideas by similar ones already in the consciousness. The widely known teaching methods advocated by Herbart were designed to facilitate this process. The first step, as may be recalled from Chapter X, is to prepare the way for new material by building up an apperceptive mass of familiar and interesting ideas. Each new idea should be offered to the child only when he is ready to assimilate it. The

---

[16] Brubacher, op. cit., p. 221.

whole curriculum may then be devised so that the child continuously passes from the familiar to the unfamiliar.

Herbart and his followers advocated the recapitulation theory of child development which was somewhat prevalent at the time. This is the theory that the child in his development passes through stages which correspond to the stages of culture through which the race has passed in its development. As it affected curriculum planning, this theory was known as the "culture epoch" theory. When the child entered school he was ready for the era of folklore. By the time he reached the seventh or eighth grades he would be ready for social, political, and scientific developments. Needless to say, this aspect of Herbartian doctrine was pleasing to those who had emphasized the transmission of culture through education. The Herbartians may be credited with introducing new materials of cultural content, particularly literature and the social sciences, into the curriculum.

Herbart also gave systematic attention to capitalizing on student interests in the promotion of learning. Being "ready" for the next stage of instruction according to the culture-epoch theory meant that appropriate and "powerful instinctive interests" were present for the teacher to seize and utilize.[17] Interest was regarded also as an outcome of apperception, a pleasurable side effect when new ideas are assimilated by old. With proper attention to the preparatory steps of this method, therefore, the problem of motivation would all but disappear. If the teacher chanced to fail in this, students could still be depended upon to pursue their studies diligently if the right ideas relating to school work in general had been built up in their past educational experience. This was considered a notable contribution to the perennial problem of how to enlist the cooperation of the child in the educational enterprise.

Herbartian concepts were influential in both general and educational psychology for a time but are now largely outmoded, except perhaps as they reappear in principles of interference and inhibition in studies of learning and remembering.

His educational theories were well known in America after about 1890. Their popularity expanded rapidly and then slowly waned. There have been several notable revivals. In the late 1920's and 1930's, for example, the Morrison plan, based primarily on Herbart's

---

[17] Charles A. McMurry, The Elements of General Method (New York: The Macmillan Company, 1903), p. 114.

ideas, won many adherents. In the initial period of popularity his methods directed teacher preparation and supervisory practices in elementary education throughout the country. Practice was provided in the preparation of daily lesson plans utilizing the Formal Steps (see Chap. X). Syllabi were prepared as a framework for the lesson plans. Textbooks were revised to include cultural content; they were then, unfortunately, often accepted as "material to be mastered bit by bit."[18] It should be noted that by and large Herbart's effect on secondary and college education was much less pronounced. At these levels formal discipline was still very much in vogue.

Despite some difference in original orientation it soon became apparent, as the preceding paragraph suggests, that Herbartian methods were to be absorbed into the prevailing assign-study-recite pattern of instruction. They provided a much needed improvement on that pattern.

American schools were still groping with the problem of mass instruction posed by the American ideal of education for all. In 1800 learning was very much an individual thing with a pupil receiving 30 or 40 minutes of instruction a day. The rest of the time he sat or amused himself while others were instructed or everyone studied. Much the same system was still in evidence as late as 1855.[19] The monitorial system was an early "improvement" that was a transition to group or class instruction. By instructing the older students first, who then taught younger children the same things in small groups, one instructor sometimes handled close to 300 pupils.[20]

Herbartian methods were introduced, then, at a time when the instruction of groups, as groups, was developing. They lent themselves admirably to the systematization of group procedures. As never before teachers had guidance, based on a definite psychology, in the organization and presentation of material. Students were prepared; new ideas were presented; new knowledge was related to the old; the students were helped to generalize; and applications in supervised study or homework were assigned. Detailed attention to lesson planning was the rule with objectives, devices for securing and holding attention, key questions, assignments, etc., all clearly formulated. It will be noted, however, that with these improvements came the

---

[18] Charles A. McMurry and Frank M. McMurry, *The Method of the Recitation* (New York: The Macmillan Company, 1909), p. 289.

[19] Thayer, *op. cit.*, pp. 1–2.

[20] *Ibid.*, p. 6.

familiar lockstep of group instruction with almost no provision for individual differences. Interests were utilized to the teacher's ends, not to direct instruction. An emphasis on cultural aims did little to promote vocational ends.

Today, Herbart's psychology is largely outmoded and his educational methods are no longer popular. Still, he led the way in the empirical study of teaching and learning and in attacking mental discipline. His influence was great in winning acceptance of principles of learning, of child development, and of children's interests as factors in educational planning. His adherents introduced new materials into the curriculum. The importance of systematic preparation, sound instructional procedures, and improved assignments was recognized, and these resulted in generally better teaching.

One is tempted not to detract from these contributions, but there were limitations to the approach of the Herbartians. They placed too much emphasis on nurture, particularly what the teacher did, and not enough on nature. A highly mechanical system of instruction emphasizing day-to-day progress developed. In the selection of content there was a tendency to worship the past and ignore the present. The masses were not improved vocationally. The Herbartian psychology was, like its predecessors, a psychology of the mind and sought to fill this mind with knowledge and information. The hands and the body and the non-intellectual phases of personality were still neglected.

To summarize the effects of Herbartian psychology on the traditional education of the times, we may point to:

1. Daily lesson plans and detailed syllabi;
2. Content emphasizing cultural developments;
3. Systematic but highly formal teaching procedures;
4. Devices to arouse pupil interest;
5. Teaching the new in terms of the old;
6. Group instruction with little provision for individual differences.
7. Emphasis on the mastery of detailed factual information;
8. Daily study and homework;
9. Texts and workbooks paralleling the Formal Steps of Herbartian method;
10. Continued neglect of personal, social, and vocational development.

Herbart's contributions are incompatible with formal discipline, yet both were popular in America at about the same time. At this time, however, formal discipline was not prominent in the thinking of elementary teachers, even though it was strongly entrenched at the secondary and college levels. Herbart's views affected educational aims at the higher levels but his methods were most popular in the elementary schools.

To add to the confusion of these changing times — the years when a developing science of education was questioning traditional subjects and methods — defenders of the *status quo* at all educational levels employed either the Herbartian or the formal-discipline point of view, as suited their convenience. Thayer suggests this use of a "double standard" by teachers when he states,

> If one challenged the utility in future life of, let us say, the classics, the teachers could plead the training value of working upon materials which developed the faculties of reason, memory, discrimination and the like. On the other hand, if the training value of specific learning materials was questioned, their usefulness as essential elements in the mental equipment of an adult could be argued.[21]

Summary and Comment

In this chapter we have been concerned with psychological views underlying older school practices. Vestiges of these "traditional" practices remain today. We think of them as relying heavily on drill and rote memorization in an attempt to teach every child of a given grade the same skills or knowledge at the same time and in the same way, although this description is probably somewhat overdrawn, or as assign-study-recite procedures.

Four "schools" of psychological thought have played major roles in our more immediate educational past. The first of these to be discussed, faculty psychology, became prominent in Germany and Scotland during the eighteenth century. There was never complete agreement among various faculty psychologists, but a popular view held that the mind was composed of various autonomous powers or faculties which could be separately trained by appropriate exercises. Something like this training of faculties, known as formal discipline, has been advocated from time to time throughout educational history and is not unknown today. In the schools, the formal

21 Thayer, *op. cit.,* p. 20.

disciplinist chose subject matter for its exercise value. Generally, the more abstract and difficult subjects were thought to be best for "honing the wits." Once a faculty, such as memory, was trained on one task it was thought fully prepared for effective use with any task. A memory trained on difficult spelling words might be expected to be equally adept at remembering names and faces, appointments, jokes, recipes, formulae, or anything at all. In a similar way there was an attempt to look upon faculties — abstractive, deductive, perceptive, inductive, aesthetic, and others — as generally useful means in the transfer of training from one area to a wide variety of school and life situations. Faculty psychology and formal discipline stressed intellectual training, difficult subjects, and intense student effort (exercise).

A school of British associationists thought that all knowledge originates in experience. Locke, the member of the group most influential in education, taught that the mind was a blank tablet at birth and that all the child learns is imprinted on this tablet by his sensations and by subsequent reflection. One's ideas are merely faint images or revivals of these sensations. Mechanistic principles or laws of association were devised to explain how these simple elements of experience were combined in more complex mental processes. Despite the different approach, Locke's educational theories resembled those of formal discipline. Association also lent support to another perennial notion that conceives of education as a process for filling the mind with ideas; it stimulated empiricism, focused attention upon the mental processes of the learner, and encouraged further attempts to develop laws of learning.

The naturalism of Comenius, Rousseau, and Pestalozzi called for conducting education in accordance with "laws" of child development. Just this idea was to have a pronounced and lasting effect upon education. Since the child's nature was thought innately good, the harsher forms of negative discipline were discouraged. Since sense impressions were thought the basis of all subsequent knowledge, some schools had students observe, manipulate, and discuss actual objects prior to their attempts to form verbal concepts or generalizations. In the United States Pestalozzi's ideas were prominent in training programs for elementary teachers after about 1850. A variety of teaching aids became popular and some new subjects, e.g., science, were introduced. For a time Pestalozzi's teaching procedures were bent, more often than not, to the purposes of those who sought to collect and organize facts for the traditional purposes of filling or training the mind. There was a lasting effect, however, that contributed to the development of the "New Education."

In the United States Pestalozzi's ideas were succeeded by those of Herbart. Herbart contributed to the scientific trend in both psychology and education. His was a brand of associationism in which similar ideas of the mind were thought to cluster through mutual attraction while dissimilar ideas were repelled. When teaching a new idea, for example, one was told to first bring a mass of similar and receptive ones to the fore in the learner's consciousness, that is, direct his attention to them. Then when the new idea was presented it would be readily assimilated. Herbart's formal instructional steps for facilitating associations brought a much needed order and system to group methods of instruction. At the same time they accentuated some soon-to-be-questioned features of these methods, such as the dominant role of the teacher and the general neglect of individual differences. The Herbartians also taught that the child in his development passes through all the stages in the racial development of culture. When the child is at a stage of his development which corresponds to a culture epoch of folklore, he is ready and able and needs to learn that folklore. Later the time will be ripe for literature, and, still later, for science. Thus schools were encouraged to concentrate on the "transmission of the culture." Herbart's educational theories were influential in elementary education around the turn of the century, about the time formal discipline held sway at the secondary and college levels. The popularity of the Herbartian methods gradually waned thereafter except for brief revivals in the 1920's and 1930's. His theories of learning and child development are also outmoded. We still follow his lead, however, in trying to base education upon a sound psychology of learning, and there are still those who see education as a process of "transmitting the cultural heritage."

The contributions of a new science of psychology and the scientific movement which it sparked within education are reviewed in the next chapter. Monroe suggests 1915 as a date which may be chosen to mark the shift in the "majority opinion" of those writing authoritatively on teaching-learning theory from the older to the newer views.[22] Any similar "turning point" in school practice is more difficult to identify, however. In your experience with the schools you will recognize the contributions of the scientific movement, but practices associated with psychological views of the past will be in evidence also. Some of these practices will continue to survive. Suitably modified, they may warrant support from the newer psychology as well as the old. A major premise of the new science is that there is no one right way of teaching in all situations. William James, a pioneer of the new psychology, made this point when he stated, "Everywhere teaching must agree with the psychology, but need not necessarily be the only kind of teaching that would agree; for many diverse methods of teaching may equally well agree with psychological laws."[23]

SELECTED READINGS

Adamson, John W. (ed.), *The Educational Writings of John Locke* (New York: Longmans, Green & Co., 1912).

    A collection of original materials published from 1690 to 1706. "Some Thoughts Concerning Education" (pp. 21–179) is a topical treatment of Locke's views on everything educational, from whipping and excuses to memorizing themes and Latin.

Brubacher, John S., *A History of the Problems of Education* (New York: McGraw-Hill Book Co., 1947), Chap. VI.

    Early views of the nature of the learner and of learning from faculty psychology and formal discipline to Thorndike and connectionism. Later chapters suggest related methods of instruction, curriculum and administrative provisions.

DeGarmo, Charles, *Herbart and the Herbartians* (New York: Charles Scribner's Sons, 1895).

    One of the most serviceable English works on Herbart despite its early date.

Froebel, F., *The Education of Man* (W. N. Hailman, trans.) (New York: D. Appleton & Co., 1887).

    Statement of the theory which he made the foundation of his educational efforts. The mystical qualities of the statement should not divert the student from the importance of the principles of: (1) free self-activity, (2) creativeness, (3) social participation, and (4) natural expression.

Herbart, J. F., *The Science of Education* (Boston: D. C. Heath Co., 1892).

    Perhaps the most complete statement of Herbart's psychological and educational principles. This work did more to psychologize educational practices than any prior publication.

---

[22] Walter S. Monroe, *Teaching-Learning Theory and Teacher Education 1890 to 1950* (Urbana, Ill.: University of Illinois Press, 1952), p. 131.

[23] William James, *Talks to Teachers on Psychology* (New York: Holt, 1920), pp. 7–11.

Kolesnik, Walter B., *Mental Discipline in Modern Education* (Madison, Wis.: University of Wisconsin Press, 1958).
A review of philosophical and psychological material on the transfer of training controversy and an analysis of experimental problems.

Mulhern, James, *A History of Education* (New York: Ronald Press Co., 1946), Chap. 10.
Brief review of the contributions of Rousseau, Pestalozzi, Froebel, Herbart, and others to the socio-psychological movement in education in the late 18th and the 19th centuries.

Murphy, Gardner, *Historical Introduction to Modern Psychology*, rev. ed. (New York: Harcourt, Brace & Co., 1949), Chaps. I–V, VII.
A full authoritative account of pre-experimental psychology for more advanced study.

Pestalozzi, J. H., *How Gertrude Teaches Her Children* (L. E. Holland and F. C. Turner, trans., 2 ed.) (Syracuse, N. Y.: Bardeen, 1898).
The clearest explanation of the author's views of education in harmony with the nature of each individual child, as carried out by Gertrude, his ideal teacher.

Rousseau, J. J., *Emile* (W. Payne, trans.) (New York: D. Appleton Co., 1906).
The author's treatise on education according to nature. His recommendations for *Emile* contain the tenets of the philosophy with which he vigorously rejected the old order in education. This book marks the beginning of an era of educational reform, not only in psychological principles but in methodology and in the relations of education to society as well.

Thayer, V. T., *The Passing of the Recitation* (Boston: D. C. Heath & Co., 1928), Chaps. I & II.
Readable discussion of the transition from individual to group teaching in American schools, including descriptions of the monitorial, Pestalozzian and Herbartian influences.

Thorndike, Edward L., "Mental Discipline in High School Studies," *Journal of Educational Psychology*, Vol. 15 (January, 1924), pp. 1–22, 83–98.
Classic study comparing the transfer value of traditional and vocational high school subjects.

Woodworth, R. S., *Contemporary Schools of Psychology*, rev. ed. (New York: Ronald Press Co., 1948), pp. 37–48.
Brief readable account of contributions to learning theory by the early English associationists and Herbart in Germany.

Chapter XIII

SCIENTIFIC PSYCHOLOGY
AND SCHOOL LEARNING

Scientific psychology reached America from Europe shortly before 1900. We could now hope to know in a precise way some of the conditions that affect knowledge and conduct, and "educational" psychologists went to work in earnest to make that dream a reality. In 1886 an outline of the application of psychology to education was entitled *Educational Psychology*,[1] and a course by the same name was offered at the University of Illinois in 1890.[2] The application of the concepts and principles of psychology to the field of education has been a major interest of an increasingly large number of psychologists since that time. In addition, these educational psychologists have promoted the use of scientific methods in the study of problems which are unique to education. Our concern in this and the remaining chapters of Part III is similar to that of an educational psychologist of the past or present, namely, contributions of the principles and methods of scientific psychology to education.

This chapter is a concise statement of psychological questions, hypotheses, and findings about learning. At this point in the teacher's preparation he should be introduced to important areas which he will examine more thoroughly and in detail in other courses. An overview here can help establish a psychological viewpoint or a predisposition to look to psychology for help with professional problems. Further courses will elaborate upon the concepts and principles

---

[1] A. A. Robach, *History of American Psychology* (New York: Library Publishers, 1952), p. 378.

[2] G. M. Blair, *Educational Psychology, Its Development and Present Status*, University of Illinois Bulletin, Vol. 46, No. 13 (Urbana, Ill.: Bureau of Research and Service, College of Education, 1948), p. 9.

introduced here and apply them in varied contexts. The simplified description of the elements of learning presented in this chapter, for example, may be likened to an introductory chapter in the study of how children learn. In subsequent "chapters," these elements will be related to the achievement of varied learning outcomes: physical skills; information, concepts, and principles; interests, motives, and attitudes; social, emotional, and personal adjustment; aesthetic behavior; and problem-solving.

THE NEW PSYCHOLOGY

Among the intellectual developments of nineteenth-century Europe which merged in the new psychology were Darwin's new conceptions of the role of environment in forming human nature, Sir Francis Galton's statistical methods for describing variations in human nature, and Wilhelm Wundt's use of the scientific method in studying human nature.

Wundt (1832–1920) founded his Psychological Institute at the University of Leipzig in 1879. He devoted the rest of his life to placing psychology on a scientific basis. More than a hundred reports of experiments on seeing, hearing, feeling, speed of response, perceptual span (the amount that one can "take in" at once), rate of learning, and the time required for complex mental tasks came from his laboratory before 1900. Each was an example of new rigor in the systematic collection, testing, and classification of evidence with respect to psychological problems. Experiments, laboratory instruments, and mathematics were used to increase the precision and objectivity (impersonalness) of his findings.

Meanwhile, Charles Darwin (1809–1882) in the *Origin of Species* (1859) had amassed an enormous quantity of data to support his theory of evolution of living forms on the basis of the survival of those individuals who could best adjust to their environment. His ideas focused attention on the individual variations which occur in all species, including man, and which make for success or failure, survival or extinction. The spirit of his theory was such, also, that it encouraged experimental study of mind, body, and behavior. Since mind and body are said to have been molded through reaction to the natural environment, they were thought to be a part of nature, subject to the mechanical laws of the physical universe, and capable of study by the methods current in physics.

A host of new psychological concerns were suggested by the "developmental" emphasis of Darwin: physical and mental development in the race and the individual; the contribution of heredity and the effects of environment on development; the measurement of individual and race differences; child psychology; animal psychology; and educational psychology.

Darwin's notion of variation implied the idea of quantity to Sir Francis Galton (1822–1911). His work resulted in measuring, tabulating, classifying, and relating data on many characteristics and abilities of men. Whereas Wundt studied the characteristics men have in common, Galton was intrigued by how they differ. He advanced the theory that such variations could be described by a bell-shaped curve, the "normal" curve, and suggested that the variation in different characteristics could be related mathematically. His attempts to measure and quantify human differences are the foundation of modern educational and psychological measurement.

Most of the pioneering psychologists of America studied in Europe. Some, like James McKeen Cattell of Columbia University (1860–1944), worked with both Wundt and Galton, and returned to found American laboratories which firmly established statistical and experimental methods as dominant characteristics of American psychology. William James of Harvard University (1842–1910), though a student of Wundt's like Cattell, preferred the biological ideas of Darwin and the role of philosopher to that of an experimenter. James held that inherited "instincts" such as fear, love, imitation, curiosity, and ambition motivate the child to react to his environment. Learning, according to his view, was the modification of these instinctive reactions, as a result of the child's experiences. This general concept of learning as active experiencing, carried into progressive education by John Dewey (see Chap. X), was incorporated also into modern learning theories.

Armed with new methods and concerned with new problems, American psychology began to break its ties with philosophy. The new laboratories stimulated new journals devoted to psychological topics; professional associations were formed; and first courses in psychology, then departments of psychology, were established by the major universities.

The new scientists still needed philosophy, however, to lend purpose and meaning to their work. Thus a typical cycle of scientific investigation included conjecture, experiment, analysis, and interpretation — beginning and ending and starting anew with activities typical of the philosopher. What was new was an emphasis on control of the conditions being studied through experimentation, and an insistence on precision, objectivity, and quantitative methods in both the collection and analysis of observations. The new psychologist did not depend on the philosopher's methods of observation of naturally occurring situations and of reflection on man and his activities.

The psychological scientist's insistence upon evidence which could be verified by observation under carefully controlled and manipulated conditions proved a limitation as well as a strength. Not all human characteristics and activities can be controlled for purposes of experimentation, or precisely and quantitatively measured for analysis, without distorting their true nature. Such characteristics and activities include matters of common experience which make for great difference in our daily lives. How, for example, can we control the will, measure human thoughts, or weigh a man's love for his family? The major contributions to our understanding of these areas continue to be those made by the philosophers.

NEW CONCEPTIONS OF THE LEARNING PROCESS

The learning process — how changes in behavior, attitude, and knowledge can be brought about most efficiently — is the central problem of educational psychology today. This is a new emphasis. The psychologists who influenced education in the nineteenth century had some general notions as to how learning takes place, but their primary concern was with the structure and contents of the mind. Following the turn of the century, E. L. Thorndike (1874–1949), who had been a student of both James and Cattell, began to study learning systematically. Gradually other psychologists followed. After the publication of Thorndike's *Educational Psychology* in 1913, learning became a major area of study. Newly discovered facts brought about profound changes in education, while different theories designed to organize and explain these facts took shape.

Recently there has been a tendency for educational psychologists to think of different theories as merely different ways of describing the facts. Each theory is useful on some occasions and for some purposes. Further, there seems to be substantial agreement among theorists with respect to a number of "practical" principles which can help to guide school learning. Learners may be observed in many different situations, attempting many different types of tasks. We should not be surprised to find that one theory of learning, designed to explain learning in a given context, differs somewhat from a second theory coming from observations in another context. These differences among theories have been magnified at times by the tendency of theorists to be preoccupied with one or two outstanding features of learning as they observed it. The use of dissimilar terms to describe essentially similar concepts has added to the confusion.

For our purposes we should recognize two major groups of theories: stimulus-response or *S-R theories* and *field theories*. The S-R theories are a scientific outgrowth of associationism (Chap. XII), but attempt to state the laws by which reactions to situations are *learned*, not merely how ideas become associated. They have frequently attempted to isolate the simplest elements of the learning situation and the learner's response. The field theories represent part of a broad trend in science and philosophy away from preoccupation with the "atoms" or simplest elements of experience and events toward the study of the overall or total situation. Field theorists regard the S-R approach as being too mechanistic and so analytical and "piecemeal" that we are unable to see the forest for the trees. The term "field" comes from the physical sciences, where it refers to the physical context of events. Events in an electrical, gravitational, or magnetic field can be understood or explained only with reference to the total field. The meaning or significance of words, actions, persons, etc., is affected by the context in which they are encountered. Similarly, field psychologists believe that the study of learning and efforts to promote learning should begin with total situations or "wholes" of experience rather than the parts.

S-R Theories

Thorndike's psychology was an S-R theory. We have noted his part in the discrediting of formal discipline (Chap. XII). In a sense this cleared the way for new and far-reaching changes in psychology and education, and Thorndike emerged as the early leader. The claims for formal discipline rapidly gave way to Thorndike's theory, which emphasized the specificity of learning. Behavior was regarded as composed of specific reactions to specific situations. Learning in one situation would be useful in a new situation only if both had identical elements or features. Schools began to report extensive efforts to identify just what situations pupils would encounter in later life so that they could be taught to react effectively to each one.[3]

Like many another psychologist, Thorndike began in the animal laboratory, while a student of James at Harvard, where Darwin's influence had stimulated the study of animals. His experiments with cats are best known and will serve to introduce his conclusions about learning.

In a typical experiment a young and hungry cat was placed in a slatted box with food outside. In such a situation the cat proved very active, threshing about, clawing, biting, and scratching at everything. If he chanced to pull a string or button (it varied with the box) a door would open, and he could eat. A cat who had to earn his supper time after time in this way, it was observed, would gradually cease his wild ineffectual clawing and biting. Finally, when put in the box, he would immediately claw the button or loop in the particular way which had previously won his release and food.

Thorndike's conclusion from his extensive observations of animals around the turn of the century and of humans somewhat later was that learning a right response is largely accidental. Through trial and error, a stimulus situation (S) is connected with the right response (R). Thorndike's cats formed a connection between the situation in which they found themselves and the response which would free them. Thus his S-R theory has been called "connectionism." Also, because this approach to learning, as that of other S-R theorists, seems to emphasize an almost mechanical explanation of how responses to various situations are acquired, it may be termed "mechanistic."

In human subjects a thought or idea may be the stimulus to action, it was said, and there is no need for a situation to be present physically. Similarly, the response does not need to be observable action; it can be a thought, idea, or feeling. Further, both the stimulus and the response may be internal and the bond one between two mental facts. Thus it was possible to reduce mental and emotional,

---

[3] Carleton Washburne, "The Philosophy of the Winnetka Curriculum," *Curriculum Making: Past and Present*, National Society for the Study of Education, Twenty-Sixth Yearbook, Part I (Bloomington, Ill.: Public School Publishing Company, 1927), p. 219.

as well as physical, behavior to a bond psychology. Interests, ideals, emotions, and complex skills, such as reading, were explained by postulating groups of related connections.

In further developments Thorndike's psychology of learning led to several laws or principles of learning governing the selection of appropriate responses for given situations and the strengthening of the connecting bonds. Initially, each stimulus situation might be connected with many possible responses. The first response could be accidental or a matter of heredity. The *law of effect* held that the connection between S and R would be strengthened if its formation and occurrence were satisfying (as when a lucky pull let the cat out of the box), weakened if the results were annoying. The *law of exercise*, or use and disuse, maintained that a connection is strengthened by exercise, i.e., by repetition. Conversely, when it is not exercised over a period of time, the connection tends to weaken.

There were several secondary laws, the most important of which Thorndike called "associative shifting." According to this law, when a new stimulus is presented along with an old one, the new stimulus is connected with any response already connected to the original stimulus. The old stimulus can be withdrawn and the new will be sufficient to produce the response. Other psychologists called this process "conditioning."

The principle of conditioning or associative shifting, was discovered quite independently by a Russian physiologist, Ivan Pavlov (1849–1936), about 1902. By some it was made the center of all learning. John B. Watson, a professor at Johns Hopkins, was a leader of the S-R theorists who adopted that view. About 1914 he rebelled against the psychologist's long concern with an unobservable mind. Rejecting the need and the ability of psychologists to study more than physical situations and physical responses, he proposed a psychology based on the scientific study of observable behavior and its modification by conditioning. The term "behaviorism" is sometimes applied to his teachings, although it may be used much more broadly to indicate any biological approach or any mechanistic and materialistic approach.

At one point Watson denied any kind of mental heredity, claiming that, if given a child early enough, he could by proper conditioning make of him whatever one might desire. Although we may discount his exaggerated claims for conditioning, we are indebted to him for clearly demonstrating how apparently irrational emotional reactions may be established. His most famous demonstration of this type was with a child of about one year.[4] When this child reached for a white rat to which he was obviously attracted, a loud noise, which he feared, was sounded. After this sequence was repeated a number of times, the child feared the rat. This provided a classic example of a stimulus (the rat) originally not associated with a reaction (fear) becoming associated with fear simply because it was present at the same time as the originally feared stimulus (the loud noise).

During the period of their greatest influence, to about 1930, S-R theories continued to emphasize the central role of the teacher in schoolroom learning. No sharp break with assign-study-recite procedures was called for. There were, as has been stated, extensive inquiries designed to break subject matter and important skills into segments or steps for easy mastery. The arrangement of these materials into progressively more difficult sequences was studied experimentally, as were the most frequent errors or obstacles to learning each step. Instructional procedures were carefully planned to minimize these difficulties. A popular pattern of instruction which emerged emphasized: (1) setting the aim or objective, (2) arranging learning activities to achieve mastery, (3) appraising results as a basis for the next lesson.[5]

The teacher's work in directing activity proceeded in accordance with experimentally verified principles for encouraging desirable responses and discouraging undesirable ones. Thorndike's early statement on the management of learning has been summarized by Thut and Gerberich:

1. Some activity is essential before learning can be directed. Hence, the individual to be taught, if he is not already an active, responding organism, must be stimulated to such activity.
2. The teacher must arrange the instructional situation so that the individual undergoing training is likely to make the right response.
3. The teacher must arrange the situation so that when undesirable responses are given, dissatisfaction will result for the learner, and

---

[4] John B. Watson, *Behaviorism*, rev. ed. (New York: W. W. Norton and Company, 1930), p. 120.

[5] Harl R. Douglas, *Modern Methods in High School Teaching* (Boston: Houghton Mifflin Co., 1962), p. 3.

when the right response is made, satisfaction will result for the learner.[6]

Others have developed S-R theories more fully and in different ways. Clark Hull of Yale University devised an elaborate, often mathematical system of postulates and corollaries, which has stimulated extensive experimentation. Conditioning and a reinforcement principle, similar to the law of effect, are central in his theory.

B. F. Skinner, now at Harvard, has built a modern behaviorism around the systematic study of the behavior of rats and pigeons in a puzzle box which is somewhat simpler than that which Thorndike used. Remarkable success has been demonstrated in controlling the behavior of animals in the Skinner box by varying the conditions under which they receive pellets of food. A number of important learning principles have been stated. Self-checking materials and "teaching machines" built around these principles are now being tried in our classrooms. With these materials and devices each new step in learning is so easy that the student seldom errs and he knows immediately how well he has done. Each student has his own materials and can proceed at his own rate. Such "self-teaching" may help provide for individual differences and make some phases of the educational process more efficient. As of this writing, Skinner is one of the very few, if not the only, major psychological theorist who is working directly on educational problems.

S-R theory enjoyed its greatest popularity among educational psychologists during the 1920's. It was increasingly under attack after the early 1920's. Although its adherents appeared quite willing to modify their earlier positions to meet all challenges, it has never quite regained its early prestige as an adequate explanation for all learning.

Field Theories

While Thorndike and Watson were describing their S-R theories in America, several Germans — Max Wertheimer (1880–1943), Kurt Koffka (1896–1941) and Wolfgang Köhler (1887–) — were working out some decidedly different views. These men were concerned primarily with intelligent behavior. For them the learner reacted to

---

[6] Edward L. Thorndike, *Elements of Psychology* (New York: A. G. Seiler, 1901), pp. 209–210. As summarized by I. N. Thut and J. Raymond Gerberich, *Foundations of Method for Secondary Schools* (New York: McGraw-Hill Book Co., 1949), p. 129.

his own inner perceptions and his own reconstruction of a problem situation, not to specific parts of the problem which are isolated by chance. Learning, they said, begins with whole situations, not, as S-R theorists seemed to claim, by associating bits of experience. They came to reject the whole concept of S-R as too unintelligent and mechanistic.

When Koffka's *Growth of the Mind* was translated into English in 1924, it found a ready reception in America. We have said enough about this new approach already to see that it would fit nicely into Dewey's logical development of learning as problem-solving (compare Chap. X). As a matter of fact, Hilgard, one of the foremost students of learning theories, has pointed out that most of the important contributions which were credited to the German school were anticipated by James, Dewey, and the progressivists.[7] Nevertheless, the theories from Germany certainly complemented American educational developments of the time and have remained an important factor in educational thought.

The German school to which we have referred is known as Gestalt psychology. Gestalt means configuration or pattern, and the perception of configurations or patterns in the field or surroundings was said to determine the learner's reactions. In experimental programs, conceived as a direct attack on S-R theories, learning appeared to take place as a result of a sudden restructuring in the learner's perception of a situation. This sudden restructuring was called "insight."

One of Köhler's famous experiments illustrates this aspect of learning. A hungry ape who found his food just out of reach was given two sticks, both too short to reach the food. But the two sticks could be fitted together like the sections of a fishpole and would then serve to reach the food. Thorndike's cats reached their food initially by means of chance or random behavior which accidentally opened their cage. No amount of such behavior seemed to provide a solution for the ape. The solution seemed to occur suddenly, like a "bright idea." When it did, the ape proceeded to obtain the food immediately. The next day the performance was repeated without hesitation. No explanation of a gradually strengthening bond between situation and response appeared satisfactory. On the contrary learn-

---

[7] Ernest R. Hilgard, "The Relation of Schools of Psychology to Educational Practice," *The California Journal of Elementary Education*, 8, 17–26, 1939.

ing appeared to be a matter of suddenly seeing a pattern in the total situation which included a way to reach the goal, that is, a matter of insight.

For the Gestalt psychologist, then, learning became chiefly a matter of coming to see relations in the field or surroundings in which the learning occurs. It appears to be more often characterized by sudden solutions than by gradual improvement of performance through trial and error. To understand learning better we should study the relationships which the learner sees. In guiding learning of reading, to cite a familiar example, field theories suggest beginning with whole thoughts, interesting and understandable to the children, rather than with unintelligible a b c's and letter-combination charts. The parts are to be studied later in relation to meaningful wholes already learned. Similar recommendations with respect to beginning with wholes from which parts are isolated later have been made in the teaching of skills, such as swimming, and in writing, in arithmetic, in art, and, in fact, in nearly every type of formal and informal instruction.

The field psychology developed by Kurt Lewin (1890–1947), like the classical Gestalt theory, held that the overall pattern or field of events was of primary importance in learning. His theory was different in that it made greater use of motivating or driving forces in drawing a parallel between psychological and physical fields. We are all familiar with how charged objects or magnets are affected by the forces in electrical and magnetic fields. Although the analogy cannot be pushed too far, Lewin's theory regards motives or drives as forces which move the learner toward goals and away from threats, and cause him to overcome or circumvent barriers which he finds in his way.

Other theorists who absorbed much of Gestalt psychology have made purpose or goal-striving the central and controlling fact in behavior. Edward C. Tolman of the University of California is currently the most important of these. His theory, often called a "sign Gestalt" or "sign-learning" theory, is that the organism is using the significant features or "signs" of mental "maps" to his goal. These "maps" and their "signs" are not easily described, but they clearly include the goal, the means to the goal, and the relationship between means and goal. What is learned is a "path" or way to achieve the goal, not specific responses to specific situations. Much may be learned rather incidentally by merely "exploring" before actually trying to reach a goal. When motivated, the learner will act on the basis of hypotheses or expectations from his previous exploratory experience. The cognitive aspects of Tolman's theory are further emphasized in evidence that alternative hypotheses may be explored vicariously or in thought before any overt goal-seeking action is taken.

Another important development closely tied to Gestalt and field theories is called "organismic" psychology. The theme is the necessity to consider the organism, that is, the learner, as a whole, not in terms of separate physical, mental, and emotional functions. This psychology is particularly opposed to Cartesian mind-body dualism, but also to any theory which gives too much or separate attention to any one aspect of the learner. Even field theories which place too much emphasis on the central role of intelligence are criticized by the organismic psychologist.

Wheeler and Perkins elaborated organismic psychology in a widely used textbook on educational psychology published in 1932.[8] The term "organismic" is of biological origin; and the theory, where it differs from other field theories, is based on biological evidence of nature and growth. This psychology has been influential in giving recognition to the essential unity of the child and his reactions. The child learns as a whole, not in parts. The mind cannot be educated without affecting the body and the emotions as well. Another contribution of organismic theories brought to the fore the role of inherited growth patterns and rates in development and learning. The term "maturation" is used to describe the process of growth and development that takes place in a child relatively independent of learning and the environment.

Clear examples of the role of maturation in learning have been presented in support of the general conclusion that it is useless to try to teach children certain skills until they are sufficiently mature. In a famous experiment by Arnold Gesell and Helen Thompson[9] one of a pair of identical twins, 46 months old, was given special training in climbing stairs and stacking cubes each day for six weeks. At the end of this time the other twin was given a two-week training

---

[8] Raymond H. Wheeler and Francis T. Perkins, *Principles of Mental Development* (New York: Crowell, 1932).

[9] Arnold Gesell and Helen Thompson, "Learning and Growth in Identical Infant Twins; An Experimental Study by the Method of Co-twin Control," *Genetic Psychology Monographs*, 6, no. 1, 1929.

period in the tasks and at the end of two weeks was equal in ability to his twin. Two weeks' training at a later stage of maturation was as effective as six weeks' training given earlier. Some things which can be taught with ease to older children cannot be learned, at least in the same way, by younger ones because of their lack of maturity. This is as true of academic skills, such as reading, as of more clearly physical ones, such as walking, swimming, and the like. Since knowledge and experience as well as physiological and mental maturity affect the progress of the learner, modern teachers plan "readiness" activities which help to insure later progress.

Field theories have received their share of criticism. The S-R-minded psychologists criticize their experimentation as being subjective and overinterpreted. Processes like "inner reorganization," for example, are difficult to demonstrate. Insight is said by critics to be the end result of learning, not an explanation of how it takes place. It may be the result of inner trial and error. As for the emphasis on wholes, the S-R theorist denies that he is as atomistic as he is pictured and claims that S has been used to refer to a complex total situation and R to complex behavior that may involve the whole individual. Neverthless, we may thank the field and organismic theories for the prominence which current educational thought and practice give to:

1. The individual and his hereditary endowment;
2. The role of physiological maturation in readiness for learning;
3. The essential unity of the individual and his reactions;
4. Respect for intelligent behavior directed by the learner's own goals and purposes;
5. Learning as seeing relationships rather than as trial and error;
6. The current situation as well as past experience;
7. Beginning learning and instruction with whole situations rather than with isolated parts of the whole.

PRINCIPLES OF LEARNING

The prevailing tendency among educational psychologists since about 1930 has been one of reconciliation among learning theories. Different theories have been seen as complementary. The emphasis has been one which teachers should appreciate — that of documenting important relations or results which have a bearing on the practical understanding and control of learning. Authors of a number of texts in educational psychology do not even discuss differences among learning theories, choosing to concentrate instead upon generally accepted principles and their application.

A simplified description of the elements of learning which has won rather wide acceptance has been presented in essentially the same way by a number of authors:

1. The learner is in a given state of *readiness*. His readiness for learning depends upon his maturity, what he has learned to do previously and what he is able to do now. It influences what he wishes to do and what will give him satisfaction, i.e., his goals. (If the further aspects of the learning process which follow do not seem to apply to a given learner in a particular situation, it may be because he has not reached an appropriate level of readiness.)

2. The learner has *goals* the attainment of which will give him satisfaction.

3. He is part of a *situation* or segment of life which includes all the persons, objects, signs, and relationships in his environment.

4. The learner *interprets the situation* by directing his attention to its parts and relating them to his past experiences and his present goals, and he anticipates what will probably happen if he does various things. (If this step is not necessary, if he reacts automatically and successfully by habit on the basis of his previous experience, he is not learning.)

5. He *responds* in a way which he thinks will help him reach his goal. His response may be tentative, if he is unsure. It may be unnoticed by an observer and consist of thought or an emotional change.

6. He *interprets the apparent consequences* of his response. If the response appears to lead to the desired goals as he predicted, he is satisfied and will tend to respond to similar future situations in the same way. If not, he may interpret this and other situations differently and try other responses until satisfying consequences are attained. (On the other hand, he may give up or act in other ways which will not help him reach his goal.)

Lists of learning principles which will help to supplement this general picture of the learning process have been published.[10] Most

---

[10] William H. Burton, "Basic Principles in a Good Teaching-Learning Situation," *Phi Delta Kappan*, Vol. 39 (March, 1958), pp. 242–248. Cf. also Ernest R. Hilgard, *Theories of Learning* 2 ed. (New York: Appleton-Century-Crofts, 1956), pp. 485–487.

learning theorists would accept the following principles and perhaps a few others:

READINESS:

1. Readiness for a given learning activity cannot be assumed.

2. Readiness is the result of previous learning, natural experience, and physiological and social development.

3. The developmental aspects of readiness cannot be forced but needed experiences may be provided and much can be done to adapt learning material to the developmental level of any learner.

GOALS AND MOTIVATION:

1. Learning proceeds more readily when the learner is motivated to achieve a goal that makes sense to him and meets his needs.

2. Individuals should be helped to set goals which are reasonable — high enough to require learning but low enough to permit success.

3. Goals which are closely related to the natural outcomes of the learner's activity are preferable to artificial goals. For example, learning to spell in order to write a letter is preferable to learning to spell for a gold star.

4. Long-range goals affect short-term ones, especially in more mature students. College students, for example, may try to relate their study to their major vocational interest.

5. Motivation that is too intense may be disturbing or distracting and may be less effective than moderate motivation.

6. The goals of competition and rivalry may encourage the learning of routine skills and factual information but may have adverse emotional effects or establish detrimental attitudes.

THE SITUATION AND ITS INTERPRETATION BY THE LEARNER:

1. A learning situation should be meaningful and realistic to the learner rather than artificial or nonsensical.

2. Learning situations should be planned to encourage progress toward the varied goals of the learner — physical, personal, and social, as well as intellectual.

3. The learning situation should be adjusted to the abilities and maturation of the learner.

4. Guidance, i.e., any help in interpretation which assists the learner rather than dominates or directs him, is beneficial.

5. A learning situation should be presented so that essential relationships are easily perceived by the learner.

6. Learning with understanding will be more permanent and more useful than learning by rote or formula.

7. The emotions and personal history of a learner influence his interpretation of a situation.

8. A wide variety of related situations of varying content promotes the learning, retention, and use of general principles.

9. For more effective learning, simple learning situations should be presented before those which are more complex. The sequence is from simple but meaningful wholes to more complex and meaningful wholes, however, and not from arbitrary or meaningless parts to wholes.

10. Frequent repetition or practice is essential in acquiring skills and in guaranteeing retention of isolated facts and will be most effective when the need is understood and accepted by the learner.

THE RESPONSE AND THE CONSEQUENCES:

1. Active, definite responses by the learner are preferable to passive reception or observation, as in a lecture or movie.

2. Immediate knowledge of results aids learning.

3. Responses during learning are modified by their consequences.

4. Learning proceeds best under conditions of reward and success, rather than punishment or failure.

5. A previous history of success helps to insure healthy reactions to failure.

6. The consequences which are understood and accepted by the learner are those which satisfy his needs or help to achieve his goals.

7. Learning outcomes are many and varied, emotional and social as well as intellectual. In its influence on later behavior learning may be of general as well as specific utility. It affects our "intuition" as well as our analytical ability.

APPLICATIONS IN SCHOOL SITUATIONS

Modern teachers want to be shown. They wish to see the applications which theories or laboratory experiments suggest tested in the classroom. Often such tests require integrating or putting together knowledge from the several major areas represented in this and the following two chapters, i.e., learning, child nature and development, and measurement and evaluation. Educational psychology courses are offered in these three areas, but the applications are most often introduced in other education courses on curriculum or methods.

Almost every phase of the school has been studied. Illustrations would include investigations of audio-visual instruction, class size, discipline, effective study habits, grouping, various teaching methods, teacher preparation and selection, parent-teacher relations, and a host of studies of the teaching of arithmetic, art, composition, handwriting, spelling, reading, English, science, social studies and various other subjects. Research relating to each of a number of the subjects or problem areas listed here has been summarized and interpreted for the teacher in a recent series of pamphlets entitled "What Research Says to the Teacher." This series has been planned cooperatively by the Department of Classroom Teachers of the National Education Association and the American Educational Research Association. About twenty-five titles have appeared in this series and others are planned.

We have chosen one of these booklets as an illustration, not just of the series but of the scope and nature of the implications of research on practical school problems. Such research began with the spelling studies of Dr. J. M. Rice in the 1890's. Our selection, appropriately, is *Teaching Spelling* by Professor Ernest Horn of the State University of Iowa. Professor Horn describes his booklet as "an effort to report to classroom teachers the most important suggestions for the teaching of spelling which have been produced by research."[11] The topics of the Table of Contents are as follows:

The Curriculum in Spelling
   The Need for Definite Objectives
   Basic Evidence for the Selection of Words
   How Many Words Should Be Taught?
   Grade Placement of Words
   The Significance of Present and Future Needs
   A Suggested Plan for Grade Arrangement

Experiences Which Help Develop Spelling Ability
   Learning to Spell thru Reading
   Learning to Spell thru Written Work

---

[11] Ernest Horn, *Teaching Spelling*, What Research Says Series, No. 3 (Washington, D. C.: National Education Association, 1954), p. 2.

The topics indicate the scope of the recommendations. A few specific examples, chosen at random from the section on "Problems of Method," will suggest their nature:

In most instances the time allotment [for spelling instruction] should not be more than 75 minutes a week, and there is some evidence that if efficient methods are used, this amount could profitably be decreased.

. . . it is more efficient to study words in lists than in context.

To teach the meaning of each word, whether it is familiar to the children or not, would seem to be a useless and formal exercise.

When corrected by the pupils and the results properly utilized, the test is the most fruitful single learning activity per unit of time that has yet been devised.

Time for the study of words missed on the test should be provided as soon as possible, preferably immediately after the test has been corrected.

Games, contests, devices, and working for school marks, if used at all, should be thought of as supplementing the more intrinsic appeals [eight are described].

. . . the only rules which should be taught are those that apply to a large number of words and have few exceptions.

Even tho the evidence is meager on some important matters, it seems to justify considerable emphasis upon phonics. . . . In extreme instances the lack of phonic knowledge is completely frustrating.

Perhaps the most frequent cause of poor spelling achievement is poor study habits [effective methods of study are described]. . . . One of the first things to do is have him explain how he proceeds in learning to spell a word.[12]

Another, perhaps more intriguing, example of research activity with implications for education will be given. This example is provided by recent study of the newer educational media. Three are attracting the most attention: (1) educational television, (2) teaching machines, and (3) language laboratories.

Interest developed in educational television as a means of compensating for the lack of competent teachers or for making a few excellent teachers or rare and costly educational experiences available to more students. In the past ten years nearly fifty stations across the country have been established, as well as many closed-circuit installations for use within a single institution.

Briefly, for the limited range of outcomes for which we have suitable measures, television instruction with superior teachers and facilities achieves better results than conventional instruction and facilities. When the quality of teachers and facilities are similar, so are the results.[13] As TV instruction is offered to larger and larger audiences — a project is now under way which uses an airplane to cover six states — it may become increasingly difficult to adapt instruction to the needs of the individual class or community. However, the problems should be no more acute for television than for the conventional textbook, if teachers are adequately trained to use programs and not be dominated by them. Television has opened up new fields of educational study in equipment, facilities, scheduling, and presentation.

A typical language laboratory has an individual booth for each student. A table in each booth has individual headphones and may have a tape recorder as well. Dictation and comprehension exercises in English or a foreign language are presented by a master voice which repeats and repeats without tiring while the students translate, listen for comprehension, or reproduce what they have heard

[12] Ibid., pp. 15–25.
[13] C. R. Carpenter, "Television," in Jack V. Edling (ed.), The New Media in Education, A Report of the Western Regional Conference on Educational Media Research held at Sacramento, California, April, 1960 (Sacramento: State College Foundation, 1960), p. 48.

orally. The individual tape recorders permit student voice recordings which may be compared with the master tape.

In a language laboratory the student may be actively and constantly participating in learning activities. In the typical classroom he might take an active part only once or twice a period. The subjective judgments of both teachers and students definitely favor the use of language laboratories. However, the lack of adequate tests of comprehension and oral production has prevented a thorough evaluation of these new procedures.

The forerunner of today's teaching machines made its debut at about the time objective tests were being introduced. In 1926 Pressey[14] described and demonstrated a simple machine which permitted the selection of one of several possible answers to multiple-choice questions by pressing a key. If the right key was pressed, a drum revolved to expose the next question; if not, the student made other choices, as necessary, until the right answer was chosen and the question disappeared. This early machine had much in common with recent devices which have been introduced to individualize instruction and capitalize on several principles of learning emphasized by B. F. Skinner of Harvard University. Self-checking texts are also being used for these purposes. Both the machines and self-checking texts present material in one of the forms commonly used for objective tests.

Further principles for modern devices and materials are:

1. The student must make an active response to each item.

2. The student progresses at his own pace.

3. Knowledge of results is given immediately.

4. The material to be learned is arranged in such small steps that failure is minimized.

A rather large number of studies have demonstrated the value of teaching machines and similar devices for supplementing instruction, whether or not the material to be learned was arranged according to the preceding principles. Research studies comparing teaching machines as the sole means of instruction with instruction by conventional methods are not conclusive. Although the schooltime re-

---

[14] S. L. Pressey, "A Simple Apparatus Which Gives Tests and Scores — and Teaches," *School and Society*, Vol. 23, No. 586, March 20, 1926. Reprinted in A. A. Lumsdaine and Robert Glaser (ed.), *Teaching Machines and Programmed Learning* (Washington, D. C.: Department of Audio-Visual Instruction, National Education Association, 1960), pp. 35–41.

quired for learning appears shorter when teaching machines are used, the effects of observing the psychologists' rules, presenting the material by a machine rather than a text, providing immediate knowledge of results, and other factors involved in the comparisons, are not clear. The comparisons are generally limited to small segments of a course, those that are most easily prepared for machine presentation. Such segments often involve simple skills or rote learning only. No one knows the future of these devices and materials for a wide variety of important instructional objectives. At least they are expected to help free the teacher from the teaching of routine information and skills for more creative work with respect to understanding, attitudes, and appreciations.

Some see the teaching machine primarily as a laboratory device for the study of teaching. Unlike human teachers these devices can be made exactly alike. When we desire to study the effect of a change in one or more characteristics of instruction, these characteristics can be systematically varied to observe the effect of learning efficiency. The desirable size of the steps in a learning sequence, the form of the responses (multiple-choice or fill-in), the treatment of errors, and the frequency and amount of review are factors which have been investigated already in attempts to make machine teaching itself more effective.

How television, language laboratories, teaching machines, and the host of other aids for teachers should be used in concert in instruction is, of course, a major unsolved problem for research.

Summary

Scientific psychology was the result of a union of philosophical psychology, a young experimental physiology, new appreciation of the role of the environment in forming human nature, and statistical concepts for the study of individual differences. Some, but by no means all, aspects of man and his nature have proved amenable to study under the controlled conditions scientists seek to establish.

In America Edward Lee Thorndike pioneered an educational psychology with the study of the learning process as its central problem. Two major groups of learning theories have since emerged — stimulus-response or S-R theories and field theories. Thorndike's connectionism was one of several S-R theories related to eighteenth- and nineteenth-century associationism. S-R theories sought to explain all behavior as responses or reactions (R) to situations (S); and learning, as the making and strengthening of S-R associations. Associations were thought to be strengthened by such factors as repetition and the reinforcing effects of satisfying consequences. Transfer was explained by previously learned responses to specific elements of the new situation. The recommended curriculum was planned around specific associations which the student would need in the future. In this view the environment appears to be acting upon the individual rather mechanically to stimulate him and to strengthen appropriate responses while weakening others. Whole situations and complex behavior are regarded as composed or determined by their elements. Although the prestige of S-R theories has declined in recent years, there is much current interest in self-checking or self-teaching materials and devices planned according to the S-R principles of B. F. Skinner.

The field theorist regards the whole learning situation of which the learner is a part as primary. Any parts derive their meaning from the whole, not vice versa. The individual is not regarded as a toy of the environment; he interacts with it. When he has a problem or is disturbed, he is motivated to find a more satisfying state of affairs. His efforts to restructure or see relationships in the situation which will enable him to accomplish this are intelligent. When he succeeds, he learns. Often his success appears the result of a sudden "insight" with little evidence of the gradual learning by repetition and reinforcement which is described in S-R theories. Accordingly, field theorists stress the need for school learning experiences which are (1) based on problems which are real for the student and (2) organized and presented so that the student understands what is before him and can see the essential relationships. There are several field theories and they differ somewhat in such matters as the treatment of the learner's goals and purposes, the essential unity of the learner's functions and reactions, and the role of maturation in learning.

Different learning theories are oversimplified in the interests of clarity. Differences arise also in the contexts and methods used to study learning and the terms used to describe it. There seems to be substantial agreement, however, on a simplified description of learning and a number of practical "principles" relating to each of the elements of the description. A learner is described as being in a given state of *readiness* because of his nature, maturation, and previous experience. He is part of a *situation* and has *goals*. He *interprets the situation* and *responds* in a way which helps him achieve his goals. He *interprets the consequences* and his interpretation affects what he does next and what he will do in future similar situations.

Almost every phase of the school has been studied by the methods of scientific psychology or research. The results of these applied studies have been summarized and interpreted often for the guidance of the teacher. In this chapter we briefly reviewed some of the research results in just two areas to illustrate what is being made available in many areas. Our two examples were related to the teaching of spelling and newer educational media, such as television, teaching machines, and language laboratories.

Students often come to the study of educational psychology, as they do to all their professional courses, anticipating that they will learn step by step the programs and methods of successful teaching. It should now be apparent that they will not and cannot. Scientific psychology and research have not produced how-to-do-it formulae and procedures for teachers, because teaching is not a skilled trade, like bricklaying, where one performs a series of acts in the same way, time after time. Teaching is an art and a profession, requiring judgment and decisions in infinitely complex situations. The related sciences supply general principles, but these must be selected, applied, or tested (for some are not much more than hypotheses) by the individual, as a professional, for particular educational situations.

SELECTED READINGS

Anderson, G. Lester, "Theories of Behavior and Some Curriculum Issues," *Journal of Educational Psychology*, Vol. 39 (March, 1948), pp. 133–140.
An interpretation of different psychological views of behavior which shows how each leads to different educational implications.
——— (ed.), *Learning and Instruction*, Forty-Ninth Yearbook of the National Society for the Study of Education, Part I (Chicago: University of Chicago Press, 1950).
This volume focuses the data and concepts from the psychology of learning upon problems of instruction. Chap. I describes the general nature of learning and Part III presents implications for the improvement of teaching.
Brubacher, John S., *A History of the Problems of Education* (New York: McGraw-Hill Book Co., 1947), Chap. VI, pp. 155–164.
Overview of changes in thinking about learning from the early behaviorists

to Gestalt psychology and the psychoanalysts. Later chapters suggest related changes in methods of instruction, the curriculum, etc.

Burton, William H., *The Guidance of Learning Activities*, 3 ed. (New York: Appleton-Century-Crofts, 1962).

An example of a text in curriculum and instruction which emphasizes understanding of the nature of learning. Chapters on the improvement of the more traditional as well as newer methods of instruction.

———— "Basic Principles in a Good Teaching-Learning Situation," *Phi Delta Kappan*, Vol. 39 (March, 1958), pp. 242–248.

A considerable list of principles of learning basic to good teaching which are supported by experimental findings.

Cole, Luella, *A History of Education* (New York: Rinehart & Co., 1950).

One of the finest accounts of the human side of educational greats such as Pestalozzi, Herbart, Froebel and Montessori with a wealth of descriptive material on the daily practices of the schools which they founded or influenced.

Colidarci, A. P. (ed.), *Educational Psychology, A Book of Readings* (New York: Dryden Press, 1955), Chap. 1.

Includes four articles relating theories of learning and behavior to curriculum issues and educational practices.

Cronbach, Lee J., *Educational Psychology*, 2 ed. (New York: Harcourt, Brace & World, 1963).

Example of an up-to-date, popular textbook in educational psychology which has learning as its principal focus. Realistic illustrations from individual or classroom episodes are featured.

Crow, Lester D., and Crow, Alice (eds.), *Readings in Human Learning* (New York: David McKay, 1963).

Comprehensive collection of source material on the nature of learning, principles and conditions of learning, various theories, types of learning, and the guidance of learning.

Dennis, Wayne (ed.), *Readings in the History of Psychology* (New York: Appleton-Century-Crofts, 1948).

Reprints of classic works in psychology, many of value for historical background in educational psychology. See especially: John Locke, "An Essay Concerning Human Understanding" (pp. 55–68); E. L. Thorndike, "Animal Intelligence" (pp. 377–387); John Watson, "Psychology as the Behaviorist Sees It" (pp. 457–471); and Wolfgang Köhler, "The Mentality of Apes" (pp. 497–505).

Department of Classroom Teachers, National Education Association and American Educational Research Association, *What Research Says To the Teacher Series* (Washington, D. C.: National Education Association, 1953–1961).

Continuing pamphlet series which seeks to bridge the gap between the advancing field of educational and psychological research and classroom teaching. About 25 titles have appeared in subject areas of the elementary and secondary schools and in personality and adjustment, homework, evaluation, parent-teacher relationships, group relations, etc. See especially No. 6 by William Clark Trow, *The Learning Process*, 1954.

Freehill, Maurice F., "Some Facts for Parents about How We Learn," *NEA Journal*, Vol. 47 (May, 1958), pp. 324–327.

Examines modern teaching methods in the light of the psychology of learning.

Garrett, Henry E., *Great Experiments in Psychology*, 3 ed. (New York: D. Appleton-Century, 1951), Chaps. 3 and 5.

An outstanding resource book which presents the classic experiments on each of a number of fundamental problems and then reviews subsequent related research to date. The chapters cited are for Thorndike's Laws of Learning and Thorndike and Woodworth's experiments on transfer of training.

Hullfish, H. Gorden, *Aspects of Thorndike's Psychology in Their Relation to Education*, Ohio State University Contributions to Learning No. 1 (Columbus, Ohio, 1926).

An excellent analysis of the implications of Thorndike's Psychology for schoolroom practices.

Kelly, W. A., *Educational Psychology*, 4 ed. (Milwaukee: Bruce Publishing Co., 1956), Part V.

A text for Catholic schools which integrates principles of scholastic and rational psychology with chapters on the soul, the will, and character formation. Part V is a standard introductory treatment of the topics of this chapter except that learning is described as mental activity and spiritual motivation is recognized.

Köhler, Wolfgang, *Gestalt Psychology*, rev. ed. (New York: Liveright Publishing Corp., 1947).

Full statement of Gestalt views and principles by one of the pioneers of this school of thought.

——— *The Mentality of Apes* (New York: Harcourt, Brace & Co., 1927).

A description of one of the most interesting experiments by the Gestalt school and one which was basic in their attack upon S-R principles.

Kolesnik, Walter B., *Educational Psychology* (New York: McGraw-Hill Book Co., 1963).

A basic text which integrates classical and Catholic philosophical and theological concepts with the findings of scientific psychology.

Meyer, A. E., *An Educational History of the American People* (New York: McGraw-Hill Book Co., 1957), Chap. XIV.

Brief but penetrating review of the psychological movement in education from Wundt to the present. Several applications of psychological developments to education are highlighted.

Morse, W. C., and Wingo, G. Max, *Psychology and Teaching* (Chicago: Scott, Foresman & Co., 1955), pp. 380–488.

Summary of material usually presented in an introductory course in general psychology prepared for students of education.

National Society for the Study of Education, *The Scientific Movement in Education*, Thirty-Seventh Yearbook, Part II (Bloomington, Ill.: Public School Publishing Co., 1938).

Brief reviews of (1) the contributions of the scientific movement to different facets of the educational enterprise, (2) the methods and techniques of inquiry in education, and (3) the contributions to education of the facts and findings of several sciences. The contributions of scientific knowledge about psychology of learning are ably presented by J. F.

Dashiell; and John Dewey examines the relationships between education, philosophy, and science.

Schramm, Wilbur (ed.), *New Teaching Aids for the American Classroom* (Stanford, Calif.: Stanford University, Institute for Communication Research, 1960).

Contains papers which show how research may contribute to the evolution and use of newer educational media. Ernest R. Hilgard discusses the principles of applying learning theory to the improvement of learning aids (pp. 19–26). Other papers review progress in television, films, and teaching machines.

Seagoe, May V., *A Teacher's Guide to the Learning Process* (Dubuque, Iowa: Wm. C. Brown Co., 1956).

A notable effort to close the gap between theory and the art of teaching by formulating and illustrating practical principles.

Thayer, V. T., *The Passing of the Recitation* (Boston: D. C. Heath & Co., 1928).

Reinterpretation of biological and S-R principles of learning as they relate to teaching methods by an author who came under the influence of John Dewey and the newer education.

Thorpe, Louis P., and Schmuller, Allan M., *Contemporary Theories of Learning with Applications to Education and Psychology* (New York: Ronald Press Co., 1954).

Follows a generally historical outline in reviewing twentieth-century lines of psychological thought that have direct bearing on the problems of learning. A strong feature is readability.

Thorndike, Edward L., *Human Learning* (New York: The Century Co., 1931).

An epoch-making book presenting considerable evidence for the revision of the author's earlier "laws" of learning. Not easy to read but rewarding for the persistent student.

Trow, William C., "The Problem of Transfer — Then and Now," *Phi Delta Kappan*, Vol. 40 (November, 1958), pp. 68–71.

Shows that the critics of modern education often have outmoded concepts of learning and transfer.

Watson, John B., *Psychology from the Standpoint of a Behaviorist* (Philadelphia: J. B. Lippincott & Co., 1919).

The clearest statement of the major tenets of Watson's behaviorism. Unlike his earlier works most examples of this book relate to the behavior of humans.

Chapter XIV

NEW KNOWLEDGE OF CHILDREN

When psychology was largely the study of the mind, it was the adult mind that was studied. Psychologists were apt to assume that children were merely unfinished adults — not as large, nor as strong, nor as fully developed, but otherwise exactly the same.

Educational reformers of the eighteenth and nineteenth centuries — Rousseau, Pestalozzi, Froebel, and Herbart — spoke out for an education which based its methods on child nature. They helped to create a demand for knowledge of children as children. Darwin's evolutionary theory helped to stimulate still greater interest in the nature and development of children, as did Wundt's occasional use of children as subjects in his pioneering laboratories. Most of all, perhaps, the systematic and serious study of children was a natural outgrowth of the enthusiasm for facts which characterizes the present century and the years immediately preceding it. This chapter reviews some of the attempts to meet new demands for new knowledge of children.

THE CHILD-STUDY MOVEMENT

Looking back, we see that some, in their eagerness for facts about children, were more enthusiastic than scientific. Under the leadership of G. Stanley Hall (1844–1924), founder and president of Clark University, societies for the study of children sprang up in a number of states during the 1890's. Journals devoted to the study of children were established, and parents everywhere became recorders of the physical and mental development of their children. After Hall met with foreign psychologists at the Chicago World's Fair in 1893, the child-study movement became international in scope and interest, spreading throughout Europe. Baby biographers were legion, here and abroad. The pink and blue baby books for parents and relatives which are still available today became a commercial item. Although a number of sound biographical studies of infants were produced in the 1890's, the method fell into disfavor because of the larger number of haphazard and sentimental accounts produced by untrained persons.[1]

Hall popularized interview-questionnaire methods of child study. Direct questioning of Boston schoolchildren led to the publication of a survey of children's information, experiences, and ideas in practically every field from nature to religion and morality.[2] He used written questionnaires to obtain vast amounts of information from children and adults as to their childhood and adolescent memories. He is well known also for a monumental work on adolescence, based in part on the personal diaries of famous persons.[3]

Hall's efforts led to a systematic body of information about children's ideas, attitudes, and personalities. Although the methods of data collection which he used or popularized were widely criticized as haphazard and undependable, as were his rather determined efforts to make his data support Darwin's theories, there is no doubt as to his massive influence on further progress in the study of children at home and abroad.

EUROPEAN RESEARCH ON CHILDREN

European research on children has been characterized by a concern with the contents of the child's mind, somewhat in the tradition of earlier centuries. In France Alfred Binet's (1857–1911) studies of the thought processes of children led in 1905 to his intelligence tests for children, and greatly stimulated study of the mental development of children and of its relationship to environment and other aspects of growth. In Vienna the studies of Sigmund Freud (1856–1939) and the psychoanalytic movement which he founded have led to an appreciation of the role of the early developmental history of the child upon adult behavior. More recently, European investigators

[1] H. D. Sheldon, "Clark University, 1897–1900," *Journal of Social Psychology*, 24, No. 1 (August, 1946), pp. 227–247.

[2] G. Stanley Hall, *The Contents of Children's Minds on Entering School* (New York and Chicago: E. L. Kellogg and Co., 1893).

[3] G. Stanley Hall, *Adolescence* (New York: D. C. Appleton, 1904).

like Charlotte Bühler in Vienna and Jean Piaget at the University
of Geneva have provided a wealth of information on child behavior,
particularly on children's views of the world.

Piaget has systematically observed the development of children's
concepts of space, time, object, number, cause and effect, right and
wrong, and the like. In the *Language and Thought of the Child*,[4]
for example, he has utilized information from observation, experiment, and clinical interviews to show how the child gradually develops an awareness of self. At first he cannot separate himself
from the rest of the world. At this stage he believes that things
are exactly as he sees them. If he thinks of his toy as broken, it is
broken. If he is sad when it is broken, you are sad and it is sad.
It is a sad world. The problem to which Piaget's research is directed
is to trace the process by which the child outgrows his self-centered
view. A point of controversy in the interpretation of Piaget's reports
is the extent to which his findings are universally applicable. Perhaps
they reflect only the culture of the Swiss with whom he works.

CHILD PSYCHOLOGY IN THE UNITED STATES

Following the turn of the century the "progressive education"
movement in the United States both stimulated and was aided by
new studies of children. Children were the new citizens of the "educational democracies," and information was needed which would
permit them to do what they wanted to do and were able to do at
each educational level.

An intensive effort was made during this time to be of service
to the child who encountered difficulties or who did not seem to be
fulfilling his promise. Binet's work on intelligence testing provided
tools which were enthusiastically received in the United States. Several
American versions of Binet's test soon appeared. E. L. Thorndike
and his students pioneered in the production of standardized achievement tests in school subjects. By 1915 there was a strong trend
toward objective measurement throughout the schools and in clinics
established to deal with children's difficulties in adjusting to school
or child life.

Watson began studying emotions in the very young child about
1916. As was noted in the preceding chapter, his laboratory experi-

---

[4] Jean Piaget, *The Language and Thought of the Child* (M. Warden trans.) (New
York: Harcourt, Brace & Co., 1926).

ments dealt with conditioning. They were probably most important in overcoming previous sentimental reluctance to use children in scientific experimentation.

After World War I large-scale studies of child development were undertaken at a series of institutes for child welfare established at major universities with the help of funds from the Lorna Spellman Rockefeller Memorial.[5]

One of the most celebrated and advanced of such centers is the Clinic of Child Development at Yale University. Directed for many years by Dr. Arnold Gesell, it has contributed, besides an impressive number of scholarly books and dissertations, less learned works for parents, films, and television programs. The study of the child has been comprehensive and painstaking, utilizing modern techniques of recording and photography extensively. Whole families have lived in the clinic while their children were scientifically observed in homelike surroundings — while eating, talking, and learning, and even sleeping.

The growth and behavior of thousands, if not millions, of our children have been checked against Gesell and Ilg's composite portrait of the development of fifty children at each age level from five to ten.[6] *The Infant and Child in the Culture of Today*[7] is another standard reference by Gesell and Ilg.

Two general approaches have been used in gathering scientific data on children and adolescents: (1) the cross-sectional approach and (2) the longitudinal approach. Composite portraits of observations and measurements of groups of children at various age levels, such as that of Gesell and Ilg, illustrate the cross-sectional approach. This approach has led to standards for each age group, such as those used when we say a ten-year-old boy should be 47 inches tall and weigh between 48 and 58 pounds. Such standards are useful in comparing a child with others of his age group. On the other hand, they often obscure the significant features of the process of development in individuals. For this reason the longitudinal approach, which observes and measures the same individuals over a period of years,

[5] Willard C. Olson, "Developmental Psychology," in Chester W. Harris (ed.), *Encyclopedia of Educational Research*, 3 ed. (New York: Macmillan, 1960), p. 372.

[6] Arnold L. Gesell and Frances L. Ilg, *The Child From Five to Ten* (New York: Harper and Brothers, 1945).

[7] Arnold L. Gesell and Frances L. Ilg, *The Infant and Child in the Culture of Today; the Guidance of Development in Home and Nursery School* (New York: Harper and Brothers, 1943).

has gained in popularity.[8] From the study of repeated measurements of the same individuals characteristic patterns of growth emerge, and individual children can be evaluated in terms of satisfactory progress or development with respect to their own rate and pattern. This approach has encouraged the study of the whole individual, as an individual, and has discouraged some absurdities in the interpretation of individual growth.

Research on children has drawn upon different sciences. The vastness and variety of the continuing contributions from various fields can only be suggested here.

Biologists have studied genetically determined patterns in the development of animals and humans and the interaction of heredity and environmental factors.

Pediatricians have described growth in gross bodily characteristics such as height and weight and have developed and applied dependable measures of dentition, the hardening of the bones, etc. Patterns of behavior accompanying the development of physiological systems and the characteristics of different age groups have been described in detail.

Sociologists have shown how the home, the school, the church, the peer group, and other social units and forces influence the behavior of children. Social anthropologists have investigated differences among different social classes and cultural groups. Studies of social relations in the school and psychological analyses of the behavior of children and adults in various social settings have been numerous and fruitful.

Psychologists have contributed knowledge and developed techniques for studying the nature, organization, and development of abilities and aptitudes; achievement and learning in such areas as language and reading; emotions, interests, attitudes toward self, and other phases of personality. Since World War II, a growing emphasis on clinical psychology has been a factor in a revolt against ultraobjectivity, and researchers have sought to look behind children's overt behavior to get at their inner feelings and values and the reasons for their actions.[9]

---

[8] W. F. Dearborn and J. W. Rothney, *Predicting the Child's Development* (Cambridge, Mass.: Sci-Art Publishers, 1941).

[9] Arthur I. Gates, *et al.*, "Educational Psychology," in "Twenty-Five Years of Educational Research," *Review of Educational Research*, Vol. 26, No. 3 (June, 1956), pp. 241–257.

From psychoanalysts and students of mental hygiene has come evidence of the effects of early childhood experiences upon later behavior and adjustment and methods of encouraging healthy development, as well as methods for dealing with personality disorders. Psychiatrists have contributed to the development of instruments for the study of personality.

Educational psychology has the task of synthesizing, interpreting, and applying to education the wealth of scientific information about children.

EDUCATIONAL APPLICATIONS

The study of the child is a major part of the teacher's professional preparation — in separate courses or incorporated as an integral part of all courses. New knowledge of the child and the manner of his development affects all teacher-pupil relations; it influences the organization, placement, and pacing of learning content and activities; it governs the administrative provisions for selection and placement, guidance and promotion; in short, this knowledge touches every phase of the educational program and its relations with the student, the home, and the community. No summary of the wealth of information available with respect to child nature and development will be attempted. Instead, a few general principles which affect the teacher's responsibilities will be briefly described. Several ways of organizing or focusing attention on data about children to make them more useful to the teacher will be presented also.

GENERAL PRINCIPLES

1. *Growth is the result of interaction between the child and his environment.* Once it was assumed that a child's heredity determined what he would become. Later, some like Watson considered environment and learning all-important. Now, however, it is an accepted principle that what happens to a child is an essential factor in what he does with his hereditary potential. Children frequently, perhaps ordinarily, do not make enough of their native capabilities. The teacher should approach his task with faith in the educability of his students.

2. *Growth and development is a continuous, orderly, and cumulative process.* The stages of life which are often described, such as

infancy, childhood, preadolescence, and adolescence, are merely a convenience for description. Actually, as the longitudinal studies have shown, any ability or other characteristic of an individual tends to change gradually and continuously in accordance with a general pattern which is inherent. An unhealthy environment will delay or stunt natural progress temporarily and may do irreparable damage, since succeeding development builds on what has gone before whether it is good or bad.

3. *Growth is especially rapid in infancy and adolescence.* Rapid physical growth, acquisition of motor skills, and development of language are characteristic of the first two years of life. Development is relatively slower thereafter in childhood; but, as puberty is approached, the rate again increases. Adolescent physical growth is striking. New motor skills are acquired. Mental development is not so easily observed, but there is general agreement that improvement of performance is rapid in the whole field of mental activity. Social skills are perfected in adolescence and many developmental tasks relating to independence and individuality are accomplished.

The development of adolescents is notable for its unevenness. Physical awkwardness often results when feet get too big and arms and legs too long too soon. Fluctuations of mood and energy mark the teen-ager, and in attitudes and behavior he is now a child, now an adult.

4. *Rates of growth and development vary among individuals and for different characteristics of the same individual.* Third graders are not all different from fourth graders. In any class there is a variety in the development of children, with the consequence that any student is further along in some respects than in others. One child may be quite mature socially but below average in physical development. Another may be average or advanced in language development, but immature socially and emotionally. Advanced development in one respect does not always reflect special opportunity or parental pushing; and relatively slow progress in others may not be a cause for alarm. Each individual has a characteristic way of developing in different respects and the slow starter may overtake his more rapid peers. Needless to say, this makes predicting the future for individuals very difficult. It also underlines the need to gear instruction to the level and pace of the individual child. It emphasizes the

importance of accepting the child where he is and helping him on his level rather than attempting to force him to the level where we think he ought to be.

5. *Girls differ from boys in their development.* Terman and Tyler have summarized the information on sex differences.[10] In childhood, girls exceed boys somewhat in school achievement and physical maturity. Boys, on the other hand, are stronger, more active, more aggressive, and more dominant. They appear to have more defects of all kinds than girls. Boys are generally taller and stronger than girls at all ages except at ages eleven to fifteen when girls reach puberty and spurt ahead of boys. All the preceding data are averages. There is, of course, great overlapping of rates of development between individuals of the two sexes.

6. *All phases of development interact.* A child's interests change with his physical development, and his school achievement changes with his interests. Interests are closely related to emotions like satisfaction, annoyance, amusement, or anger. Emotions and interest are potent factors in school learning, as are health and mental ability. All these affect the overall pattern of behavior, attitudes, interests, feelings, etc., which we call personality. This principle is closely related to the concept that the child develops and reacts as a whole.

WAYS TO STUDY AND HELP CHILDREN

Several schemes of presenting findings from the study of children have helped to make it more meaningful to teachers. At first, much of the information was organized by age or grade level to suggest the physical, mental, and emotional characteristics of each age. Such norms have helped with some aspects of the teacher's work, such as physical education, but by and large have failed to give teachers a workable understanding of children. More useful approaches include: (1) study of the child's basic needs, (2) the developmental task approach, (3) personality theory, (4) readiness for learning, and (5) individual differences.

According to a theory of *basic needs,* the child is endowed with natural drives — needs for affection, belonging, recognition, self-re-

[10] L. M. Terman and E. Tyler, "Psychological Sex Differences," in Leonard Carmichael (ed.), *Manual of Child Psychology* (New York: John Wiley and Sons, Inc., 1954), pp. 1064–1114.

spect, and others. A child's behavior may be studied and understood in terms of the success or failure of his attempts to satisfy his basic needs. Problems arise when children fail to satisfy their needs or when they satisfy them by undesirable means. They can be helped if they are given opportunities to satisfy their needs in morally and socially desirable ways.

Developmental tasks refer to learning and adjustments which all children and adults have to accomplish as they grow older and more mature.[11] These tasks arise from their psychobiological nature and the demands of the society in which they live. At each age level the individual must play his expected role. With regard to independence, for example, the preschool child must learn to be separated from his parents, choose among activities, and make suggestions to his group. He must become increasingly independent through childhood and early adolescence, and in later adolescence make serious decisions without relying on adults. Still later he is expected to make and hold to decisions even against parental opposition.

Similar developmental tasks relate to physical accomplishments, intellectual achievements, approval by authority figures and peers, self-respect, and others. The various tasks fit together into a continuous pattern. The accomplishment of each task at the proper time paves the way for those to come. Each task unachieved at the proper time is an obstacle in the path to maturity. The teacher's responsibility includes an awareness of the tasks with which her group is struggling and the progress or lack of it evident in the behavior of each child. More than this, the teacher and the classroom culture which she helps to create play an important role in providing opportunities for optimum achievement with respect to developmental tasks. Take tasks relating to social acceptance as an example. The elementary teacher who makes class offenders an object of ridicule is inviting rejection of these "bad" children by the group. On the other hand, the high school teacher who shows favoritism toward a student likewise makes it more difficult for him to be accepted by his older peer group. Other and wiser teachers will be able to help the unpopular child win acceptance through accomplishments admired by his fellow students.

Psychoanalytic theory and clinical practice have encouraged a view

---

[11] Robert J. Havighurst, *Human Development and Education* (New York: Longmans, Green, 1953).

of development which we may term *personality theory*.[12] This approach emphasizes the consideration of inner feelings and urges and their control and utilization by the individual in satisfying, "healthy" ways. The process of growing up is conceived to be in large part the resolution of conflicts between one's self and his growing body and between both of these and society.[13] The more difficult the resolution of these conflicts the less energy the individual has for learning. The task of the school — and of the home and the community — is in large part the provision of opportunities to resolve satisfactorily the fundamental conflicts characteristic of each level of development. These conflicts are sequential and age-related. It is instructive to describe one which is characteristic of ages four and five. Haan[14] has called this "initiative versus guilt about purposing." The child of this age has found out he is an individual, now he needs to find out what he can be by himself. His immaturity and physical limitations prevent him from actually striking out on his own but in fantasy he can disobey, reject, or even abandon his parents and take on adult roles and functions. He does this in play but not without a sense of guilt for even thinking about it. Here is the conflict which he needs to work through so that he can preserve his initiative and not be overly restricted or burdened by guilt. His imaginative enterprise and initiative must be encouraged and not restricted or punished if he is to be prepared for later creation and accomplishment. We are reminded of the small boy in a cartoon who tells his young friend, "Of course I'll marry you but we'll have to live at my house. I'm not allowed to cross the street."[15]

Educational psychologists have emphasized the use of developmental information in understanding *readiness for learning*, a basic concern of the teacher. Trow, for example, asks, "When are children ready to learn?" The answer he suggests is "when they are healthy, well adjusted, mature enough, and interested."[16] He emphasizes that

---

[12] A useful statement similarly oriented is *A Healthy Personality for Every Child: A Digest of the Fact Finding Report to the Midcentury White House Conference on Children and Youth* (Raleigh, N. C.: Health Publications Institute, Inc., 1951).

[13] Erik H. Erikson, *Childhood and Society* (New York: W. W. Norton & Co., Inc., 1950), Chap. 7.

[14] Aubrey Haan, *Elementary School Curriculum: Theory and Research* (Boston: Allyn and Bacon, Inc., 1961), p. 35.

[15] Fred Neher, *The Milwaukee Journal*, June 25, 1961.

[16] William Clark Trow, *The Learning Process*, What Research Says Series, No. 6 (Washington, D. C.: National Education Association, 1954), pp. 6–12.

"teachers must be acquainted with all aspects of development and with all periods of life." Cronbach uses information and concepts of physical development, cultural pressures and opportunities, developmental tasks, and need satisfaction to illustrate four principles related to readiness: (1) all aspects of development interact, (2) physiological maturing prepares one to profit from experience, (3) experiences have a cumulative effect, (4) certain times in one's life are formative periods when basic readiness for a particular activity is established.[17]

Some reviewers regard new knowledge of *individual differences* as the greatest contribution of developmental psychology to education.[18] Trow's recent textbook,[19] for example, has "the teacher relates to individuals" as a principal focus. Information on children who differ in psychological characteristics, school achievement, aptitude, cultural background, and personality is systematically presented. The ability to recognize the differences among children and to do something about them is a major responsibility of the teacher.

Concepts of evolution, concern for the exceptional child and especially the development of quantitative and measurement methods (reviewed in Chap. XV) have been factors in our clearer recognition of individual differences and their significance for education. Standardized tests are most useful in the determination of individual differences in intelligence and school progress. Physical differences are apparent or picked out with the help of the school nurse or doctor. The teacher must be able to detect personality or adjustment difficulties. Here she may have the help of specially trained personnel — social workers, psychologists, and psychiatrists.

In large groups of students of any age, abilities, achievement, and other characteristics are distributed somewhat like the intelligence quotients in Figure 10. The intelligence quotient (IQ) is a common measure of the kind of mental ability needed to succeed in many school situations. Here it can be considered "school ability." You will note the small percentage of children of extremely high or low ability and the large percentage at the middle who are of average ability. A similar distribution would be found for other mental,

---

[17] Lee J. Cronbach, *Educational Psychology* 2 ed. (New York: Harcourt, Brace and World, 1963), p. 89.

[18] Olson, op. cit., p. 375.

[19] William Clark Trow, *Psychology in Teaching and Learning* (Boston: Houghton Mifflin Co., 1960).

Fig. 10. Distributions of Composite Stanford-Binet IQ's
(Forms L-M) of Standardization Group

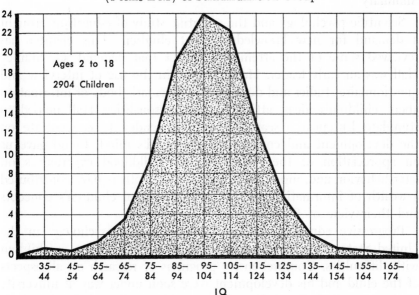

Ages 2 to 18

2904 Children

IQ

* Adapted from Lewis M. Terman and Maud A. Merrill, *Measuring Intelligence* (Boston: Houghton Mifflin Co., 1937), p. 37, Fig. 1.

physical, or personality characteristics. Further, there is a low relationship between intellectual and physical abilities or either of these and personality characteristics. Different characteristics may vary widely within the same individual, and a student who is highly developed or advanced in one respect may lag behind in another.

Schools share the responsibility for the optimum development of each child — intellectually, socially, emotionally, physically, and morally — with the home, the church, and the community at large. Schools have the primary responsibility for intellectual development. Examination programs, various forms of classification and grouping, special remedial materials and methods, and our extensive group and individual guidance programs are examples of the ways schools provide for individual differences in meeting their responsibility to each child. The individual teacher must be a serious student of the makeup of each child in her classroom as well as of childhood in general. She must know the specific ways in which her children differ and find ways to provide the best experiences for each.

Summary

Scientific psychology and the scientific study of education brought a demand for new knowledge about children. This chapter has reviewed some of the attempts to meet that demand. G. Stanley Hall was an early leader. He pioneered in the use of interview and questionnaire studies and developed a systematic body of information about children's ideas, attitudes, and personalities. Hall helped to stimulate European research which has tended to concentrate on the development and contents of the child's mind. Freud gave us an appreciation of the effect of early childhood experiences on later behavior; and, more recently, Piaget and others have contributed a wealth of information on the development of children's concepts and their view of the world.

Progressive education helped stimulate child psychology in the United States as did a concern for exceptional children or children with difficulties. Comprehensive programs of research on all aspects of the child and his development were soon under way at university clinics, e.g., that directed by Dr. Arnold Gesell at Yale. Work in these clinics has benefited from the cooperation and contributions of scientists from different disciplines. Cross-sectional studies have yielded composite portraits of the "average" child at each age level, and longitudinal studies of individual children over a period of years have led to a greater understanding of patterns and individual differences in growth and development.

Several principles which teachers need to understand and observe in their work with children have emerged, e.g.: (1) growth is the result of interaction between the child and his environment; (2) growth is a continuous, orderly, and cumulative process; (3) growth is especially rapid in infancy and adolescence; (4) rates of growth and development vary among individuals and for different characteristics of the same individual; (5) girls differ from boys in their development; and (6) all phases of development interact.

Teachers have found several approaches useful in studying children: (1) *basic needs* which every child strives to satisfy, (2) *developmental tasks* which the child's nature and society set for him at each age level, (3) *personality theory*, which emphasizes the child's need to resolve satisfactorily age-related conflicts between his self and his growing body and between both of these and society, (4) *readiness for learning* any particular activity at any given time, and (5) *individual differences* in rates of growth and development. The several approaches need not be conflicting or confusing. Like the different tools of the mechanic, one approach will "fit" or be most useful on one occasion, while another time a different one will be best — all in the service of better understanding the children we teach that we may better help them develop as they are capable of developing, achieve as they are capable of achieving, become what they are capable of becoming.

SELECTED READINGS

Blair, Glenn M., Jones, R. Stewart, and Simpson, Ray. L., *Educational Psychology* (New York: The Macmillan Company, 1954), pp. 114–122.

An excellent treatment of the varied factors of maturation and previous learning in readiness for learning.

Commission on Teacher Education, *Helping Teachers Understand Children* (Washington, D. C.: American Council on Education, 1945).

Chaps. 1–3 emphasize important factors in understanding children. In all this is a very helpful, well-illustrated guide to the observation and reporting of children's behavior.

Cook, Walter W., "Individual Differences and Curriculum Practice," *Journal of Educational Psychology*, Vol. 39 (March, 1948), pp. 141–148.

The author indicates some invalid assumptions about individual differences and surveys some of the related research.

Erikson, Erik H., *Childhood and Society* (New York: W. W. Norton & Co., 1950), pp. 219–233.

Description of the conflicts to be solved by children at each of eight stages of ego development postulated in the author's modification of Freudian theory.

Frank, Lawrence K., "The Fundamental Needs of the Child," *Mental Hygiene*, Vol. 22 (July, 1938), pp. 353–379.

A statement of the fundamental needs of the developing child, as they are seen by an author whose views have influenced many educators, psychologists, and parents.

Garrett, Henry E., *Great Experiments in Psychology*, 3 ed. (New York: Appleton-Century-Crofts, 1951), Chap. 7.

Describes Watson's pioneering studies of the behavior of the human infant and reviews subsequent related research.

Haan, Aubrey, *Elementary School Curriculum: Theory and Research* (Boston: Allyn & Bacon, 1961), Chaps. 1 & 2.

A description of child growth in terms of personality theory. Clear explanations of the inner conflicts which children face at each stage of development and an extensive bibliography of related readings about each.

Hall, G. Stanley, "The Contents of Children's Minds," in Dennis, Wayne (ed.) *Readings in the History of Psychology* (New York: Appleton-Century-Crofts, 1948), pp. 255–276.

An important early paper which first appeared in 1883. The results of an inventory of concepts held by school beginners are reported with recommendations, that sound quite modern, for readiness activities to overcome deficiencies.

Havighurst, R. J., *Human Development and Education* (New York: Longmans, Green & Co., 1953), Chaps. 1, 2, 4, 8–11.
Overview of the developmental tasks of childhood and adolescence with implications for the school curriculum. Chap. 8 treats developmental tasks as objectives of education.

Hymes, James L., Jr., *The Child Development Point of View* (New York: Prentice-Hall, 1955).
A book for parents and teachers that discusses what children are like, how they feel and how they learn and grow.

Jenkins, Gladys Gardner, *Helping Children Reach Their Potential* (Chicago: Scott, Foresman & Co., 1961).
In Part one extensive case material on individuals and classroom situations is used to illustrate principles and procedures in providing for five basic needs of children. Parts two and three answer questions frequently asked by teachers about growth and development and about home and family.

Lee, J. Murray, and Lee, Doris M., *The Child and His Development* (New York: Appleton-Century-Crofts, 1958).
A book of principles and ways of working with children consistent with the point of view that each individual is an integral whole and that his basic drive is for increasing self-realization. Divisions on understanding development, understanding the individual, helping children learn and working with groups. Each division has several chapters and each of these is introduced by a useful list of understandings needed by the teacher.

Midcentury White House Conference on Children and Youth, *A Healthy Personality for Every Child* (Raleigh, N. Carolina: Health Publications Institute, 1951), pp. 6–25. Reprinted in Coladarci, A. P. (ed.), *Educational Psychology: A Book of Readings* (New York: Dryden Press, 1955), pp. 147–169.
Defines a "healthy personality" in terms of the eight stages of personality development postulated by Erik Erikson.

Murphy, Gardner, *Historical Introduction to Modern Psychology*, rev. ed. (New York: Harcourt, Brace & Co., 1949), Chap. 26.
Historical review of the origins and growth of systematic and serious study of children.

National Society for the Study of Education, *Individualizing Instruction*, Sixty-First Yearbook, Part I (Chicago: University of Chicago Press, 1962).
Broad issues and general principles in the origin and development of individual differences and practices intended to provide for individual differences in the classroom. See especially Chap. XIV by Theodore Glymer and Nolan C. Kearney, "Curricular and Instructional Provisions for Individual Differences."

Ojemann, Ralph H., *Personality Adjustment of Individual Children*, What Research Says to the Teacher, No. 5 (Washington, D. C.: Department of Classroom Teachers, N.E.A., 1954).
Reports to the classroom teacher the most important suggestions indicated by recent studies for the personality adjustment of individual children.

Ojemann, Ralph H., and Wilkinson, Francis R., "The Effect on Pupil Growth of an Increase in Teachers' Understanding of Pupil Behavior," *Journal of Experimental Education*, Vol. 8 (December, 1939), pp. 143–147.
 Experimental evidence of a direct relationship between the level of children's school achievement and the degree to which their teacher is willing and able to see children as individuals.
Olson, Willard C., and Hughes, Byron O., "Concepts of Growth: Their Significance for Teachers," *Childhood Education*, Vol. 21 (October, 1944), pp. 53–63.
 Suggests several factors that are significant in understanding the growth of children. For each factor implications are offered for teaching methods, administrative practices and educational policy.
Piaget, Jean (Margaret Cook, trans.), *Construction of Reality in the Child* (New York: Basic Books, 1954).
 An attempt to understand the child's view of the universe through historical study of the development of the concepts of object, space, causality, and time in several young children.
Trow, William C., *Psychology in Teaching and Learning* (Boston: Houghton Mifflin Co., 1960).
 An example of a current text which finds a principal theme in the teacher's treatment of individual differences in physiological characteristics, school achievement, aptitude, cultural background, and personality. See especially Chaps. 5–9.
Wright, Herbert F., "How the Psychology of Motivation is Related to Curriculum Development," *Journal of Educational Psychology*, Vol. 39 (March, 1958), pp. 149–156.
 An analysis of the use and meanings of the concept of "pupil needs" in education.

Chapter XV

PROGRESS IN MEASUREMENT

AND EVALUATION

Our knowledge of the child and how he learns and matures would still be fragmentary and speculative were it not for the progress in measurement and evaluation which is reviewed in this chapter. For convenience the contributions of the past are classified into six periods, from a period of early invention to the present day.

New knowledge has helped us to redefine the aims of education in terms of the optimum development for each child. It has also aided our efforts to achieve these aims. Finally, we continue to use measurement and evaluation to guide and check our efforts and to measure the quality of our student product. Now, more progress is needed.

THE PERIOD OF INVENTION

We have noted how psychologists like Wundt, Galton, and Cattell began to measure and quantify human characteristics in the closing years of the nineteenth century. We may consider these men, and several others whom we will not introduce, inventors in the field of psychological and educational measurement.

The characteristics measured in the early psychological laboratories were nearly all concerned with the accuracy with which sounds, colors, weights, sizes, etc., could be discriminated or with the strength and rapidity of movements. Attempts to relate performance on these tests to practical concerns like academic achievement were largely negative, responsible in part, as later research suggested, to their simple nature, and in part to the crudeness of the measurement techniques.

The work of the French psychologist, Alfred Binet, was notable, however, because of the practical nature of his aims and interests. In 1904 he was appointed to a commission to identify pupils who would require instruction in special classes for the retarded. A number of his initial proposals for tests to meet this practical need were rather vague and general. He spoke of the simple processes measured by other psychologists but also of comprehension, suggestibility, aesthetic feeling, and moral sentiments.[1] It was the continued attempts of Binet to measure some of these more complex processes, however, which led to his mental age scale, a milestone in the development of tests of general scholastic aptitude, which we usually call intelligence tests, and the prototype for many of our modern tests.

The first scale which Binet and his associate Simon put out in 1905 was a series of thirty short tests, ranging from the very easy task of following with the eye a lighted match passed in front of the face to the difficult one of telling the difference between words like "remorse" and "chagrin." The tests were arranged to form a ladder of difficulty, and Binet's studies enabled him to describe how far up the ladder children of different ages should be able to go.

This early scale provided the approach which nearly all tests of general aptitude have followed. Performance was measured on a variety of complex tasks designed to sample the many types of tasks which call for mental ability of the type needed in school. The tasks were arranged in order of difficulty, and differences in ability were determined by the number of tests which were passed successfully. In a later 1908 scale Binet and Simon classified each test at a separate age level, and a child's mental age (MA) was determined by the most difficult tasks he could pass. The MA represented, as it does today, a kind of average score which corresponds to the chronological age at which the average child will do as well. Binet published one more revision of his scale (1911) just before his death.

Binet and Simon conducted several types of studies with their tests which have become standard practice.[2] They studied the consistency of repeated measurements of the same individuals. Today

---

[1] Frank N. Freeman, *Mental Tests, Their History, Principles, and Applications*, rev. ed. (Boston: Houghton Mifflin Co., 1939), p. 57.

[2] Alfred Binet and Th. Simon, *The Development of Intelligence in Children*, translated by Elizabeth S. Kite (Vineland, N. J.: The Training School, 1916).

this would be considered an effort to determine the test's reliability — a most important characteristic of any measuring instrument, second only to validity or the value or usefulness of the instrument for the purpose for which it is being used. Binet and Simon checked their test's validity by studying its worth as a predictor of academic achievement, obtaining results very similar to those which have been obtained in hundreds of more recent studies. They found a moderate relationship between the test results and school achievement.

Illustrations from the tasks for two of the years from Binet and Simon's 1908 scale follow:[3]

Five Years

1. Comparison of two weights, one pair three and twelve grams respectively, the other pair, six and fifteen grams respectively.
2. Copying a square with pen and ink.
3. Putting together two triangles so as to make the same form as a rectangle.
4. Counting four pennies.

Eleven Years

1. Detecting the absurdity of a series of statements.
2. Building a sentence out of three words.
3. Naming any sixty words in three minutes.
4. A definition of abstract terms.
5. Arranging a number of words which have been disarranged so as to make a meaningful sentence.

Two nineteenth-century educators should be given recognition, along with the psychologists who have been mentioned. As early as 1845 Horace Mann, secretary of the Massachusetts Board of Education, severely criticized the Boston schools for their custom of examining students orally. He reinforced his criticism with the results of a uniform written examination. It is clear from the procedures used in this early survey, the first that was anything like our modern testing programs, that he recognized the advantages of written examinations, of substituting a large number of specific questions for a few general ones, and of uniform conditions of test administration and scoring. Still, there were no immediate and widespread reforms.[4] It was not until much later in the nineteenth century, probably as a result of rising enrollments more than of Mann's vision, that writ-

---

[3] Freeman, op. cit., pp. 88–89.
[4] Otis W. Caldwell and S. A. Courtis, Then and Now in Education, 1845–1923 (Cleveland: World Book Co., 1924).

ten essay tests began to replace oral examinations in any number of schools.

Dr. J. M. Rice had studied in Europe and had come under the influence of the new experimental psychologists. He was convinced that progress in education required quantitative measurement of results rather than speculation. In 1897 he reported the results of his efforts to demonstrate a new approach to educational problems. He had devised and used standard spelling tests to study the effectiveness of methods of teaching spelling. His tests were very nearly objective; that is, they were composed of items that required no judgment in scoring. A given answer was scored exactly the same, right or wrong, by anyone with a predetermined key.[5]

Rice revised his tests several times and tested, all in all, some 30,000 children, finding great variation in achievement from class to class, from school to school, and from city to city. Among other things he concluded that students who spend as much as 40 minutes a day studying spelling achieved no better than those who spent only 15 minutes a day. Rice subsequently devised similar studies with arithmetic and language tests,[6] but progress is slow, and for nearly a decade practically no one followed his lead or recognized the merit of his contributions.

Some of the same names reoccur if we examine the early history of efforts to study nonintellectual characteristics. Galton and Binet were among the early experimenters in the area of personality assessment. Galton[7] proposed rating scales for the study of character in 1884, and Binet[8] used a crude test to study differences in the personality of his two daughters in 1903. Another psychological innovator, Carl Jung, experimented with a word-association technique about 1906.[9] He looked for significant characteristics of the responses which persons give, quickly, without thinking, to a series of 100 words in order to identify their problems or concerns. Among the contributions of G. Stanley Hall, whom we have noted for his

[5] J. M. Rice, "The Futility of the Spelling Grind," Forum, Vol. 23 (April and June, 1897), pp. 163–172, 409–419.

[6] J. M. Rice, Scientific Management in Education (New York: Hinds, Noble and Eldredge, 1914), Chaps. 5–11.

[7] Francis Galton, "Measurement of Character," Fortnightly Review, Vol. 42 (1884), pp. 179–185. Cited by C. C. Ross and Julian C. Stanley, 3 ed., Measurement in Today's Schools (New York: Prentice-Hall, Inc., 1954), p. 46.

[8] Alfred Binet, L'Etude experimental de l'Intelligence (Paris: Costes, 1903).

[9] C. S. Jung, Studies in Word Association (New York: Dodd, Mead & Co., 1919).

early work in the study of children, was a questionnaire study of the interests of children.

THE PIONEERING PHASE

Shortly after the initial period of exploration or invention, E. L. Thorndike emerged as the guiding genius in the application of scientific principles from psychology to the building of educational tests. Thorndike and a few others were the pioneers who by the end of World War I had established the principles and methods and provided the examples which later workers were to follow.

Thorndike's 1904 textbook on educational measurement showed the way in this field, just as his 1913 *Educational Psychology* revolutionized the study of learning. He and his students built the first standardized tests in school subjects with methods and principles learned in the psychological and statistical laboratories. The term *standardized*, as applied to these first instruments, means: (1) they were tried out and refined by administration to a large "norm" group of appropriate age and grade levels; (2) they were administered under carefully controlled and uniform conditions; and (3) statistical information on the performance of the norm group was provided to facilitiate interpretation of test scores.

Among the first tests produced by Thorndike and his associates were the *Stone Arithmetic Reasoning Test* (1908), the *Courtis Arithmetic Computation Test* (1908), the *Thorndike Scale for the Handwriting of Children* (1910), and the *Buckingham Spelling Scale* (1913).

Meanwhile Starch and Elliott[10] reported a well-known series of experiments which revealed great differences among teachers in scoring essay examinations and lent a sense of urgency to the work on objective examinations.

Binet's work on intelligence testing was now received enthusiastically in the United States. Several American revisions of his test soon appeared. The most widely known and accepted was the Stanford revision known as the Stanford-Binet, published by Lewis M. Terman

10 Daniel Starch and Edward C. Elliott, "Reliability of Grading Work in Mathematics," *School Review*, Vol. 21 (April, 1913), pp. 254–259. Daniel Starch, "Reliability and Distribution of Grades," *Science*, Vol. 38 (October 31, 1913), pp. 630–636.

in 1916.[11] For many years the Stanford-Binet was the standard measure of intelligence to which all others were compared. The Stanford-Binet used the Intelligence Quotient or IQ as an index of brightness. This is the ratio of the measured mental age (MA) to the actual chronological age (CA) multiplied by 100 to eliminate decimals. William Stern (1871–1935) proposed this measure several years before the publication of the Stanford-Binet. The MA, but not the IQ, was used by Binet himself.

Other individual intelligence tests which require little or no knowledge of English were developed for use with very young children, deaf children, immigrants, and similar groups. The *Pintner-Paterson Performance Scale*, which was of this type, appeared in 1917.[12]

Although individual diagnosis by a competent psychologist specially trained in intelligence testing is highly desirable, it is too expensive and time-consuming for routine use in school or when large groups must be tested rapidly. One such situation, which arose in 1917 when large numbers of men were inducted into the armed services, led to the first test of intelligence designed for use with groups. The test was a written one, the *Army Alpha*.[13] It was designed by a committee of psychologists who drew heavily on an unpublished work by Arthur H. Otis. *Army Beta*, which did not require reading or writing, appeared shortly thereafter. *Beta* could be administered entirely by pantomine. The two army tests were administered to several million men during World War I, clearly demonstrating the practicality of mass testing for the classification of normal persons. Several sample items from each of the army tests are reproduced in Figure 11.

Little progress was made in this period on tests of aptitude for specific fields of study or work, although a beginning may be seen in the Seashore Test of Musical Talent (1915)[14] and the trade tests

[11] Lewis M. Terman, *The Measurement of Intelligence* (Boston: Houghton Mifflin, 1916). Lewis M. Terman and Maud A. Merrill, *Stanford-Binet Intelligence Scale, Manual for the Third Revision, Form L–M* (Boston: Houghton Mifflin, 1960).

[12] Rudolph Pintner and Donald G. Paterson, *A Scale of Performance Tests* (New York: D. Appleton Co., 1917).

[13] Henry E. Garrett, *Great Experiments in Psychology* (New York: The Century Co., 1930). Includes an account of the development of the Army Alpha.

[14] C. E. Seashore, *The Psychology of Musical Talent* (New York: Silver, Burdett and Co., 1919).

Fig. 11. Sample Items From the Army Alpha and Army Beta

Subtest	Alpha Sample Items

Subtest

Alpha Sample Items

2. Arithmetic Problems

1. How many are 5 men and 10 men? . Answer (15)
2. If you walk 4 miles an hour for
3 hours how far do you walk? . . . Answer (12)

4. Vocabulary

1. good — bad . . . . same — <u>opposite</u>
2. little — small . . . . <u>same</u> — opposite

6. Number Series

1. 2   4   6   8   10   12   <u>14</u>   <u>16</u>
2. 1   7   2   7   3   7   <u>4</u>   <u>7</u>

7. Analogies

1. sky — blue :: grass — table   <u>green</u>   warm   big
2. fish — swim :: man — paper   time   <u>walks</u>   girl

Beta Sample Items

1. Maze Test

(Examinee draws shortest route from left to right.)

2. Cube Analysis

(The examinee counts the number.)

3. XO Series

(The examinee completes the series in the same pattern.)

4. Geometrical Construction

(The examinee draws lines to show how the smaller pieces fit into the square.)

of World War I. One of the trade tests, a mechanical information test, was quite similar to later aptitude tests.

Personality assessment was in a highly experimental stage in 1917 when R. S. Woodworth developed the first of the group personality tests.[15] The *Personal Data Sheet* (sometimes referred to as the *Woodworth Psychoneurotic Inventory*) helped in diagnosing the ability of inductees to adjust themselves to military life. It was an attempt to standardize a psychiatric interview by using questions which differentiated normal individuals from known neurotic patients. The *Data Sheet* was used as a screening device to identify those in need of psychiatric attention. It became a pattern for many other instruments of the same type. Several items which serve to illustrate the questions of this and similar inventories follow:

1. Do you usually sleep well?   Yes   No
2. Did you have a happy childhood?   Yes   No
3. Do you make friends easily?   Yes   No
4. Do you daydream frequently?   Yes   No

Getting the facts about schools and teachers was an old American custom. Horace Mann's 1845 inquiries have been noted. It had become quite common for school systems to import experts to conduct a survey and make recommendations for improvement. The development of measurement techniques enabled surveyors to become more objective and scientific. A survey of the New York City schools in 1911–1913 using the Courtis arithmetic tests marked the beginning of survey techniques which were to contribute substantially to the improvement of school practice. The Cleveland Survey of 1915–1916 was another milestone. Tests of reading were developed and applied on a large scale for the first time in this survey.[16] Ruediger and Strayer in 1910 and Boyce and Elliott in 1915 were among the first to introduce rating scales for systematizing judgments concerning the efficiency of teachers.[17]

Evidence of the unreliability of teachers' marks set off a rash of studies of marking and reporting systems about this time. One of

---

[15] R. S. Woodworth, *Personal Data Sheet* (Chicago: C. H. Stoelting Co., 1918).

[16] Charles H. Judd, "Contributions of School Surveys," *The Scientific Movement in Education*, National Society for the Study of Education, Thirty-Seventh Yearbook, Part II (Bloomington, Ill.: Public School Publishing Co., 1938), p. 15.

[17] A. S. Barr, "Teaching Competencies," in Walter S. Monroe (ed.), *Encyclopedia of Educational Research* (New York: The Macmillan Co., 1950), p. 1447.

the most extreme findings was that of Meyer at the University of Minnestoa.[18] Over a period of five years he discovered such variations as 55 percent A's in philosophy and 1 percent in chemistry. Thorndike, writing in 1922, referred to the situation as "scandalous."[19]

Research suggested that classifying achievement according to a few symbols was more reliable than using many.[20] As a result, the percentage, of "points out of 100" system of marking, which was in general use at the time, lost a good many adherents to the procedure of arranging scores in order from high to low, then assigning each of the now well-known letter symbols to an agreed upon proportion of the students. The advisability of deriving these proportions from the normal probability curve, which had been found to describe the distribution of many human characteristics, was debated. There appears to have been theoretical agreement, at any rate, about the necessity of having agreed-upon standards to which all teachers of a given school would adhere.

In 1918, near the end of what we have termed the pioneering phase, the Seventeenth Yearbook of the National Society for the Study of Education[21] reviewed previous accomplishments in measurement and made predictions for the future. The stage had been set for real progress.

THE MEASUREMENT ERA

The years from World War I (1918) to 1930 brought rapid advances. There were numerous books on measurement and statistical methods. Tests were developed for all the skill and content areas of the schools. The army tests were released for general use and other language and nonlanguage group tests of general ability were published in large numbers. A whole line of personality questionnaires and inventories followed Woodworth's *Personal Data Sheet*.

---

[18] Max Meyer, "The Grading of Students," *Science*, Vol. 28 (August 21, 1908), pp. 243–250.

[19] E. L. Thorndike, "Measurement in Education," *Intelligence Tests and Their Use — The Nature, History and General Principles of Intelligence Testing*, National Society for the Study of Education, Twenty-First Yearbook, Part I (Bloomington, Ill.: Public School Publishing Co., 1922), p. 2.

[20] Daniel Starch, *Educational Measurement* (New York: The Macmillan Co., 1916).

[21] *The Measurement of Educational Products*, National Society for the Study of Education, Seventeenth Yearbook, Part II (Bloomington, Ill.: Public School Publishing Co., 1918).

Instruments designed to measure attitudes and the Strong interest inventory appeared.

Another interesting movement was a series of developmental schedules for infants and preschool children. Gesell was the first in this field with a *Pre-School Child Development Scale* (1925).[22] It consisted of an inventory of activities which is compared with a schedule of ages at which the activities normally appear.

The *Stanford Achievement Test* (1923) was the first of a series of test batteries for surveying the achievement of students in the basic elementary and secondary school subjects. It has undergone numerous revisions and remains a leader in the field today.[23]

The individual and group tests of intelligence previously described were designed to predict success in school-like situations. They sought to sample the many types of tasks required in school. For this reason they are often referred to as general ability, general aptitude or, more accurately, scholastic aptitude tests. Now a number of tests of more specific abilities or aptitudes began to appear. They sampled tasks similar to those found in areas of work or study in which achievement was to be predicted. Early examples include the test of musical aptitude by Seashore, already noted, and one of mechanical aptitude by Stenquist.[24] Of a somewhat different nature was Rogers' test of mathematical ability,[25] which was followed by tests designed to predict success in specific courses, such as algebra and geometry. A related type of test which has appeared much more recently is designed to measure a child's fitness for the reading instruction of the first grade.

McCall in 1920[26] had urged the adaptation of the objective item types used in standardized tests to the uses of the classroom teacher. By this time the deficiencies of the older essay examinations were

[22] Arnold Gesell, *The Mental Growth of the Pre-School Child* (New York: The Macmillan Co., 1925). The further development of this approach is represented by Arnold Gesell and others, *Gesell Developmental Schedules* (New York: Psychological Corporation, 1949).

[23] Truman L. Kelley and others, *Stanford Achievement Tests*, Primary, Elementary, Intermediate, and Advanced (New York: Harcourt, Brace and World, 1956). Truman L. Kelley and others, *Stanford Achievement Test* (Yonkers-on-Hudson, N .Y.: World Book Co., 1923).

[24] J. L. Stenquist, *Stenquist Mechanical Aptitude Tests* (Yonkers-on-Hudson, N. Y.: World Book Co., 1922).

[25] Agnes Low Rogers, *Experimental Tests of Mathematical Ability and Their Prognostic Value* (New York: Teachers College, Columbia University, 1918).

[26] William A. McCall, "A New Kind of School Examination," *Journal of Educational Research*, Vol. 1 (January, 1920), pp. 33–46.

well known. Soon teacher-made objective tests were widely and rather uncritically used, and mimeographed sheets of "true-false" and "cafeteria-style" questions became a standard classroom item.

In these years school surveys — local, statewide, and national — became so numerous that they threatened to exhaust the supply of qualified surveyors. Special aspects of the school, such as buildings, finances, or the curriculum were sometimes the subject of study. Tests became a standard item in the surveyor's kit for comparing classes, schools, and school systems.

Teachers were studied from every angle. Their scores on generally available and specially designed tests, attitude scales, and interest inventories were scrutinized, as were biographical characteristics, such as age, sex, marital status, experience, and professional and recreational activities. By 1930 Barr and Emans[27] were able to identify 209 rating scales used quite extensively in judging the desirable characteristics of teachers and future teachers. Other approaches included: identifying causes of failure; collecting opinions of administrators, teachers, parents, and pupils; and studies of the differences between good and poor teachers.

There was no slackening of debate or research which suggested confusion with respect to marking and reporting practices. Although the value of informal notes and letters to parents was being recognized by a few authors, Roelfs found that all of the schools he surveyed in 1925 used the formal, traditional type of report.[28] Letters or words had replaced percentages as symbols for achievement in about 80 percent of the schools.[29] New attempts to adapt instruction to individual differences raised additional problems. What should be the distribution of letter grades in a high-ability group or in a low one? The answer to this question was complicated by the fact that teachers consciously considered not only achievement and ability in assigning marks but also effort, attitude, and progress.

In the 1920's education was seeking the status of a science; and educational systems were looking for the efficiency of a modern industry with precise methods for custom tailoring operations to

---

[27] A. S. Barr and L. M. Emans, "What Qualities Are Prerequisite to Success in Teaching?" Nation's Schools, Vol. 6 (September, 1930), pp. 60–64.

[28] R. M. Roelfs, "Trends in Junior High School Progress Reporting," Journal of Educational Research, Vol. 49 (September, 1955), pp. 241–249.

[29] Roy O. Billett, Provisions for Individual Differences, Marking and Promotion, U. S. Office of Education Bulletin, No. 17, 1932.

the individual and measuring the quality of the product. Standardized tests were made to order for these times and they were used with enthusiasm rather than discrimination. Buckingham states that the *test makers* became professionals in 1919.[30] But the majority of *users* were still amateurs, if not novices, and many sins were committed in the name of measurement.

THE RISE OF EVALUATION

About 1930 there was a widespread reaction against some emphases of the measurement movement. Thus an era of unqualified enthusiasm and acceptance of objective measurement came to an end. We may think of the new emphasis as one of *evaluation.* This term implies not only the determination of degrees or quantities but a judgment with respect to the value or significance of measurement data as related to established standards or criteria. A homely example will help to clarify the difference. With a gauge you measure air pressure in the tires of your car. This measurement might be 24 pounds per inch. Evaluation requires a further judgment as to the adequacy or inadequacy of this value by comparing it with some standard. In this case the standard would be the recommendation of the auto or tire manufacturer. Perhaps your owner's manual recommends 28 pounds per square inch and your evaluation tells you that 24 is not enough. More air will have to be added.

In education the outcomes that suggest achievement of our stated objectives are the standards with which we evaluate. One objective might be "interest in solving problems scientifically." Sample outcomes in terms of student behavior which would indicate progress toward this objective include: (1) willingness to spend extra time on scientific projects, (2) refusal to be discouraged by initial failures with experiments or projects, (3) curiosity about the cause and reasons for result, (4) voluntarily reading science material, and (5) voluntarily spending time on projects of their own. The data provided by conventional tests were inadequate as a basis for judging the achievement of this and many other important educational outcomes.

The conventional test emphasized the traditional outcomes of achievement, such as factual knowledge and academic skills, to the

---

[30] R. B. Buckingham, "Our First Twenty-Five Years," *Proceedings* of the National Education Association, 1941, p. 354.

neglect of interest, appreciation, understanding, or the ability to use knowledge effectively. Little attention had been given to the assessment of personal, social, and emotional characteristics — important in the newer education but less susceptible to objective measurement. In short, the evidence provided by tests of the time was inadequate. Furthermore, it was feared that the available tests, uncritically used, would narrow and focus educational efforts on achieving what the tests were measuring to the actual neglect of other outcomes. In 1930 this was a very real danger, for tests were being used to compare schools and set the standards for graduates, sometimes on a statewide basis.

Widespread criticism during the 1930's and 1940's forced a reappraisal of existing instruments and serious attempts to develop other kinds of measures. Achievement tests were now published in more than one form to lessen the effect of practice when retesting the same group. Diagnostic tests were designed specifically to identify the students' strong and weak points; and practice tests, whose function was to teach rather than test, appeared. A thorough revision of the Stanford-Binet was published in 1937,[31] and in 1939 David Wechsler brought out an intelligence scale designed specifically for adults — the content was fairer to adults, and so was the method for computing the IQ.[32]

In the effort to measure less tangible factors, interest inventories, such as the Kuder Preference Record,[33] were devised especially for high school groups. Attitude scales and methods of analyzing the social structure of groups (sociometric techniques) were used. Another instrument, The Bernreuter Personality Inventory (1932)[34] was the first of a number of questionnaires designed to measure several aspects of personality simultaneously — neurotic tendency, self-sufficiency, introversion-extroversion, and dominance-submission. Clinical instruments for diagnosing personality, such as the well-known inkblot or Rohrschach test, appeared. Student products and

---

[31] Lewis M. Terman and Maud A. Merrill, Stanford-Binet Intelligence Scale, Manual for the Third Revision, Form L–M (Boston: Houghton Mifflin, 1960).

[32] David Wechsler, Wechsler Adult Intelligence Scale (New York: Psychological Corporation, 1955); The Measurement of Adult Intelligence (Baltimore: Williams and Wilkins, 1944).

[33] G. Frederick Kuder, Kuder Preference Record — Vocational, Manual, and Kuder Preference Record — Personal: Manual (Chicago: Science Research Associates, 1953).

[34] Robert G. Bernreuter, The Personality Inventory: Manual (Stanford, Calif.: Stanford University Press, 1935).

methods of systematic observation were studied also as evaluation techniques.

Evaluation efforts begin with a comprehensive statement of educational objectives in terms of the behavior expected. Then a variety of tests and less formal techniques are selected or devised to gather evidence of this behavior. This approach is well illustrated in several large-scale studies undertaken in the 1940's. Perhaps the best example is provided by the Eight-Year Study of the Progressive Education Association,[35] which was designed to show that departures from traditional practices did not reduce graduates' ability to do college work. Tests, attitude scales, rating scales, pupil reports and records, and still other techniques were utilized to provide evidence on students' reasoning; social sensitivity; civic and social beliefs; appreciation of literature and art; personal, social, and school interests; and personal and social development.

A notable step in the evaluation of school programs and school systems was taken in 1933 when the Cooperative Study of Secondary School Standards was formed.[36] This is an organization of representatives of the several regional agencies which study and accredit schools. From the beginning this group emphasized the evaluation principle that each school should be judged in terms of its own philosophy and objectives. The *Evaluative Criteria* of the Cooperative Study of Secondary School Standards are the best known and most useful of a rather large number of statements of criteria and standards for use as norms in surveying a school. These are based on current practice and research findings. New editions of the *Evaluative Criteria* have appeared in 1940, 1950, and 1960.

The 1960 *Criteria* contain forms or schedules for use by committees of the school being evaluated and by a visiting committee of teachers, administrators, and specialists. Each form or schedule is used to record data and judgments on a different aspect of the school's philosophy, facilities, personnel, or program. The data, thus collected, are the basis for decision and recommendation by the visiting committee, state committees and ultimately an association-wide committee.

The approach of the *Evaluative Criteria* is in terms of what is

[35] Eugene R. Smith, Ralph W. Tyler, *et al.*, *Appraising and Recording School Progress* (New York: Harper and Brothers, 1942).

[36] In June, 1959, its name was changed to National Study of Secondary School Evaluation.

available and what is done rather than in terms of the measurement of results. It is an evaluation of what Hagen and Thorndike refer to as "structural" and "process" outcomes rather than "products."[37] Structural outcomes refer to provisions of equipment, materials, facilities, etc.; process outcomes refer to procedures; the best criterion, presumably, would be that of student performance which demonstrates the accomplishment of the school's objectives. The variability in school objectives and situations has made progress in the use of product outcomes difficult.

Earlier approaches to the identification of desirable teacher characteristics were continued, with more attention to how well they predicted student-teacher ratings, in-service ratings, college grades, and the consensus of judges. With few exceptions we can say that a low but not particularly useful relationship with criteria such as these has been found for any characteristic that would seem, on common-sense grounds, to be desirable in teachers.[38] A small amount of experimental work with pupil growth as a criterion of teaching effectiveness was reported but the question of a universally most effective teacher was raised more and more insistently. Different communities, different subjects, different age levels, and different objectives may influence the characteristics desired in a teacher, and his chances for success.

Marks of any kind were often questioned in the 1930's, but they continued in use. Perhaps the consensus of expert opinion is represented in reports by Norsted and Crooks. Norsted[39] reported that marks of some kind were considered essential, that they did motivate students, and that some undesirable attitudes and behavior were being incorrectly attributed to the practice of marking. Crooks[40] concluded that marks are sometimes misused, but are not objectionable in themselves, and that opinion favored using them for achieve-

---

[37] Elizabeth P. Hagen and Robert L. Thorndike, "Evaluation," in Chester W. Harris, Encyclopedia of Educational Research, 3 ed. (New York: The Macmillan Co., 1960), p. 482.

[38] Charles W. Sanford and J. Lloyd Trump, "Teacher Education — IV. Preservice Selection," in Walter S. Monroe (ed.), Encyclopedia of Educational Research, rev. ed. (New York: The Macmillan Co., 1950), pp. 1390–1395. A. S. Barr, "Teaching Competencies," in Walter S. Monroe (ed.), Encyclopedia of Educational Research, rev. ed. (New York: The Macmillan Co., 1950), pp. 1446–1454.

[39] Roy A. Norsted, "To Mark or Not to Mark?" Journal of Education, Vol. 121 (March, 1938), pp. 81–84.

[40] A. Buryee Crooks, "Marks and Marking Systems: A Digest," Journal of Educational Research, Vol. 27 (December, 1933), pp. 259–272.

ment only with supplemental ratings for other aspects of behavior. There was agreement on the need for specific definition of marking symbols and considerable support for establishing these definitions in terms of percentages of the normal curve.[41] There were several well-considered proposals for overcoming difficulties in using a normal curve distribution for small groups and students grouped according to ability.[42] In general, these proposals required the definition of the proportion of students to receive each letter grade in terms of all the students taught by a teacher or all the students enrolled in a particular course of study.

The traditional report card has been criticized severely and often since the concepts of evaluation became well known. There is no doubt that the report card with a single percentage or letter grade for each subject is just as inadequate to report progress toward the various objectives of the school as is the test of factual recall to measure them. School practice, however, lags far behind recommendations contained in the literature. Perhaps this is why Messenger and Watts[43] reported that in many schools formal report cards were being replaced entirely by notes or letters, while Roelfs[44] found that the letter was advocated but not used. Another investigator reported that 80 percent of 443 report cards studied did carry a written message to the parents to supplement the subject marks.[45]

WORLD WAR II

World War II, like World War I, brought an upsurge of activity to the measurement field. One wartime emphasis which carried over

---

[41] Edna E. Lamson, "Problems of Adequate Evaluation of the College Student's Achievement," *Educational Administration and Supervision*, Vol. 26 (April, 1940), pp. 495–507. Arch O. Heck, "Contribution of Research to the Classification, Promotion, Marking and Certification of Pupils," *The Scientific Movement in Education*, Thirty-Seventh Yearbook, Part II, National Society for the Study of Education (Bloomington, Ill.: Public School Publishing Co., 1938), pp. 187–199.

[42] Warren C. Middleton, "Some General Trends in Grading Procedure," *Education*, Vol. 54 (September, 1933), pp. 5–10. Thomas C. McCormick, "Precautions and Procedure in Normal Grading," *School and Society*, Vol. 35 (February 29, 1932), pp. 298–299.

[43] Helen R. Messenger and Winifred Watts, "Summaries of Selected Articles on Report Cards," *Educational Administration and Supervision*, Vol. 21 (October, 1935), pp. 539–550.

[44] R. M. Roelfs, "Trends in Junior High School Progress Reporting," *Journal of Educational Research*, Vol. 49 (December, 1955), pp. 241–249.

[45] George E. Hill, "The Report Card in Present Practice," *Educational Method*, Vol. 15 (December, 1935), pp. 115–131.

into civilian tests was the development of batteries of aptitude tests. During the war a great deal of work was done on tests for placing personnel in special fields of work. The Air Force, for instance, selected men for training as navigators, bombardiers or pilots, as well as for many technical maintenance jobs.

A statistical technique, "factor analysis," was used to identify a few basic factors which account for a person's performance on a great number of the different tests or test items being developed. Thus, performance on the variety of tasks which have been put together to measure general intelligence was described in terms of a few basic factors and related tests in the *Primary Mental Abilities Tests* developed by L. L. Thurstone.[46]

Success in each different course area — such as English, mathematics, and science — was found to require different levels of ability in the basic factors measured by such tests. Similarly, success in each different job or occupation appears to require different combinations of ability with respect to these same factors plus a number of others relatively unimportant in most schoolwork.

Some of the main abilities measured by one or more of the most popular aptitude batteries — such as the *Differential Aptitude Battery* for high school students or the *General Aptitude Test Battery* of the U. S. Employment Service — are listed in the following paragraphs. Brief descriptions of some selected tests are included:

1. *Verbal ability.* Understanding words and written material. This definition item might be used independently or after the examinee has read a paragraph in which the word questionnaire is used:

Questionable means

A. curious
B. doubtful
C. inquisitive
D. true
E. false

2. *Number ability.* Solving easy number problems quickly. Sample computation items are:

Add	Subtract	Multiply	Divide
403	302	34	8 / 604
53	− 27	× 72	
26			

---

[46] The research origins of the Primary Mental Abilities Tests were published in L. L. Thurstone, "Primary Mental Abilities," *Psychometric Monographs*, No. 1, 1938; and L. L. Thurstone and Thelma G. Thurstone, "Factorial Studies of Intelligence," *Psychometric Monographs*, No. 2, 1941.

3. *Verbal reasoning.* Solving word problems, such as this analogies item:[47]

.... is to water as eat is to ....

1. continue	2. drink	3. foot	4. girl
A. drive	B. enemy	C. food	D. industry

4. *Nonverbal reasoning.* Solving problems using symbols instead of words, as in the following figure sequence item:

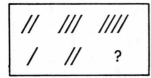

5. *Space relations.* Seeing which of several three-dimensional figures can be made by folding a flat, two-dimensional figure, for example:[48]

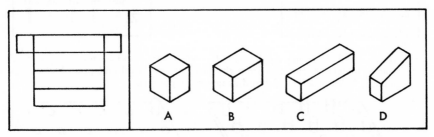

6. *Mechanical comprehension.* Having mechanical information and figuring out how mechanical devices work. The following item is an example of the type often used to measure this factor:

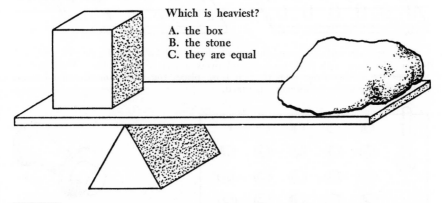

---

[47] Reproduced by permission from the *Differential Aptitude Tests,* Form L, Verbal Reasoning, copyright 1947, 1961, The Psychological Corporation. All rights reserved.
[48] *Ibid.,* Space Relations, Form L.

7. *Clerical ability.* Carrying out clerical tasks and determining errors or checking items in lists, as in the following excerpt from the directions for the *Differential Aptitude Tests:*[49]

These examples are correctly done. Note that the combination on the Answer Sheet must be exactly the same as the one in the Test Item.

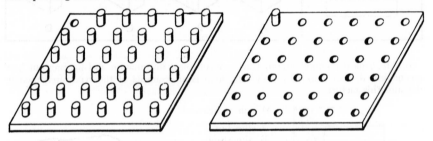

Test Items						**Sample of Answer Sheet**				
V.	<u>AB</u>	AC	AD	AE	AF		AC	AE	AF	AB	AD
W.	aA	aB	BA	Ba	<u>Bb</u>		BA	Ba	Bb	aA	aB
X.	A7	7A	B7	<u>7B</u>	AB		7B	B7	AB	7A	A7
Y.	Aa	Ba	<u>bA</u>	BA	bB		Aa	bA	bB	Ba	BA
Z.	3A	3B	<u>33</u>	B3	BB		BB	3B	B3	3A	33

9. *Motor speed.* Working rapidly with the hands. An examinee might be required, for example, to remove the pegs from the holes of one board and place them in the corresponding holes of a second board as rapidly as possible.

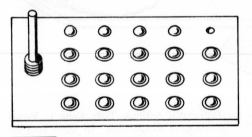

10. *Finger dexterity.* Manipulating small objects quickly with the fingers. One such test uses a board with pins, washers, and rivets similar to that shown. The examinee removes the washer from each rivet in turn, places the washer on the spindle, and replaces the rivet. His performance is timed.

---

[49] *Ibid., Clerical Speed and Accuracy, Form L.*

Although the development and refinement of measures of specific ability or aptitude were the outstanding contributions of wartime programs, much work was done on most of the other major information-getting or assessment procedures including: achievement batteries, personality and interest inventories, clinical instruments for personality analysis like the Rohrschach, biographical data blanks, rating scales, and performance tests. In addition, the personnel programs of the services produced a number of penetrating analyses on the educationally important topics of objectives and teacher evaluation.

The prestige and success of the wartime personnel programs greatly accelerated postwar developments, particularly since the wartime leaders quickly won positions of influence in education, government, and business.

MEASUREMENT AND EVALUATION TODAY

Evaluation for the optimum total development for every individual gained new popularity as a result of postwar concern for youth as a national resource. The international competition in education has been felt almost as keenly as the race for outer space. Further, psychologists and educators, familiar with wartime personnel programs, have the professional prominence, the know-how, and the enthusiasm to promote testing and evaluative efforts on a national scale.

The National Defense Act of 1958[50] authorizes federal grants to educational agencies in support of testing in secondary schools under state-developed plans. The same act provides funds for institutes to prepare school personnel to participate in such programs. The agencies which accredit and approve schools are actively encouraging each school to have teachers specially trained in test use and interpretation on their staff.

Testing Programs

History may know our time as the era of testing programs. The nationwide programs of the College Entrance Examination Board,[51] the American College Testing Program of Science Research Associ-

---

[50] Theodora E. Carlson assisted by Catherine P. Williams, *Guide to the National Defense Education Act of 1958*, rev. ed., Office of Education, OE–10000 (Washington, D. C.: U. S. Government Printing Office, 1960). See also Chapter III.

[51] College Entrance Examination Board, *College Board Score Reports, A Guide for Counselors* (Princeton, N. J.: Educational Testing Service, 1961).

ates,[52] and the National Merit Scholarship qualifying tests[53] help to determine eligibility for college and for scholarships. Elementary and secondary schools use test scores to group students according to ability, to identify exceptionally advanced or retarded students for special classes, and to provide a basis for personal, educational, and vocational guidance. Still other programs, large and small, help to determine eligibility for opportunities in business and industry, the government, and the armed forces.

A national survey conducted by the University of Pittsburgh under contract with the United States Office of Education is the most ambitious of numerous programs undertaken for research purposes.[54] This project is a census of the aptitudes, achievements, and talent potentials of American youth. First, committees of nationally prominent scientists and educators spent three years planning the study. Then in the spring of 1960, nearly 500,000 scientifically selected secondary school students took a comprehensive battery of aptitude, achievement, and information tests. At the same time information was gathered on the personal characteristics, background, and interests of the students, and the characteristics of the schools which they attended. This census of "talent" is to be followed up with surveys of students' education, vocational success, and many other aspects of their adult lives — one, five, ten, and twenty years after they are graduated from high school. Among many anticipated outcomes of this long-range research project are:

1. An inventory of the human resources represented in our youth;

2. A set of standards for educational and psychological measurement to which other tests and instruments may be compared;

College Entrance Examination Board, *The College Board Today* (Princeton, N. J.: Educational Testing Service, 1962).

College Entrance Examination Board, *A Description of the College Board Achievement Tests* (Princeton, N. J.: Educational Testing Service, 1961).

College Entrance Examination Board, *A Description of the College Board Scholastic Aptitude Test* (Princeton, N. J.: Educational Testing Service, 1961).

College Entrance Examination Board, *A Guide to the Advanced Placement Program, 1961–62* (Princeton, N. J.: Educational Testing Service, 1961).

[52] American College Testing Program, Inc., A. C. T. (Iowa City, Iowa: The American College Testing Program, Inc., 1960). Science Research Associates, ACT, *Student's Booklet* (Chicago: Science Research Associates, 1960).

[53] National Merit Scholarship Corporation, *Guide to the National Merit Scholarship Program* (Evanston, Ill.: National Merit Scholarship Corporation, 1961). Science Research Associates, *National Merit Scholarship Qualifying Test, Technical Report* (Chicago: Science Research Associates, 1960).

[54] John C. Flanagan, John T. Dailey, et al., *The Talents of American Youth: I. Design for a Study of American Youth* (Boston: Houghton Mifflin Co., 1962).

3. Guides to the patterns of aptitude, ability, and experience which help to insure success in various careers;

4. Increased knowledge of how young people choose their lifework;

5. Increased knowledge of the educational experiences which best prepare students for their lifework.

Test Developments

The concepts of evaluation have had major influence on postwar developments in measurement. New tests, as well as a variety of less formal techniques, have resulted from efforts to know more about more aspects of the total development of the individual.

The recently published achievement batteries, such as the *Iowa Tests of Educational Development* (ITED)[55] and the *Sequential Tests of Educational Progress* (STEP)[56] emphasize the measurement of understanding, interpretation, application, and synthesis of information. These batteries focus on more general and important outcomes of formal and informal educational experiences rather than the memory of facts from specific courses. Two examples of the ITED test of literary interpretation are reproduced in Figure 12. New attention has been given to the merits of improved essay examinations, and an essay test is included in the *Sequential Tests of Educational Progress*.

Similar emphases in the preparation of the teacher's own tests are evident in professional journals, measurement tests, and measurement and evaluation courses for teachers. Teachers are being taught to approximate the techniques of the professional test maker, and the trend is toward increased use of teacher-made tests for classroom evaluation purposes. In the *Taxonomy of Educational Objectives*,[57] for example, a committee of distinguished educators recognize three domains of achievement: (1) the cognitive — intellectual knowledge, skills, and abilities; (2) the affective — interests, attitudes, values, appreciation, etc.; and (3) psychomotor — manipulation and motor skills. They have succeeded in providing definitions

---

[55] E. F. Lindquist (ed.), *Iowa Tests of Educational Development* (Chicago: Science Research Associates, Inc., 1951).

[56] Educational Testing Service, *Sequential Tests of Educational Progress, Teacher's Guide* (Princeton, N. J.: Educational Testing Service, 1958).

[57] Benjamin S. Bloom and others, *A Taxonomy of Educational Objectives, Handbook I, Cognitive Domain* (New York: Longmans, Green, 1956).

Fig. 12. Sample Exercises for *Iowa Test of Educational Development*, Test 7 — Ability to Interpret Literary Materials*

And so on Sunday morning before noon, Rose and Missie were dressed, ready to go. Missie hardly knew Rose in her fine flowered purple muslin. It stayed in the trunk in the shed room. Rose had on a corset, too, and her wrapped hair was completely covered with a black wool wig she had bought from the crossroads store. This fitted smooth and tight and it had a knot right in the back. It made Rose's black sailor hat almost too small for her head, but it looked very grand.

Rose had no shoes that were whole, so she borrowed a pair from Mary West, and Mary sent along her gold-rimmed spectacles, too, for Rose to wear. Mary was a sinner. She hardly ever bothered to go to church, but she was very kind about lending her things. Rose's feet were short and thick, and Mary's were long and narrow, but that didn't make much difference, because Rose didn't put the shoes on until she got in sight of the church. Shoes were just for looks.

1. How did Rose probably think she looked when dressed for church?
1) Ordinary.
2) Shabby.
3) Funny.
4) Elegant.

2. Mary sent her spectacles to Rose because
1) she did not need them any longer herself.
2) she considered them as finery.
3) Rose had poor vision.
4) Rose had broken her own.

3. The author's feeling toward these characters is
1) indifferent.
2) sympathetic.
3) pitying.
4) scornful.

4. These characters are best described as
1) childish.
2) sophisticated.
3) stupid.
4) crazy.

Loveliest of trees, the cherry now
Is hung with bloom along the bough,
And stands about the woodland ride
Wearing white for Eastertide.

Now, of my threescore years and ten,
Twenty will not come again,
And take from seventy springs a score,
It only leaves me fifty more.

And since to look at things in bloom
Fifty springs are little room,
About the woodlands I will go
To see the cherry hung with snow.

5. How old was the poet when he wrote this poem?
1) 20.
2) 50.
3) 70.
4) One cannot tell.

6. Which of these words is used as a descriptive figure of speech rather than in its usual meaning?
1) "snow" (last line).
2) "twenty" (sixth line).
3) "woodlands" (next to last line).
4) "bloom" (second line).

7. What feeling does the poet express in this passage?
1) Delight in beauty.
2) Religious faith.
3) Fear of death.
4) Enjoyment of old age.

8. What is an outstanding quality of the style of this poem?
1) Unusual rhythm.
2) Richness of language.
3) Simplicity of expression.
4) Variety of images.

---

* Reproduced from *How to Use the Test Results*, "A Manual for Teachers and Counselors," *Iowa Tests of Educational Development* (Chicago: Science Research Associates, Inc., 1949), pp. 26–27.

and examples of items designed to measure such cognitive outcomes as knowledge, comprehension, application, analysis, synthesis, and evaluation.

Commercial aptitude batteries have resulted from wartime beginnings and the continued application of factor analysis. The *Differential Aptitude Tests* and the *General Aptitude Test Battery*, which have already been noted, are described as "ready for use in counseling."[58] In designing general ability tests, attempts are being made to construct tests which are relatively unaffected by the differences in cultural and socioeconomic backgrounds among students. New personality inventories have been developed by the factor-analysis methods used with aptitude tests. There is a trend, evident in all types of tests, to provide more information through part scores, for diagnostic purposes and use in assessing progress toward more specific objectives. Great strides have been made also in the application of electronic devices to facilitate test scoring and data processing.

We might identify as another trend the increased production of professional articles on test theory, test construction, and the use of test results. A number of unusually fine textbooks in measurement have appeared recently. Professional organizations, such as the American Psychological Association, the American Educational Research Association, and the National Council on Measurements Used in Education, have formulated standards to encourage more responsible practices in test development and use. The test makers have responded by maintaining higher standards with respect to test construction, factual information on the essential characteristics and limitations of their instruments, and aids to interpretation for the users of test results.

Nontest Techniques

Nontest techniques for appraising the nonacademic aspects of student development, experimental before World War II, have been simplified and explained as practical procedures for teachers. These include procedures for the observing and recording to student behavior, rating scales and checklists for teachers and for student self-reports, conference and interview techniques, and procedures for evaluating student products.

---

[58] Donald E. Super, "The Multifactor Tests: Summing Up," *The Use of the Multifactor Tests in Guidance* (Washington, D. C.: American Personnel and Guidance Association, 1958), pp. 88–91.

Science Research Associates' "Teacher Guidance Handbooks" for the elementary and secondary school, entitled *Identifying Children with Special Needs*, will be cited to illustrate practical informal procedures for gathering evidence about student characteristics. These publications were designed to show teachers how to supplement the information provided by tests and more formal procedures. The authors, Jack Kough and Robert F. DeHaan, drew heavily upon their experiences with the Youth Development Commission of Quincy, Illinois, in a long-term project to identify and help children with special abilities or handicaps. Companion materials include a second volume at each level, elementary and secondary, called *Helping Children with Special Needs*, and a Roster Workbook in which the characteristics which identify a child having special needs or abilities are recorded. A list of identifying characteristics is provided for students with each of three kinds of ability — intellectual, scientific, or leadership — and each of several kinds of talent, such as artistic, writing, dramatic, and musical. Similar lists are provided for each of a number of common maladjustments found in school-children. One of the shorter lists is for dancing talent (elementary school edition):

1. Responds to rhythm of music by swinging arms or tapping feet.
2. Is well coordinated, limber, light on feet.
3. Uses whole body to respond to feelings or experiences. Skips when happy, shuffles when sad, leaps for joy.
4. Responds to the sense of music; can tell whether to skip, run, or hop, by the mood of the music.
5. Can pantomine easily — using only motions; can depict emotional and dramatic situations.
6. Enjoys tapping out rhythms with fingers, sticks, or feet.
7. Enjoys some form of dancing.[59]

The handbooks include suggestions for situations which can readily be arranged to get the information needed with respect to each child. Statistical results of the use of such procedures, in comparison with other evaluation procedures, are reported in a *Technical Supplement*.

------

[59] Reprinted by permission from *Identifying Children With Special Needs, Teachers' Guidance Handbook: Elementary Edition*, by Jack Kough and Robert F. DeHaan 1955, Social Research Associates, Inc.

Evaluation and Instruction

More and better information about students makes for better teaching. The complementary and interdependent nature of evaluation and instruction has been emphasized repeatedly in the educational literature of the past decade. The statement, "Evaluation is an integral part of instruction," appears again and again in the 1960 edition of the *Evaluative Criteria* which is used by the several regional associations for accrediting secondary schools and colleges. The implications of this point of view, as stated by G. Max Wingo in the *Encyclopedia of Educational Research* are: "(a) evaluation must always be done in terms of the recognized objectives of the group; (b) a variety of kinds of data are [sic] necessary; (c) appraisal should always be diagnostic in the sense that results obtained should be used to improve subsequent learning."[60] Clearly this is not just a matter of determining what has been accomplished after instruction, but a part of the teaching-learning activity.

Records and Reporting

A continuing problem has been that of devising marking and reporting procedures which will increase the effectiveness of student learning rather than merely record results. From this point of view a single mark per subject is obviously inadequate, and there has been widespread demand for reports which give more specific information with respect to a range of instructional objectives.

Many schools have sought to work cooperatively with parents in changing reporting methods, at least to the extent of finding out what they would like to know about their children's progress. One high school conducted a poll of parents and found that they wished reports to answer the following questions:

1. In comparison with his group, how well is my child mastering subject matter?
2. Considering his over-all ability and potential, is my child working up to that level?
3. What strengths and weaknesses does my child evidence in his class work?

[60] G. Max Wingo, "Methods of Teaching," in Chester W. Harris, *Encyclopedia of Educational Research*, 3 ed. (New York: The Macmillan Co., 1960), p. 858.

4. How is my child progressing in social development, such as citizenship, conduct, attitudes, etc.?[61]

It is evident that these parents agree with the proponents of evaluation in wishing a wider variety of information, and also that they want it from at least two points of view — how does my child compare with others and how does his performance compare with his potential? Still another basis of comparison is often mentioned, that of progress or improvement in comparison with previous status.

Experimentation is widespread with no indication that a single completely satisfactory method of reporting will emerge. The high school that conducted the poll we have just referred to devised a report card to try to answer the first three questions parents asked. This card used letter grades to show the comparison with others; numbers (1 for excellent, 2 for satisfactory, and 3 for unsatisfactory) for rating a student's work with respect to his potential; and S (satisfactory) and U (unsatisfactory) for indicating strengths and weaknesses on a list of various aspects of schoolwork, such as assignments, recitations, and special projects. Letters, telephone calls, and parent-teacher conferences were used for reports with respect to social development. This approach is perhaps typical of recent experimentation, but it is more complex than procedures followed in the typical high school or elementary school. High schools have tended to remain quite traditional, using competitive marks in the belief that such marks have weight in determining college admissions. The trend for elementary schools is toward marks based on ability with supplementary checklists and parent-teacher conferences.

There is at least clear recognition of the requirements for an improved grading system. The grading system should:

1. Be uniform through the school or school system;
2. Be understandable to students, parents, and teachers;
3. Be clearly defined in terms of the evidence of progress toward objectives;
4. Provide for significant comparisons of the student with others or with his potential;
5. Indicate accomplishment of specific goals rather than the results of an ill-defined global or omnibus appraisal:

---

[61] Louis T. Camp, "Improving Reporting Techniques," *NEA Journal*, Vol. 48, No. 9 (December, 1959), p. 26.

6. Be based on comprehensive measurement and evaluation;

7. Entail no more time than is available for the purpose (a major stumbling block).

Traxler[62] reports the systematic recording of the results of standardized tests and other evaluation information on cumulative records as another current trend. In the early 1950's, 94 percent of 1300 high schools were using such records, as compared with only 50 percent ten years earlier. Traxler does not view this development as surprising, but as a necessary development to unify and utilize the results of the school's appraisal program.

Guidance Programs

More and better ways of studying individuals contribute directly to the school guidance program. Testing and evaluation is one phase of guidance, a process of helping individuals to understand themselves better and plan more effectively for the future. Guidance personnel also provide information about opportunities, orientation to programs and institutions, individual counseling, and placement services. Frequently they follow up to see how the individual's plans have worked out. Although guidance services are not new, the need for specially trained "guidance persons" to help teachers has increased with concern for the development of the whole child, with the multiplication of specialized evaluation techniques, and the growing national concern for the development and conservation of manpower. Undoubtedly the prestige and success of the large-scale personnel programs of World War II were also stimulating factors. As a trained personnel worker, the guidance counselor contributes significantly to education. He works closely with others even more highly trained, such as the school psychologist and psychiatrist, to help see that students achieve their potential. In so doing they serve the national need for the maximum development and utilization of human resources.

Evaluating Schools and Teachers

Recent approaches to the evaluation of teacher personnel and school programs recognize that what is quite different may be equally good.

---

[62] Arthur E. Traxler, "Twelve Current Trends in Testing," *Clearing House*, Vol. 28 (September, 1953), pp. 3–6.

The basic principle here, as in other areas of evaluation, is that what is good depends upon the objectives of the local school situation. Objectives may vary and still be acceptable; and, hence, practices and activities vary also. To take an extreme example, we don't expect to find the same thing in a class or school for students especially gifted in sciences that we find in a vocational school designed to provide immediately salable skills. A related trend is toward self-evaluation. The experience of studying one's program in terms of one's own objectives is a valuable learning experience.

In the opinion of many, the emphases of current school evaluations have an undesirable side also. The procedures quite frankly depend upon self-study of facilities and procedures which appear designed to achieve objectives, rather than evidence of desired changes in students. In other words, there has been rather less effort to use improved measurement techniques — to appraise the student product in terms of objectives, than to utilize the less adequate criteria relating to what is provided and what is done. All in all, recent efforts to study teachers and school programs are more commendable from the standpoint of providing learning experiences for individual school staffs than from the standpoint of scientific measurement and evaluation. It seems probable that recent clear thinking about the desirable characteristics of educational criteria will result in more intensive criticism and revision of current procedures in this phase of evaluation.

Summary and a Word of Caution

In a relatively brief period of educational history, measurement and evaluation have won acceptance as research tools and essential features of school practice. Modern concepts and methods of measurement originated in a period of invention which accompanied the rise of scientific psychology. Simple processes, such as reaction time, were measured in the early laboratories. Binet and Simon's intelligence test (1905) and Rice's spelling scale (1897) brought measurement out of the lab and put it to work on school problems. The first work on rating scales and questionnaires for the study of personality, character, and interest were devised about the same time.

Shortly after 1900 E. L. Thorndike emerged as the most vigorous of the pioneers who were to show the way to further progress. He and his students developed concepts and procedures for "standardizing" tests and gave us examples in arithmetic and language arts. Tests and scales were used to study schools and school systems. Teachers were rated. Evidence of the unreliability of teacher's marks shocked some and encouraged the use of standardized tests. Marking "on the curve" was debated and letter grades became more popular than percentage marking systems. American revisions of Binet's test and performance tests of ability appeared. The Army Alpha and Beta group tests were developed in response to the demands for mass ability testing during World War I. The first of the group personality questionnaires, Woodworth's Psychoneurotic Inventory, was also developed at this time.

What we have called the Measurement Era followed World War I. The 1920's brought a rapid, somewhat uncritical expansion in the production and use of tests and inventories of all kinds. Achievement test batteries were a new development. The objective test forms were adapted for use by the classroom teachers. School surveys were numerous, and every available technique was used in attempts to identify or select better teachers. Marking and reporting problems were magnified by the concern for effort, attitude, and progress and by attempts to adapt instruction to individual differences. The evaluation movement began with the 1930's. New emphasis was now given to defining objectives in terms of the behavior expected and to finding improved ways of measuring personal, social, and emotional behavior, as well as more tangible achievements. Interest inventories, new personality inventories, clinical instruments, and observational records were among the techniques used. Large-scale studies using the new techniques and approaches were a feature of the early 1940's. The Cooperative Study of Secondary School Standards developed uniform criteria for use in evaluating schools. Although traditional marks and report cards were widely questioned, schools were slow to change.

World War II produced and popularized batteries of tests for the measurement of specific abilities or aptitude tests. Since the war, progress has been rapid in developing and refining earlier approaches. Most notable is the increase in testing programs for selection, to form instructional groups, and for use in personal, educational, or vocational guidance. Achievement tests, both teacher-made and standardized, are emphasizing the understanding and use of knowledge. In the classroom, evaluation is being accepted as an integral part of instruction and a method for improvement of instruction, not merely a ritual for marking and reporting. The teacher-made tests are more popular for classroom use than standardized tests, and teachers have available excellent guides and examples for the construction and use of nontest techniques to evaluate progress in the noncognitive or nonacademic aspects of development. The requirements of improved marking and reporting procedures are well known, and experimentation with revised procedures is spreading. Trends in the evaluation of schools and teachers are toward recognizing excellence in adapting to local situations and objectives and away from standardization. Self-evaluation is being encouraged as a valuable method of self-insight and self-improvement.

Our brief review should leave no doubt of progress if we accept the assumption that wiser decisions result from every increase in the completeness and accuracy of information pertinent to those decisions. Complete information would mean that we could correctly predict what a person would and should do in every situation. This we have not achieved and never will; but our "batting average" can be improved by the full and appropriate use of what we do know.

At the same time we should recognize that misuse of tests and other techniques can nullify the progress that has been made. An overemphasis on tests, coaching students on particular tests, teaching only for test results, interpreting a test or other measure apart from other available information, careless procedures in administration and scoring, and regarding scores or the decisions based on them as fixed and unchangeable are some of the practices to be avoided. Where such practices are found, widespread and general criticism of tests may be expected to follow. One schoolteacher, for example, feels so strongly about the misuse of classification and selection tests that he has written a book telling parents and students how to defend themselves.[63] Under circumstances like these, teachers, counselors, and administrators must learn to understand, use, and interpret measurement and evaluation procedures correctly. Courses designed to guide such learning are an important part of professional training.

SELECTED READINGS

Alexander, W. M., Teel, Dwight and Eugenia, and others, "Special Journal

---

[63] David Engler, *How to Raise Your Child's IQ* (New York: Ballantine Books, 1961).

Feature — Reporting," *NEA Journal*, Vol. 48, No. 9 (November, 1959), pp. 15–29.

Experienced teachers and specialists give their views on the why, what, and how of reporting. The experiences of selected schools with parent-teacher conferences, abolishing grades, and improving grading and reporting procedures are featured.

Ayres, Leonard P., "History and Present Status of Educational Measurements," *The Measurement of Educational Products*, Seventeenth Yearbook of the National Society for the Study of Education, Part II (Bloomington, Ill.: Public School Publishing Co., 1918), Chap. I.

One of the best statements of the early history of educational and psychological measurement.

Beecher, Dwight E., *Evaluation of Teaching* (Syracuse, N. Y.: Syracuse University Press, 1949).

A review of methods of appraisal in the evaluation of teaching and an overview of related problems and issues.

Bloom, Benjamin S., and others, *A Taxonomy of Educational Objectives, Handbook I, Cognitive Domain* (New York: Longmans, Green & Co., 1956).

A scholarly classification of educational objectives that goes far beyond simple recall and gives illustrations of how the achievement of these objectives may be measured with tests.

Caldwell, O. W., and Courtis, S. A., *Then and Now in Education, 1845–1923* (Yonkers-on-Hudson, N. Y.: World Book Co., 1924), Chaps. 3 and 7.

Notable for a report on Horace Mann's 1845 Boston Survey. Contains similar data for 1919.

Ebel, Robert L., "Eight Critical Questions About the Use of Tests," *Education*, Vol. 81, No. 2 (October, 1960), pp. 1–32.

Six specialists give their answers to questions parents and teachers ask about tests and their use.

Freeman, F. N., *Mental Tests, Their History, Principles, and Applications*, rev. ed. (Boston: Houghton Mifflin Co., 1939).

Excellent summary of developments and trends before 1940.

Garrett, Henry E., *Great Experiments in Psychology*, 3 ed. (New York: D. Appleton-Century, 1951), Chaps. 11 and 12.

Describes the pioneering studies of individual and group intelligence testing and reviews related developments to date.

Kough, Jack, and DeHaan, R. F., *Teacher Guidance Handbooks*, elementary and secondary school editions (two volumes each) (Chicago: Science Research Associates, 1955–1957).

Practical and concrete suggestions to aid the teacher in identifying and helping the gifted and talented; the emotionally, socially, and educationally maladjusted; and the physically handicapped.

Meyer, A. E., *An Educational History of the American People* (New York: McGraw-Hill Book Co., 1957), Chap. XV.

Background and development of the scientific movement in education which highlights the role of mental testing, the measurement movement, curriculum reconstruction, and child study.

Morgan, H. G., Traxler, A. E., and others, "Special Journal Feature — Testing and Evaluation," *NEA Journal*, Vol. 48, No. 8 (November, 1959), pp. 15–30.

Specialists report on standardized tests — what they are; how they are used and misused; self-evaluation; interpreting test results to parents and the community; text anxiety in students.

Orata, P. T., "Evaluating Evaluation," *Journal of Educational Research*, Vol. 33 (May, 1940), pp. 641–661.

A stimulating early paper calling attention to the shift from measurement to evaluation.

National Society for the Study of Education, *The Scientific Movement in Education*, Thirty-Seventh Yearbook, Part II (Bloomington, Ill.: Public School Publishing Co., 1938), Chaps. 29–31.

Discussions of factors influencing the development of tests, observational procedures, questionnaires, and rating scales prior to 1930.

Ross, C. C., and Stanley, J. C., *Measurement in Today's Schools*, 3 ed. (New York: Prentice-Hall, 1954).

A standard text on educational measurement.

Rothney, J. W., *Evaluating and Reporting Pupil Progress*, What Research Says to the Teacher, No. 7 (Washington, D. C.: Department of Classroom Teachers, N.E.A., 1955).

An attempt to select from research material the items of most help to the classroom teacher in her efforts to evaluate and report pupil progress.

Scates, D. E., "Fifty Years of Objective Measurement and Research in Education," *Journal of Educational Research*, Vol. 41 (December, 1947), pp. 241–264.

Comprehensive survey of the development and status of educational measurement to 1950.

Smith, E. R., Tyler, R. W., and others, *Appraising and Recording Student Progress* (New York: Harper & Bros., 1942).

Report of the appraisal program of the Eight-Year Study which provides a description of the development of non-test techniques for the evaluation of major high school objectives.

Strang, Ruth, *How to Report Progress* (Chicago: Science Research Associates, 1955).

A concise summary of marking and reporting principles and procedures which is well illustrated with examples from various schools.

Traxler, A. E., "Twelve Current Trends in Testing," *Clearing House*, Vol. 28 (September, 1953), pp. 3–7.

Discusses twelve policies that large city schools were following in the 1950's to get better results from their testing programs.

Traxler, A. E., and others, *Introduction to Testing and the Use of Test Results in Public Schools* (New York: Harper & Bros., 1953).

Excellent introductory book on establishing and using testing programs.

Tyler, Ralph W., "Educational Measurement: A Broad Perspective," *The National Elementary Principal*, Vol. 6, No. 1 (September, 1961), pp. 8–12.

Illustrations of the uses of educational measurement in the school and an overview of the origins and progress in measurement and evaluation.

Wrightstone, J. W., Justman, Joseph, and Robbins, Irving, *Evaluation in Modern Education* (New York: American Book Company, 1956).

Excellent discussion of the origins and trends in measurement and evaluation; the principles, scope and methodology of evaluation; and the types, uses and qualities of major evaluation techniques.

Chapter XVI

ISSUES IN THE PSYCHOLOGY
OF EDUCATION

The preceding chapters of Part II have examined the changing role of psychology in education. In tracing psychological developments we also dealt with issues, for issues stimulate change and change produces new issues. Thus theorists of the Stimulus-Response group challenged faculty psychology on the issues of formal discipline and transfer; in turn they were challenged by the field theorists on such issues as learning by parts versus learning by wholes, insight and learning by trial and error, and the essential unity of the individual. Whenever possible, we have identified the bases for decision or reconciliation insofar as schools are affected.

The present chapter reviews a small sampling of the many current issues related to the psychology of education. Issues, like principles, may be presented at several levels (Chap. I). The first two issues presented here are closely tied to theory but have implications for general educational policy. These relate to: (1) learner discovery versus teacher exposition, and (2) specific versus general transfer. The first of these issues has been chosen to represent a group of closely related issues emerging with the "New Education" (Chap. X) and scientific study of the learning process (Chap. XIII). Among those noted in the present treatment of discovery, for example, are teacher-centered versus child-centered education, education as problem-solving, rote versus meaningful learning, active versus passive learning, and the place of learner interests. One may be surprised to find that general transfer is still fighting for recognition after its earlier defeat by S-R theorists. New evidence and a revised theoretical basis have again made it a contender. Either the discovery or the transfer issue may be omitted without violence to the continuity of the text. The authors have found these two issues of special interest to more advanced students and sometimes reserve them for individualized assignments.

Next, four specific issues illustrating conflicts among educational psychologists with respect to educational policy or practice are included. Those we have chosen are timely and are likely to be encountered in both professional and popular literature. Such issues often arise in practice rather than in psychological theory, but research in educational psychology may hasten their resolution. The four we have picked relate to such diverse matters as teaching machines, phonics in reading instruction, promotion practices, and essay versus objective examinations.

Since it is impossible to present enough examples to give an adequate notion of the number and variety of current issues relating to measurement and evaluation, we present instead what is perhaps the real issue — our progress with respect to several educational purposes for which evaluation is undertaken. A number of specific issues which this approach should help the student to answer for himself are listed.

LEARNER DISCOVERY VERSUS TEACHER EXPOSITION

In learning by discovery the method followed is one in which concepts or principles are inferred from specific facts or experiences. At times this method is called problem-solving, independent inquiry, or the laboratory method; but in any event the substance or content of what is learned must first be discovered by the learner. This notion of pupil discovery is itself exciting, and is one of the more enduring emphases of the "New Education" (Chap. X). Persons currently working on curriculum revision in mathematics and science, for example, have been stressing the educational value that results when a student discovers generalizations for himself. They contrast this approach with that in which the teacher first states a generalization and then attempts to prove it.[1]

Ausubel has identified several "major strands in the design of the

---

[1] Jerome S. Bruner, *The Process of Education* (Cambridge, Mass.: The Harvard University Press, 1960), p. 20 ff.

discovery method."[2] Progressive education had problem-solving as both its principal objective and method. An uncompromising rejection of drill methods and memorization of facts which were unrelated to the experience of the student led to suspicion of all verbal learning that is not immediately preceded by direct and active experience with real persons or objects. The belief that the verbal and general must follow directly from the concrete and specific, and this in the process of solving problems, led to an overemphasis on pupil discovery of concepts and relations as a result of inductive or incidental learning. Furthermore, and this is important to note, the extreme progressivists made no exceptions for the more mature student with his extensive prior experiences and greater ability for abstraction. What is good for the child was thought equally good for the man.

Progressive education adopted the child-centered approach to instruction from Rousseau and Froebel. The educational environment should not, it was stressed, interfere with natural maturation. One point of view held that the child himself was in the best position to choose the objectives and activities suited for him at any given time. Any form of teacher direction ran the risk of violating the natural laws of child development. Pupil autonomy and self-discovery were held to be most conducive to optimal growth. Somehow, facts which were discovered independently were to come with a full-blown understanding, and this understanding could be achieved in no other way. A related point of view was that teachers who communicate their superior knowledge directly violate the rights of younger citizens and are "authoritarian" or "undemocratic."

The popularity of the discovery method was also due in part to a vigorous reaction to attempts to project laboratory explanations of rote learning to the verbal learning of the classroom. For many this meant that verbal learning and rote learning were identical. Since rote learning was undesirable, so, it was argued, was verbal learning. The alternative was nonverbal learning which, through long association, was identified with independent self-discovery.

Another factor contributing to the popularity of discovery methods was the hope that every child could be made a productive and crea-

---

[2] David P. Ausubel, "Learning by Discovery: Rationale and Mystique," *Bulletin, National Association of Secondary School Principals*, Vol. 45 (December, 1961), pp. 18–58.

tive thinker. An especially militant group would make him a productive and creative scientist. Perhaps the initial concern was only for the gifted, but the more "democratic" notion was that everyone has the capacity to be creative in some way. There was an obligation, the progressivists urged, to help each student develop this alleged creativity. Somewhat naïvely, it was assumed that this is best done by simulating in the classroom the conditions and methods of work of the mature thinker and researcher.

Some bitter experiences and second thoughts have helped the modern proponent of discovery to avoid such excesses and absurdities. Today, no one advocates letting the child with his "natural wisdom" design the curriculum without interference from adults. Few believe that more mature learners must independently discover all they learn by manipulating concrete, physical objects or "props." Verbal concepts may have meaning for the more mature learner because of his extensive background of experiences. In the development of relationships, for example, learners with a sufficiently large repertoire of meaningful concepts and recalled experiences may manipulate and relate these symbolically rather than actually. This much is usually granted.

Advantages Granted

The critics of discovery have become more tolerant also. Thus it is readily granted that several of the advantages claimed for the discovery method have at least logic to recommend them. Perhaps the most important of these probable advantages are:

1. *Discovery with the aid of concrete materials is invaluable in the early stages of abstract learning, particularly for young children.* The young child is severely limited in his ability to find meaning in abstract, verbal, or symbolic materials. Until he has an easy familiarity with a large number of verbal concepts based on personal experience, and until he can relate these concepts directly, in the abstract, without reference to the concrete or physical, he obviously finds the purely verbal or symbolic meaningless. He must build his concepts by experience with concrete physical objects. He often senses, rather than verbalizes, relationships among his experiences. Modern instruction in arithmetic provides for many experiences with groups of objects until the understanding of the essential nature of these objects develops. Generations of children, for example, have used

their fingers to add meaning to number concepts. A limited amount of concrete experience may help learners of greater maturity get off to a better start in a field of learning which is new to them.

2. *The discovery method is an effective way to teach the techniques of and appreciation for independent inquiry or discovery.* The best way to appreciate the power and limitations of science and to learn the method of scientists, for example, may be to practice the formulation of hypotheses, to collect relevant evidence, etc., while solving real problems.

3. *The active role of the learner in discovery and his personal reactions of frustration or success promote retention.* This we deduce from accepted principles of learning. Nevertheless, other methods of learning may also be in accord with these principles.

4. *When rules or relationships are discovered through experience with multiple and diverse specific situations, transfer is greater.* Here again we are guided by accepted principles; but, once more, other methods may also provide experiences in numerous situations similar to those to which transfer is expected.

Universal Claims Refuted

A place for discovery learning has been won or granted. But there are signs that some proponents of discovery will only be satisfied with the total surrender of those who have defended teacher exposition. Hence today the issue seems to be the future of teaching that begins with exposition. Is there any place for the expository lecture? May we, for example, sometimes boldly state a rule or relationship which we hope to make evident by examples and explanations, or must we always arrange things so that the student, as a result of firsthand examination of a number of specifics, gains his first knowledge of a principle or a relationship by his own insight? Should every new item of knowledge be a personal act of discovery — like that of Kohler's apes who suddenly found food within their reach? Are we always to be schemers and arrangers of experiences, luring students to rediscover our hard-won knowledge, or may we sometimes stand right up and speak the truth as we see it?

We may be accused of erecting a straw man here, for we all know that there is no lack of exposition by teachers. The issue, however, is what *should* be done, not what *is* done. Is at least some of our exposition desirable or should we consider it a weakness and apologize?

Discovery has some logic on its side, but a number of assertions which have been advanced in support of discovery as the universally best way of learning appear unwarranted. Some of these will now be examined:

1. *All knowledge must be self-discovered.* This conclusion may be traced to those who earlier saw all education as problem-solving or child-centered. It receives emphasis in lofty sentiments more recently expressed.[3] To understand, we must make knowledge our own by translating it into our own words (thoughts) and by relating it to previous experience, concepts, and conclusions. This much seems true. On the other hand, the very nature of human culture denies that every generation must actually rediscover all that became known before. A fragment, yes, but anything more must be communicated and explained. A continuing culture is made possible because communication and explanation is a quicker and more economical process than discovery.

2. *Meaning is a product of discovery, obtainable in no other way.* This assertion results primarily from identifying the question of rote memorization with that of teaching by verbal exposition. They are really quite separate things. Purely arbitrary associations gained through rote learning are of very limited value. Learning through teacher exposition, however, can be meaningful. It is, in fact, perhaps the most common form of meaningful learning in our experience.

Both Craig,[4] working with college students, and Kittell,[5] working with sixth graders, report experimental evidence that giving the rule before examples is at least as effective a way to teach principles as is arranging a series of examples to enable students to discover the rule themselves; and, the "rule-first" method is much more efficient in terms of time. To state a rule and follow it with examples is a proven and efficient method of organizing material for presentation by teaching machines.[6] Student activity and clearly understood exam-

---

[3] Jerome S. Bruner, "After Dewey What?" *Saturday Review* (June 17, 1961), pp. 58 f, 76 ff.

[4] Robert C. Craig, "Directed versus Independent Discovery of Established Relations," *Journal of Educational Psychology*, Vol. 47 (April, 1956), pp. 223–234.

[5] Jack E. Kittell, "An Experimental Study of the Effect of External Direction During Learning on Transfer and Retention of Principles," *Journal of Educational Psychology*, Vol. 48 (November, 1957), pp. 391–405.

[6] Lloyd E. Homme and Robert Glaser, "Problems in Programming Verbal Learning Sequences," in A. A. Lumsdaine and Robert Glaser (eds.), *Teaching Machines and Programmed Learning, A Source Book* (Washington, D. C.: Department of Audio-Visual Instruction, National Education Association, 1960), pp. 486–496.

ples seem to be important variables in meaningful learning. It is relatively unimportant whether the rule is given first followed by examples or the procedure reversed. However learning is much faster and fewer examples are required when the rule is presented first. There are those who argue, however, for organizing the entire curriculum, even on secondary and college levels, along the lines of inductive discovery.[7] Since these methods are so much more time-consuming, this hardly seems feasible. Nevertheless, the proponents of this view argue that the acquisition of a large number of concepts is not so important as learning a smaller number better. This is another issue; but even if the point is granted, there is no evidence that the methods of discovery and induction result in learning even a fewer concepts better. As things now stand, the actual evidence, from experiments with relatively mature learners (Grade 6 to college), suggests that by exposition and explanation one can teach more concepts, with just as good retention and transfer, than one can by adopting the approach of inductive discovery.

3. *Discovered knowledge is the only permanent knowledge.* Granted that discovery methods may aid retention, there is no reason to believe that discovery per se is essential for good retention. The accepted principles of learning favor meaning and activity, but both can be provided in several ways. The statement of principle, for example, may be followed by extensive examples, and applications which require learner activity. Research evidence on this question was cited in the preceding paragraph. Bruner also notes a different experiment which he says supports the value of discovery for retention.[8] In this experiment a group of learners who were told to remember word pairings by "producing a word or idea that will tie the pair together in a way that will make sense to them" recalled the associations better than a group who were given the ideas to be used in relating the words. A third group utilizing no connecting relationships had the poorest retention. Since the connecting words which students provided themselves probably had more meaning for them than those provided by the experimenter, this study is interpreted as supporting the value of meaningful associations rather than the merit of self-discovered ones.

---

[7] J. A. Easley, Jr., "The Physical Science Study Committee and Educational Theory," *Harvard Educational Review*, Vol. 29 (Winter, 1959), pp. 4–11.

[8] Jerome S. Bruner, "The Act of Discovery," *Harvard Educational Review*, Vol. 31 (Winter, 1961), pp. 21–22.

Still, don't the results reported by Bruner suggest that self-discovered associations are always the more meaningful? Not at all. The true relationship or even the best arbitrary one may never occur to the unaided learner. Gilbert, for example, has described how other arbitrary pairs can be "taught" in "one trial to practically any unpracticed student with assurances of perfect recall after six months, a year, and even longer."[9] This method is to provide a relational scheme meaningful to all learners, one which they would be unlikely to discover without direction.

4. *Methods of inquiry and discovery are the primary goals of education.* The progressivists and, more recently, others have said that the process and goal of education are the same — problem-solving.[10] This is an overstatement. We cannot even be sure that a learner who spends all his time solving problems at his level will learn all the facts and principles he needs to know to solve problems effectively in the future. The inadequacies of problem-solving as the *sole* method of transmitting knowledge have been noted.

Knowledge must be considered a separate and major goal of education, if for no other reason than that the more knowledgeable person, given problem-solving skills and experience, will be the better investigator, the better searcher for truth. Adept problem-solvers with no depth of knowledge in a field must be limited, it may be argued, to skillful attacks on shallow problems. It is unlikely that they will even recognize the significant problems. For instance, a high school with a special reading program was eminently successful in teaching students to be skillful, rapid readers. A survey of this school's graduates disclosed that they applied their superior skills almost exclusively to reading comic books.

Many persons are highly motivated by a need to understand, even if they do not actively try to advance the frontiers of knowledge. Who is to say that this is not a worthy goal? Both problem-solving ability and knowledge and understanding are recommended as educational objectives; and, although teaching for one supports the teaching for the other, we should probably plan for both, systematically and separately.

5. *Discovery nurtures creativity.* Here the term "creativity" is

---

[9] Thomas F. Gilbert, "On the Relevance of Laboratory Investigation of Learning to Self-Instructional Programming," in Lumsdaine and Glaser, *op. cit.*, p. 475.
[10] Bruner, "After Dewey What?" *op. cit.*, p. 77.

not limited to the singularly original achievements of a few persons. This is obviously a more general use of the term which includes any discovery new to the individual, regardless of how commonplace it is to others. When seen in this light, the assertion is much the same as saying that the discovery method of learning teaches methods of inquiry, which we have acknowledged. We even suggested that discovery may be the best method for this, although there is evidence from short-term experiments that there is little difference between students who learn principles by exposition and explanation and those who learn by discovery with respect to the production of "original" solutions to new problems.[11]

When we think of creativity in its more restrictive meaning, there is no evidence that the most extreme verbalism has prevented the development of even a single genius. It seems improbable, moreover, that many powerful intellects would disregard the knowledge and experience of the past as set down in journals and books, for example, in favor of a point-by-point personal rediscovery.

6. *Discovery methods motivate the learner.* The argument here is that a student identifies himself with the task in searching for its solution, and that task completion consequently becomes the goal rather than external approval or high marks. It would appear that some successful discovery experiences have this effect. Unsuccessful experiences may not. Inspiring lectures have been known to motivate students also, although the likelihood of this may be less.

The whole question of greater motivation by the use of discovery methods is practically untouched by research. The relative novelty of discovery approaches in many educational settings might be sufficient to account for initial motivational differences. It is hard to believe that more mature and able learners would continue to gain satisfaction from being indirectly pushed or led to discover facts and principles which they know the instructor could explain to them in a minute. Certainly, the thrill of discovering the instructor's predetermined answer is in no way comparable to that of the scientist's genuinely original discovery. Who is really motivated — the person who demands that the teacher get to the heart of the matter and explain a relationship or the one who says give me some more examples so that I can guess the answer? Games of this sort are

---

[11] Robert C. Craig, *The Transfer Value of Guided Learning* (New York: Teachers College, Columbia University, 1953).

interesting for a time, but they are hardly the methods we would pick for serious study of a field of knowledge.

7. *Exposition is undemocratic.* This is the final assertion which we shall mention. It is utterly without foundation except in the extreme case where an instructor not only presents ideas but insists that they be accepted without question because "I say so." This may be characteristic of some teachers, but not of the method. There is nothing inherently dogmatic, authoritarian, or stultifying about presenting and explaining ideas to others by word of mouth or in writing. There has never been a more efficient way of transmitting large bodies of accumulated knowledge.

In our examination of discovery as an issue we have recognized that it is a legitimate technique which may be used to advantage with young learners, to teach appreciation and methods of problem-solving, to add variety to classroom methods, and perhaps in other ways. Nevertheless, because learning by discovery requires so much time, we do not hesitate to say that it will never replace exposition as the most prevalent instructional approach.

When the exaggerated claims for discovery have been discounted, there appears to be no reason to make discovery the *only* instructional method. Meaning and activity appear to be far more important factors in learning than discovery *per se*. Both meaning and activity can be provided by methods that begin with exposition by presenting a rule and then requiring the learner to apply it in diverse and meaningful situations.

Since several types of research studies which are usually cited in support of discovery have not been mentioned, a word of explanation is needed. Our reason is that most of these investigations, for example, the well-known Gestalt studies (Chap. XIII), have not really studied discovery. They have contrasted rote learning with meaningful learning, but this is not the present issue. We also admire the work of the various curriculum projects that call for increased use of discovery in learning. These projects are bringing new enthusiasm and vigor to the teaching of science and mathematics. They have produced authoritative instructional materials which have been systematically organized around explanatory and integrative relationships. So much has been done all at once in these programs, and in use they vary so much from school to school, that we shall never know either the extent or the effect of their use of discovery learning.

GENERAL OR SPECIFIC TRANSFER

A student makes a perfect score on a spelling test but misspells some of the same words in a theme. Other students make no change in their reading habits after a course emphasizing the appreciation of literature. A geometry course is designed to teach students to reason, but there is apparently no carry-over by the students to biology or social-science courses. An algebra course teaches students to dislike mathematics. American soldiers who drive trucks in England have difficulty in keeping to the left side of the road. The students of public and Catholic schools are found to be very similar with respect to attitudes and moral values. These are problems in the transfer of original training (learning) to new situations.

That education is best which has maximum transfer value, but how is this to be achieved? The theory of formal discipline held that the influence of what is learned in one situation is very widespread. The mind was thought to be like a muscle (or a group of muscles each corresponding to a different faculty such as memory, reasoning, etc.). A person could strengthen his mind by many kinds of difficult exercises. This person would then excel in a wide variety of school tasks and be equipped to think through problems of life.

The theory of formal discipline was an early attempt to explain the effect of past learning in new situations (compare Chap. XII). We now reject it as an explanation for transfer because many studies, beginning with those of Thorndike about 1900, showed that students of equal initial mental ability taking so-called "formal" discipline courses (foreign language, mathematics, science, etc.) and "informal" discipline courses (shop, commercial subjects, art, etc.) made about the same gains on mental tests. Moreover, practice on assumed faculties, such as memory, with one type of material didn't help students to perform better in other fields.

After discrediting formal discipline and massive general transfer Thorndike was one of the first to show the effects of transfer to a narrow range of situations, clearly related to those of the original learning. His was a theory of specific transfer which took place because of "identical elements" in related or similar situations.

A widely quoted experiment by Judd emphasized that it is important for the learner to see the similarity in the learning and transfer situations. One group of learners was given instruction concerning the refraction of light in water. Another group was not. Both groups practiced throwing darts at an underwater target and proved equally proficient. The group that had received instruction on the principle of refraction was superior, however, when the target was moved to a different depth. Judd's theory is easily combined with Thorndike's if one considers that a principle may be an element of identity relating two situations.

Gestalt psychologists have made much of the fact that students may not apply their learning to new situations if they do not see these situations as similar to the old. Transfer, they point out, takes place whenever an individual recognizes a new situation as similar to one for which he has learned responses. Transfer to a wide variety of situations can be anticipated with confidence if certain conditions, which help the student to recognize the possibilities, are met.

Scientific psychology discarded a theory of massive transfer through strengthening of the faculties in favor of one which recognizes transfer within a narrow range of specific knowledge, skills, or habits. Psychological thought like that of the Gestaltists has again suggested that general transfer is a distinct probability. Orata[12] and Kolesnik[13] have provided excellent analyses of the extensive literature on several aspects of the transfer of training controversy.

Castiello also contends that transfer takes place through abstraction and generalization. He holds that man is able to solve new problems or reason to new conclusions because he has the power to abstract the similarities which unite varied specific situations and recognize the differences which distinguish them. Education which facilitates transfer does so because it increases a person's interest and ability for abstract reasoning. Castiello holds that man can form ideas of universal applicability because the soul is a spiritual, not a material, entity (see Nature of the Learner, Chap. XIII). Ideas belong to the spiritual realm, and transfer is the "spiritualization of learning."[14]

Castiello presents evidence to support the common-sense observation that a person's entire approach to learning and life is influenced

---

[12] Pedro T. Orata, "Transfer of Training and Educational Pseudo-Science," *Mathematics Teacher*, Vol. 28 (May, 1935), pp. 265–289, and "Recent Research Studies in Transfer of Training with Implications for Curriculum Guidance and Personnel Work," *Harvard Educational Review*, Vol. 11 (May, 1941), pp. 359–378.

[13] Walter B. Kolesnik, *Mental Discipline in Modern Education* (Madison: University of Wisconsin Press, 1958).

[14] J. Castiello, S.J., *Geistesformung* (Berlin: Ferd. Dummlers Verlag, 1934), p. 136.

by his prior learning. He shows how a humanistic-philosophic outlook may come from one school background, a scientific outlook from another. One learner will look to the will for explanations of typical human behavior, such as raising the hand in greeting; another, the scientist, explains the same act in terms of physiology, psychology, and sociology.

A 1959 conference of scientists, educators, and historians, reported by Bruner, reached conclusions which are somewhat similar to those of Castiello. They spoke of the fact of "massive general transfer," when students grasp the "underlying structure or significance" of subject matter. "Grasping the structure of a subject is understanding it in a way that permits other things to be related to it meaningfully."[15] This seems to be in part the understanding of broad principles or recurrent ideas which have wide application. At one point the indirectness of information in science and the need for an operational definition of ideas in measurement are cited as an example. "We do not see pressure or the chemical bond directly but infer it indirectly from a set of measures. So too body temperature. So too sadness in another person."[16] Unifying principles or ideas are not always verbalized or even conscious. One example mentioned is that of the child who demonstrates mastery of the structure of sentences by generating many in different content areas without consciously knowing or using rules.[17]

Another problem faced by the conference which presupposes general transfer was intuitive thinking in a subject field. In analytical thought one is fully aware of his plan of attack, his reasons, etc., and usually can relate them to another. The intuitive thinker, on the other hand, may jump to surprisingly good conclusions with little awareness of process. While intuitive thinking is hard to define, it is demonstrated both by the individual who, after working for a long time on a problem, suddenly achieves a solution without knowing quite how and by the person who can make good guesses about the solution to a problem quickly, without detailed analysis.

Intuitive thinking is very highly regarded among scientists, but not enough is known about the development of this talent. It is believed to be fostered by practices which encourage: (1) the use of

[15]Jerome S. Bruner, *The Process of Education* (Cambridge: Harvard University Press, 1960), pp. 6–7.

[16] *Ibid.*, p. 26.

[17] *Ibid.*, p. 8.

hunches and guesses, (2) self-confidence and independence, and (3) a good grasp of the structure of a subject field. It may be important to discourage dependence on excessively formal techniques, proofs, and the like.

The fact of transfer has not been questioned recently. The issue appears to be the generality of transfer, although arguments such as those that follow result more often than not either from misunderstanding, or from a failure to agree on definitions.

For Specific Transfer Only	For More General Transfer
1. Teach the specific skills, attitudes, knowledge, appreciation, or other responses which will be needed in the future.	1. The most important transfer is nonspecific and general.
2. No subjects or courses have special merit for sharpening the intellect, increasing reasoning ability or memory.	2. Certain subjects, particularly college preparatory or academic ones, teach students to be better thinkers.
3. The study of a foreign language, for example, helps students to use English only to the extent that English is taught in the foreign-language course.	3. A foreign language, for example, helps students to use English more effectively and may improve international understanding as well.
4. Social problems of the present are best solved by the methods of scientific inquiry.	4. Study of the wisdom of the past (the great books) prepares one to solve present social problems.
5. Our best scientists and scholars may be inept reasoners in other areas of life.	5. There is more to the educated man than a repertoire of specific skills or items of knowledge.

There are those who feel that the argument over transfer is mostly sound and fury when it comes to actual classroom practice. Much seems clear. We know that transfer is a function of the relation between learning and later situations. We know that transfer is greatest when the learner can be helped to anticipate and see such relationships. Learners differ in their ability to see relationships, but any student is helped if the teacher: (1) points out the possibilities for transfer, (2) uses varied teaching materials and creates situations as similar as possible to those to which the learning is expected to transfer, (3) strives for student understanding of the common features or recurrent ideas in varied experiences, and (4) provides practice in transfer.

How a subject is taught makes the difference for transfer. As Andrews and Cronbach have said:

. . . From a study of Latin, one can probably improve his English, or become aware of the problems of man and the state, or establish a lifelong enjoyment of Roman poetry, or become antagonistic to Latin, the teacher, the school, and "culture" in general. There is no superior subject matter for transfer, there are only superior learning experiences. No doubt, under skilled teaching, educational psychology, art, or cooking can be made the vehicle for developing reasoning, a sense of values, or superior study habits.[18]

The Machine Versus the Teacher

Here we present the first of four rather specific issues whose solution will be facilitated by the contributions of educational psychology. The four are typical of many which teachers face today. The psychological rationale of teaching machines and the evidence of their educational value were given in Chapter XIII. Though brief, that presentation should have dispelled any fears that the newer instructional devices are mechanical monsters which threaten the existence of all present texts, methods, and teachers. Still, since the topic is timely and likely to provoke lively debate, it will be of value to consider some extreme views of the desirable relationship between the teacher and teaching machines.

Arguments For

One view, somewhat exaggerated, holds that the teacher's role should become one of scheduling, distributing, and servicing materials prepared by experts for presentation by machine or "do it yourself" textbooks. Persons of this view contend that with machines:

1. There will be precise and systematic control of the conditions of learning.

2. The lessons will be prepared by experts with full knowledge of the subject and fully aware of the laws of learning.

3. No student will be penalized because he happens to get a poor teacher.

4. Each student will have a very superior and personal tutor.

5. Excellent diagnostic opportunities will be produced by the step-by-step progression in student performance.

6. Research on the improvement of learning can be continuous and much more adequately controlled.

---

[18] T. G. Andrews, Lee J. Cronbach, Peter Sandiford, "Transfer of Training," in Walter S. Monroe (ed.), *Encyclopedia of Educational Research*, rev. ed. (New York: The Macmillan Co., 1950), p. 1488. Reproduced with the permission of the publisher.

Arguments Con

A different view is that the machine threatens all that is "best" in education. Some of the hazards noted are:

1. Teaching machines are based on a Stimulus-Response psychology which is inadequate as an explanation of human learning.

2. The human teacher, but not the machine, can be a model as well as a communicator, a personal symbol of worthy goals to be reached by the student.

3. Machines can provide verbal learning, but this is apt to be superficial. Experience with concrete things is essential, as are field trips, supervised practice, etc.

4. Much important learning is social. We are motivated, guided, and receive our evaluations from others. Machine learning is impersonalized.

5. The most important intellectual experiences cannot be gained by following a prearranged program step by step. What of independent inquiry requiring the selection and synthesis of information?

6. Some "wholes" are the more effective learning material. Cutting a literary masterpiece or a vigorous description by an able scientist into little pieces for spoon (machine) feeding is a revolting idea.

7. Contrary to the claims of some teaching-machine enthusiasts, no tutor worth his salt spends his time asking one very easy question after another. Rather he stimulates discriminating thinking, prompts when necessary, gives assurance, and encourages independent progress. That this is inconsistent with the theory on which teaching machines are based merely indicates that the theory needs to be reexamined.

8. Contrary to other claims, most teaching-machine materials are not completely individualized. Every learner, bright or slow, regardless of his previous achievement, may be forced through the same set of steps. This can be as frustrating and wasteful as any "lock step."

9. Individualized materials of the teaching-machine type spell trouble for the teacher. Hundreds of different charts or frames may have to be kept in order in multiple sets, distributed, collected, and stored. This is the type of "housekeeping" that teachers abhor.

10. The mechanical capabilities of the machine rather than human intelligence may come to dictate the instructional program. The

type of association learning for which programs are most readily drafted may stultify the students' capacity for original and productive thinking.

11. Programs cannot be rapidly or economically modified to keep instruction up to date or adapt it to local needs.

12. Some see an additional danger in the pressure which a multi-million dollar teaching-machine industry might bring to bear on educational planners at all levels — local, state, and national.

A Point of View

Both the advantages and the limitations of machines are so apparent that compromise seems inevitable. It may be human vanity, but we think the teacher will continue to determine how a subject will be presented and what devices and materials will be used, resisting any unwarranted encroachment by either machines or the manufacturers of machines. Teachers will be remiss, however, if they do not use teaching machines as additional tools to help them in their work.

Several advantages in addition to those previously listed may be expected when machines are used as adjuncts to other instruction:

1. The teacher may be freed from some types of routine instruction for greater attention to those phases of learning, too often neglected at present, which require a "human" touch.

2. Classwork will be more efficient since the prior completion of related factual or skill programs can be required. There will be no need to waste class time correcting errors gained in unguided study.

3. A store of flexible programs for machine "tutors" can be the backbone of remedial programs for those who have inadequately mastered basic knowledge or skills.

PHONICS AND THE TEACHING OF READING

Here is an issue that is mentioned only because no controversy of recent years has sparked more strongly stated opinions. Ironically, the real issue probably has nothing to do with either reading or phonics. Phonics simply provides a handy point of attack for those who believe the schools are neglecting the traditional subjects. Rudolph Flesch provided ammunition when he told his readers that "learning to read means learning to sound out words."[19] This concept is erroneous, of course. Sounds without meaning are truly empty — no more than nonsense syllables. Sounding out words is only one method of recognizing words, and one that helps very little in understanding what they mean.

Flesch and other critics of current reading instruction condemn what they call the "look and say" method of teaching. This is a reference to the practice of teaching readers to recognize on sight some words that have meaning for them without excessive attention to word mechanics or pronunciation. This is only one technique of a whole assortment used by the modern teacher. Phonics, far from having been forgotten, is another technique used by almost all — though never exclusively. Here is a controversy which most teachers can well afford to ignore, since they have probably been teaching both phonics and sight reading for years. It would be a mistake to limit the reading teacher to one tool — no matter how effective. She has a tough job and needs as many tools as there are.

Those who have joined the argument recently are not really for or against phonics but merely for or against Flesch, his allegations, and his prescriptions.

If you think reading instruction needs the Flesch "cure," you say:	If you think that current methods are sound, you say:
1. Large numbers of students are not learning to read adequately.	1. Students are learning to read better than ever before.
2. Reading is easy if you can sound out the letters.	2. Reading is getting meaning from the printed page, not merely sounds.
3. Schools do not teach phonics, just word-guessing.	3. Practically all schools teach phonics; all basic readers include it.
4. Colleges have started remedial programs because students are no longer taught to read.	4. All objective measures of students "then and now" show present college students superior.
5. Flesch's methods teach students to read words, not just memorize them.	5. Flesch's drills may produce "word callers" and "word by word" readers.
6. Flesch has made an important contribution to the betterment of teaching methods.	6. Flesch overemphasizes one of many techniques now used by teachers; he neglects others of proven value.
7. College and university teachers of English support Flesch.	7. Flesch ignores the testimony of linguists and psychologists.
8. Flesch has documented his claims.	8. Flesch uses histrionics, not facts.

[19] Rudolph Flesch, *Why Johnny Can't Read and What to Do About It* (New York: Harper & Bros., 1954).

Nila B. Smith has prepared a summary of research answers to several questions about the teaching of phonics:[20]

1. Are schools teaching phonics? One study indicates that 98% of elementary school teachers do.
2. Should we teach phonics? Most research indicates that phonics instruction is effective.
3. When should we teach phonics? Formal phonics instruction is of great value after the beginning of Grade II, of less value earlier.
4. How should phonics be taught? The better methods are closely tied to and applied in the child's daily reading. Emphasize only those rules which have few exceptions.

CONTINUOUS PROMOTION VERSUS RETENTION

What should be the school's policy with respect to grade-to-grade promotions? The hottest argument has been between those who would retain children who fall behind in the work of a grade and those who believe it better for the child's total development if he is promoted continuously with his age-mates. The arguments are as follows:

Arguments for Retention

1. A graded-school organization has no meaning without standards which must be met for placement at each level.
2. Retention makes for classes that are more homogeneous, prevents extremes of achievement level in a single grade.
3. Children will not try to do their best if they know promotion will be automatic.
4. Children who cannot do the work of the higher grade become disciplinary problems.
5. Nonpromoted children have less anxiety about continued progress and home security (a research finding).
6. Repetition of a grade leads to greater mastery of the work of that grade (a research finding).

Arguments for 100% Promotion

1. Standards are highest in schools with high promotion rates (a research finding).
2. Whether homogeneous classes are desirable or not, retention does not significantly reduce the range of abilities with which the teacher has to cope.
3. Praise and success, not threats and failure, are the most effective incentives.
4. Retention leads to large numbers of overage and retarded problem children and more dropouts.
5. Children promoted with their age group make better social adjustments.
6. In later grades repeaters achieve no better than children of like ability who were promoted continuously (a research finding).

[20] Nila B. Smith, "What Research Says About Phonics Instruction," *Journal of Educational Research*, Vol. 51 (September, 1957), pp. 1–9.

7. When underachievers are promoted, gaps of information and skill may lead to more serious failures later.	7. If teachers work with individual students at their ability and achievement level, gaps in information and skill can be corrected at any grade level.

Arguments settle few questions. Objective summaries of research and theory lead to the conclusion that, while completely automatic promotion is not wise, both factual evidence and informed opinion favor promotion over retention as a general policy.[21] Well over half of a group of superintendents, chosen for the excellence of their elementary schools, favored continuous promotion except in "highly unusual circumstances."[22] A temperate and cautious use of retardation is suggested which considers:

1. Each child as an individual problem with his optimum total development the goal;

2. A wide variety of factual information about each child; measures of intelligence and achievement only are not sufficient.

3. The needs of the child rather than administrative expediency.

ESSAY VERSUS OBJECTIVE EXAMINATIONS

The argument over the use of essay or objective examinations in schools tends to be an issue separating measurement "experts" and classroom teachers. Despite repeated attacks by those who study measurement as a science, the essay continues to be widely used and hotly defended. What may be said of each type?

Objective Tests

True-false, multiple-choice, and matching items, which can be answered by choosing one of several options, and completion or "fill-in" items, which require the examinee to supply only a single word or phrase, are called "objective." As applied to these test types, and several others, the term means only that the answer has been determined in advance, usually when the test was written. Thus scoring is not subject to the judgment of the person who

---

[21] John J. Goodlad, "Research and Theory Regarding Promotion and Non-Promotion," *Elementary School Journal*, Vol. 53 (November, 1952), pp. 150–156.

[22] Harold G. Shane and James Polychones, "Elementary Education, Organization and Administration," *Encyclopedia of Educational Research*, 3 ed., Chester W. Harris (ed.) (New York: The Macmillan Co., 1960), p. 427 f.

corrects the test. As a matter of fact, a strictly impersonal machine can sometimes do it. Of course, someone's judgment does determine what topics will be covered, what abilities will be tapped, and which of many possible items will be used to measure a particular ability.

The interest in objective tests was stimulated by evidence that essay tests are difficult to score consistently. Examples are common. The February, 1961, issue of *ETS Developments*, a professional news bulletin published by the Educational Testing Service, tells how two judges reading the same college freshman's essay differed. One discovered many "serious errors" and gave it the lowest possible score of 1 on a scale of 9. The other described it was "well thought out," and gave it a score of 8. A host of factors contribute to such differences and to others, almost as dramatic, which are found when the same person scores the same paper at two different times. Different readers, or the same reader at different times, may give different weight to such factors as handwriting, spelling, effectiveness of expression, organization, and even the general reputation and personality of the student. Differences in scoring are often magnified by the lack of a definite scoring key. Many readers have only a vague notion of what they expect in a good answer or a poor one, and this notion is apt to change from time to time and paper to paper. The advantage of the objective test is clear. With a predetermined key every paper is scored by the same standard regardless of who does the grading or when it is done.

It is possible to overemphasize the scoring advantage of objective items. When essay items have other advantages, the consistency with which they can be scored can be much improved if several precautions are taken: (1) make the questions definite and detailed so that everyone knows what is expected; (2) when the item is written, decide just what factors will be considered in scoring; (3) prepare a tentative answer showing the number of score points which can be earned for each factor and how these points are to be assigned — a checklist or rating scale is often helpful; (4) try the tentative key with a random and anonymous group of answers and revise it if necessary; (5) if there are several questions, score all answers to one question before going on to the next; (6) keep the papers anonymous; (7) recheck papers occasionally to make sure you are being consistent; (8) when feasible, have the paper scored by several different people and average their ratings.

Although ease and consistency of scoring are the most obvious advantages of objective items, they are not the most important. The principal virtue of objective tests is that a much better sample of the students' achievement can be obtained in the testing time available. Since objective items can be answered quickly, a test for a single period can contain many items. Several or more items can be planned for each major topic studied and each major ability, such as knowledge of facts and reasoning about causes. The several items on each topic or ability can be of differing difficulty. Contrast this sampling of achievement with that provided by an essay test of three or four general items. The objective test is almost certain to be fair to all, with no student lucky enough to be asked the few questions he knew, or so unlucky that the exam covered only the two or three topics he didn't study. A major step in the improvement of essay examinations is often the use of a larger number of questions, each of which demands a relatively short answer.

Since a large number of objective-test items may be asked or answered in a relatively short time, this type of test surveys students' knowledge of terms, formulas, facts, and relationships efficiently. Objective tests are not limited to the measurement of factual recall or knowledge, however. Practically all recent textbooks and current evaluation courses for teachers describe the preparation of objective items to measure understanding, such as required to explain, illustrate, compare, and infer. Do objective tests also measure these outcomes more efficiently and adequately than essay tests? The answer probably depends on the skill of the examiner. Many teachers, as well as test publishers, prepare objective tests which are excellent measures of understanding.

It is very important but very difficult to insure that all examinees interpret a test question in the same way. Since the objective item is more completely structured than the essay items, it is more apt to present the same task to all. This is particularly true for multiple-choice items when it is understood that one is to select the best answer of those presented — not necessarily the best that exists when all things are considered.

One other probable advantage of objective tests will be given separate attention. This is the use of data from an administration of the test to improve the test for future use. Such data are more readily obtained and used with objective than with essay tests. The proportion of students missing an objective item is a clue to its difficulty. Items which are too easy or too difficult may be revised or discarded. We may also learn something of how well an item helps with the task of distinguishing students of high achievement from students of low achievement. If students are divided into high and low groups, for example, we can compare the number in the high group who miss a given item with the number in the low group who miss it. If the item is a good one, fewer students in the high group will miss it. If the number missing the item is about the same for both groups, or if low students seem to succeed more often than high ones, we will want to study the item closely to see if we can improve it. Failing this, we may drop it from consideration for use in further testing. We can develop a pool of objective items with data on how well each has worked in the past. By selecting and revising items from this pool, we can steadily improve our tests. As we add to the pool, it will be unnecessary to use the same items too frequently.

We probably can adapt the item analysis procedures used with objective tests to essay tests. We can, for example, tabulate the number of above- and below-average students who miss each part of an essay question. Even so, however, it will be harder to reuse essay-test items. The few broad questions of the essay test are more easily remembered and communicated to other students than are the specific items of an objective test.

The Essay Test

In an essay test the teacher supplies the questions and the students compose the answers in their own words. A rather free and extended response is required, and two or three questions may be the whole test. An example of an essay question is:

> State the major advantages and disadvantages of essay tests from the point of view of measurement theory and practice.

The advantages claimed for essay tests are of two types — those related to the improvement of learning and those related to the measurement of learning outcomes. There is little argument about the fact that essay tests encourage students to learn how to organize their own ideas and express them correctly. In studying, the student attends to larger wholes or segments of the subject, if he expects an essay test. He tries to synthesize information from different sources as he reviews, to see implications and applications, and to put his conclusions into his own words. He does, in short, what he expects he will have to do on the examination. We should like to think that he does this not only to earn a grade, but also because he believes the examinations emphasize the important outcomes of learning. This is all to the good. On the other hand, the student preparing for an essay test may not be as thorough in his attempts to build up a broad and comprehensive background of knowledge and abilities as the student preparing for an objective examination. The objective test will surely cover a wide range of material; the essay test will probably be limited to several major topics or abilities especially emphasized in course work. There is little to the argument of recall versus recognition, incidentally, except as the students' study habits are affected. For grading purposes, students will be ranked very much the same on recognition and recall tests.

Essay items can measure some important outcomes of instruction more adequately than objective items. The most obvious example is the student's ability to express himself in his own words. Other examples occur whenever the desired response cannot be entirely anticipated by the examiner. This is true when we attempt to measure original and productive thinking, as in organizing or reorganizing, postulating or hypothesizing, or synthesizing material from several sources in a unique way. These qualities or abilities can be evaluated in class assignments other than tests, however; and some argue that the nontest approach is better here, since originality and productivity probably cannot be turned on instantly or brought to bear on this question or that at the whim of the examiner. The test may not be an ideal situation for demonstrating writing ability either.

Generally speaking, the measurement of attitudes and personality traits is not considered part of achievement testing, but this may depend on the teacher's objectives. In answering an essay question a student may reveal his attitudes without intending to do so. The examiner or teacher may be able to draw some inferences about personality characteristics of examinees from the study of a student's responses. Any such insights or inferences must, of course, be checked. Here the evidence from the examination is used like any chance observation, not as tests usually are. The students' answers to appropriate essay questions may provide some additional opportunities to study children thoroughly.

Essay tests may offer some diagnostic opportunities that objective items do not. A student may do well on an objective test without revealing significant weaknesses in spelling, grammar, or effectiveness of expression. Moreover, the student's responses to an essay question can be analyzed to find out why he succeeded or failed. Is a low score, for example, due to erroneous, insufficient, or irrelevant facts; failure to see relationships among known facts or principles; inability to generalize; or other factors? In subjects like mathematics the student's work may help to pin-point a failure to grasp or note an essential aspect of the skill or content very precisely. The teacher's comments on the essay response may be a valuable aid to the student. It is true, of course, that if we can anticipate the errors which may occur, we can construct objective tests to do the same thing. We can, for example, construct some items to measure only knowledge or facts, others to measure only the ability to recognize relationships among facts, etc. Success in this is directly dependent upon skill in preparing objective tests, however, and so is related to the next advantage of the essay test.

Essay tests are easier to prepare. They require less time and special training and experience on the teacher's part than do objective tests. We believe these points to be true. It is clear, however, that the preparation of *good* essay questions is harder and more demanding of time and skill than is popularly supposed. To make the most of the inherent advantages of the essay test we have to make every effort to counteract its obvious weaknesses as much as possible. The general ways in which this can be done have been indicated in arguments raised in rebuttal of advantages claimed for objective items.

Summary Comparison

This brief summary of the advantages and disadvantages of each type of item should make it absolutely clear that we should be asking, "When should essay questions be used and when the objective?" The answer cannot be categorical. We should use the type which has the most advantages and fewest disadvantages for a par-

ticular purpose and situation. It is here that professional training and judgment must be exercised.

"X" MARKS THE ADVANTAGE

Factor or Characteristics	Essay	Objective
Measures knowledge efficiently.		X
Measures original and productive thinking, as in organizing and reorganizing, in hypothesizing and synthesizing *in ways not anticipated.*	X	
Reveals skill in language usage, writing, and expression.	X	
May provide insight into attitudes and personality.	X	
Sets a uniform task for examinees.		X
Samples outcomes adequately.		X
Encourages students to learn how to organize knowledge and express it effectively.	X	
Encourages students to build up a broad background of knowledge.		X
Prevents bluffing.		X
Discourages guessing.	X	
Easier and quicker to prepare.	X	
Easier and quicker to score.		X
Scored more reliably and consistently.		X
More easily improved from year to year by the analysis of test results.		X

THE REAL ISSUE IN MEASUREMENT AND EVALUATION: ADEQUACY

The basic assumption in measurement and evaluation is that judgments are wiser and decisions sounder when they are based on relevant and dependable information. But just how adequate are our instruments and procedures? What are our accomplishments and limitations with respect to such important purposes as: (1) evaluating student progress, (2) studying the effectiveness of educational programs, (3) diagnosing learning deficiencies, (4) adjustment counseling, (5) helping students and parents to plan realistically, (6) selecting students for educational opportunities, and (7) grouping students for instruction? These are the real issues we will examine in concluding the present chapter. An instructor or reader may elect to concentrate on some combination of these issues rather than all of them.

In the preceding sections of the chapter we presented the pros and cons of several rather specific issues, including some related to measurement and evaluation. Now, by using a different approach we hope to challenge the reader to find his own position with respect to such questions as:

1. Can we measure the noncognitive outcomes of education?
2. Are marks and report cards necessary?
3. Should test results be used to group students for instruction?
4. Should standardized tests be used to judge teachers?
5. Are interest and personality tests of value in counseling?
6. What do ability tests really measure?
7. Can we raise a child's IQ?
8. What is the proper role of IQ tests in selecting students for educational opportunities?
9. Can tests predict future occupational success?
10. Should we reveal scores on standardized tests to students and their parents?

Evaluating Student Progress

Measurement and evaluation are closely related processes but they are not identical. Measurement, for example, may result in scores which describe a student's performance in arithmetic, but a conclusion regarding the student's learning requires more. In order to determine the meaning of these data or draw from them a sound conclusion or plan of action, a teacher must relate them to objectives and a variety of other information about this student and others — a process which will require him to bring all his professional intelligence and experience to bear. Not the least of our achievements of recent years is a clearer understanding of the proper role of descriptive information in professional decisions.

We have (1) more knowledge and better techniques for determining what information we need to check the progress of students toward our objectives for them and (2) improved methods and instruments for collecting this information. Much credit is due Tyler,[23] who in the early 1930's focused attention on the formulation of instructional objectives and their definition in terms of observable, hence more measurable, pupil performance or behavior. In essence, each objective is studied to determine just what things

---

[23] Ralph W. Tyler, *Constructing Achievement Tests* (Columbus: Ohio State University, Bureau of Educational Research, 1934).

can be seen, heard, reported by students, or otherwise detected to indicate progress. Further steps demand, of course, the identification of situations and methods for observing and recording this evidence and interpreting it in light of the objective.

Now, many examples of the process of determining what to measure are available. The *Eight Year Study*,[24] Bloom's *Taxonomy*,[25] a guide by Gerberich,[26] the *Forty-Fifth Yearbook of the National Society for the Study of Education*,[27] and many excellent texts offer suggestions and illustrations for a wide variety of objectives and content areas.

Instruments and procedures for the collection of evidence are most adequate for the measurement of cognitive outcomes. We may be able to utilize standardized tests. These are often excellent if they have been designed to measure the outcomes related to our particular objectives. This is often not the case, but very acceptable written or performance tests can be prepared by teachers who can approximate the proven procedures used by the test publishers.

We are concerned also with what persons do typically, in contrast to what they can do when tested, and with their interests, attitudes, values, and appreciations. The opportunities of the teacher to observe typical behavior are often limited, especially since persons will not behave typically if they know they are being observed. By their nature feelings are internal; and a person's reports on his attitudes, values, and the like are not always dependable. Greater dependence must often be placed on indirect evidence. Interest, for example, may be suggested by voluntary activities. Not enough is known about how to do this for all of our objectives. Some useful and ingenious ideas are provided by the sources previously mentioned. The newer texts in the field of measurement and evaluation review these and other contributions fully.

The principles of effective reporting on student progress are known and experimentation with improved methods of reporting is spreading (Chap. XV).

Two principal limitations on further progress in evaluating stu-

---

[24] Smith, *op. cit.*
[25] Bloom, *op. cit.*
[26] J. Raymond Gerberich. *A Guide to Achievement Test Construction: Specimen Objective Item Types* (New York: Longmans, Green and Co., 1956).
[27] National Society for the Study of Education, *The Measurement of Understanding*, The Forty-Fifth Yearbook, Part I (Chicago: University of Chicago Press, 1946).

dent progress may be identified. The first limitation is a problem of communication. By and large, teachers do not know what can be done or lack the training and experience to do it properly. This underlines the need for pre- and in-service courses in evaluation. The second limitation is one of feasibility. The present demands on the teacher's time and effort make it impossible for her to develop and use the best possible methods of collecting information on her students even if she knows how to. This problem can be solved only if administrators and the communities they serve recognize the importance of evaluation and allow teachers time for it. This problem is in part also one of communication.

Studying the Effectiveness of Educational Programs

The best criterion of the effectiveness of our programs is the progress of our students. The achievements and problems considered in evaluating student progress are to be considered here also. An added difficulty in evaluating a course or other program in terms of student progress consists in isolating that part of the observed progress which should be credited to the program from the part which is due to other factors, such as student ability and previous experiences. Psychologists and others engaged in educational research know how this can be done, not perfectly but accurately enough for most purposes. Their procedures, however, pose additional problems of feasibility and the education of local personnel. Careful planning, the development of special data-collection methods, and the collection and evaluation of data over an extended interval of time may be required. As a result, pupil progress has not been widely used for the evaluation of educational programs or important aspects of those programs, such as textbooks and teachers, except in limited research studies.

The question of using standardized tests for the evaluation of teachers or programs is frequently raised. Recently, the opinions of six experts ranged from "only with extreme caution" to "definitely not."[28] As has been noted, standardized tests can provide only a part of the evidence that might be needed and, as one of the six experts, J. Raymond Gerberich, notes, "There are so many important and unmeasured — even unmeasurable — factors involved that the desired

[28] Robert L. Ebel, "Eight Critical Questions about the Use of Tests," *Education*, Vol. 81, No. 2 (October, 1960), pp. 1–32.

evaluations can be made reliably only if elaborate research procedures are substituted for testing programs."[29] Pointing to the need for "elaborate research procedures" is another way of questioning the present feasibility of evaluating programs or teachers by the criterion of student progress.

We must conclude that procedures and techniques for securing the best evidence of the effectiveness of our educational programs are not yet ready for use. In previous sections we have pointed to the availability of guides for collecting evidence of provisions and practices which are *likely* to make it possible to achieve our objectives. These guides are the result of careful and serious studies by outstanding educators. They are comprehensive and systematic. Even though they are "second best" as evidence of the effectiveness of programs, those who use them consider them of great value for self-study and improvement.

Diagnosing Learning Difficulties

Individuals or groups are often studied to identify their weaknesses and to plan preventive or remedial programs. When a learning difficulty occurs almost any characteristic of the student or of the situation may be important. Thus, a thorough study of the individual with respect to his physical, intellectual, emotional, or educational development may be required. His environment, in or out of school, may be at fault.

For help in identifying the point in learning where failure occurs, we have useful research analyzing the learning of skills into sequential steps, studies of common errors, and techniques for the study of individual performance. These are especially valuable in mathematics, spelling, reading, handwriting, and language. Little has been done of this nature in other fields. Illustrations of error studies which a teacher may use are given by Newland[30] and by commercial diagnostic tests. A number of diagnostic tests include remedial suggestions which may be effective if the difficulty is merely that of failure to grasp or note an essential aspect of the skill or content. Failures due to more deep-seated problems may challenge all our resources. A rather large number of tests provide part scores, some-

---

[29] *Ibid.*, p. 25.

[30] T. Ernest Newland, "An Analytical Study of the Development of Illegibilities in Handwriting from the Lower Grades to Adulthood," *Journal of Educational Research*, Vol. 26 (December, 1932), pp. 249–258.

times on a very few items, for which diagnostic value is claimed. The user should be skeptical of such claims. The interpretation of part scores should be tentative and used primarily as a starting point for more thorough study of individuals.

Adjustment Counseling

Research in child development and clinical experience has suggested the characteristics of children who need special help. There is a fair amount of agreement on such characteristics, although different theorists may postulate different causal conditions, such as the failure to satisfy basic needs, inadequate achievement of developmental tasks, or the unacceptable resolution of conflicts. Woodworth's pioneering research on personality assessment emphasized differences between "normal" persons and patients. The handbooks of Kough and DeHaan, described in a previous section, provide especially practical lists of characteristics for identifying: (1) general maladjustment, (2) aggressive maladjustment, (3) withdrawn maladjustment, (4) potential dropouts, (5) slow learners, (6) undermotivated students, and (7) students with a variety of handicaps.

Experienced counselors find standardized tests of ability useful in some problems of adjustment, for example, when a pupil is attempting courses of study too difficult for him. The personality, adjustment, and temperament inventories are useful in helping students study themselves, and they may help others identify students likely to profit from counseling. The limitations of these instruments as "tests" include the student's failure to (1) understand the item, (2) understand himself, and (3) give frank and honest answers. Furthermore, most inventories have been developed for the middle-class American culture and may not be entirely appropriate for other groups. Intensive study of the student's responses by psychologically trained persons may be fruitful; in the hands of most school personnel the same responses could be dangerously misleading. Thorndike and Hagen refer to a number of studies in concluding that "inventory scores have generally failed to predict anything much about the future success of the individual either in school, on the job, or in his personal living."[31] It should not be necessary to add, in view

---

[31] Robert L. Thorndike and Elizabeth Hagen, Measurement and Evaluation in Psychology and Education, 2 ed. (New York: John Wiley and Sons, Inc., 1961), p. 344.

of varying contemporary standards, that such tests cannot be used
to assess the "worth" of a person's personality.

The obvious importance of personality and adjustment in all
aspects of living calls for continued attention from psychologists
and educators. Students needing special help can often be identified
as failing to make satisfactory progress through nontest techniques.
Increasingly, school systems are employing psychologically trained
personnel to study and counsel such individuals intensively. Specialized evaluation instruments of value have been developed for use
by clinicians.

Helping Students and Parents to Plan Realistically

This purpose underlies the school's guidance program. The educational and vocational decisions which face youth are far more complex and difficult today than a generation ago. We have come to
regard the help we can give the individual in his planning as both a
moral obligation and a national necessity.

What measurements are of most worth when we wish to judge
a person's potential with respect to the requirements of a future
educational program or job or to help him make his own decisions?
To really know, we would have to make our measurements and
tentative predictions and then follow up to see if our predictions
came true. We have to start, however, with measurements of some
kind. We might begin by identifying the requirements of the educational or vocational situation for which predictions are to be made.
Binet and his followers identified intelligent tasks which they
thought would involve the abilities demanded for success in school.
Early tests of mechanical and musical aptitude sampled performance
on tasks similar to those of mechanical and musical areas. A recent
and much more sophisticated approach to "job analysis" is illustrated
by the work of Flanagan in developing the *Flanagan Aptitude
Classification Tests*. He has identified a number of elements of
ability which are apparently important in varying degrees and
combinations for success in a number of occupations.

A somewhat different approach, which is illustrated by the factor
analysis studies, attempts to identify the fundamental ways in which
individuals may differ in ability, interest, or personality. We try all
the test types available and devise new ones to tap other hypo-
thetical characteristics. Statistical analysis suggests a number of

factors which appear to differ and indicates the tests which seem the purest measures of each factor. The naming of a factor depends on logical analysis of the apparent nature of the tests which best measure it.

What measures available to the counselor have proven worth for predictive judgments? For educational counseling the test of general scholastic ability or intelligence is our best tool. Such tests have been thoroughly studied. The scores they yield have a substantial relationship to educational success at every level and in a wide variety of programs. Data are frequently available so that the counselor can show the student his chances for success in a particular college or university. Typically, for example, if his intelligence score ranks among the upper 25 per cent for high school students who go on to college, he has about 5 to 6 chances in 10 of being in the upper 25 per cent with respect to college grades. Of course, the chances are still almost 50–50 that he will get lower grades in college. There are even about 5 chances in 100 that his college grades will be among the lowest 25 per cent. If we consider present achievement, as well as intelligence test scores, we can be somewhat more accurate. Other factors are obviously important in success, and the intelligence score itself may be inaccurate for a number of reasons.

Early educational decisions are often a first step in narrowing down the range of occupations from which more specific choices will be made. At the senior high school and college levels choices must become progressively more definite because of the specialized education or training required for different vocations.

There is research evidence indicating differences in average intelligence (scholastic ability) between occupational groups for a number of professional and semi-skilled occupations. Professional groups have an average IQ of 120 or above; unskilled laborers, 100 or lower.[32] Some of these differences are undoubtedly due to academic requirements or experience and the overlap between groups is perhaps as significant as the average difference. Some laborers score as high in scholastic ability as some university professors. The relationship of general intelligence scores to success within occupations is low or negligible. Such relationships are perhaps highest for skilled workers, as judged by supervisor ratings.

---

[32] Naomi Stewart, "A.G.C.T. Scores of Army Personnel Grouped by Occupations," *Occupations*, Vol. 26 (October, 1947), pp. 5–41.

There are insufficient data to support the claimed contributions of specific aptitude tests in educational situations. Among the aptitude batteries, the *Differential Aptitude Tests* present the most predictive data. With but a few exceptions — mechanical reasoning for science subjects, numerical ability for mathematics, and spelling for shorthand — the separate tests probably do not add much to a general measure of scholastic ability. For individual students judgments based on differences in the part scores, unless supported by a variety of other data, should be quite tentative.

Perhaps the most extensive study of the predictive value of more specific aptitude measures in the world of work has been provided by Thorndike.[33] He studied the occupations and occupational success of 10,000 men thirteen years after they had been given an aptitude battery in the Air Force during World War II. For 125 occupational groupings Thorndike reports no convincing evidence of any relationship of test scores to success within an occupation. There were, however, real and marked differences between occupations in average test scores. He identified significant ways in which jobs vary in their demands for different aptitudes. Studies of the *General Aptitude Test Battery* used by the U. S. Employment Service also identify such differences for about 25 occupational groupings. Although the evidence is far from being as complete as we could wish, we may conclude that counselors may make use of both general intelligence and more specific aptitude measures in helping individuals narrow down their occupational choices. At present, however, the evidence concerning these measures does not warrant attempts to predict relative success within a particular field of work.

Early educational choices may concern subjects or areas for which special prognostic tests have been developed. We have such tests for music, art, algebra and geometry, foreign languages, and several commerical subjects or skills, such as shorthand and stenography. The authors of these tests claim better prediction of achievement in related studies than can be obtained using tests of general scholastic ability. General scholastic ability and previous achievement combined will probably give equally good results, however.

Interest measurements have been shown to have some validity for the prediction of occupational choice, and hence choice of edu-

---

[33] Robert L. Thorndike, and Elizabeth P. Hagen, *10,000 Careers* (New York: John Wiley and Sons, 1959).

cational programs among students with professional interests at the high school senior or college level. Below this level they are of most value for encouraging self-study and the exploration of various opportunities. They probably should not be used as definite cues for early curricular choices since they are subject to change with maturity and experience. The relationship of measured interests to academic achievement in corresponding areas is generally quite low.

Other factors are obviously important for educational and vocational choices. Personality judgments are often given weight, but there is little evidence of any relationship between our personality judgments and measurements and success in different educational programs. Of fourteen factors studied for their contribution to academic achievement in a Connecticut study mentioned by Gerberich,[34] indices of socioeconomic status and intelligence test scores were most highly related to academic achievement. Drive or ambition, parental support and financial resources are evidently reflected in socioeconomic measures and should be studied in considering the wisdom or feasibility of tentative choices.

Biographical information about individuals should be studied in vocational as in educational counseling, but at present no generally useful data are available to indicate the predictive value of items concerning family background and out-of-school activities. Several World War II and business programs have developed information that indicates the predictive value for a number of items of background information for particular jobs or positions. For some years life insurance companies have used a questionnaire of this type for selecting salesmen.

In review it is apparent that our knowledge and the procedures for providing youth with the information they need for decisions are far from perfect. Too often we operate as best we can by using information which *seems* *likely* to have predictive value. Progress continues, however. The follow-up phases of surveys of secondary-school students which have been completed should, in the next few years, provide evidence of the long-range predictive value of a variety of test and nontest factors. There is no doubt that full and appropriate use of even our present "guidance" resources would result in a better "batting average" — more right choices for youth than could be made without them.

---

[34] Ebel, *op. cit.*, p. 25.

A word of caution should be added at this point, however. Averages are for groups, and we must often deal with an individual who will gain small comfort from the fact that our overestimate of his success is balanced by our underestimate of another's. Our best hedge against errors in dealing with individuals is complete information. Many types and sources of information may be relevant. None should be neglected. None should be interpreted in isolation. Serious errors have resulted from neglect of these precepts — perhaps most often with one of our most valuable tools, the general ability test from which the IQ is calculated. We will use the "IQ test" as an example.

Have you wondered why schools may be reluctant to reveal a student's exact test score or IQ even to his parents? Our schools do have an obligation to tell both the student and his parents about his abilities, opportunities and progress in as useful and meaningful a way as possible. But test scores and indices, as the doctor's blood counts or metabolism rates, are not very useful or meaningful to students or parents. The teacher or counselor, as well as the physician, must explain the significance of his findings.

When untrained persons are given an isolated piece of information, such as the IQ, they are too apt to consider it separately, as a brand which finally gives the individual's merit and opportunities. Even in conferences, where explanations are possible, it is probably best to speak of ability in terms of a group classification (in the upper quarter of the class, above-average, low, etc.). Insist upon full consideration of other important assets not included in a measure of general ability. The usual ability test does not reflect even some very important aspects of intellect, such as originality and creativity; and the creative student is likely to succeed in school or life far better than would be predicted from an IQ.

Different ability tests, it should be noted, differ so widely from one another at times that the IQ's they yield should be referred to by the name of the test — that is, a Stanford-Binet IQ, an Otis IQ or a California Mental Maturity Test IQ. Tests may be administered improperly or under distracting conditions or when the student is in poor health or spirits. Clerical errors may occur in scoring. Even under the best of conditions changes of from 1 to 10 points in IQ can be expected when a student is retested. For all of these reasons it is very important that test results be re-checked and verified.

We now know also that some apparently low IQ's, verified by several tests, can be raised. A student's test IQ will change if he changes with respect to the following:

1. Verbal ability, which penalizes those with a language handicap.

2. Reading comprehension, which can be increased with training.

3. Ability and willingness to follow directions, which changes with practice and motivation.

4. Test "wiseness," which comes from experience in taking tests.

5. Memory, which may be organized or disorganized.

6. Ability to concentrate under test conditions, partly a matter of practice.

7. Cultural background, which may be rich or poor in ideas and breadth of experience.

Selecting Students for Educational Opportunities

Tests and other data are being used increasingly in selecting students for college preparatory programs, colleges, and professional schools and scholarships. A selection program is based on the knowledge that there are more people than places to be filled, and that it is possible to identify those who are most likely to profit from the opportunity.

The problems here are similar to those of helping individuals plan. To be sure, in selecting we are often quite insistent that he not choose our program, but ideally we are still concerned with the wisdom of the choice for the individual. The information and procedures used in selection are also similar to those used by the counselor and the reader may wish to review that section at this time. Greatest dependence is placed upon measures of general scholastic ability and previous achievement for, as we indicate elsewhere, these measures are known to have the greatest predictive value for educational or training programs.

Self report inventories of personality and interest are not appropriate for selection purposes. They are too "fake-able." There is little evidence to support the use of your reaction to a person's personality in this context, and biographical inventories have not been studied sufficiently to determine their worth. Where scholarship money is involved, of course, officials are justified in considering the applicant's financial need. Reference should be made to the preceding section for an estimate of how successful our predictions of academic success are likely to be with the use of general scholastic and achievement measures. Again bear in mind that we could not do nearly so well without such measures. Tests of specific aptitude may add slightly to the information provided by general scholastic ability tests for a few fields. The batteries developed by professional schools for engineering, law, medicine, nursing, accounting and others are, with but minor variations, tests of reading ability, general scholastic aptitude and achievement. The variations are designed to fit the field. For example, engineering tests emphasize quantitative materials. There is a chalk-carving test for dentistry.

Grouping Students for Instruction

There is evidence that academic learning can proceed more efficiently when students of relatively uniform scholastic ability or achievement can be grouped together for instruction. The intent of such plans is to reduce the range of individual differences for which a teacher or program need provide. They should be more able to provide adequately for a group that is uniformly bright, for example, than they can for a group that includes individuals of all degrees of brightness or dullness.

Grouping has been attempted by classes, subjects, or entire schools. At the elementary level students are most often grouped for reading within each classroom. The arguments against this grouping have centered about their failure to reduce materially individual differences and their social desirability. There has been less opposition at the secondary level than at the elementary. It is recognized that general ability grouping is not so effective as grouping according to talent or achievement in each different area. Evidence for socially undesirable side effects has not been convincing. Today, the precautions which should be observed in the use of groups are generally well-known and grouping in one form or another is definitely on the increase.

Since grouping for instruction, like guidance in educational choices or selection for educational opportunities, depends upon a judgment as to probable future success or rate of learning, similar evidence and procedures are used. Typically, general scholastic ability, previous achievement and teacher opinion are considered. Those selected for a particular group usually must meet some standard with respect to at least one or two of these measures. Provisions for regrouping help to counteract the effects of initially erroneous judgments.

For grouping, as for selection and guidance, there is no great amount of evidence that special prognostic tests for music, art, foreign language, mathematics, or commercial studies result in better judgments of future success in related course work than the combination of general scholastic ability and achievement measures. A school might well use such special tests if their value can be checked by follow-up studies of the students in a particular school situation.

Effective tests to aid us in one early grouping or selection situation, that of reading readiness, have proved effective. The available tests vary in the extent to which they resemble general intelligence tests and, therefore, in the extent to which they provide information to supplement that provided by such tests. Readiness tests based on tasks which resemble those faced by the beginning reader — such as perceiving and matching words, selecting rhyming words and completing stories — have proved most useful.

Summary

Actually, few informed persons have extreme views on the issues of educational psychology. They know that both discovery and exposition have their place, for example. They realize that transfer has its general aspects, but can't be confident of general transfer from one field of endeavor to another and realize the need for giving proper attention to specifics. It is no secret that teaching machines, phonics, and both essay and objective tests are useful but not omnipotent. Decisions with respect to promotion are being kept flexible and responsive to the needs of students. Measurement and evaluation techniques give information needed for decisions, but they offer no substitute for wisdom.

The extremists are a vocal minority who mark the road and help to keep the schools on a generally healthy middle course with respect to each issue. The middle of the road is not always safe and smooth, however. Evidence from psychology and research can mark the path more clearly, telling us of conditions which make it desirable to veer for a time toward one side or the other. This, we are beginning to realize, is a far more constructive goal than trying to prove one side or the other utterly impassable.

SELECTED READINGS

Alexander, W. M., Teel, Dwight and Eugenia and others, "Special Journal Feature — Reporting," *NEA Journal*, Vol. 48, No. 9 (November, 1959), pp. 15–29.
    The experiences of selected schools with parent-teacher conferences, abolishing grades, and improving grading and reporting procedures are reported.

Anderson, G. Lester, "Theories of Behavior and Some Curriculum Issues," *Journal of Educational Psychology*, Vol. 39 (March, 1948), pp. 133–140.
    An interpretation of different psychological views of behavior which shows how each leads to different educational implications.

Andrews, Thomas G. and Cronbach, Lee J., "Transfer of Training," in Monroe, Walter S. (ed.), *Encyclopedia of Educational Research* (New York: Macmillan Co., 1950), pp. 1483–89.
    Selective survey of research including a discussion of topics that can be improved through transfer and the procedures that will produce the greatest amount of transfer.

Ausubel, D. P., "Learning by Discovery: Rationale and Mystique," *Bulletin, National Association of Secondary School Principals*, Vol. 45 (December, 1961), pp. 18–58.
    A complete, readable and objective review of the historical antecedents and rationale and the claims, both warranted and unwarranted, for discovery in learning.

Bruner, Jerome S., "The Act of Discovery," *Harvard Educational Review*, Vol. 31 (Winter, 1961), pp. 21–32.
    The author presents a case for discovery in learning based on hypothesized benefits in information gathering and processing, motivation, problem-solving abilities and the improvement of memory.

Bruner, Jerome S., *The Process of Education* (Cambridge, Mass.: Harvard University Press, 1960).
    Report of a conference of scientists, scholars and educators on the improvement of science education. Develops four themes: (1) the role of structure in learning, (2) readiness for learning, (3) the use of intuition, and (4) the desire to learn. The understanding of structure is seen as a major factor in transfer of training and the method of discovery is given a prominent role in such learning. See especially Chap. 2.

Coffield, W. H., and Blommers, P., "Effects of Non-promotion on Educational Achievement in the Elementary School," *Journal of Educational Psychology*, Vol. 47 (April, 1956), pp. 235–250.
    An analysis of the problems and issues of automatic promotion and an experimental study of the effectiveness of nonpromotion at the elementary level.

Doll, Edgar A., "The Four IQ's," *International Journal for Exceptional Children* (October, 1957), pp. 56–57, 66. Reprinted in Crow, Lester D., and Crow, Alice, *Readings in Human Learning* (David McKay Co., 1963), pp. 267–270.

The author urges recognition of four I.Q.'s to counteract a tendency to place too much faith on the first. These are: (1) *intelligence quotient,* (2) the *inner quest* of aspirations and values, (3) the *ideal qualities* or personality traits and (4) the *innate quirks* in ourselves or our environment.

Ebel, Robert L., "Eight Critical Questions about the Use of Tests," *Education,* Vol. 81, No. 2 (October, 1960), pp. 1–32.
Six specialists give their answers to questions parents and teachers ask about tests and their use.

Goodlad, J. I., "Research and Theory Regarding Promotion and Non-promotion," *Elementary School Journal,* Vol. 53 (November, 1952), pp. 150–156.
Survey of research and thinking on the controversial question of the effects of nonpromotion which concludes that universal promotion is not justified but that the evidence favors promotion over nonpromotion.

Hendrix, Gertrude, "Learning by Discovery" *Mathematics Teacher,* Vol. 54 (May, 1961), pp. 290–299.
An analysis of some methods of teaching by a proponent of discovery in an attempt to clarify the meaning of discovery in learning.

Humphreys, L. G., "Transfer of Training in General Education," *The Journal of General Education,* Vol. 5 (April, 1951), pp. 210–216.
An interpretation of the literature on transfer of training with a focus on general (nonspecialized) education.

Kelly, W. A., *Educational Psychology,* 4 ed. (Milwaukee, Wis.: Bruce Publishing Co., 1956), Chap. XIX.
The author distinguishes between the historical scholastic meaning of formal discipline and faculty psychology and points out the implications for theories of transfer of differing views of the nature of man and of learning.

Kolesnik, Walter B., *Mental Discipline in Modern Education* (Madison, Wis.: Univ. of Wisconsin Press, 1958).
A review of philosophical and psychological material on the transfer of training controversy and an analysis of experimental problems.

Loomis, Mary J., Wilhelms, F. T. and others, "Special Journal Feature — Grouping," *NEA Journal,* Vol. 48, No. 6 (September, 1959), pp. 17–28.
A close look at types of grouping for instruction and some problems and principles at the elementary, junior high and senior high school levels with the general conclusion that the teacher makes the difference.

Lumsdaine, Arthur A., and Glaser, Robert (eds.), *Teaching Machines and Programmed Learning, A Source Book* (Washington, D. C.: Department of Audio-Visual Instruction, N.E.A., 1960).
A comprehensive reference source of reprinted material on teaching machines and related techniques of instruction. The articles particularly relevant to the present discussion are, "Some Perspectives and Major Problems Regarding Teaching Machines" by Sidney L. Pressey (pp. 497–505), and "Some Issues Concerning Devices and Programs for Automated Learning" by Lumsdaine (pp. 517–539).

Monroe, Walter S., *Teaching-Learning Theory and Teacher Education, 1890 to 1950* (Urbana, Ill.: Univ. of Illinois Press, 1952), Chap. IV.
After a summary comparison of teaching-learning theory in 1850 to 1950, the author clarifies current agreements and disagreements on such matters

as child nature, individual differences, learning outcomes, maturation, goals of pupil activity, organization of learning activites and teaching devices.

Morgan, H. Gerthon, Traxler, A. E., and others, "Special Journal Feature — Testing and Evaluation," NEA Journal, Vol. 48, No. 8 (November, 1959), pp. 15–30.

> Specialists consider the question, "Has Testing Gone Too Far?" and describe how standardized tests are used and misused, interpreting test results to parents and the community, text anxiety in students and the pros and cons of a nationwide testing program.

Morris, William, and Betts, Emmett A., "Teaching Johnny to Read," Saturday Review (July 30, 1955). Reprinted in Scott, C. Winfield, Hill, C. M., and Burns, H. W. (eds.), The Great Debate, Our Schools in Crisis (New York: Prentice-Hall, 1959), pp. 44–50.

> A summary of Rudolph Flesch's controversial book Why Johnny Can't Read, and two opposing views of it.

Nordberg, Robert B., "What Teaching Machines Can and Cannot Do," The Catholic Educational Review, Vol. 59 (September, 1961), pp. 361–367.

> An examination of what teaching machines can and cannot do, what opportunities and dangers they pose, and what should be done about them.

Sims, Verner M., "Questioning Some Assumptions Underlying Current Achievement Testing, Educational and Psychological Measurement, Vol. 8, No. 4 (1948), pp. 565–574.

> The author feels that at least five assumptions implicit in measurement are unfortunate and indicates the educational consequences.

Smith, Nila B., "What Research Says about Phonics Instruction," Journal of Educational Research, Vol. 51 (September, 1957), pp. 1–9.

> An objective summary of research with respect to four questions about phonics: (1) Are schools teaching phonics? (2) Should we teach phonics? (3) When should we teach phonics? (4) How should phonics be taught?

Thorndike, Robert L., and Hagen, Elizabeth, Measurement and Evaluation in Psychology and Education, 2 ed. (New York: John Wiley & Sons, 1961).

> Comprehensive and authoritative measurement text including clear and cogent presentation of evidence on (1) the advantages and limitations of essay tests (pp. 41–50), (2) marking and reporting systems (chap. 17), (3) the uses of tests detailed descriptions of the characteristics and interpretation of measures of intelligence, special aptitudes, achievement, interests and other personality characteristics (chaps. 9–15).

Thurstone, Thelma Gwinn, Gerberich, J. Raymond, and others, "Special Journal Feature: Your Child's Intelligence," NEA Journal, Vol. 50, No. 1 (January, 1961), pp. 34–48.

> A briefing for parents and others by several authorities on the fundamental questions of: What is intelligence? How is it tested? Is it the same as talent? Should parents be told their child's I.Q.? How are test results used?

Trow, William C., "The Problem of Transfer — Then and Now," Phi Delta Kappan, Vol. 40 (November, 1958), pp. 68–71.

> Shows that the critics of modern education often have outmoded concepts of learning and transfer.

THE TEACHING PROFESSION

Part IV

THE TEACHING PROFESSION

Chapter XVII

TEACHING AS A CAREER

At some time or other in life every person must be a teacher. The future parent will have the primary responsibility for the preschool education of his children. The foreman, office manager, even clerical workers will have the responsibility for training the people under their supervision. Farmers and craftsmen will be the "educators" of the apprentices or beginners in their respective fields. If you go out for an evening of card playing and some member of the party does not know the game, you immediately become a teacher.

However, our concern in this chapter is with the person who will devote his life to teaching in formally organized educational institutions.

TEACHING — A PROFESSION

The 2,125,000 people working in education like to look upon themselves as the members of a profession. Whether teachers and other educational personnel constitute a profession in the same sense that medical doctors, lawyers, and clergymen do is a moot question. In order to determine whether teachers can claim for themselves the prerogatives of a professional status, the following criteria of professionalism proposed by the TEPS commission might be of help.

The professional person

Is a liberally educated person.
Possesses a body of specialized skills and knowledge related to and essential for the performance of his function.
Is able to make rational judgments and to take appropriate action within the scope of his activities, and is responsible for the consequences of his judgments and action.
Places primary emphasis upon his service to society rather than upon his personal gain.

Actively participates with his colleagues in developing and enforcing standards fundamental to continuous improvement of his profession and abides by those standards in his own practice.

Practices his profession on a full-time basis.

Is engaged in a continuing search for new knowledge and skill.[1]

In the United States of one hundred years ago, teaching would not have been able to meet any of these rigorous criteria. But today all of the requirements have become at least the goal of "professional-minded" teachers. To illustrate, there are organizations for teachers such as the National Education Association, even though no one organization speaks for all teachers. There is a "code of ethics" generally accepted and followed by administrators and teachers (N.E.A. Code of Ethics). The selection and professional training of teachers is vested in the hands of teacher-education institutions recognized by the various states in the Union, by regional accrediting agencies, or by the National Council for the Accreditation of Teacher Education. All of the institutions and accrediting groups insist that the teacher be a liberally educated person. All public school teachers are granted licenses or permits to teach by the states in which they work only upon meeting the requirements of those states. At present, the requirements may vary somewhat from state to state, but there is a common core of professional preparation for all teachers. Most people who prepare for teaching plan on careers in teaching, although a relatively large number leave the field for various reasons, such as marriage or better-paying jobs. Certainly, teaching renders a service to society, both idealistically and realistically.

There are several organizations devoted primarily to raising professional standards in education. In 1946, the National Education Association instituted the National Commission on Teacher Education and Professional Standards (NCTEPS). The purpose of this commission is to develop a program for the teaching profession in the areas of selection and recruitment of teachers, preparation and certification of teachers, in-service growth, raising standards within the profession and within the teacher-education institutions. As the members of the commission worked, they decided to organize their activities around five basic areas: (1) advancement of professional

[1] Margaret Lindsey (ed.), *New Horizons in Teacher Education* (Washington, D. C.: National Commission on Teacher Education and Professional Standards, N.E.A., 1961), p. 6.

standards (in general); (2) preservice and in-service education; (3) accreditation of teacher-education institutions; (4) certification of teachers; (5) identification, selection, and retention of all professional personnel in education.

In 1959, the group was prepared to launch a project of national scope to improve the teaching profession. The purpose of the project is:

> To develop definitive statements in the areas of responsibility assigned to NCTEPS that would serve as guides for action programs at the local, state, and national levels by TEPS and other professional organizations and individuals toward the complete professionalization of teaching.[2]

In 1960, seven regional conferences were held, each of which submitted recommendations in the five basic areas mentioned above. These recommendations were distributed widely in pamphlet form and were critically analyzed and discussed throughout the teaching profession. A year later NCTEPS published *New Horizons for the Teaching Profession*, presenting recommendations for raising standards, giving the rationale for these recommendations and proposing programs for the complete professionalization of teachers. This report covers the: (1) present status of the teaching profession, (2) responsibility of the profession in this decade, (3) preparation of professional personnel, (4) accreditation of professional education programs in colleges and universities, (5) licensing of professional personnel, (6) identification, selective admission, and retention of professional personnel, (7) advancement of standards, and (8) plans for the profession in the decades ahead. This organization and its state and local affiliates are now exerting all their efforts to bring about the recommended changes in the area of professional standards.

A movement within the independent schools (committed to raising the standards for Catholic parochial school personnel) is the Sister Formation Conference of the National Catholic Educational Association. This organization launched a four-phase program for the improvement of the professional training of Sister teachers. The first phase investigated both the strengths and weaknesses in content and methods of teacher-training programs among the various communities of Sisters and the areas in which a need for change and

---

[2] *Ibid.*, pp. viii–ix.

improvement was felt. The second phase consisted in a "curriculum construction project," in which the members of the various congregations, with the assistance of consultants, actually drew up an "ideal curriculum" (at the bachelor's degree level) for Sister teachers. This phase was completed at the Everett (Washington) Curriculum Workshop from June 1 to August 30, 1956. The third phase consisted in the establishment of two demonstration centers where the recommended curriculum was put into practice. The final phase of the project brought the results of the entire study to the superiors of the congregations of teaching Sisters in the United States through the Regional Sister Formation Conferences.

In general, the Sister Formation movement demands that all Sister teachers possess: (1) the bachelor's degree; (2) and a sound general educational background in the fields of theology, philosophy, English, speech, classical and modern languages, the fine arts, social sciences, natural sciences, mathematics, and psychology. In addition every Sister teacher should work in the psychological, historical, sociological, and philosophical foundations of education and in an integrated program of curriculum and directed teaching (including work in elementary and secondary methods).

Besides those organizations which have the raising of standards as their primary goal, all teachers' organizations consider such activity as one of their major functions. For example, the American Federation of Teachers, an affiliate of the A.F.L.-C.I.O., lists the "raising of standards of the teaching profession as one of its major objectives.[3]

All in all, the above summary tends to indicate that teaching is eligible for professional status even if it has not already achieved such status. Perhaps the weakest link in the whole chain in the "professionalization" of teaching is the organization of the practitioners. On this particular aspect, teaching differs somewhat from medicine. One of the "issues" in the next chapter will treat this problem in more detail.

QUALIFICATIONS FOR TEACHING

Indirectly, the criteria listed above imply some screening or selection of candidates for the profession. A basic list of minimum qualifi-

[3] See below, "Issues in Professional Education. The Teachers' Union vs. the Professional Organization," p. 462 ff.

cations might help the student to determine whether or not he possesses the necessary qualifications for teaching. It seems that the most important qualification for the future teacher is superior intelligence. How can a teacher stimulate young minds if he himself is not capable of dealing with or interested in the world of ideas? It is extremely difficult to state this quality in terms of intelligence quotients because of their relative nature. Perhaps a negative approach will be more helpful. Thus, if one were not able to cope with the academic subjects in high school or the first few college semesters or found them boring or unchallenging, either his intellectual abilities are limited or his interests lie in fields other than teaching. In the past, a significant number of such people have gained entrance to the teaching field, and no doubt everyone has been subjected to their lack of intelligence and enthusiasm; they constitute the "dead wood" of the profession. Certainly, one would not want to join their ranks. A person simply cannot be a good teacher if he does not have the ability or interest necessary to master the subjects he will teach. *One cannot teach what he does not know.*

The second qualification might be measured in terms of one's interest in, and ability to get along with, children or adolescents. If a person simply "can't stand those little monsters," he does not belong in teaching. Perhaps an individual will not discover this weakness until he does his student teaching because of limited opportunity to work with children or adolescents prior to that time. It is suggested, therefore, that the future teacher seek opportunities to work with children and youth in summer camps, scout work, etc., as early in his college career as possible. Such experiences will not only help him decide whether he wishes to spend his life working with youngsters but will afford excellent preparation for courses in educational psychology, methodology, and student teaching.

The third qualification demanded of teachers is good physical and mental health. Because teaching usually does not involve a great amount of physical labor, is does not follow that less physical energy is required. As most teachers who have worked at manual jobs during the summer will verify, it takes more energy to keep up with a day's teaching duties than it does to perform the typical factory job. In addition, certain types of physical defects such as incorrigible speech impediments might render a person incapable of obtaining a teaching position because of the very nature of the impediment. Certain other types of physical handicaps, such as lameness, are not considered deterrents to teaching effectiveness.

Just as important as good physical health is sound mental health. Emotional stability viewed in terms of patience, kindness, good humor, and mastery of one's temper will make teaching relatively pleasant. Without these qualities, the youngsters will drive the teacher to despair. No doubt you have heard adolescents boasting how "they drove the teacher out of the room in tears." The pupils have ways of finding the teacher's emotional weaknesses and making the best of them for their own merriment. College courses can help a person learn "what to teach and how to teach it"; they can give him an understanding of children and help him develop a sound philosophy of conduct and life; but course work cannot change a person's emotional makeup or temperament. The National Commission on Teacher Education and Professional Standards suggests approximately the same qualifications: emotional maturity, the ability to communicate, mastery of basic skills, moral and ethical fitness, academic aptitude (intelligence), academic achievement, ability to work with others, understanding the teacher's role in a democratic society, and, finally, health.[4]

This short list of qualifications for teaching indicates that every candidate for the teaching profession must be screened carefully by the teacher-education institutions. It is a crime against the youth of our country to admit to the profession those who lack intelligence, those who do not know their subject-matter fields, or those who are emotionally unsuited for the teaching profession. Intelligent parents would not think, for a moment, to put their sick child in the hands of an incompetent surgeon. Why, then, should they be asked to place the education of their children in the hands of incompetent teachers? The candidate for teaching should also analyze his own potentialities and weaknesses to determine his fitness for the profession. Such self-analysis might save him the discouragement and frustration that results from failure.

Screening and selection for teaching, then, is the responsibility of the teacher-education institutions, the teachers in the field, the state departments of education, the students themselves, and the public they will serve.

---

[4] *Ibid.*, pp. 188–192.

Fig. 13.   The Teacher Shortage — 1962

Teachers needed, Sept., 1961

1. To replace teachers leaving   125,000
2. To serve increasing enrollment   35,000
3. To relieve overcrowding to eliminate part-time
   sessions   30,000
4. To give instruction and services not now provided 25,000
5. To replace the unprepared   25,000
                                            _____
            Total needed   240,000

College graduates of 1962 likely to enter teaching
   (approximately 74½ percent of the new supply)   .   106,000
                                            _____
            Net shortage   134,000

An overall shortage of teachers is likely to continue for some years although the actual figures change. In 1961–1962 an estimated 97,000 teachers held only emergency certificates which makes the above estimate of unprepared teachers seem conservative. For some time the most acute shortages have been in elementary schools. Moreover, these figures do not include the heavy demand that independent schools will make on teacher-education institutions.

(Estimates from National Education Association, *Teacher Supply and Demand in Public Schools, 1962*, Research Report 1962-R8 [Washington, D. C.: N.E.A., 1962], p. 21.)

OPPORTUNITIES IN EDUCATION

The cost of preparing oneself for teaching is the equivalent of the cost of a college education. In general, there are no fees over and above tuition, as are assessed in other professional programs such as medicine or dentistry, and living expenses. If a person attends a state-supported school in his home town, tuition may run as low as $500 for the entire four years of college. If he attends one of the more "exclusive" private colleges $5,000 may be needed for tuition alone.

Once a candidate has completed his approved teacher-education course in college he becomes eligible for a teacher's license. In general, baccalaureate degree programs prepare teachers for kindergarten, elementary, and secondary school teaching (a few states require the master's degree for secondary school teachers). At present, the greatest shortage is in the lower grades and this situation exists throughout the nation. Such is not true of all secondary fields. For example, in some parts of the country there is a sizable surplus of social-studies and men's physical-education teachers. On the other hand, there is a great demand, nationwide, for mathematics and physics teachers, although there may be a small surplus in these two fields in some areas of the country. But in spite of the regional imbalance in suppy and demand, the overall picture for job placement in teaching is excellent, since at least one half million teachers will have to be added in the next decade to the profession to keep up with increased enrollments and the retirement and death of teachers presently in the field. The enrollment figures in Chapter II are a good indication of the great demand for teachers. Figure 13 presents an estimate of the teacher shortage in one recent year. Under any circumstances it is wise to consult the teacher-placement office of your college to get the latest information on the supply and demand picture.

Most of the other positions in education require work beyond the bachelor's degree. College teachers, for example, must have at least a master's degree in the field in which they will teach; most large universities require the doctor's degree. School administration, guidance and counseling, remedial reading, psychometry, supervision, and hosts of other specialties usually require at least one year of work beyond the bachelor's degree. Acceptance for most of these positions usually is dependent upon several years of successful teaching in elementary or secondary schools or in colleges.

In addition to positions in schools there are opportunities for teachers in government, industry, publishing houses, and the like. The fact that such a large number of teachers leave the classroom for other jobs seems to indicate that preparation for teaching is one of the best forms of general education a person can acquire. At any rate, if after several years of teaching you become convinced that "it's just not for you," there will be many job opportunities outside the field.

SALARIES AND BENEFITS

Much has been said in recent years about low salaries for teachers. As with all other general statements, this one is correct "in general," but there are many exceptions. To illustrate, beginning salaries for women with the four-year college degree are higher in teaching than in most other fields. Furthermore, there are greater opportunities for advancement in pay for women in teaching than there are for women in industry and business. The number of college women holding responsible and high-paying jobs in business and industry is relatively small. But in teaching they progress on the salary schedule at the same rate as men. Teacher's salary schedules do not discriminate against women.

Men, however, do not compare as favorably as women to their counterparts in business and industry, even though beginning salaries in teaching may compare favorably with those paid by business and industry. The discrepancy is evident after ten to fifteen years of experience have been acquired. Then the average salaries for male college graduates working in fields other than teaching are significantly higher. Certainly, this is one of the problems the teaching profession must solve if it is to attract more men to the field.

It is extremely difficult to give an accurate salary range because of the rapid changes effected every year in the local salary schedules. Beginning salaries in elementary and secondary schools, however, seldom fall below $4,000 (ten-month basis) and seldom over $6,000 for the holder of the bachelor's degree with no teaching experience. Top salaries range from $6,000 to $12,000 for teachers with three years of work beyond the bachelor's degree (doctor's degree or the equivalent) and many years of teaching experience. Salaries in college teaching in some parts of the country and certain types of institutions are approximately the same as in secondary schools. In professional schools such as medicine, they are, of course, much higher. But again, the absolute amount paid does not necessarily give the true picture. For example, $5,000 might provide a good living in a small town where rent is only $30 a month or where a home can be purchased for $6,500, whereas the same salary would involve real hardship in a large city where rental on an apartment is $200 a month or the purchase price of a small home is $22,000. Consequently, when a prospective teacher considers the problem of salaries, he should look at the "whole picture," not merely the dollars and cents figures given on salary schedules.

In addition to beginning teachers' salaries comparing favorably with those in other areas, such benefits as tenure and job security, retirement plans, and sick leave are usually a part of every contract. After a trial period of two to five years a teacher is usually granted tenure in the school system.[5] Once a teacher has tenure he cannot be dismissed unless very serious charges are proved against him

---

[5] In 1961 thirty-seven states had tenure laws. In those without tenure laws, such legislation measures are being taken to have such laws enacted.

(incompetence or malfeasance). Besides this legal tenure the teacher enjoys special job security because the "ups and downs" of the business economy have little effect on schools. Similarly, retirement benefits for teachers, and all states have them,[6] are very secure, even though they are not the highest in the professions. Social-security benefits are often added to local and state retirement plans, giving them the added assurance of raises in social-security payments due to rises in the cost of living or inflation. Sick-leave benefits, too, are augmented by the mutual assistance rendered among teachers and administrators. Even after a teacher has used all the sick-leave time to which he is entitled, the principal and other teachers may take over for him so that a substitute will not have to be hired for the day.

To leave monetary concerns aside for the moment, the future teacher must give serious consideration to the less tangible advantages and disadvantages of teaching. If one likes to work with people (especially young people) rather than things or machines, there is no more psychologically rewarding profession than teaching. Since the classes change every year, there is no danger of becoming bored because you are working with the same people all the time. Even if one teaches the same subject year after year, each class of students is different enough to require a different treatment of the subject matter. Transfers within the same school system or to other systems are frequent among teachers, for they are a highly mobile group. If "variety is the spice of life," teaching really has spice.

Long summer vacations, also, add to the teachers' opportunities to broaden his intellectual and vocational horizons by travel, study, or work in fields other than teaching. Many teachers who spend the entire three months of summer working at other jobs feel that the very change constitutes a vacation which leaves them mentally refreshed and eager to return to the classroom and its intellectual challenges. Then, too, actuarial figures are very favorable for the teaching profession.

Finally, there is the appeal of what might be called "religious motivation." Too many of our young people believe that unless an education "pays off" in a large salary it is not worth the trouble or effort. Of course money is essential to conduct normal lives in our

---

[6] New Jersey adopted the first statewide teacher-retirement system in 1896. By 1946 all states had adopted retirement plans.

highly technological society. But money should never become the be-all and end-all of existence for the religious person. Protestants, Catholics, and Jews alike maintain that the ultimate purpose of life is happiness hereafter with God.

With the possible exception of parents, who has more influence upon the youth of this country than the teacher? Certainly the teacher is the channel whereby the great religious and intellectual heritage of our civilization is transmitted to youth. Thus, to be a teacher is to have a "mission in life," not merely a job. By word, and most of all by good example, the teacher can mold the moral and spiritual life of youth as well as their intellectual life.

Not only does the teacher with high religious and moral standards influence his students; he can also be a force for good in the professional organizations of which he is a member. Many teachers have bemoaned the fact that "secularism is taking over" the schools and professional organizations. If such be the case, those of religious conviction cannot remedy the evil by fleeing the profession or by keeping aloof from the professional organizations.

On the negative side of the ledger, it must be noted that teaching is not an eight-hour-a-day job. One usually cannot leave the classroom and wend his way home to evenings of complete relaxation or the pursuance of other activities. Often the teacher will have to correct papers, prepare lessons for his classes, or work on courses he is taking toward an advanced degree. There are PTA meetings, parent conferences, athletic and social events which are part of his duties as a teacher. Furthermore, the teacher is expected to exercise some leadership function in the community through work in religious, fraternal, charitable organizations. If a person is looking for a short workweek, teaching is not for him.

Summary

In summary, then, one might say that teaching not only is one of the greatest challenges of our times but also one of the greatest services a person can render to God and country. Furthermore if one possess the intellectual, moral, and emotional qualities necessary for teaching it also can give the greatest degree of self-satisfaction. The responsibilities are great, but the rewards are correspondingly tremendous; sweat and tears go into a day's work but joy and satisfaction are the warp and woof of the teaching fabric.

You may not become rich (although some teachers have), but you shall receive other rewards; you may not "live fast," but you will probably "live long."

SELECTED READINGS

Gauerke, Warren E., *Legal and Ethical Responsibilities of School Personnel* (Englewood Cliffs, N. J.: Prentice-Hall, 1959).

A comprehensive statement of the legal and ethical responsibilities and rights of teachers, administrators, and school board members.

Harris, Chester (ed.), *Encyclopedia of Educational Research* (New York: The Macmillan Company, 1960): "Teachers' Organizations," pp. 1491–1496; Supply and Demand," pp. 1378–1382; "Certification," pp. 1354–1357; "Tenure," pp. 1382–1385; "Salary Schedules," p. 1178 ff.

Gives current information on teacher supply and demand, tenure and salary schedules.

Kearney, Nolan C., *A Teacher's Professional Guide* (Englewood Cliffs, N. J.: Prentice-Hall, 1958).

A handbook for teachers covering all the professional aspects of teacher-administration, pupil-teacher, and parent-teacher relations.

Lieberman, Myron, *Education as a Profession* (Englewood Cliffs, N. J.: Prentice-Hall, 1956), Chaps. 1, 4, 5–9, 13.

A very comprehensive study of teaching as a profession. Treats the issues involved in professionalism such as professional autonomy, accreditation, certification, membership in professional organization, and teacher qualification.

Lindsey, Margaret (ed.), *New Horizons for the Teaching Profession* (Washington, D. C.: NCTEPS, N.E.A., 1961).

A blueprint for raising standards in the teaching profession through the upgrading of preservice preparation and in-service activities.

Mayer, Martin, *The Schools* (New York: Harper & Bros., 1961), Chap. 19.

A critical discussion of teacher-training programs in U. S. colleges, standards of the profession, certification and licensing of teachers.

National Education Association, *Handbook* (Washington, D. C.: N.E.A., 1960).

A helpful *vade mecum* for the teacher and administrator offering suggestions for a successful career in teaching.

National Education Association, *Teachers' Ethics* (Washington, D. C.: Committee on Professional Ethics of the N.E.A., 1958).

Presents the approved N.E.A. code of ethics, the rationale and the implications of the code for the teacher and other professional personnel in education.

Richey, R. W., *Planning for Teaching* (New York: McGraw-Hill Book Co., 1958), Chaps. 1–3.

Gives good background material on teachers and their work, planning a career in education, and the economic aspects of teaching.

Wynn, Richard, *Careers in Education* (New York: McGraw-Hill Book Co., 1960), Chaps, 1, 4, 5–10.

Provides excellent information on choosing a career, teaching as a profession, the work of a teacher, job opportunities, salaries and benefits, and preparing for teaching.

Chapter XVIII

ISSUES IN PROFESSIONAL EDUCATION

There are many occasions for controversy within the teaching profession. Much of the time, the difficulties arise because of differences of opinion among teachers and administrators. However, because the average citizen often considers himself an "expert" in education and because the schools belong to the people, numerous professional problems originate outside the profession. Obviously, only a few of the issues in professional education arising from within the profession and from the lay public can be treated in this chapter. But a listing of typical issues might be of interest to the future teacher.

1. Should there be a single salary schedule for both elementary and secondary teachers?

2. Is a four-year college degree necessary for primary grade teachers?

3. Should teachers be permitted to hold another job during the school year in addition to their teaching duties?

4. Should teachers be expected to be church members?

5. Should Communists, ex-Communists, or "left-wingers" be permitted to teach in the nation's schools?

6. Should teachers be permitted to strike?

7. Is union affiliation (AFT) to be preferred to membership in professional organizations such as the National Education Association?

8. Are merit ratings for teachers possible?

9. Is the teacher's relation to the school board one of employee or is it that of a civil servant?

10. Should liberal arts or professional education courses constitute the bulk of the teacher-education program?

11. Is teaching a profession in the same sense as medicine and law are professions?

12. Should a "family" increment be paid to married teachers who are the family breadwinners?

13. Should educational experts control the curriculum of American schools?

Following is a discussion of several of the more significant professional problems facing future teachers.

THE PROFESSIONAL EDUCATION OF TEACHERS

Within the past few decades the professional education of teachers has been severely criticized by many people, both lay and professional. No doubt, you already have heard much about the "mickey-mouse" courses in education. "All you do is 'play school' in that methods class" is the lament of many a teacher-education candidate. On the other side of the ledger, you might hear it said of some education course that it was one of the best courses a student had in his college career (the latter comment is less frequently heard than the others).

There seems to be general agreement that a teacher needs some professional training for his career, just as a lawyer or engineer must take certain courses that are designed to give them specific preparation for their profession. All European countries require a certain amount of professional coursework and practice teaching under the supervision of an experienced teacher. The question then seems to be, "Does the future teacher now have to take too many education courses?" rather than "Should he take any education courses?" The pros and cons of the case for and against professional education follow.

Arguments Against Too Much Professional Education

1. The chief criticism against the professional education of teachers is that students are required to take so many courses concerned with "how to teach" that inadequate time remains to study "what to teach." The future teacher is told he should teach children, not subjects. In order to understand children he must have a large accumulation of credits in general psychology, child growth and development, educational psychology, adolescent psychology, and educational tests and measurements. Since the child lives in society, more credits are

acquired in such courses as school and society, education in a democracy, principles of elementary or secondary education, introduction to education. A great deal of the content of these courses duplicates that of the sequence of psychology courses except that the emphasis is on social development rather than physical development.

After spending one third of the time of the freshman and sophomore years on the courses listed above(or their equivalents) the student is faced with a long series of methods courses. The elementary teacher piles up more credit in methods of teaching arithmetic, language arts, reading, science, social sciences, art, music, and others. A secondary teacher of business education might face the following array: principles of business education; methods of teaching bookkeeping; methods of teaching basic business subjects; methods of teaching shorthand, typewriting, transcription; methods of teaching office practice; methods and materials in business education; student teaching in business education. Business education is not the only secondary teaching field plagued by this proliferation of professional courses. Home economics, physical education, industrial arts and driver training, art and music curricula are packed with "how-to-do-it" courses.

2. Needless duplication is the second most crucial argument against education courses. With such a proliferation of education courses, the duplication of content (or lack of content) becomes unbearable to the intelligent student. The psychology sequence contains at least 50 percent duplication from course to course. One course in business methods will be "short" on intellectual content; obviously a whole series of courses will be so repetitious as to be wholly indefensible. Further, the presence of such redundancy has a most deadening effect on the intellectual curiosity of the student.

3. In addition to the repetitiousness of education courses, many are concerned with a "profound treatment of the obvious." For example, educationists spend a great deal of time telling future teachers that individual differences exist among pupils. Any first grader could give you the same information after one semester in school. Also, the instructor might give profound lectures on adjusting the shades in the classroom, optimum room temperature, ventilation, seating arrangements, etc. Certainly such topics are not legitimate content for a college class.

4. A very frequent criticism leveled against education courses, especially by students, is that they are too theoretical and ideal. Instead of being practical and realistic, the lectures and discussions are based on situations that are not found within the context of the "living classroom." Rather, they are based on the favorite theory about teaching held by the instructor. For example, an instructor might propound the theory that a teacher will have no discipline problems if he "motivates" his

students properly. Then he proceeds to list a whole series of motivational devices which will make all the pupils eager to learn and therefore easy to discipline. But the future teacher does not have to glance too far back to his own high school and grade school experiences to recognize the vacuous nature of such statements. If he has a short memory, he might be quickly disillusioned when he enters his first practice-teaching classroom. The same might be said for many other facets of the professional preparation of teachers.

5. It is not bad enough, the critics say, that the undergraduate program of the teacher is diluted by such courses, but even masters' and doctors' degrees are given in most of the areas of professional education. Because of the pressure of the "educational hierarchy," teachers take a master's degree in "education" instead of their teaching field. Oftentimes, teachers are not able to take work leading to a master's degree in an academic field simply because the necessary undergraduate background is lacking. The only course open to them is to pile up more credits in child development, educational psychology, educational methods, etc., to get a master's degree entitling them to an increment on the salary schedule. The courses at the master's level are merely "warmed-over" versions of the undergraduate courses. Consequently, almost anyone can acquire a master's degree, and the end result is that the master's degree no longer represents the first step along the road of serious scholarship.

But this travesty of scholarship extends even to the exalted doctor's degree, the critics lament. To avoid the difficulties involved in acquiring the traditional doctor of philosophy degree with its foreign language and research thesis requirements, the educationists have concocted their own doctor of education degree. These Ed.D. degrees are usually sought by high officials in the educational hierarchy, such as superintendents of large school systems, state department officials and by "professors of pedagogy" in teachers' colleges, colleges of education, and departments of education in liberal arts colleges. The degrees might be acquired by enrolling in courses such as organization and administration of American education, school finance, school budgeting and accounting, public relations in administration, elementary school supervision, secondary school supervision, school plant, construction and maintenance of school buildings, and a host of similar titles. (In fact, some colleges of education had, at one time, as many as ninety courses in educational administration.) With all these offerings to be used for a "major" in administration, the "minor" usually consists of more courses in child development, educational psychology, testing, etc. In lieu of the doctoral thesis or dissertation, the candidate for the Ed.D. usually does some "practical project" on the job. "Scholarly" topics such as the *Ratio of Plumbing Fixtures to the Number of Pupils in Selected Schools* (any intelligent janitor could make the same observations), *Teacher Load in Secondary Schools* (the secretary might determine these figures in her free time), *The Organization of PTA's in State "X"* (the state president of the PTA could have given this information over the phone).

The granting of these advanced degrees, say the critics, is not the most disastrous aspect of the whole fiasco. The most dire result is that the holders of these "titles" are the principal creators of educational policy in the United States. It is they who are responsible for the low-caliber education received in elementary and secondary schools. They have forced "life-adjustment" education down the throats of parents and pupils alike. It is because of their educational shenanigans that students entering college cannot read or write beyond the seventh-grade level. They are the anti-intellectuals who have made the United States a second-rate intellectual power. Unless teacher-education institutions eliminate the top-heavy requirements in professional education courses and insist that the future teacher spend the greater portion of his college time mastering the subject matter of his teaching field (and related fields), the United States never shall realize its intellectual potential.

Arguments in Defense of the *Professional* Education of Teachers

1. Those who defend the relatively large course requirements in professional education contend that the presence of such courses in the modern teacher-education curriculum would never have been necessary (especially for secondary teachers) if the academic professors had demonstrated the least interest in the preparation of the teacher. Instead, the academicians were concerned primarily with preparing the research specialists in their respective fields. The science departments designed their curriculum to prepare the student to take his place in the science laboratories of the nation (not the classroom); the history departments wished their products to be "historians" rather than history teachers. In many instances the students began "specializing" in one narrow field within the major area. For example, the student's whole major program might be in zoology whereas the teacher, both elementary and secondary, is expected to teach botany, zoology, physiology, and hygiene. Obviously the academic departments were not designed to prepare teachers.

In addition to the extreme specialization within the academic departments, no attention was given to the methods and materials necessary for teaching the various subjects. It was assumed that if a student knew his subject, *ipso facto*, he knew how to teach it. Sad experience had convinced those running the elementary and secondary schools that this assumption was false. A lack of understanding of child and adolescent development often made the teacher unable to bring his subject matter to the developmental level of the pupils; he knew little or nothing about test construction or the valid use of standardized tests; his standards for the ten-year-old were the same as those employed in his college courses; he was completely oblivious to the great range of individual differences in his classes. In fine, he was just *not* prepared for teaching, albeit he might know his subject matter.

2. It is true that many teachers are graduated from teachers' colleges or colleges of education with over half of their college credits in professional education. But a closer scrutiny of the college catalogs and courses of study will reveal that many of the courses bearing an *Education* number and title are actually subject-matter courses. For example, certain elementary education courses cover the mathematics, science, geography, history, etc., taught in the elementary schools. Similarly, many secondary education courses such as those listed above in business education cover the content of the courses as well as the methods of and materials for teaching them in the high schools.

That this situation exists is partly due to the historical development of teachers' colleges in the United States as well as to the factors mentioned in point 1 above. If all of these courses were credited to academic fields such as mathematics or science or history, the total number of credits in professional education would be reduced immensely. In fact, many teachers' colleges (now converted to state colleges) are following this procedure, with the result that the total number of semester hours in professional education for secondary teachers ranges from 18 to 24 or about 12 to 15 percent of the total requirements for the bachelor's degree. The elementary teacher's professional education requirements account for 20 to 25 percent of the total requirements for the degree mainly because of the specialized nature of teaching elementary school subjects such as reading and language arts, elementary school music and art, health education, and the like.

3. The critics of professional education lament the granting of master's and even doctor's degrees in "education." The "educationist" will respond that if the graduate schools had designed graduate degree programs for *teachers* as well as research experts, the master of education degree might never have come into being. But most master's degree programs in the academic fields were so specialized as to be wholly unsuited to improve either the subject-matter background or the teaching effectiveness of the classroom teacher of elementary and secondary subjects.

Yet another valid reason for the introduction of advanced degrees in professional education flows from the complex nature of the modern public school. A school superintendent or principal, for example, needs to know much more than his teaching field such as history or mathematics. The legal complications of running a modern school demand a thorough knowledge of school law; the intricacies of school finance demand that the school administrator be familiarized with the highly complex accounting and management of federal, state, and local funds. To say that a business manager should be hired for such matters does not solve the problem, for businessmen do not understand the total educational structure of the modern school. Therefore, the school administrator needs specialized training for his job. The same position can be argued for guidance workers, psychometrists, and remedial reading specialists. Simply because these specialties were not demanded in the schools of a century ago does not warrant the assertion that they have no place in the modern educational structure. Remember that the master's and doctor's degrees in science are of relatively recent origin!

Much ado is made by the critics about dropping the foreign-language requirements for some professional education degrees. The artificiality of the foreign-language requirement is also attacked by many people outside the field of education. An unofficial survey made among holders of advanced degrees (who passed the foreign-language requirements) reveals that those foreign languages were used so seldom that they were soon forgotten. The reasons are fairly simple. Almost all research or scholarly work of note is translated into English. Second, an accurate translation of such works demands far more knowledge of the language than is required to pass the foreign-language examinations for the master's and doctor's degrees. Third, the foreign languages required of doctoral candidates (usually French and German) are not necessarily the one needed in the field. For example, much more literature in the field of pure science appears in Russian than in French. Consequently the language requirement constitutes an artificial hurdle or barrier to scholarship rather than an aid to it.

4. The critics who object to granting advanced degrees in professional education are not consistent. They do not fuss and fume when advanced professional degrees are given in business administration or commerce, engineering, law, medicine, dentistry, and architecture. Nor do they object to the very inane topics of master's and doctoral theses in other fields. A close scrutiny of the master's and doctoral theses in many fields will reveal that at times they are simply "exercises in research methodology" of the specialized area. "The pot should not be calling the kettle black!"

MERIT RATINGS

Although the subject of merit ratings has been a controversial one since the beginning of the public school system in the United States, it has caused much more discussion in recent years. Critics of the "automatic increment" system, now in common use, feel that too much "dead wood" has accumulated in the ranks of teachers and the only means of rewarding outstanding faculty members is by paying them more than other teachers or showing other signs of recognition for quality staff.

Arguments for Merit Ratings

1. Those who favor merit ratings for teachers realize that the greatest objection to such ratings in the past has been the alleged impracticability of devising and administering any merit system acceptable to the large majority of teachers. In response to this difficulty it is asserted that teachers are constantly being rated by pupils, parents, and administrators, but no use is made of such ratings for rewarding the good teacher. All that is needed, then, is a measuring technique more systematic than the informal ratings of pupils, parents, and administrators. This measurement can be done in several ways.

    a) *In Terms of the Product.* Business and industry measure an employee's effectiveness by the product. If the employee is a salesman, his effectiveness is judged by the amount of goods he sells. If he is a plant worker, evaluation is in terms of the number and quality of the products he makes. Why, then, should a teacher not be evaluated in terms of the product, the student? For example, a battery of tests might be administered to the class at the beginning and end of the school year to determine the amount of change the teacher effected in the students. Granted that a certain amount of improvement in the student might be due to factors other than the teacher's influence, it is not illogical to assume that the teacher is one of the most important factors in the improvement of the student.

    b) *Evaluation of the Teacher.* One of the most frequently used techniques for establishing norms for teacher tenure is based on an appraisal of traits presumed to make up a good teacher. Intelligence, objectivity, emotional stability, drive, the ability to stimulate and hold student interest, effectiveness in lesson planning and directing learning activities, and effective appraisal of results, are some of the traits of a good teacher. Evaluation of these traits is usually carried on by supervisors and administrators, and a teacher must possess them to some degree before tenure is granted by a local school system.

    Those favoring merit rating maintain that this same type of evaluation might be one of the means to determine promotions and salary raises even after the teacher has become a member of the permanent staff.

Simply because merit-rating systems are difficult to design and administer is no valid reason for not having them.

2. Not to use merit ratings of one sort or another is to fail to capitalize on the competitive nature of human beings. In those school systems with no merit-rating programs, even teachers with exceptional ability will not put forth their best simply because they will receive no recognition for their work. True, a significant number of teachers will do an outstanding job in spite of the fact that no reward will result from their performance. But they are the exception rather than the rule.

3. Any organization without some form of merit rating tends to attract the "security-seeker" rather than the truly professional teacher. This type of teacher is quite evident in school systems with the automatic increment salary schedule. A teacher of this kind will do what is minimally essential to retain his position. Certainly American youth need more than a "clock puncher" to guide them to the heights of educational excellence. Only when school systems recognize and reward outstanding teachers will there be a general upgrading of teaching personnel.

4. Single salary schedules and automatic increments place teachers in the same class as common or skilled laborers. In the latter, all laborers receive the same hourly rate regardless of the quantity or quality of their work. Most employers will agree that "equal pay for equal time" spent on the job encourages laziness, sloppiness, and procrastination. On the other hand, when a worker is put on a competitive program such as piecework he is much more diligent because he is paid according to the amount produced. Thus, when teachers insist on a single pay scale they are lowering themselves professionally — in fact they are indirectly stating that they should not have the status of the profession.

5. "Professionalism" can never be achieved by teachers unless there is some provision for rewarding quality performance. All of the established professions have earned their high status by emphasizing quality and correspondingly higher remuneration. American communities are accustomed to paying higher fees to the most competent people within each profession. The parent who wishes to have the best surgeon operate on his child expects to pay a higher fee for such expert services than he would give the "average" surgeon. Similarly, no parent should object to have his child taught by an outstanding teacher simply because this teacher is paid more than the "average" teacher.

Thus, rewarding outstanding professional performance will never harm the status of the profession, it can only raise it.

6. An argument related to the one given above refers to job mobility within the teaching profession. In most school systems today, the only avenue to higher pay lies in obtaining administrative or supervisory positions. Because of this situation many outstanding classroom teachers take postbachelor's degrees in the area of administration and supervision in order to qualify for such positions that might appear in their own or other school systems. In this manner a large number of excellent teachers leave classroom teaching in spite of the fact that it is their "first love." Certainly, the schools need good administrators, but the caliber of a school is determined by its teaching staff more than by its administrative personnel. If outstanding teachers would receive salaries commensurate with their teaching ability they would not be tempted to leave the classroom for administrative posts. (Most administrators will admit that running a modern school is not a picnic.)

In summary, then, those favoring some form of merit rating do not deny that there are many complex problems involved in inaugurating and directing any kind of program, especially when salaries are involved. But the advantages accruing from such programs far outweigh the disadvantages. And, unless American school systems inaugurate some system of merit rating, teaching will never be listed among the honored professions and most outstanding people will abandon classroom teaching. There may be a few "bruised heads" as a result of such action, but the long-term gains will be worth the blood and sweat required to achieve the necessary results.

Arguments Against Merit Rating

1. One of the very convincing objections to any form of merit rating proffered by the "opposition" is based on the subjectivity of all methods of evaluating. It is argued that "good teaching" is so intangible that only one of its results, acquisition of knowledge on the part of the student, is measurable. And even this criterion is unusable because of the increased amount of incidental learning acquired through such means as television, radio, and inexpensive paperback books. The teacher's ability to foster proper attitudes and behavior in his students is out of the range of objective evaluation, even though it is one of the important objectives of modern education.

2. Merit ratings foster "cutthroat" activities among teachers rather than the cooperative spirit needed among teachers to function as a harmonious unit. Thus many teachers might attempt to tear down the reputation of fellow teachers in order to improve their own chances for advancement. This unsavory side of human behavior is evident in highly competitive situations and is more apt to be absent when no personal gain can result from undermining one's fellow workers.

3. Besides, the negative effects of "cutthroat" behavior merit ratings

discourage original and creative behavior. A teacher might fear to use new teaching methods or introduce controversial issues into his teaching lest he offend those who will rate him. Such restrictions on teacher freedom should be found only in dictatorships, not in a democracy.

4. Since most merit-rating systems involve the administrators and supervisory staff of the school, the professional relationships between teachers and administrators will deteriorate. The teacher will no longer be able to view his principal or supervisor as a guide or helper; he will be reluctant to ask for assistance lest his request be considered an admission of weakness.

5. In order for any merit-rating plan to be effective a greatly increased amount of time must be spent by those who will do the rating. The evaluation process is usually lengthy and cumbersome; additional records must be kept. Such activities will entail employing additional supervisory and clerical help or add to the load of the already overburdened supervisory and administrative staff.

6. Merit ratings remove one of the most attractive aspects of teaching, namely security. Even though teachers' salaries are below those received by people with equivalent educational background at least teachers know the beginning salaries, increments, and maximum salaries. Their mode of living can be geared to the salary schedule, and securing part-time work is left to the teacher's discretion according to his needs or desires. If prospective teachers are to be denied any assurance of "automatic increments," there can be no security in the profession. It is fallacious, therefore, to assume that merit ratings will relieve the teacher shortage. In reality the opposite result might be expected.

7. Merit ratings fail to take into account many variables in the teaching profession. For example, a teacher working in a slum area where students are hostile or apathetic toward education will have little to show for all his efforts. On the other hand, a teacher in an upper-class suburban school where most students are college bound will have little difficulty in obtaining outstanding results. Teachers with excellent laboratory equipment for science classes have a definite advantage over those with poor facilities.

A very dangerous side effect of such variables in the teaching environment is that teachers who fall into disfavor with the administrators for any reason whatsoever will be assigned the difficult classes where they cannot possibly achieve the success required to earn a merit promotion.

8. Collective bargaining, and the many advantages that accrue from it, is practically nullified by any system of merit rating. Teachers are placed in the position of bargaining individually with the superintendent or

school board. The memory of the days of the "great depression" should be ample warning to the evils of such bargaining. It was not uncommon for a teacher's contract to be voided simply because another had agreed to work for less.

9. No convincing evidence has been produced to indicate that merit ratings improve the quality of teaching or teachers' salaries. For example, no studies of significant scope have been made which show that higher average salaries exist in school systems with merit promotion. Only a few instances can be pointed to as evidence that teachers do not leave the teaching field because of merit ratings. In fact, most of the arguments for merit ratings are based on analogies from business and industry. But are such analogies valid? Can teaching be compared to a business operating for profit? Can teachers be compared to foremen, office managers, or industrial executives? Surely not! The aims of business and education are entirely different!

TEACHERS' UNIONS VERSUS PROFESSIONAL ORGANIZATIONS

In Chapter XVII it was noted that one of the weakest links in the professionalization of teaching was the lack of adequate organization within the ranks of the practitioners. No one organization can speak for teachers as the American Medical Association speaks for medical doctors. Perhaps the large number of educational practitioners (over two million in the early 1960's) and the diversity of functions they fulfill make it very difficult to form one organization. But even more crucial is the fact that the practitioners cannot decide what type of organization they want. There are two main points of view about the kind of organization needed for teachers: the unaffiliated professional organization, such as the National Education Association, and the Teachers' Union, usually affiliated with a labor union. Following are some of the arguments for each position given by its proponents.

Arguments for a Teachers' Union

1. The proponents of teachers' unions contend that an independent professional organization such as the American Medical Association for doctors of medicine can have no counterpart for teachers because of the essential differences between the two groups. The most significant of these differences is that the relationship between teachers and administrators is fundamentally one of employer-employee. In this respect, teachers resemble labor rather than the medical profession.

Teachers must bargain with members of their own professional organization, the administrators, in regard to salaries, working conditions, and benefits. Thus, when both teachers and administrators are in the same professional organization such as the National Education Association, there must necessarily be a basic conflict of interest. Such is not the case in the medical profession, even when one doctor happens to be in the employ of another, for such arrangements are accidental rather than essential to the practice of medicine.

2. The present structure of the N.E.A. with the affiliated state and local units lends itself to dominance by school administrators. As such, it can never be truly representative of the rank and file of teachers. The teacher's job is at stake if he disagrees with the administrators in the school system in which he is employed. Therefore an organization for teachers and low-level administrators *only* is needed if their professional interests are to be safeguarded.

3. The American Federation of Teachers (a union) is one such organization made up almost exclusively of classroom teachers. A teachers' union, such as the A.F.T., must and does have the welfare of its clientele (the children), as its major objective. Other objectives, subsidiary to this one, are:

   a) To bring associations of teachers into a relationship of mutual assistance and cooperation;
   b) To obtain for teachers the rights to which they are entitled;
   c) To raise the standards of the teaching profession by securing the conditions essential to the best professional service;
   d) To promote such a democratization of the schools as will enable them better to equip their pupils to take their place in the industrial, social, and political life of the community;
   e) To promote the welfare of the children of the nation by providing progressively better educational opportunities for all.

4. Affiliation with any existing professional organization such as the N.E.A. was not considered beneficial by the A.F.T. Consequently, American Federation of Labor affiliation was sought and obtained. Such affiliation is not a hindrance to professionalization but a boon because:

   a) Organized labor has always been the champion of education in America, especially of the cause of "equality of opportunity";
   b) Other professional groups such as symphony conductors and airline pilots have achieved their professional objectives by affiliating with organized labor without lowering their status;
   c) Backing from a powerful organization like the A.F.L. assures teachers of support they cannot get elsewhere.

5. The organizational structure of the only large professional association for teachers, the N.E.A., is such that no constitutional amendments can be made by the members without the approval of the Congress of the United States. In other words, the N.E.A. is not a truly professional organization because it lacks autonomy. But teachers' unions can inaugurate changes for improving professional standards from the grass roots via their elected representatives — no governmental approval is needed. Nor does the parent organization, in this instance the A.F.L., dictate policy and procedures to the A.F.T. Consequently, the teachers' union has more autonomy than the N.E.A. and in fact is independent of the parent organization, the A.F.L.

6. One of the criticisms of the A.F.T. or any teachers' union has been based on an occasional strike by some A.F.T. locals. The strike, it is contended, is a weapon of the laboring class, but should not be used by professional people. In response to this criticism, it is pointed out that strikes have been consistently renounced by the A.F.T. on several occasions, even though a no-strike policy is not found in the union constitution.[1] (In fact, the N.E.A. also does not have a constitutional provision against strikes.) The only exception to the A.F.T. "no-strike" policy is that the right to strike is believed essential to the collective bargaining power of teachers. Since the services of the teacher are not essential to the health and safety of the people in the same sense that the services of firemen, policemen, and government employees are, teachers should not be denied the right to strike.

Arguments Against Teachers' Unions

When criticisms are voiced against teachers' unions, they usually imply arguments for membership in a professional organization such as the N.E.A. Therefore, the arguments against teachers' unions may be construed as arguments for a nonunion organization.

1. The vocation of teaching is different from, though not necessarily more honorable than, other callings with which unionism is usually associated. Consequently, teachers should achieve professionalization outside the framework of the American labor-union movement.

2. Teachers are primarily a public-service group, whereas unions are concerned primarily with the welfare of the members. Because of this conflict in major objectives teaching and unionism are incompatible.

3. Membership in the organized labor movement builds bias into the teaching of many subjects. Such bias is unbecoming to the professional person, especially the teacher who owes his allegiance to the people rather to any political philosophy. No organization affiliated with the labor movement can be said to be unbiased — it is prolabor.

---

[1] See the American Teacher, Vol. 36, February, 1952, p. 8 ff.

4. A.F.T. standards of admission are not professional, for anyone who is *de facto* teaching can become a member regardless of what his professional training might be. For this reason the malcontents, the professionally unqualified, the morally unfit, and the academically incompetent seek protection in the union. Such people are clever enough to realize that union membership has saved the job of many an unfit laborer or craftsman and might one day save them from dismissal because of incompetence.

5. Teachers' unions have not formulated codes of professional ethics for their members. The major concern of the union has been the defense of all paying members rather than the weeding out of incompetents by strict adherence to a professional code of ethics. Until measures are taken to establish and enforce standards the teachers' unions cannot be considered "professional."

6. All professions which have achieved true professional stature such as medicine, dentistry, and law have done so because they have been completely independent of nonrelated organizations. Medical doctors, dentists, and lawyers did not achieve professionalization by affiliating with labor. They have been scrupulous about admission to the profession; they have formulated a code of ethics unique to their profession; they have been rigorous in disciplining members who have deviated from the code of ethics. By these means, they have convinced their clientele that the best possible professional service is rendered. And they have proved to the members of their own profession that they do not need the support of organized labor or any other outside agency — they have achieved self-discipline and self-determination, through their own independent organization.

From the foregoing instances of controversy within the teaching profession, the student can learn that all problems are not settled within the profession. Also, some circumstances that give rise to controversy in the 1960's will cease to exist in the next decade. But one thing is certain: teachers, administrators, and the public must begin in earnest to solve some of the more pressing problems facing the profession. The intellectual and moral welfare of the pupils, the future citizens of our country, demand it. If the members of the profession and their supporting public do not resolve the problems, some governmental agency will do so. Then the prized freedom and independence of American education will be lost, perhaps, forever.

SELECTED READINGS

Bestor, Arthur, Jr., *The Restoration of Learning* (New York: A. Knopf Co., 1955), Chaps. 7–9, 12–14.

A statement of the ills affecting professional education and suggestions for their remedy.

Chandler, B. J., *Education and the Teacher* (New York: Dodd, Mead & Co., 1961), Chap. 5.
Discusses the issues in professional education utilizing up-to-date materials and arguments.

Kennedy, E. E., "Advantages and Disadvantages of Teacher Merit Rating Plans," *National Association of Secondary School Principals-Bulletin*, Vol. 42, September, 1950, pp. 38–40.
A good summary of the pros and cons of merit-rating plans and the rationale of the positions presented on such plans.

Kline, Clarice, and Megel, Carl, "Should Teachers Unionize?" *Teachers College Record*, Vol. 63, No. 2, November, 1961, pp. 115–127.
A debate between representatives of the N.E.A. and the American Federation of Teachers on the advisability of affiliation of teachers with organized labor.

Lieberman, Myron, *Education as a Profession* (Englewood Cliffs, N. J.: Prentice-Hall, 1956), Chaps. 10–12, 14–15.
A comprehensive study of teachers' unions, collective bargaining, the economic and occupational status of teachers, and the challenge of professionalization.

Lynd, Albert, *Quackery in the Public Schools* (New York: Little, Brown & Co., (1950), Chaps. I, V, VI, VII.
A scathing criticism of professional education courses and American progressivism.

Mayer, Martin, *The Schools* (New York: Harper & Bros., 1961), Chap. 18.
Faces some of the practical issues involved in teaching techniques, promotion, salary schedules, and use of mechanical aids to teaching.

Moore, Sheldon, "Administrative Problems Under a Merit Plan," *Journal of Teacher Education*, Vol. 10, March, 1959, pp. 28–34.
Points up the problems which arise in administering merit plans for promotion and salary increases for teachers.

National Education Association, "Merit Salary Plans," *Research Bulletin*, Vol. 39, May, 1961, pp. 61–63.
Lists representative merit-rating plans in use throughout the United States pointing up the difficulties involved in them.

Scott, W. C., Hill, G. M., Burns, H. W., *The Great Debate* (Englewood Cliffs, N. J.: Prentice-Hall, 1959), Chap. 7.
Presents both sides of the picture on the value of the professional education of teachers in the United States.

"Special Feature on Merit Rating and Pay," *Phi Delta Kappan*, Vol. 42, January, 1961, pp. 149–153.
Contains articles, pro and con, on merit-rating plans for teachers.

Stamper, O. B., "Let's Quit Dodging the Issue of Merit Rating," *Nations Schools*, Vol. 59, May, 1957, p. 57.
Calls for a realistic look at the present system of continuous promotion and automatic salary increases prevalent in most school systems.

Stiles, Lindley, Barr, A. S., Douglass, R., and Mills, H. H., *Teacher Education in the United States* (New York: Ronald Press Co., 1960).

An excellent review of teacher education programs in the United States.
Good discussions of the issues in professional education.

Walcutt, C. C., *Tomorrow's Illiterates* (New York: Atlantic — Little, Brown &
Co., 1961).
A critical treatise on professional education in the United States.

Wessel, H. M., and Miller, B. R., "What are the Pro's and Con's of Teacher
Merit Rating Plans?" *National Association of Secondary School Principals
Bulletin*, Vol. 43, April, 1959, pp. 149–153.
A thorough summary of the advantages and disadvantages of merit-rating
plans.

Chapter XIX

THE ROAD AHEAD

In the preceding chapters we have tried to give the student an over-view of the American school systems and the teaching profession. The historical, philosophical, and psychological foundations of education and the crucial issues involved have been discussed as objectively as possible. The student must have noted that even when apparently minor matters in education were under consideration, there seemed to be the ever present conflict of opinions. Is education the world over such a controversial subject as it is in this country? It seems not, for American education is, indeed, in a class by itself. A study of European systems will reveal substantial agreement between the various European countries on most of the points that cause such heated controversy in America. For example, even though the administrative structure of the school systems of France, Germany, Italy, Spain, and Sweden is quite different, the essential purpose of the elementary and secondary school and higher educational in-situations is practically identical in all these countries. The elementary school weeds out those unfit to attend secondary academies, lycées, and gymnasia. The secondary schools have as their goal the preparation of their clientele for the university and the weeding-out process is very stringent. Because of this basic agreement on goals there are very few attacks on public education as we know them in America.

But in America no such agreement can be found. Some want the schools to be like European schools, and they criticize American schools for not achieving the same results as the European schools. Others argue that European educational ideals should not be those of the American school. *All* students should be educated, they contend; it is antidemocratic to permit only the intellectual elite to attend secondary schools and colleges; schools must meet the needs of all youth.

And so the battle rages! Is it possible to harmonize such conflicting points of view? Is it necessary to harmonize them? The answers to such questions are not easy to derive. But one thing seems to be certain: the bitterness of the present conflict must be mitigated to enable American educators to achieve some unity within the great diversity found in the educational patterns of this great country. Certainly the existence of different points of view is healthy, just as constructive criticism is essential to the growth of any educational organism. But education, like man, cannot go in all directions at the same time and ever expect to achieve the minimal amount of unity necessary for success.

Perhaps an illustration might suggest a possible approach to achieving at least some convergence toward national unity on the basic educational issue of "intellectualism vs. life adjustment." The American people, with few exceptions, are committed to giving all the children of all the people all the schooling possible. In fact most states expect children to remain in school at least until they are sixteen years old (mentally defective children are the only exceptions to this general rule). The teachers have a captive audience for at least ten years! What should they do with this mass of youngsters? At one extreme, the intellectualists (rational humanists) insist that they be given a rigid diet of intellectual disciplines in the form of the well-known subjects, mathematics, English, foreign languages, the sciences, history, etc. At the other extreme are those theorists who maintain that "life adjustment" is the only realistic goal for such a large, diversified assortment of pupils.

How can these seemingly antagonistic points of view ever be synthesized? Obviously such books as Lynd's *Quackery in the Public Schools*, A. Bestor's *Educational Wastelands*, J. Keat's *Schools Without Scholars*, and R. M. Hutchin's *The Conflict in Education* do not represent an attempt to solve the conflict. Similarly, the many partisan responses to these criticisms published by the advocates of the "new education" do little to ease the tensions between the conflicting parties. In fact, the approach of both parties tends to widen the breach between the two camps.

The only approach to this problem, from the point of view of the writer, is a movement in American education similar to the

"Christian Dialogue Movement" (Ecumenism) in Europe. What lessons might the ecumenical movement have for American education? As the student will recall from his high school and college study of history, the various religious denominations of Europe have been in serious conflict for the past four hundred years. There seemed to be little desire to get together to heal the ruptured unity of Christendom. But the rise of secularism and Communism gave all Christian groups a common enemy. Here, at last, was the one point that all could agree upon — the combined forces of secularism and Communism might destroy Christianity within a relatively short time unless Christians united for the battle for men's hearts and minds. To achieve that unity, essential, at least, to hold their own against the enemy, the leaders of the Christian denominations (both Catholic and Protestant) have organized seminars, meetings, and conferences. The results, thus far, have been most gratifying. The delegates "discuss" rather than "quarrel"; common elements are sought in the various theological systems represented; very little personal animosity is displayed by the participants. Such cordial relations among religious groups have never before been witnessed. Yet the participants are very realistic and do not expect to resolve all differences in a short time. In fact most of them realize that they will not see a united Christendom in their lifetime. Such a realization does not deter them from their endeavor.

Does American education have any rallying point capable of generating interest in educational ecumenism? On the positive side, American educators, with few exceptions, are committed to the democratic ideals of their forefathers. On the negative side, Americans must unite educationally to combat the serious threat from without posed by totalitarian Communism. All neutral observers will admit that the Soviet Union has made great strides, especially in fundamental education and the sciences, because of unity of purpose. Granted, a great many of the figures on educational achievement published by the Soviet Union are exaggerated for propaganda purposes. But there is no denying the fact that from a state of almost complete illiteracy, Russia has achieved nearly universal literacy in a short twenty-five years. It has risen from the position of a medieval agricultural nation to one of the powerful industrial giants of the world. Both Russians and outsiders have agreed that education is chiefly responsible for both achievements.

Can America meet the threat from without if its educational leaders are going in all directions? Will not the lack of unity of purpose tend to negate the great gains made by American schools in the past? Only history will give the final answer to these questions! But it seems plausible that very little progress will be made on the American educational scene unless there is some solution found for the deep-rooted conflict in education. The solution seems to lie in the search for some unifying force in the American school.

Unity of purpose for the American school, some argue, implies complete conformity or uniformity in education. Such a concept of unity is wholly alien to the American democratic tradition. This writer contends that the school in Texas need not be identical to those in New York; not every secondary class in science need be studying the same topic on the same day in every school of the nation (as is done in the Soviet Union); not every teacher must hold and teach the same political philosophy (as teachers must in the Soviet Union); not even the curriculum and teaching methods must be alike in every school. It seems that sufficient unity can be achieved if educators could agree on the role of the schools (elementary, secondary, collegiate, and professional) in modern American society. A very broad statement of the major role of the schools in society would leave great freedom for the various state and local systems to develop their own educational programs within this broadly stated national goal. Parochial and private schools, it seems, also would be able to operate within the same context without doing violence to the ideals of the specific groups they serve. In other words, a *national system* of education is not necessary to achieve unity. Certainly, such a system makes it easier to do so, as is evident from the highly centralized educational systems of Russia and France. But Britain seems to have accomplished this unity of purpose without an educational dictatorship of the central government. British education has demonstrated that there can be unity within diversity; there can be "conformity in essentials" coupled with "freedom in nonessentials." If educators do not cooperate to bring unity into American education, someday they may have to swallow the bitter pill of nationally enforced unity.

INDEX

Academic freedom, definition of, 275; legitimate restrictions, 277

Academies, decline, 83; founding and early expansion, 24 f; "new," 83 f; in new nation, 83 f

Achievement, diagnostic tests, 374; prediction of, 426 ff; test batteries, 371, 382 f; testing, 364 f, 366; see also Tests, achievement

Activity, in learning, 335

Adolescence, education for, 241; effect of prolonging, 126 f

Adult education, 42 ff; American Association for, 43; characteristics, 43 f; course offerings, 42; early history, 42 f; enrollments, 36, 43; factors in growth, 43

Adults, as examples, 120 f

Advantages, of professional work, 448 f

A.F.T. (American Federation of Teachers), and professionalism, 463; professional standards of, 442; and school administrators, 463

Aims, educational, 249 ff; educational, and Dewey, 256; see also Objectives

Apperceptive mass, Herbart's, 311

Aptitude tests, see Tests, aptitude

Aquinas, St. Thomas, and Aristotelianism, 213; and faculty psychology, 301; and intellectualism, 213; opponents of, 215; view of relationship of philosophy and theology, 212

Aristotelianism, and Christian education, 209

Aristotle, influence on education, 209, 213; and faculty psychology, 301 f

Army tests, Alpha and Beta, 367 f

Associationism, dynamic, 310 ff; effects, 307

Augustine, St., on educational methods, 202; on secular learning, 202; on the teacher, 203

Authority, need for, 165; of teacher, 163

Baby biographers, and child study, 346 f

Barnard, Henry, and early public schools, 18

Behavior, measurement of, 422; scientific study of, 299

Behaviorism, of B. F. Skinner, 328; of Watson, 326

Binet, Alfred, and child study, 347; mental-age scale, 362; personality measures, 365

Boards of education, state level, 57; see also School board

Bode, B., view of democracy, 259 f

British educators, and humanism, 226

Camps, summer, 127

Carter, James, and early public schools, 18

Catechetical school, aims of, 200

Catechumenal schools, aims of, 199

Cathedral schools, aims of, 207 f; curriculum of, 207

Catholic Church, educational role, 115 ff

Catholic schools, administration, 93; current colleges, 103; development of colleges, 89 ff; early colleges, 77; early leaders, 88; early missions, 75; and early public schools, 179; early secondary, 75 f; First Plenary Council of Baltimore, 79; frontier colleges, 87 f; lay teachers, 97; nineteenth-century secondary, 84 f; parish school movement, 80; recent college enrollments, 103; recent enrollments, 92 f; teacher training, 90 f; Third Plenary Council of Baltimore, 80; vocational, 101

Cattell, James McKeen, and new psychology, 322

Censorship, advocates of, 289; and creativity, 289 f; and freedom, 290; impracticality of, 290 f; of mass media, 129; and morals, 288; organizations favoring, 287; and truth, 288

Certification of teachers, 57; independent schools, 97

Character education, Herbart's theory of, 244

Charlemagne, educational influence of, 208 f

Child clinics, founded, 349